The Politics of Energy Security

Energy security is known for its 'slippery' nature and subsequent broad range of definitions. Instead of another attempt to grasp its essence, this book offers a critical reflection that problematizes the use of energy security itself.

After a short historical and methodological analysis of the proliferation of energy security, *The Politics of Energy Security* unpacks three social practices that drive energy security. These include an analysis of the logics of security, a study of the relation between the materiality of sociotechnical (energy) systems and the knowledge people have over such systems, and a reflection on the power and politics behind (energy) security. Each of these is discussed and ultimately illustrated in the last chapter to show how energy security works, how it is shaped, and what role it plays within political processes.

Based on a novel performative reading of energy security with its focus on ontological politics and an in-depth look at the often implicitly accepted social practices that determine how people shape and are shaped by energy security, this book will be of great interest to students and scholars of energy security and policy, political theory, international relations, critical security studies and environmental studies more broadly.

Johannes Kester is a postdoctoral researcher at the University of Aarhus working on the social barriers and acceptation of electric mobility and vehicle-to-grid integration in the Nordic countries. His primary interest lies in the governance of sociotechnical energy systems and their stabilization and transformation, drawing on social theory with a focus on the role of the politics of security and risk in these processes. He has published articles in *Energy Policy*, *Energy*, *Energy Research and Social Science* and *Mobilities*, and defended his PhD, *Securing abundance: The politics of energy security* (2016), at the University of Groningen in the Netherlands.

Routledge Explorations in Energy Studies

Energy Poverty and Vulnerability
A Global Perspective
Edited by Neil Simcock, Harriet Thomson, Saska Petrova and Stefan Bouzarovski

The Politics of Energy Security
Critical Security Studies, New Materialism and Governmentality
Johannes Kester

The Politics of Energy Security

Critical Security Studies, New Materialism and Governmentality

Johannes Kester

Routledge
Taylor & Francis Group

LONDON AND NEW YORK

First published 2018 by Routledge

2 Park Square, Milton Park, Abingdon, Oxfordshire OX14 4RN
52 Vanderbilt Avenue, New York, NY 10017

Routledge is an imprint of the Taylor & Francis Group, an informa business

First issued in paperback 2020

British Library Cataloguing-in-Publication Data
A catalogue record for this book is available from the British Library

Library of Congress Cataloging-in-Publication Data
A catalog record has been requested for this book

ISBN: 978-1-138-03747-2 (hbk)
ISBN: 978-0-367-50766-4 (pbk)

Typeset in Goudy
by Wearset Ltd, Boldon, Tyne and Wear

Contents

Illustrations

Figures

Table

Acknowledgements

This book is based on my PhD thesis *Securing abundance: the politics of energy security*, which I defended in 2016 at the University of Groningen. It would not have come into fruition without the helpful advice, patience and occasional friendly push from a range of people. First, I would like to thank my wife, Vimke, for joining me on a journey that was not of her choosing but which she supported as if it was her own. Special thanks as well to both my PhD supervisors. To Jaap de Wilde for his insightful comments and critique, his guidance through university politics, and his initial trust in an MA student who wanted to write 'something' about energy and constructivism. Thanks to Benjamin Herborth for his encouragement and his enthusiasm to share an almost-encyclopedic breadth of theoretical knowledge with me. The book also builds in large part on the international relations bubble at the Oude Boteringestraat. I feel lucky to have been part of this group and would like to thank Stef Wittendorp, Lennart Landman and Kars de Bruijne for their willingness to suffer as a critical sounding board, one that has seen quite some use over the years. Add to them the others with whom I started my PhD journey and shared many of the joy and pains of writing a thesis, Petra Boudewijn, Margriet Fokken and Simon Halink, and you have an environment in which it is a pleasure to go to work each day, every day. Lastly, I would like to thank Benjamin Sovacool for his support and generosity to use some of the precious time of our project on the sociotechnical transition behind electric mobility to rewrite the thesis into the book before you. Of course, I have encountered many others throughout my research, close by and far off, who in one way or another have enriched my thinking. The list is long and, if you feel you are on it, you probably are and I thank you. I can only hope that this book properly reflects all the lessons and insights that you all shared so freely.

1 Introduction

1.1 Introduction

I have never considered myself wealthy. Luckily, I have also never known hunger or thirst and the longest period I have been without electricity involuntarily has been half a day at most. In other words, I have had the fortune to grow up and live in a society with the norms, institutions and markets that cater for an abundance of natural resources. In fact, as this book shows, I live in a society that has completely structured its political markets to ensure this. That said, these same political markets produce several adverse effects for those at its fringes. Climate change, energy poverty, scarcity, food banks and a degrading biodiversity are but some of the terms that indicate the negative sides of our current political economy. A political economy that has benefited many, but not without excluding some and harming others.[1] Simultaneously, this political economy is constantly defended and secured against the threats and dangers that its beneficiaries believe to exist. This calls for a need to understand the security processes at work in the production, distribution and consumption of energy, food and other natural resources. While the security processes behind each of these resources (and their nexus) is important, 'nothing exists that is not energy, or not affected by energy'.[2] This book will therefore focus on the concept, practice and politics of *energy security*.

There are many ways to study energy security. Some scholars approach it conceptually, historically or quantitatively, a lot take a policy-oriented route, and a select few offer a broader social critique.[3] What many of these analyses have in common is that they search for an answer to what energy security *is* or *ought to* be – often simultaneously. What is studied are questions like how energy security should be defined, what exactly needs to be secured, what the threats are, who is in need of energy security, what needs to be done to counter the threats, and so on.[4] This book is not concerned with such questions. Instead it argues that the studies asking these questions only partly help us understand what energy security is, because it does not allow for an understanding of what energy security *does* politically. The book thus shifts the question to: what does energy security do? A question which it pursues by studying how energy security is approached in current scholarship and then further unpacks with another shift in focus from the current energy security literature to the security politics around energy security and by answering a different set of questions: what is security and what does security do? How does energy security relate to the materiality of energy, its infrastructure and resources? How does energy security work politically as a form of governance? And how can we operationalize such a performative approach to energy security?

Following these questions, the book promotes a shift away from a pre- and descriptive understanding of the concept of energy security towards an understanding of energy security as performative: to see the designation and use of the concept of energy security as an act in itself.[5] By seeing energy security as an act, the repeated practice of its use 'constitutes', 'maintains' or 'changes' the meaning of the concept itself and the enactment of its material effects, and thereby the potential involvement and identity of the actors behind it and the possible routes of action that are open to them.[6] Such a performative approach forces scholars to move away from the 'quest for certainty' inherent in studies that want to understand what energy security is, and replace this with the acceptance that the concept of energy security is embedded, structured, productive, malleable and used differently by different people in different places at different times.[7]

The performative reading of energy security (PRES) that is proposed in this book builds primarily on critical international relations (IR) theory and critical security studies (CSS), but also draws on insights from new materialism, development studies, political geography, sociology and philosophy. By unpacking the concept of energy security with the help of these different literatures, a reflexive stance is imposed on both the author and reader towards the triangle of political economy, security and natural resource policies and their trade-offs (closely related to the energy trilemma within energy studies depicting the trade-offs between economic concerns, security concerns and environmental concerns).[8] Importantly, these trade-offs point to the fact that energy security is only one aspect within the wider debate on energy, which also includes discussions that start from an energy transition or energy justice perspective.[9]

To be clear, the goal here is not to offer a specific performative reading that explains energy security, but to problematize current understandings of energy security through a rigorous theoretical reflection on the concept and the practices that shape it. These include the different security logics (Chapter 4), the interaction between energy security concerns and the materiality of the actual energy infrastructures (Chapter 5) and a deeper understanding of the politics and power relations behind the organization of energy (Chapter 6). These three, in all their intricacy and heterogeneity, explain part of how people approach and secure the production, transportation and consumption of current and future energy use.

1.2 Argument, contribution and approach

One of the main problems identified within the energy security literature involves the realization that any definition of energy security is inherently unstable, which leads ensuing research to question the 'slippery', 'blurred', 'polysemic', 'multidimensional', 'deepening and widening', 'totality or banality' of the concept itself.[10] Those few studies that do reflect upon the concept either quantify, categorize or try to find logics behind different forms of energy security (Chapter 3). Instead of problematizing this openness, this book argues for an acceptance of its inherent empty and contextualized nature and calls for an understanding of energy security as a security practice that is always already political, in line with earlier work from Ciută and Bridge.[11] It calls for a performative understanding of energy security that does not stop at the identification of the threat and the success or failure of its countermeasures. Instead it moves beyond such questions to the acts that are needed to make energy security come into being in the first place and the subsequent broader socio-material implications and effects that follow from this becoming.

Such an approach immediately highlights three alternative insights for energy security. First, the proliferation of energy security does not stand on its own. It is for example mirrored in food security, where the concept has also kept expanding to include ever more elements.[12] Likewise, the analyses of security (Chapter 4) highlight multiple logics that can all be used to approach energy security. However, to repeat, instead of seeing this as a challenge that needs to be overcome we can also accept the multiplicity of it. That might add a layer of complexity, yes. But, if anything, such complexity should strengthen the need for a different way of thinking about energy security. Second, the acceptance of such a multiplicity imposes a reflective stance on energy security scholars, on how their work acts politically as well. This follows the red line of this book, about the importance of knowledge gathering on and within sociotechnical energy systems and the normative and ethical dimension inherent to these observations. A third, but not final, insight centres on the self-referential aspects of the theories that are used to examine and explain energy and energy security, like neorealism and neo-liberalism. From a performative approach, these theories are not just explaining energy security but are actively involved in producing its future through what they observe and the assumptions that they justify, for example on whether to trust the state, the market or humankind.

In short, by unpacking some of the underlying practices and assumptions behind energy security and by offering a performative understanding of energy security, this book contributes to a deeper understanding of energy security based firmly in the otherwise overall deplorably absent humanities literature in energy studies.[13] In the process, it opens up the concept of security, reflects on the role of the material world in social research and argues for more reflexivity and attention to the knowledge practices behind energy security practices. In addition to its contributions to the energy security literature this book also contributes to the CSS literature, which currently is mostly absent from energy and other natural resource debates, while in turn these sociotechnical systems around natural resources hardly return within the CSS literature.[14] True, CSS has excellent contributions on the relation between finance and security,[15] but always in relation to terrorism or migration, not in relation to natural resources, even though there are clear connections, especially with the recent research into the materiality of security.[16]

Besides CSS, another notable absence from this book is international political economy (IPE). This is notable considering this book studies the security processes behind the political economy of energy, a topic for which IPE has very little if anything to add. Yet, it is also notable because of the origins of the discipline of IPE itself, as this field traces its own roots to the 1973 oil crisis.[17] This absence can be explained by a combination of the relative independence of natural resource debates and the overwhelming focus on economic and financial institutions, globalization, and the organization of markets in IPE. As Strange remarks in her 1988 classic *States and Markets*, energy is a 'classic case of the no man's land lying between the social sciences, an area unexplored and unoccupied by any of the major theoretical disciplines'.[18] Recent work by Hughes and Lipscy shows that this mismatch remains valid, as current energy issues are still conspicuously absent in top-tier IR/IPE journals.[19] Hancock and Vivoda explain this through the preselection practices in the publication strategies of energy scholars, which make them bypass IR and IPE journals and thus the debates and agenda-setting functions of these journals.[20] Interestingly, Hancock and Vivoda still refer to energy as part of IPE and do not see it as a separate field that follows its own progression, nor do they see it as a topic that belongs to a broader natural resource debate. What is more, their future research options for energy cover a range of issues, but a focus on security and the politics energy security is not one of them. Instead, they argue for a move away from the focus on oil to other energy resources and issue areas like renewables, biofuel, electricity and sovereign wealth funds. That they feel the need to mention such basics is shocking, and further evidence of the lacking integration between energy studies and the research in IPE and IR.

Lastly, a brief reflection on methodology and methods in this book. First, many of the theories discussed in this book are not applicable positivist theories and do not offer inductive or deductive explanatory schemes. They are not models predicting behaviour but ways to trace actions, interpretations and relationships. Moreover, the scope and intent of this book is such that there is not one theory or method(ology) that is appropriate for its subject. In fact, as Aradau and Huysmans argue in a recent critical reflection, methods inherently fixate specific epistemological and ontological positions.[21] Choosing a method (or a theory) as a 'neutral' way to analyse an event is therefore a self-defeating exercise as methods and methodologies are effectively a politics of ontology (see Chapter 5). They help shape a specific world the moment they are used to analyse that world. The theoretical scope of this book and more precise the shifting ontological positions within these theories thus inhibit it from clearly taking up one theory or method over another (of course, the decision not to choose is also a decision that performs a specific reality).

Still, that does not mean that the analysed critical theories do not offer tools to study their subjects. Most of the theories below make assumptions on ontology (what exists in the world) and epistemology (what we can know of this world) and thereby offer an interpretation of how reality works. In terms of methods, it could therefore be argued that this book, in an equally loose manner, combines – but does not apply – aspects of deconstruction, discourse analysis, genealogy, 'pearl-fishing', diffractive reading, disclosure, actor-network accounts and so forth. Additionally, the book discusses multiple explicit performative approaches, ranging from the speech acts in Section 4.4 and the performativity of Butler in Section 5.3 to Barad's interpretation of intra-action in Section 5.5 and Foucault's insights on the power/knowledge nexus in Section 6.4. What is shared by all these methods and approaches is a critical stance towards ontology and epistemology, or the awareness that the knowledge we have of the world helps shape it. In other words, they are all, to some extent, performative.

To repeat, this book does not offer *the* performative reading of energy security and the performative reading it offers should be read in *addition* to the existing energy security literature as the reflexivity advanced by a performative reading of energy security actually needs positivist studies to be able to reflect in the first place (see the conclusion). Nevertheless, because all the theories are performative, the conclusion offers a brief reflection on how I personally operationalize across these theories with security in mind, a view that primarily builds on the intra-action between events, observation and assemblages, or how we observe events and gather things together in response. This is still rather general, but an unspecified performative reading offers the openness and self-reflexivity to understand and cope with the world of energy security as it is performed from a wide range of perspectives.[22] Doing so offers scholars the ability to come to a more extensive, although always temporal understanding of the socio-material drivers behind the concepts and practices of energy security.

What is more, even an unspecified and temporal performative reading of energy security offers a range of conclusions for energy security. For instance, it shows that energy security proliferates not because it cannot be defined, but because (1) it is relative and its meaning can be different for different people at the same time, because (2) its usage and context changes continuously and because (3) it is based on empty security logics wherein failure and success always lead to more security. Moreover, the search for a central definition itself acts politically as a form of closure and hides the true virtuality and differences of energy security and is therefore inhibitive of a deeper understanding of the phenomenon and its underlying social processes. Basically, once defined as *the mode through which people identify undesirable energy futures and act upon them in the present*, energy security is no longer solely something to be achieved but emerges as a governance technique aimed at energy circulations that consist of a set of materialdiscursive relations which are constantly performed and disrupted and which consist of humans, things, knowledge, morality, practices and so on. Energy security becomes a performative act which simultaneously is produced and is producing a specific understanding of energy security and the materialdiscursive world around it.[23]

1.3 Overview of chapters

The chapters in this book are divided into three parts. The next two chapters set the stage by introducing the concept of energy security and by problematizing current approaches to energy security. The subsequent three chapters unpack energy security theoretically to come to a deeper understanding of the drivers behind energy security. Finally, the last chapter provides an illustration of an alternative performative reading of energy security, while the conclusion offers a reflection on these insights based on a short summary.

Chapter 2 provides a brief historical conceptualization of energy security. It traces the evolution of the concept in line with its expanding referent object, from a concept focused on security of physical supplies via economic and ecological security towards an understanding of energy security that includes ethical considerations and focuses on energy systems. Chapter 3 subsequently discusses how the current literature approaches energy security. It discusses the categorization of the growth of the number of referent objects behind energy security, the role of geopolitical and neo-liberal theoretical understandings of energy security and some recent theoretical developments within the field of energy security, including the search for underlying logics and contextualization. After concluding that a constant search for the perfect definition of energy security is a neverendingly and highly normative struggle, this book moves on to the question of what energy security *does* politically.

To make this performative move and to come to an understanding of the constant proliferation of energy security, this book draws on three distinct literatures in the next three chapters. Chapter 4 moves from energy security, with its emphasis on energy, to the security practice labelled energy *security*. This chapter offers a theoretical discussion of security along a two-track approach that first discusses how the security literature describes security and then moves on to analyse what security does. Even at first glance this chapter reveals the emptiness of security as well as the multiple different logics behind it that all revolve on the will to know the future and to decide upon its undesirability. This chapter also offers two ways to approach a performative reading of energy security with its discussion of securitization theory and the governmentality of risk. Where the first can be found within studies on energy security (and is briefly illustrated here with the securitization of Russian gas imports by the European Commission), its attention to exceptionality dismisses the routine everyday security questions that make up most of today's energy systems, which is why this chapter introduces the governmentality of risk as an unexplored alternative.

Chapter 5, on the relationship between materiality and knowledge, tries to come to terms with the social understandings of security in relation to the geological and sociotechnical infrastructure that underpins energy systems. This chapter first analyses the linguistic arguments and the performativity of concepts, and then continues by introducing new materialist understandings of the role of matter within such a performative epistemological understanding. Matter here becomes both an impediment (technical solutions to social concerns) and a driver (technological change like the electrification of society) for security arguments towards energy and other fields. Nevertheless, in line with security, this chapter ends by highlighting the importance of knowledge gathering practices and the ethics of observation behind these practices, as materiality offers both the surprise of socio-material events as well as the achievement of closure following the interpretation of these events.

Chapter 6 returns to security by introducing the work of Michel Foucault on biopolitics. Specifically, this chapter studies the broader political effects behind the chapters on security and materialization, which primarily look at the politics inherent to security and ontological politics (how it works and how people get it to work). For these political effects, Foucault offers another theoretical understanding of security. He sees security as a form of political power that is both negative and productive, which enables him to see security as a form of governance that organizes freedom and the continuous circulation of goods and people. However, while Foucault thus offers yet another explanation for security, his reflections on security, knowledge and materiality do enable us to combine some of the insights from the previous chapters and simultaneously show how security acts politically in relation to economic markets, society and the environment.

After these theoretical chapters, Chapter 7 offers an illustration that utilizes some of these theoretical insights to reflect on the constitution and reification of energy security, including its practical consequences. Specifically, it discusses the Dutch debate about the earthquakes that result from natural gas extraction in the north of the Netherlands. This illustration shows how the insecurity of the persons living above the gas fields conflicts with the risk assessments and energy security concerns of the authorities and how the subsequent debate unconsciously reifies current understandings of natural gas supply security. What's more, besides this novel study of these conflicting security logics, this chapter highlights the importance of security processes for the knowledge practices over uncertain material events.

Finally, the conclusion will summarize some of the main findings of this book on energy security. After a summary, it offers a first general assemblage of the performativity behind all the theories discussed in relation to security – focusing on events, observation and assemblages. It subsequently reflects on some of the broader aspects of a performative reading of energy security, about politics, the desire for knowledge, the question of who acts and the always-inherent resistance that breaks materialdiscursive assemblages. The chapter ends with five research topics that deserve further attention and four implications for energy security scholars, policymakers and performative scholars.

Notes

1 Le Billon 2005, 5.
2 Ciută 2010, 124.
3 Conceptually, qualitatively or historically: Winzer 2012; Chester 2010; Cherp and Jewell 2014; Yergin 1991. Quantitatively: Kruyt *et al.* 2009; Jansen and Seebregts 2010; Brown *et al.* 2014; Narula and Reddy 2015. More policy-oriented: Luft and

Korin 2009; CIEP 2004; Kalicki and Goldwyn 2005; Bahgat 2006; Vivoda 2009. And from a social critique: Sheller 2014; Illich 1974; Shove and Walker 2014; Byrne and Toly 2006.
4 Cherp and Jewell 2014.
5 Butler 2010; Barad 2003; Bialasiewicz *et al.* 2007.
6 Aalberts 2006, 3.
7 Herborth 2012.
8 On the energy trilemma, see Figure 3.2 and its discussion in Chapter 3.
9 Goldthau and Sovacool 2012; Sovacool 2013.
10 Chester 2010; Löschel, Moslener and Rübbelke 2010; Sovacool and Brown 2010; Dyer and Trombetta 2013; Ciută 2010; Cherp and Jewell 2011.
11 Ciută 2010; Bridge 2015. See also the broader work on 'energopower' by Boyer 2011; Boyer 2014; Mitchell 2013. Other critical discursive articles include: Smith Stegen 2011; Byrne and Toly 2006; Campbell 2005; Cooper 2013; Fischhendler and Nathan 2014; Herbstreuth 2014; Kurze 2008; Lovell 2008; Nyman 2014; Teschner and Paavola 2013.
12 Jarosz 2011; Smith, Pointing and Maxwell 1992.
13 Sovacool 2014, 11. Also, Urry 2014.
14 Kester 2018.
15 Amoore and De Goede 2008; De Goede 2012.
16 Aradau 2010; Schouten 2014; Walters 2014; Aradau, Coward *et al.* 2015.
17 Gilpin and Gilpin 2001. Gilpin's classic handbook only mentions energy four times: either as a side note or in relation to the 1973 origin of IPE. An exception is Keohane 2009.
18 Strange 1994, 195. See also: Stoddard 2013, 2.
19 Hughes and Lipscy 2013.
20 Hancock and Vivoda 2014.
21 Aradau and Huysmans 2014; Aradau, Huysmans *et al.* 2015.
22 See also: Cooper 2013.
23 Barad 2003.

Bibliography

Aalberts, Tanja E. 2006. *Politics of Sovereignty*. PhD thesis, Amsterdam: Vrije Universiteit.

Amoore, Louise, and Marieke de Goede. 2008. Transactions after 9/11: The banal face of the preemptive strike. *Transactions of the Institute of British Geographers* 33 (2): 173–185.

Aradau, Claudia. 2010. Security that matters: Critical infrastructure and objects of protection. *Security Dialogue* 41 (5): 491–514.

Aradau, Claudia, Martin Coward, Eva Herschinger, Owen D. Thomas and Nadine Voelkner. 2015. Discourse/materiality. In *Critical security methods: New frameworks for analysis*, edited by Claudia Aradau, Jef Huysmans, Andrew Neal and Nadine Voelkner, 57–84. London and New York: Routledge.

Aradau, Claudia, and Jef Huysmans. 2014. Critical methods in international relations: The politics of techniques, devices and acts. *European Journal of International Relations* 20 (3): 596–619.

Aradau, Claudia, Jef Huysmans, Andrew Neal and Nadine Voelkner, eds. 2015. *Critical security methods: New frameworks for analysis*. London and New York: Routledge.

Bahgat, G. 2006. Europe's energy security: Challenges and opportunities. *International Affairs* 82 (5): 961–975.

Barad, Karen. 2003. Posthumanist performativity: Toward an understanding of how matter comes to matter. *Signs* 28 (3): 801–831.

Bialasiewicz, Luiza, David Campbell, Stuart Elden, Stephen Graham, Alex Jeffrey and Alison J. Williams. 2007. Performing security: The imaginative geographies of current US strategy. *Political Geography* 26 (4): 405–422.

Boyer, Dominic. 2011. Energopolitics and the anthropology of energy. *Anthropology News* 52 (5): 5–7.

Boyer, Dominic. 2014. Energopower: An introduction. *Anthropological Quarterly* 87 (2): 309–333.

Bridge, Gavin. 2015. Energy (in)security: World-making in an age of scarcity. *The Geographical Journal* 181 (4): 328–339.

Brown, Marilyn A., Yu Wang, Benjamin K. Sovacool and Anthony Louis D'Agostino. 2014. Forty years of energy security trends: A comparative assessment of 22 industrialized countries. *Energy Research & Social Science* 4: 64–77.

Butler, Judith. 2010. Performative agency. *Journal of Cultural Economy* 3 (2): 147–161.

Byrne, John, and Noah Toly. 2006. Energy as a social project: Recovering a discourse. In *Transforming power: Energy, environment and society in conflict*, edited by John Byrne, Noah Toly and Leigh Glover, 1–32. New Brunswick, NJ, and London: Transaction.

Campbell, David. 2005. The biopolitics of security: Oil, empire, and the sports utility vehicle. *American Quarterly* 57 (3): 943–972.

Cherp, Aleh, and Jessica Jewell. 2011. The three perspectives on energy security: Intellectual history, disciplinary roots and the potential for integration. *Current Opinion in Environmental Sustainability* 3 (4): 202–212.

Cherp, Aleh, and Jessica Jewell. 2014. The concept of energy security: Beyond the four As. *Energy Policy* 75: 415–421.

Chester, Lynne. 2010. Conceptualising energy security and making explicit its polysemic nature. *Energy Policy* 38 (2): 887–895.

CIEP. 2004. *Study on energy supply security and geopolitics – Final report*. CIEP Study for DGTREN. The Hague: Clingendael International Energy Programme.

Ciută, Felix. 2010. Conceptual notes on energy security: Total or banal security? *Security Dialogue* 41 (2): 123–144.

Cooper, Christopher. 2013. Physics envy: Why energy policy is more art than science. *The Journal of World Energy Law & Business* 6 (1): 67–82.

De Goede, Marieke. 2012. *Speculative security: The politics of pursuing terrorist monies*. Minneapolis, MN: University of Minnesota Press.

Dyer, Hugh, and Maria Julia Trombetta. 2013. *International handbook of energy security*. Cheltenham: Edward Elgar.

Fischhendler, Itay, and Daniel Nathan. 2014. In the name of energy security: The struggle over the exportation of Israeli natural gas. *Energy Policy* 70: 152–162.

Gilpin, Robert, and Jean M. Gilpin. 2001. *Global political economy: Understanding the international economic order*. Princeton, NJ: Princeton University Press.

Goldthau, Andreas, and Benjamin K. Sovacool. 2012. The uniqueness of the energy security, justice, and governance problem. *Energy Policy* 41: 232–240.

Hancock, Kathleen J., and Vlado Vivoda. 2014. International political economy: A field born of the OPEC crisis returns to its energy roots. *Energy Research & Social Science* 1: 206–216.

Herborth, Benjamin. 2012. Theorising theorising: Critical realism and the quest for certainty. *Review of International Studies* 38 (01): 235–251.

Herbstreuth, Sebastian. 2014. Constructing dependency: The United States and the problem of foreign oil. *Millennium – Journal of International Studies* 43 (1): 24–42.

Hughes, Llewelyn, and Phillip Y. Lipscy. 2013. The politics of energy. *Annual Review of Political Science* 16 (1): 449–469.

Illich, Ivan. 1974. *Energy and Equity*. New York: Harper & Row.

Jansen, Jaap C., and Ad J. Seebregts. 2010. Long-term energy services security: What is it and how can it be measured and valued? *Energy Policy* 38 (4): 1654–1664.

Jarosz, Lucy. 2011. Defining world hunger: Scale and neoliberal ideology in international food security policy discourse. *Food, Culture and Society: An International Journal of Multidisciplinary Research* 14 (1): 117–139.

Kalicki, Jan H., and David L. Goldwyn. 2005. *Energy and security: Toward a new foreign policy strategy*. Washington, DC: Woodrow Wilson Center Press.

Keohane, Robert O. 2009. The old IPE and the new. *Review of International Political Economy* 16 (1): 34–46.

Kester, Johannes. 2018. Governing electric vehicles: Mobilizing electricity to secure automobility. *Mobilities* 13 (2): 200–215.

Kruyt, B., D. P. Van Vuuren, H. J. M. De Vries and H. Groenenberg. 2009. Indicators for energy security. *Energy Policy* 37 (6): 2166–2181.

Kurze, Kristina. 2008. The changing discourse of energy security. Creating new momentum for energy policy integration in the European Union. Conference paper presented at 'Energy in Europe and North America: From National to Human Security'. In *Energy in Europe and North America: From National to Human Security*. Trento.

Le Billon, Philippe. 2005. The geopolitical economy of 'Resource Wars'. In *The geopolitics of resource wars: Resource dependence, governance and violence*, 1–28. London and New York: Frank Cass.

Löschel, Andreas, Ulf Moslener and Dirk T. G. Rübbelke. 2010. Indicators of energy security in industrialised countries. *Energy Policy* 38 (4): 1665–1671.

Lovell, Heather. 2008. Discourse and innovation journeys: The case of low energy housing in the UK. *Technology Analysis & Strategic Management* 20 (5): 613–632.

Luft, Gal, and Anne Korin. 2009. *Energy security challenges for the 21st century: A reference handbook*. Santa Barbara, CA: Praeger Security International.

Mitchell, Timothy. 2013. *Carbon democracy: Political power in the age of oil*. London: Verso.

Narula, Kapil, and B. Sudhakara Reddy. 2015. Three blind men and an elephant: The case of energy indices to measure energy security and energy sustainability. *Energy* 80: 148–158.

Nyman, Jonna. 2014. 'Red storm ahead': Securitisation of energy in US–China Relations. *Millennium – Journal of International Studies* 43 (1): 43–65.

Schouten, Peer. 2014. Security as controversy: Reassembling security at Amsterdam Airport. *Security Dialogue* 45 (1): 23–42.

Sheller, Mimi. 2014. Global energy cultures of speed and lightness: Materials, mobilities and transnational power. *Theory, Culture & Society* 31 (5): 127–154.

Shove, Elizabeth, and Gordon Walker. 2014. What is energy for? Social practice and energy demand. *Theory, Culture & Society* 31 (5): 41–58.

Smith, Marisol, Judy Pointing, and Simon Maxwell. 1992. Household food security: Concepts and definitions – an annotated bibliography. In *Household food security: Concepts, indicators, and measurements. A technical review*, edited by Simon Maxwell and Timothy R. Frankenberger. Rome: Unicef/IFAD.

Smith Stegen, Karen. 2011. Deconstructing the 'energy weapon': Russia's threat to Europe as case study. *Energy Policy* 39 (10): 6505–6513.

Sovacool, Benjamin K. 2013. *Energy & ethics: Justice and the global energy challenge*. Basingstoke: Palgrave Macmillan.

Sovacool, Benjamin K. 2014. What are we doing here? Analyzing fifteen years of energy scholarship and proposing a social science research agenda. *Energy Research & Social Science* 1: 1–29.

Sovacool, Benjamin K., and Marilyn A. Brown. 2010. Competing dimensions of energy security: An international perspective. *Annual Review of Environment and Resources* 35 (1): 77–108.

Stoddard, Edward. 2013. Reconsidering the ontological foundations of international energy affairs: Realist geopolitics, market liberalism and a politico-economic alternative. *European Security* 22 (4): 437–463.

Strange, Susan. 1994. *States and Markets*. 2nd edn. London: Continuum.

Teschner, Naama, and Jouni Paavola. 2013. Discourses of abundance: Transitions in Israel's energy regime. *Journal of Environmental Policy & Planning* 15 (3): 447–466.

Urry, John. 2014. The problem of energy. *Theory, Culture & Society* 31 (5): 3–20.

Vivoda, Vlado. 2009. Diversification of oil import sources and energy security: A key strategy or an elusive objective? *Energy Policy* 37 (11): 4615–4623.

Walters, William. 2014. Drone strikes, dingpolitik and beyond: Furthering the debate on materiality and security. *Security Dialogue* 45 (2): 101–118.

Winzer, Christian. 2012. Conceptualizing energy security. *Energy Policy* 46: 36–48.

Yergin, Daniel. 1991. *The prize: The epic quest for oil, money & power*. New York: Simon and Shuster.

2 The historic proliferation of energy security

2.1 Introduction

The crux behind debates on energy security is that the insecurity of someone living in a European country differs from those living elsewhere in the world, as well as from those within the same country. Different geographical, temporal and environmental circumstances dictate different energy needs, while different market and regulatory structures dictate the options people have to fulfil these needs. Yet, despite these differences, almost everybody is connected through global energy systems and markets of coal, oil, natural gas, uranium, wood pellets, corn, renewable technology, battery storage and so on. Not a single country can run from the climate effects of these markets nor can it be entirely independent from them. Simultaneously, energy is closely connected to the production, trade and consumption of other resources, while those same resources enable the production of energy, be they water (cooling/hydro), food (biofuels) or rare earth minerals (renewable technologies).[1] Furthermore, the current transformation from a traditional fossil fuel system into a renewable electrified energy system is changing the earth's topography, physical infrastructures, market structures, social habits and power structures.

This complexity returns in debates on the concept of energy security. In fact, Hildyard, Lohmann and Sexton rightly remark that there are two things confusing about energy security: the concept of energy and the concept of security.[2] For Hildyard, Lohmann and Sexton, both of these concepts hide many of the underlying sociopolitical and economic choices behind energy consumption and production, as they only implicitly touch upon the actual choice for a particular energy source or the decision who is in need of security. These latter choices are often foregone conclusions in most policy-oriented energy security debates whose prime focus it is to secure the resulting situation in the first place. In relation to the energy side of energy security,[3] a quick reflection on the meaning of the word already shows that a physicist's definition of energy differs from an economic or a political conceptualization.[4] Physicists understand energy as the work (joules) needed to lift something over a fixed distance and they observe that energy cannot be created or destroyed in closed systems, only transformed into other less useful types of energy.[5] This clearly contrasts with an economic understanding of energy as a commodity to be produced, sold and wasted, let alone with a political understanding of energy as a strategic resource that needs to be acquired and controlled. In this respect, Jansen and Van der Welle remark how it is not energy itself that is in need of securing, but *useful* energy: the energy that fits current sociotechnical energy systems.[6]

Then again, ever more energy sources are useful or made to be useful. Hence, the concept of energy security has evolved along the cyclical whims of the expanding energy markets, in particularly the global oil market. Over the years, the concept 'has quietly slipped into the energy lexicon and assumed a relatively prominent position' as evident by a range of definitions (see Table 2.1).[7] The International Energy Agency (IEA) provides one of the most accepted and basic definitions of energy security and defines energy security as 'adequate, affordable and reliable supplies of energy'.[8] Implicit in this definition is the sense that an agent is energy-*in*secure when the supplies of energy are not adequate, affordable or reliable. However, who defines what is adequate, affordable or reliable? What kind of energy is needed? Who needs to make sure that energy is secure? It seems that the simplicity of the concept quickly breaks down under questioning. An alternative definition is provided by Ciută, who describes energy *in*security as 'the product of the contradiction between a general trend of increasing energy consumption and a contradictory trend of decreasing energy reserves'.[9] Easily grasped in its simplicity and a core logic behind many of the geopolitics-oriented considerations on energy security, such neo-Malthusian thinking is not self-evident and neither is this definition (see Chapter 4).[10] In other words, these definitions break down under scrutiny. So, instead of discussing these and the other definitions in Table 2.1 (to which we will return later on in this chapter), the rest of this chapter provides a history of the evolution of energy security and highlight its expansion by identifying five themes that have become inherent to energy security.

Looking back, most of the literature that studies energy security retraces its origin to the 1970s oil crises, not only for its political and economic import-ance but also because the actual concept of energy security originates from around that period. Of course, this does not mean that the concerns captured by the concept of energy security did not exist before the 1970s. For instance, *security of supply* concerns have a long history, arguably from the moment that people became dependent on others for their tools (in the Bronze Age).[11] However, the political meaning of the concept of *energy*, as denoting a combi-nation of coal, oil, gas and electricity industries and supply chains, only emerged in the early second half of the twentieth century.[12] Before this polit-ical understanding of energy, the discussions focused simply on the resource in question. There was a coal problem or an electricity problem, never an energy problem. The difference becomes clear when one compares Jevons's 1865 argu-ment on the importance of coal with Schumacher's 1964 argument on the importance of energy:

Coal in truth stands not beside but entirely above all other commodities. It is the material energy of the country – the universal aid – the factor in everything we do. With coal almost any feat is possible or easy; without it we are thrown back into the laborious poverty of early times.[13]

There is no substitute for energy. The whole edifice of modern society is built upon it. Although energy can be bought and sold like any other commodity, it is not 'just another commodity' but the precondition of all commodities, a basic factor equal with air, water, and earth.[14]

In comparing these two quotes, three things become apparent. First, the current understanding of energy (and thus energy security) is a relatively modern understanding that has evolved in tandem with developments in markets, society and technology. Second, while the meanings and content might change and concerns can be added to the concept of energy security, some of the primary concerns, like security of supply, seem to remain stable over time. Lastly, the importance and all-pervasiveness of energy in modern societies make any security argument that calls for the protection of energy a self-evident argument, for how can one not secure 'the factor in everything we do' or 'the precondition of all commodities'?

Table 2.1 Definitions of energy security

Source*	Definition
Yergin 1988, 112	'The objective of energy security is to assure adequate, reliable supplies of energy at reasonable prices and in ways that do not jeopardize major national values and objectives.'
Bohi and Toman 1996, 1–2	'Energy insecurity can be defined as the loss of economic welfare that may occur as a result of a change in the price or availability of energy.'
European Commission 2000, 2	'[E]nergy supply security must be geared to ensuring, for the well-being of its citizens and the proper functioning of the economy, the uninterrupted physical availability of energy products on the market, at a price which is affordable for all consumers (private and industrial), while respecting environmental concerns and looking towards sustainable development.... Security of supply does not seek to maximise energy self-sufficiency or to minimise dependence, but aims to reduce the risks linked to such dependence.'
Bielecki 2002, 237	'Energy security is commonly defined as reliable and adequate supply of energy at reasonable prices.'
Barton *et al.* 2004, 5	'as a condition in which a nation and all, or most of its citizens and business have access to sufficient energy resources at reasonable prices for the foreseeable future free from serious risk of major disruption of service.'

Table 2.1 Continued

Source*	Definition
APERC 2007	Four As: *Availability* (physical); *Accessibility* (political-economic barriers); *Affordability* (costs and prices); and *Acceptability* (environmental).
WEC 2008, 4	'Energy security is defined as an uninterruptible supply of energy, in terms of quantities required to meet demand at affordable prices.'
Patterson 2008, n.p.	'The energy security that worries politicians concerns supplies of imported oil and natural gas, not the secure delivery of energy services, such as keeping the lights on.'
Hughes 2009, 2461	'The four 'R's of energy security explain the actions needed to improve energy security, beginning with understanding the problem (review), using less energy (reduce), shifting to secure sources (replace), and limiting new demand to secure sources (restrict).'
Kleber 2009, 2	'Energy security is the capacity to avoid adverse impact of energy disruptions caused either by natural, accidental or intentional events affecting energy and utility supply and distribution systems. [it] possess[es] five characteristics: surety [access], survivability [resilient and durable resources/supply chains], supply [having resources], sufficiency [adequate to demand] and sustainability [limit environmental impact].'
Sovacool and Brown 2010, 81	'We argue … that energy security should be based on the interconnected factors of availability, affordability, efficiency, and environmental stewardship.'
IEA 2010a, 559	'Energy security, broadly defined, means adequate, affordable and reliable supplies of energy. It matters because energy is essential to economic growth and human development. No energy system can be entirely secure in the short term, because disruptions or shortages can arise unexpectedly, whether through sabotage, political intervention, strikes, technical failures, accidents or natural disasters. In the longer term, under-investment in energy production or transportation capacity can lead to shortages and consequently unacceptably high prices. So energy security, in practice, is best seen as a problem of risk management, that is reducing to an acceptable level the risks and consequences of disruptions and adverse long-term market trends.'
Chester 2010, 893	'These findings lead to the contention that the concept of energy security is inherently slippery because it is polysemic in nature. The concept has many possible meanings. Energy security may be delineated through multiple dimensions and it takes on different specificities depending on the country (or continent), timeframe or energy source to which it is applied.'

continued

Table 2.1 Continued

Source*	Definition
Jansen and Seebregts 2010, 1655	'Let us coin the certainty level of enduring, uninterrupted access of the population in a defined region to affordably and competitively priced, environmentally acceptable energy end-use services by the term *energy services security*.'
Sovacool and Mukherjee 2011	Divide APERC's four As into five dimensions: Availability, Affordability, Technology Development, Sustainability, and Regulation.
Jansen and Van der Welle 2011, 241	'We propose to use the term *energy services security* (ESS) instead of energy security as the notion that covers the central topic of this chapter. Hereafter, ESS refers to *the extent to which the population in a defined area (country or region) can have access to affordably and competitively priced, environmentally acceptable energy services of adequate quality*.'
von Hippel *et al.* 2011, 78	A nation state is energy secure to the degree that fuel and energy services are available to ensure: (1) survival of the nation, (2) protection of national welfare and (3) minimization of risks associated with supply and use of fuel and energy services.
Goldthau and Sovacool 2012, 235	'Energy security, defined as the way of equitably providing available, affordable, reliable, efficient, environmentally benign, proactively governed, and socially acceptable energy services to end-users, is gaining ever more prominence on contemporary policy agendas. Energy security has supply-side and demand-side components.'
Winzer 2012, 36	'we suggest narrowing down the concept of energy security to the concept of energy supply continuity. This reduces the overlap between the policy goals of energy security, sustainability and economic efficiency.'
Yergin 2012, 269	'The usual definition of energy security is pretty straightforward: the availability of sufficient supplies at affordable prices. Yet there are several dimensions. The first is physical security.... Second, access to energy is critical.... Third, energy security is also a system.... And finally and crucially, if longer-term in nature – is investment.'
Metcalf 2013, 2	'Energy security is the ability of households, business, and government to accommodate disruptions in supply in energy markets.'
Cherp and Jewell 2014, 415	'We define energy security as low vulnerability of vital energy systems.'

Source: author

Note

* For similar overviews and tables see: Sovacool 2011; Cherp and Jewell 2011; Sovacool and Mukherjee 2011; Winzer 2012; Hughes 2012, 228–229; Boersma 2013. I'm grateful to Jaap de Wilde for pointing out that many of these definitions do not discuss consumers explicitly but implicitly take them as passive consumers, as a people who need to be pleased and are in need of governance. From a critical position, this reinforces the position of the policymakers and scholars discussing and organizing energy security in a top-down manner.

In reality, the public and scholarly attention to energy and energy security concerns fluctuates. The oil crises of the 1970s spurred an increase in attention, but declined in the late 1980s when the market dynamics changed back from the 1970s' producer's market (where producers are able to dictate the market price) to a buyers' market (where demand sets the price). This buyers' market lasted until the rise in prices from 2003 onwards and culminating in the price hike of 2008 following unrest in producing countries, increasing demand from Asia and other developing countries, tightening refinery markets and decreasing production in non-OPEC countries. Together these market developments brought back energy security concerns and fears for a competition over the remaining fossil resources (and renewable technologies).[15] While the general opinion was that this particular producer market was structural, the same price hike of over $140 per barrel in July 2008 coincided with the beginning of the financial crisis that plummeted economic growth and the global demand for energy. This drop in demand, in turn, coincided with an increase in investments in renewables and shale gas technology after the increase in oil and gas prices between 2003 and 2008, in a situation comparable to the responses to the oil crises in the 1970s, which spurred deep-sea non-OPEC oil and gas field exploration. Together these factors have reduced fossil fuel prices and thereby many of the energy *insecurity* concerns in Western energy policies. Even such a brief overview already shows that, when analysing energy security, one constantly has to be aware that energy has both physical (geographic, technologic, infrastructural, environmental), economic and sociopolitical aspects.

The concerns captured with the concept of energy security are wide-ranging and proliferating. In a recent prominent analysis, Chester captures this proliferation by arguing that energy security is a 'polysemic' concept, by which she refers to an understanding of energy security that differs depending its context.[16] In arguing for a contextual approach to energy security, whole-heartedly supported here in this book, it is no longer possible to see the concept as a neutral policy goal. Energy security instead is a 'plastic phrase used by a range of different interest groups to signify many often contradictory goals'.[17] Below this polysemic complexity will be introduced through a brief sketch of the historical shifts in the meaning of energy security. While impressionistic and impossible to date precisely, it is possible to identify five general shifts in this brief overview of the evolution of the energy security literature.[18] Section 2.2 discusses the shift from a physical to a political security of supply; Section 2.3 embraces the economics of energy security; Section 2.4 adds the concerns and complexity of climate change and sustainability; and Sections 2.5 and 2.6 move away from a state-centric focus, respectively downwards towards the individual and upward to the protection of energy systems. The range and complexity of the energy supply chain and all its perceived threats will be analysed more closely in Chapter 3. Furthermore, note that most of the energy security definitions in this chapter share a Western outlook and are thus partial to an energy consumer and market focus, as they consider *security of supply* over the *security of demand* of producers.[19]

2.2 From physical to political security of supply

The availability of and access to natural resources, like water and food, have in some form always been a concern for individuals and governments. In the late nineteenth century, Jevons and Lord Kelvin raised such concerns in relation to the increasing reliance on coal for shipping, production, heat and electricity.[20] However, while Jevons and Lord Kelvin discussed the future of British coal supplies, oil was gradually gaining in significance with the development of the combustion engine. Consequently, concerns over the availability of domestic coal decreased while security of supply concerns over (foreign) oil increased. Churchill's decision to shift the complete British navy to oil before World War I led to one of the first debates that fits a modern understanding of energy supply security.[21] Weighing the increased speed and capacity of the Royal Navy in favour of a dependency on foreign oil from Persia, the British navy tried to minimize that dependency as much as possible. On the one hand, the Admiralty decided to control as much as possible of the supply line itself, among other things by taking ownership of a company nowadays known as British Petroleum (Anglo-Persian), by using that same naval power to secure its own supply lines, and by simultaneously building a domestic reserve. On the other hand, in line with Churchill's claim that '[s]afety and certainty in oil, lie in variety and variety alone', it promoted a global competition of oil suppliers by entering into supply contracts with other companies and their access to oil resources elsewhere in the world.[22]

While the modern energy security literature picked up on the diversification argument, the main argument in Churchill's speech is actually not one of dependency but one of price volatility and market manipulation by a small group of companies.[23] He feared that the navy would become dependent on volatile oil markets and, more precisely, would be overcharged for its oil needs. In Churchill's own words: 'The problem is not one of quantity; it is one of price' and if we are not careful '[i]t would mean, however, that we should be made to pay an excessive price for it'.[24] Still, while Churchill clearly points towards the economics of oil markets, he does so in regards to the military and from within a frame of national security concerns. Hence, the argument is still based on national security of supply concerns – as is the energy security literature at this point.

In fact, this military security of supply argument remained dominant up until the oil crisis of 1973, even though oil became increasingly important in other sectors of society, including mobility, industry and electricity generation.[25] Heavily influenced by two World Wars and the early years of the Cold War, energy security was mainly interpreted in terms of its military value: as a necessity to win wars and thus as something in need of protection.[26] During World War II, many resources, including oil, were heavily regulated. These restrictions only relaxed after the war with the realization that the oil flowed quite abundantly and prices remained low. The Cold War, in turn, highlighted the (strategic) military vulnerability of energy infrastructure (oil refineries, pipelines, electricity plants etc.) and gave birth to the field that nowadays is called critical infrastructure protection.[27]

This changed with the 1973 oil shock when the Organization of the Petroleum Exporting Countries (OPEC) reduced its production level and extended an export restriction towards Israel, the United States and the Netherlands. This first use of the 'oil weapon' against industrial consumer countries reinforced two insights: a strong feeling of foreign dependency and a realization of the importance of energy for economic and social life.[28] The first insight was an acute and broadly shared feeling of dependency across publics in industrialized countries and a longing for the 1960s' uninterrupted flows of low-priced oil.[29] The crises also brought forth the public realization that oil consumption had long trumped coal by tripling in total volume since the end of World War II.[30] Moreover, it led to the recognition that decolonization meant that many of these oil sources no longer fell under colonial rule or under Western markets as they were increasingly being nationalized.[31] Contrary to the public, this was less of a surprise to energy experts, who had been noting the incidents leading up to 1973. These include the European security of supply concerns raised in relation to the Suez Crisis in 1956, the nationalization of Western-owned extraction and transport facilities in former colonies, and the American debate in the 1950s in which domestic oil producers called for and received import quotas against cheap foreign Middle Eastern oil (lasting from 1959 until 1973).[32]

Still, the 1973 oil crisis and its 1979 sibling following the Iranian Revolution shook the world. In response, the industrial countries initiated a number of practical measures to support their continuing oil consumption. This includes the installation of the IEA in 1974 (planned by Kissinger in 1969) and the support from Western governments for the development of new non-OPEC-controlled oil and gas fields, new technological development as well as the shift to alternative energy sources (nuclear).[33] It also initiated a spur in energy security research.[34] For Yergin, who later became known for his book *The Prize* on the evolution of the oil industry, the 1970s' oil shocks and the following energy policies of consumer countries showed that '[t]he focus of energy security concerns is on the shocks – interruptions, disruptions and manipulations of supply – that can lead to sudden, sharp increases in prices and can impose heavy economic and political costs'.[35] Up to this day, politically engineered supply disruptions remain at the core of energy security concerns.

2.3 Securing the economics of energy

A popular solution to such political supply disruptions is independence. However, already in the 1970s after the second oil crisis Nye argued against such a position, as a country will always be part of the global oil market, where the price for a product is set by the last barrel that is sold, meaning that, even with very few imports, those imports still influence domestic price levels and one is still dependent on international affairs and energy markets.[36] Equalling imports with vulnerability therefore only works up to a point and neglects the insight that trade also offers an instrument to dampen supply shocks. This link between global energy markets and the economic and political costs of supply shocks relates to a second insight gained from the 1973 oil crisis: the central importance of oil for economic and social life in general.

The economic crisis that followed the increase in oil prices extended Churchill's earlier military concerns about price volatility to the economy as a whole. The concept of security of supply subsequently broadened to include price fluctuations and their effects on the overall economy besides the existing concerns for uninterrupted physical flows of supplies.[37] In a key text on the link between economics and energy security, Bohi and Toman define energy security as 'the loss of economic welfare that may occur as a result of a change in the price or availability of energy'.[38] To this day, the IEA uses a similar starting point for its definition of energy *in*security: 'Energy insecurity stems from the welfare impact of either the physical unavailability of energy, or prices that are not competitive or overly volatile'.[39] Initially, however, the welfare impacts of oil disruptions remained framed in terms of a dependency on foreign countries. This changed with the privatization and liberalization of consumer countries' energy markets in the 1980s and 1990s, after Thatcher's struggle with the coal miners in Great Britain.[40] In line with Churchill's early concerns about a British dependency on a limited number of oil companies, the meaning of energy security extended to an overall economic vulnerability of consumer countries. In this broadened understanding of vulnerability, not only are foreign countries and companies deemed problematic, but so are domestic companies (investment decisions) and acts (labour strikes) that might hamper the flow of oil, gas, etc.[41]

With the shift in referent object towards the broader economic impact of a supply disruption, the solution to prevent and minimize potential negative impacts of such a disruption shifted as well. Following the neo-liberal-inspired privatization and liberalization programmes, consumer governments increasingly relied on independently operating markets and international institutions to prevent supply disruptions. This market-based understanding of energy security has become quite influential and lies at the core of modern definitions of energy security.[42] The main argument for a market-based energy security policy is that in a well-functioning market 'economic costs may rise but physical shortages do not materialize' due to the self-correcting nature of the market.[43] In a neo-liberal perspective, markets are seen to be delivering security in two ways.[44] In the short term, they prevent physical shortages by shifting supplies to where they are needed based on fluctuating price levels, while in the long term markets promote security because they allow for the free flow of finance and thereby enable investments when and where they are needed to supply future demand.[45] The greater efficiency promised by markets, which in theory leads to lower end user prices, is seen as a welcome bonus to this self-correcting nature.

Because energy markets are seen as the main option to prevent and level out supply disruptions, their future existence is itself cause for concern. This returns in relation to the functioning of markets as well as to the idea of free markets. On the one hand, scholars working on the economics of energy study the markets themselves and ask whether they are operating as they should (they never do). Bohi and Toman, for example, focus on 'energy security externalities' or why energy prices do not reflect all costs and benefits associated with the product. They pay attention to the level of oil imports (either directly in volumes and prices or indirectly through inflation or the trade balance), to the fluctuations in prices and to security expenditures.[46] A more recent contribution by Metcalf reflects on the economics behind energy taxes, the quest for independence and the economic value of diversity and strategic reserves.[47] Similarly, the IEA's attention to 'regulatory failures' in more recent reports on energy security shifts the problem from innocent markets to imprudent governments.[48]

On the other hand, on a more abstract level the idea of neo-liberal markets itself needs protection. For example, one of the reasons why the recent surge in resource nationalism, from both the state-owned producer companies in Russia and the Middle East and the state-owned consumer companies in China and India, is perceived as a threat by Western consumer countries is because it endangers the *idea* of free energy markets (see Section 4.4).[49] Interestingly, there are calls to install a consumer cartel to level this playing field (in addition to the IEA). The recent proposal for a European Energy Union for instance included the idea to negotiate collectively on natural gas with external suppliers.[50] As Labban argues: somehow '[c]artel behavior on the part of the producers … justifies a consumers' cartel; but whereas the former appears to undermine the security of the energy market, the latter appears to guarantee it, as it paradoxically promotes market principles'.[51] From proposals like the one above, the impression rises that free markets are just an instrument for Western consumer countries to govern their security of supply by playing on their primary strength, namely purchasing power.

While the market delivers a way to flatten supply shocks and is seen to organize a long-term balance between supply and demand, it also creates insecurity. Price volatility is one insecurity, but so are the price hikes of bull (upward trend) and bear (downward trend) markets. Both point to the inherent uncertainty of markets. While markets only work when left to their own device, that same lack of control together with the speed of unpredictable and emotion driven shocks leads to calls for intervention. As Mitchell argues, '[t]he paradox for policymakers is that extensive and open energy networks both provide resilience and transmit shocks to physical supply and short-term price'.[52] While the relation between security and markets has never been an easy partnership, the choice for privatization and competition has created a situation wherein the search for lower costs leads to underinvestment on spare capacity, back-up installations and new long-term viable technologies. This is said to have contributed to the Gas Bubble in the UK and to the power blackouts in both America (California, New England) and north-western Europe in the early 2000s.[53]

These local blackouts point to another shift in the concept of energy security. Although extended over time to include gas, the concept of energy security still focused mainly on oil markets at this stage. For example, in his 1988 article

Yergin defined energy security as 'ensuring the availability of oil at reasonable prices'.[54] However, the increasing reliance on nuclear energy and the development of renewable energy sources, the Gas Bubble in the UK and the more recent blackouts of the early 2000s all point towards electricity as a major source of energy on its own. At present, electricity, from whatever source, is counted as the second source of all globally consumed energy.[55] What is more, the extensiveness of the electricity grid, ranging around the globe, is seen as highly vulnerable to external influences, both man-made and natural. In extending the referent object of energy security and the number of energy sources, the quite narrow concept of security of supply evolved into a broader concept of energy security.

2.4 Sustainable energy security

Environmental concerns are another externality of energy markets that simultaneously result from the use of fossil energy fuels and affect the future of those energy systems and markets. Environmental and climate change concerns can be traced to the neo-Malthusian literature of the late 1960s and their official acknowledgement in the report of the Brundtland Commission in 1987.[56] At stake in this third thematic proliferation are not the short-term security of supply concerns but the security of the livelihoods of future generations.

The link between energy security and climate change is strong but not always as obvious as stated. In an overview, Mulligan describes four phases. For Mulligan it starts in the 1960s and 1970s, when there was a clear link between energy scarcity and the impact of energy use, a link that was captured with the term 'ecological security'. In the 1980s and 1990s, he sees the attention shifting to the conflict potential of these environmental impacts under the heading of 'environmental security'.[57] The third phase, in the late 1990s, shifted the discussions back to the global level with a focus on climate change and the Anthropocene. This move to 'climate security' includes the fourth phase of renewed attention to questions of energy resource scarcity, which became prevalent again around 2005 and 2006.[58] The complex relationship between climate change and energy security highlighted by these shifts led some authors to conclude that this link is an 'unnecessarily broad extension' of the concept of energy security.[59] There are in fact two reasons to incorporate sustainable energy in the concept of energy security, but also two that question it.

First, there is a clear relationship between global energy consumption and its negative impacts on climate change and environment degradation. This includes CO_2 and methane emissions that result from fossil fuel consumption but also biodiversity impacts of large-scale infrastructure projects like hydro dams, open-pit mining and first-generation biofuels (including indirect land use change). In turn, climate change is affecting potential future energy production and extraction. There are three main areas where climate change is said to impact energy supplies. First, there is the direct link between energy and climate change impacts. This is exemplified by extreme weather that disrupts electricity distribution or by the need for fresh water in the production and extraction of energy resources (e.g. coal, shale gas, biofuels, etc.) and for the cooling of energy plants. France, for example, was forced to shut down a number of its nuclear reactors in the summers of 2003 and 2009, as high summer temperatures resulted in a rising temperature of the river water, which in turn made cooling of the reactors impossible.[60] Second, a more indirect relationship focuses on the impact of climate change and environmental degradation on vulnerable areas, most often poor and less developed regions.[61] In these circumstances and through its impacts on water, air and food, climate change is said to act as a threat multiplier, causing migration and increased pressure on the resources that are left. Third, a last link can be found in the consequences of the measures against climate change upon future energy production. This link returns especially in the argument of a 'Carbon Bubble'.[62] This financial argument builds on the premise that the remaining carbon fuels that can be safely burned without an increase of global temperatures above the agreed 2°C is not equal to the fossil fuel reserves the major oil and gas companies deem financially viable and upon which they built their investment portfolios. Simply put, according to this argument, the companies are not worth what they and the financial markets think they are.

Second, climate change is part of energy security because the solutions to climate change reflect the solutions for a future secure energy supply. In principle, both build on a sustainable energy supply (a reduction in greenhouse gases) from renewables and passive energy (efficiency, isolation etc.). By expanding the volume of locally produced renewable energy sources and by increasing the efficiency of equipment, the CO_2 emissions and total demand for energy are reduced, as well as the level of dependency from external energy sources. While this argument is correct in that decentralized and domestically produced renewable energy could prevent physical shortages, there are some drawbacks from an energy security perspective. These include the intermittent nature of renewable energy that requires the construction of conventional back-up capacity, storage capacity or demand-side management programmes.[63] It also needs to come to terms with the fact that renewables favour electricity production, whereas transportation is still mainly reliant on oil.[64] The transformation of both sectors is a challenge that will take decades, with fossil fuels remaining prominent in the near future. During this transformation, cultures of consumption but also cost imperatives and the difficulty of providing public goods within private markets might undermine the optimal solution to both climate change and energy security.[65] For example, the recent downward pressure on German wholesale electricity prices is one of the contributing factors to the resurgence of coal as a major input source for electricity (together with the decision to close nuclear power plants and the shale gas revolution in the US that also put downward pressure on global coal prices). Again, countries and individuals are not isolated from the global energy markets. It hardly matters whether you import a little or a lot of an externally produced source of energy, in the event of a tightening market international prices will go up and so too will domestic prices.[66]

This argument goes in fact both ways. It also makes it impossible for a country – especially in the EU – to stimulate domestic renewable production directly as these effects spread out over other countries.[67]

The link between climate change and energy security is clearly a complicated one. In this respect, Luft, Korin and Gupta make two critical remarks.[68] First, although they do not question the direct linkages between climate change and energy supplies, as in the example of rising temperatures/adverse weather impacts on French energy production, they do question the usefulness of including second-order effects of climate change, like migration and civil conflict, to the concept of energy security. For Luft, Korin and Gupta these indirect effects open the definition of energy security to many other second-order concerns. They mention religion, which could easily be ascribed a role in energy security analyses as well.[69] Second, they critically reflect upon the inherent negativity of the relationship between climate change and energy supply. From an energy security perspective, they argue that theoretically there could be positive developments as well. In this respect, they point to the recent surge in interest towards the Arctic, where higher temperatures enable new trade routes and deep-sea oil and gas exploration.[70] Bad for the environment, but potentially increasing the security of a fossil fuel-based energy system. The fact remains that both are linked very closely in a multitude of ways. Hence, this rethinking of the relationship between climate change and energy security highlights a third general reflection on the constant struggle between the short-term urgency of energy supply shocks and its long-term sustainability.[71]

2.5 Human energy insecurity

Together with the surge in environmental awareness, the energy security literature also moved away from its state-centric approach to human-centric appraisals of energy security. Among others, the 1994 UNDP report on human security helped codify the focus shift towards the individual as a referent object in energy security discussions by arguing that:[72]

> Of the world's six billion people, one-third enjoy the kind of energy on demand that Americans take for granted … and another third have such energy services intermittently. The final third – two billion people – simply lack access to modern energy systems.[73]

This geographical inequality is further complicated by the realization that in energy-secure nations too there are individuals who do not enjoy such provisions. The resulting break with a state-centric understanding of energy security is captured with the concept *energy poverty*, a concept that comes in three flavours.[74]

The first interpretation of energy poverty focuses on the individual from an economic developmental perspective and is used especially in relation to individuals in underdeveloped countries. In these countries and regions, the energy security of the poor is centred on the availability of and access to modern electricity and cooking equipment. This interpretation stems from a developmental engineering perspective that, on the one hand, analyses the health consequences of traditional biomass energy consumption and, on the other hand, emphasizes the construction, improvement and affordability of a minimum energy infrastructure (based on an appraisal of basic energy needs in that particular environment).[75]

A second understanding of energy poverty is largely favoured in developed Western countries. Here access and availability are not the core problem but affordability is. Also called fuel poverty, this idea, which Moore traces back to the early 1980s, considers everybody who spends more than 10 per cent of their income on energy as energy poor.[76] Discussions range on what counts as income, how fuel costs are calculated and at what percentage or threshold someone can be considered energy poor. This latter benchmark is often connected to considerations of minimum energy needs, predominantly in terms of minimum room temperatures during winter and subsequent social support programmes for those who fall below this line.

Together these two readings lead to a third overarching understanding of energy poverty. At a more abstract and global level, energy poverty is discussed comparatively in terms of global energy justice.[77] This perspective also starts with the actual access to and affordability of energy, without which there is no justice at all. However, the ideal type of energy justice goes further. In a recent contribution, Sovacool argues that a just energy world is based on intergenerational (between generations) and intragenerational (within a generation) *equity*, in terms of *availability* and *affordability* of energy, access to high-quality *information*, and decision makers following *due process* and acting with *prudency* and *responsibility* when deciding on energy investments.[78] Heffron and McCauley make a similar distinction between distributional justice (dealing with access and affordability) and subsequent procedural justice in relation to collective decision-making processes.[79] Comparable to the other two approaches to energy poverty, the focus on distributional justice implies that in this case as well the core question remains 'how much and what kind of energy enables a person to live a truly human life without interfering with or diminishing the ability of others to do the same'.[80]

Two general remarks can be made about this literature. First, the shift towards individuals is not uniform. While energy justice is often discussed in favour of an individual's access and affordability to energy, the measurement of this often caps at a household level, as household are easiest to measure. This however obscures the intra-household and family disparities. Then again, without physical access for the household as a whole the individual has no access either. In this respect, Pachauri defines *household* energy security:

> In terms of access to secure, stable, and reliable supplies of modern energy
> at affordable prices in amounts adequate to meet demands for energy

services in full so as to ensure human health and well-being. In contrast, energy insecurity can be seen as a lack of, or inconsistent access to, sufficient affordable energy of the type and quality necessary for a healthy life.[81]

To be fair, this is a relatively comparable definition of energy (in)security to other more national and state-centric definitions.

However, second, Pachauri's definition does introduce the importance and difference between energy supplies and energy services. 'As energy expert Amory Lovins has long pointed out, people do not want energy or kilowatt hours; they want "hot showers, cold beer, lit rooms"'.[82] People are not interested in oil; they are interested in the services that are made possible by burning oil: movement, light, heat, cooling etc. Whereas most of the state- and market-oriented perspectives discussed above focus on the access, availability and affordability of energy supplies and the markets that deliver them, the focus on individuals and the returning question of what needs to be considered as basic energy needs highlights the services to which those supplies are put to use.[83] For this reason, Patterson expressly starts from energy services and shows how such a departure enables the inclusion of alternative ways to reach those services that have nothing to do with commoditized fuel supplies, like an optimal use of ambient energy.[84] In doing so, the referent object of energy security shifts once more to a point between the security of supplies and the impact on economic and social life.[85]

2.6 Securing energy systems

A last shift in perspective (and referent object) can be found in discussions on the protection of energy systems. Difficult to pinpoint to a particular publication or time, this perspective builds on ideas about complex systems in the environmentalist literature and the protection of vital systems in the 1950s and 1960s strategic defence literature.[86] With these, energy security again moves away from a state-centric understanding of energy security, but not down to the individual but up to the complexity of vital energy supply chains and systems. When analysing the energy security literature from a systems perspective, the protection of total supply chains as well as the interaction with adjacent vital systems often return. However, besides these much-discussed vital energy systems there is another considerably smaller systems reading, a critical one, that reviews the self-referentiality in current energy systems. For authors like Illich and Bryne, discussed below, the system of energy production and consumption itself is problematic as the current organization of energy is inherently pushing for more of the same, and consequently, in terms of the above-discussed sustainability and equality concerns, threatening from a security perspective.

Regarding the first 'traditional' energy system debate, it should be clear that a focus on energy systems disregards individuals and nations except as part of the overall system. Often the physical infrastructure is the focal point of energy security analyses, especially in relation to the vulnerability to military or

terrorist attacks, but also in relation to extreme weather, human error or insuffi-
cient maintenance.[87] Under the general heading of critical infrastructure
protection (CIP), the physical infrastructure of electricity grids and power
plants, oil and gas pipelines or refineries is protected against intentional disruptions.[88] These disruptions can be aimed at the infrastructure itself (nuclear
power plant) or indirectly at the services that the infrastructure enables (dis-
rupting socio-economic life through the electricity grid).[89] Two reflections are
in order. First, in an energy system where there are always nodes or parts of the
system that are less protected than others, the desire to defend against unpredictable attacks from either a physical or cyber origins results in the desire to
protect the entirety of the infrastructure system.[90] This includes the infinitely
small-scale daily objects and practices that lie at the base of these large-scale
assemblages.[91] At the same time, knowing that total protection is not possible,
the aim is to build a resilient system that can handle adverse disruptions with
minimum impact. To speed this along, attention is paid to those installations
that are prioritized as most vulnerable or are likely to have the highest impact.[92]
Second, although prioritization is useful, the core characteristic of a system as a
referent object is that it is never closed. For example, the electricity grid, when
seen as a system, links to other infrastructure systems – telecommunications,
finance, water, public services and transportation – and is hence vulnerable to
potential cascading effects between them. This leads to the urge to control those
systems too and thereby highlights the constant tension between a search for
control and a sense of vulnerability (see Chapter 4).

If a 'system' is interpreted more broadly, it becomes possible to engage with
the critical literature that discusses the energy system as part of society in what
it calls an 'energy regime'.[93] Scholars working from such a critical Marxist-
inspired perspective study the internal logics of the physical energy infrastructure, energy markets, regulatory regimes and production and consumption habits
of individuals in relation to the lock-in effects that uphold the status quo of
current energy regimes.[94] This perspective argues that the technological path
dependency of increasingly complex systems and the neo-liberal market incentives within this system constantly work to reinforce the desire for more energy
consumption and thereby foreclose any serious reflection upon consumption
itself. For these critical authors, the energy regime is a regime that builds upon
failures and externalities by patching the holes, thus adding more of itself in a
constant reinforcement of its basic tenets. In other words, it argues that current
energy regimes do not reflect upon the underlying dynamics that help cause
those externalities and insecurities. In addition, new solutions, like modern-day
renewable energy, only seem to gain general reception because of their direct
link towards the existing regime, for example as they gain financial viability.[95]
As Hildyard, Lohmann and Sexton remark:

> If fossil-fueled capitalism has defined what we mean by energy, then merely
> to use the word uncritically is to make a commitment to certain assump-
> tions about scarcity, foreclose certain alternatives and cover up some of the

most important issues that need to be discussed. Paradoxically, having a serious discussion about 'energy security' requires taking a therapeutic step back from the modern concept of Energy itself.[96]

From this perspective, energy security or general security practices are not something to be achieved but an 'administrative logic' (Chapter 6) that is part of the self-reinforcing nature of the current neo-liberal energy regime.[97] In other words, this energy regime literature argues that any understanding of energy security would not be complete without a critical reflection on what energy security *does* in terms of possible consequences and effects, besides questioning the essence of what energy security *is*.

2.7 Reflection: defining energy security

The brief historically oriented analysis of the concept of energy security above clearly highlighted the proliferations of the different themes and forms that are captured by a broad policy-oriented reading of the concept of energy security. The main conclusion that can be drawn from this overview is that energy security is an empty concept, but an empty concept with strong political and social impacts and one that is always filled by someone with a reference to something or someone. Although the meaning of energy security itself evolves over time (from individual resources to energy), what mainly shifts are the referent objects that are in need of security (supplies, services, human health, national wealth, environmental sustainability, infrastructure systems etc.). With the growing importance of energy in all aspects of socio-economic life, this means that by now almost all of our lives are subject to and in need of energy security.[98]

Many definitions of energy security try to capture this proliferation by adding aspects to the core definition of the IEA on 'the uninterrupted availability of energy sources at an affordable price'.[99] Table 2.1 listed a number of definitions, but two are worth mentioning in lieu of their extensiveness. The European Commission's green paper on energy security (supplies), from 2000, provides one of the most extensive definitions of energy supply security available to date:

> Energy supply security must be geared to ensuring, for the well-being of its citizens and the proper functioning of the economy, the uninterrupted physical availability of energy products on the market, at a price which is affordable for all consumers (private and industrial), while respecting environmental concerns and looking towards sustainable development.... Security of supply does not seek to maximise energy self-sufficiency or to minimise dependence, but aims to reduce the risks linked to such dependence.[100]

Likewise, Barton *et al.* in a 2004 legal discussion of energy security (services) define it as:

A condition in which a nation and all, or most of its citizens and business have access to sufficient energy resources at reasonable prices for the foreseeable future free from serious risk of major disruption of service.[101]

Despite their extensiveness, these definitions primarily highlight what is missing. There is no agreement on *what needs protection* (the source of energy or energy in general, the infrastructure, the supplies, the services, the markets that deliver them). There is no agreement *whose energy needs are protected* (the state, the market or business, the individual or the system as whole). Moreover, they leave open *who decides on the relativeness* of these definitions (the level of affordability, sufficiency, proper functioning, respectful environmental behaviour, and seriousness of risk). In addition, the definition from Barton *et al.* leads to the question whether it is truly possible to achieve the goal of energy security at all. While the European Commission searches for energy security for *all*, Barton and colleagues offer a definition where energy security is reached when *most* of the citizens and businesses are secure, not all of them.

Following similar lines of argumentation, the general conclusion by energy security scholars seems to be that energy security cannot be defined universally and that the referent objects will keep expanding.[102] One exception includes a recent reflection by Cherp and Jewell, who argue that, even though the meaning of energy security is contextual, there is still some shared core meaning behind it.[103] They point towards the values behind energy, the 'acquired values' of modern life, but do not explain these further.[104] In response, Ciută disagrees with such a hidden and shared understanding of energy security (as well as the search for a perfect all-encompassing definition) by asking whether it is actually the totalizing tendency of energy that makes energy security a banality.[105] If everything is energy and hence part of energy security, than its security becomes in essence unexceptional (banal) and consequentially no longer a form of security. However, Ciută argues that the totality of energy should not be translated to its security side.[106] While energy is everywhere, security should not be in line with its prioritization function. Which, in line with this book, points to the need to study energy security *as* a security practice.

Furthermore, definitions of energy security not only contain assumptions about referent objects or particular teleology of security that explain what energy security is and ought to be, but also hide another layer of assumptions and value judgements on a range of issues that include economic growth, progress, technological development, scarcity and abundance, trust in markets and so forth.[107] In this respect, even the cursory glance above highlights the difference between two dominant readings of energy security: on the one hand, a geopolitical interpretation of nation states caught in a zero-sum game of conflict over the last remaining scarce resources and, on the other, a neo-liberal market interpretation of energy security that puts its faith in energy markets to distribute resources and develop substitutes. Such differences in core assumptions on conflict (yes, no), scarcity (yes, no), control (politics, markets) and potential technological development (unimportant, substitution) are what separate the different readings of energy security. Still, these two readings dominate the discussions on energy security, and although they differ on important assumptions, the capital-intensive and central-ized decision-making tendencies behind both of them have historically implied that energy security is a concern for national governments. This state-centrism in turn leads Hildyard, Lohmann and Sexton to differentiate between the high pol-itics of 'Energy Security' (state-centric, geopolitical readings of free markets) and the low politics of 'energy security' (individualized services, sustainability and system maintenance).[108] In other words, while the five evolutions identified in this chapter might add to a broader and deeper understanding of energy security, they are not read, discussed and rated with equal importance.

In sum, the brief overview above shows that what started as a political security of supply concern quickly evolved into a set of concerns on political and military intervention, market externalities, environmental consequences, health, affordability and the resilience of systems. The continuing evolution of the concept of energy security shows a proliferation of concerns and referent objects that follows the evolving technological application of energy in our lives. The subsequent discussion brought to light the empty and polysemic nature of energy security and thus the need for contextualization. Such an evolving conceptualization makes for a banal understanding of energy security on two accounts. First, because it spreads a simplistic binary understanding of security that stems from the two dominant theoretical readings of energy security (geopolitics and neo-liberalism). Neither of these provides an actual reflection of the broader (ethical) security theories and questions behind energy security; they simply observe and reflect the normative logic and power politics behind current energy markets. Second, it keeps including new (commoditized) referent objects as a way to tackle newly identified shortcomings. Consequently, energy security is something that will never be reached, as it will always fail the next shortcoming. However, as Bridge argues, precisely in this failing '"energy" when conjoined with "security" creates a potent discursive couplet that is reduc-tive and performative in equal measure'.[109]

Notes

1 Andrews-Speed *et al.* 2012; Beisheim 2013; Beddington 2009.
2 Hildyard, Lohmann and Sexton 2012, 6. For a similar argument, see: Bridge 2015.
3 Chapter 4 will discuss the intricacies of the security side of energy security.
4 Stern and Aronson 1984, 14–21. In their work, Stern and Aronson identify four perspectives besides a physicist understanding of energy. These include energy as a commodity (economics), as an ecological resource, as a social necessity and as a strategic material. See also Illich 2009, 13.
5 In turn, power denotes the work done per unit of time (joules per second = watt). In terms of the discussion on materiality in Chapter 5, energy is an interesting phe-nomenon as it escapes clear categorization and is neither matter nor force nor social construction, but all of them together.
6 Jansen and Van der Welle 2011, 240. For politicians and those working from a security perspective, the referent object of energy itself (that which needs securing) is never the issue; it can be anything. See also Chapter 4.

7 Chester 2010, 887.
8 IEA 2010a, 559. More generally, the IEA defines energy security as 'the uninter-rupted availability of energy sources at an affordable price' – see IEA 2015.
9 Ciută 2010, 126.
10 Hirsch 1976; Xenos 1989; Achterhuis 1988; Mehta 2010.
11 Buijs, Sievers and Tercero Espinoza 2012, 201.
12 Patterson 2008, 2; Illich 2009.
13 Jevons 1866, chap. I-Introduction and Outline. See also Yergin 1991, 543.
14 Schumacher and Kirk 1977, 1–2. See also Yergin 1991, 559.
15 Hoogeveen and Perlot 2005; Yergin 2006; Mallaby 2006; Klare 2008.
16 Chester 2010.
17 Hildyard, Lohmann and Sexton 2012, 5. For similar arguments see: Winzer 2012, 36; Labban 2011, 327.
18 Interestingly, the positions themselves were already identified by Stern and Aronson 1984. Yet, when analysing the energy security literature many of these positions have only been incorporated at later stages. Also, the five themes are here inter-preted inclusionary, as only together they make up the definition of energy security (in line with the multiplicity behind a politics of ontology – see Chapter 5).
19 Chester 2010, 891.
20 Jevons 1866; Yergin 2012, 3.
21 Yergin 1991, 153–164.
22 Ibid., 160; Parliamentary Debates, Commons 1913, 1477.
23 Parliamentary Debates, Commons 1913, 1473.
24 Ibid., 1473, 1474.
25 Mitchell 2000.
26 Ibid.; Cherp and Jewell 2011.
27 Collier and Lakoff 2008b.
28 Cherp and Jewell 2011. Stern 2006, 1650, argues that the 'oil weapon' was first termed by the League of Nations debating possible sanctions against Italy in 1935, and first applied by the United States when it sanctioned Japan over its occupation of China in 1941 (80 per cent of Japanese imports).
29 Mitchell 2000.
30 Yergin 1991.
31 Cherp and Jewell 2011.
32 Stern 2006; Yergin 1991, 535–540.
33 On Kissinger see: Labban 2011.
34 See for example: Akins 1973; Bradley 1973; Levy 1973; Pollack 1973; Gordon 1974; Kemp 1978; Stobaugh and Yergin 1978; Deese 1979; Lieber 1980.
35 Yergin 1988, 112, 1991.
36 Nye 1981, 12–13. For an earlier take on dependency see: Lubell 1961. For a more recent discussion see: Verrastro and Ladislaw 2007; Greene 2010.
37 Bohi and Toman 1996, 3.
38 Ibid., 1–2.
39 IEA 2007, 12.
40 Bohi and Toman 1996, 3; Cherp and Jewell 2011.
41 See Mitchell 2013 for an alternative interpretation of these strikes.
42 IEA 2007, 12 and 32.
43 Bohi and Toman 1996, 4.
44 Labban 2011, 331.
45 WEC 2008.
46 Bohi and Toman 1996. They also conclude that except for the trade balance, which depend on the country in question, none of the indirect price effects have been proven.
47 Metcalf 2013. See also Mulder, ten Cate and Zwart 2007 on strategic reserves.

48 IEA 2007, 33–34.
49 Labban 2011.
50 European Commission 2015, 6; Beckman 2015.
51 Labban 2011, 335.
52 Mitchell 2000.
53 Mitchell 2002, 6; Bielecki 2002, 236.
54 Yergin 1988, 114. To be fair, in the same article his main conclusion was based on the importance of energy efficiency, which he claimed had 'turned out to be the most important incremental energy "source" of all' during the 1970s and 1980s; see ibid., 114–115.
55 Chester 2010, 889; Bielecki 2002, 247–248.
56 Brundtland 1987; Meadows *et al.* 1972; Ehrlich 1970; Carson 1981; Dalby 2006, 2014. For an historical overview, see: Mulligan 2010.
57 See: Homer-Dixon 1991, 1994.
58 Mulligan 2010; La Branche 2013, 403–404.
59 Wright 2005, 2273; Luft, Korin and Gupta 2011.
60 Pagnamenta 2009.
61 Brown and Dworking 2011.
62 Carbon Tracker Initiative 2011.
63 Kester 2016.
64 Kester 2018.
65 Brown and Huntington 2008; Luft, Korin and Gupta 2011, 48–51.
66 Mitchell 2000.
67 Mallaby 2006.
68 Luft, Korin and Gupta 2011.
69 Ibid., 46.
70 Ibid., 47.
71 La Branche 2013, 412.
72 UNDP 1994.
73 Wirth, Boyden Gray and Podesta 2003, 138.
74 Bhattacharyya 2013, 424.
75 Bhattacharyya 2013; IEA 2010b; Kaygusuz 2011; Prasad 2011; Sokona, Mulugetta and Gujba 2012; Okereke and Yusuf 2013.
76 Moore 2012; Hills 2012; Middlemiss and Gillard 2015.
77 Pachauri 2011b; Goldthau and Sovacool 2012; Sovacool 2013; Sovacool, Sidortsov and Jones 2014; Heffron and McCauley 2014. For an early discussion, see: Illich 1974.
78 Sovacool 2013, 12.
79 Heffron and McCauley 2014.
80 Sovacool, Sidortsov and Jones 2014, 197.
81 Pachauri 2011a, 191.
82 Hildyard, Lohmann and Sexton 2012, 8, quoting Lovins 1990, 21.
83 Patterson 2008, 2010; Jansen 2009; Jansen and Seebregts 2010.
84 Patterson 2008. Ambient energy refers to the energy already available: sunlight, body heat, the shadow of trees and so forth.
85 See also: Winzer 2012, 37.
86 For an analysis on the origins of CIP see Collier and Lakoff 2008b, 2008a, 2015; Lakoff and Collier 2010. For one of the earliest systematic reflections, see Lovins and Lovins 1982. Collier and Lakoff have described its genealogy by analysing the correlation between the 'invention' of scenario studies and the protection of large-scale infrastructure systems following World War II. What they show is how the growing material development of vast and connected infrastructures – of energy, communication and mobility – together with a deeper scientific understanding of biological and chemical flow processes has led to a governing of complex

interconnected infrastructure systems. A governing of systems, which in turn has been heavily influenced by scenario techniques, which led to an understanding of inherent vulnerability that nowadays supports all approaches to infrastructure systems. For an interesting reflection, see Coward 2009.

87 Cherp and Jewell 2014.
88 Farrell, Zerriffi and Dowlatabadi 2004.
89 Labban 2011.
90 Ibid., 338.
91 Mayer and Acuto 2015, 678; Voelkner 2011, 2012. In this respect, Graham and Thrift discuss the mundane activities of maintenance and repair of the electricity grid, and in particular how, while often overlooked in political debates, the organization of these activities is a highly political affair that influences the future direction of the grid, and consequently our electricity consumption. See Graham and Thrift 2007; see also Bennett 2005.
92 Farrell, Zerriffi and Dowlatabadi 2004, 440.
93 Byrne and Toly 2006; Hornborg 2013; Illich 1974, 2009; Nye 2014; Huber 2009, 2011a, 2011b; Labban 2010.
94 Byrne and Toly 2006.
95 Ibid., 15–16.
96 Hildyard, Lohmann and Sexton 2012, 19–20.
97 Bridge 2015, 3.
98 Ciută 2010, 124.
99 IEA 2015; Cherp and Jewell 2014, 417.
100 European Commission 2000, 2.
101 Barton *et al.* 2004, 5.
102 Winzer 2012; Chester 2010.
103 Cherp and Jewell 2014.
104 Ibid., 416.
105 Ciută 2010, esp. 138.
106 Ciută 2010.
107 Von Hippel *et al.* 2011; Valentine 2011.
108 Hildyard, Lohmann and Sexton 2012.
109 Bridge 2015, 1.

Bibliography

Achterhuis, Hans. 1988. *Het Rijk van de Schaarste: van Thomas Hobbes tot Michel Foucault.* Baarn: Ambo.

Akins, James E. 1973. The oil crisis: This time the wolf is here. *Foreign Affairs* 51 (3): 462–490.

Andrews-Speed, P., R. Bleischwitz, Tim Boersma, Corey Johnson, Geoffrey Kemp and Stacy D. VanDeveer. 2012. *The global resource nexus: The struggles for land, energy, food, water, and minerals.* Washington, DC: Transatlantic Academy.

APERC. 2007. *A quest for energy security in the 21st century: Resources and constraints.* Tokyo: Asia Pacific Energy Research Centre.

Barton, Barry, Catherine Redgwell, Anita Ronne and Donald N. Zillman. 2004. Introduction. In *Energy security: Managing risk in a dynamic legal and regulatory environment,* edited by Barry Barton, Catherine Redgwell, Anita Ronne and Donald N. Zillman, 3–16. Oxford, NY: Oxford University Press.

Beckman, Karel. 2015. The plan behind the EU Energy Union. *EnergyPost.eu.* Available from www.energypost.eu/energy-union-now-never-european-energy-policy. Accessed 9 June 2015.

Beddington, John. 2009. *Food, energy, water and the climate: A perfect storm of global events.* London: Government Office for Science.

Beisheim, Marianne. 2013. *The water, energy & food security nexus: How to govern complex risks to sustainable supply?* SWP Comments. Berlin: Stifting Wissenschaft und Politik.

Bennett, Jane. 2005. The agency of assemblages and the North American blackout. *Public Culture* 17 (3): 445–65.

Bhattacharyya, Subhes C. 2013. Energy poverty: Access, health and welfare. In *International handbook of energy security*, edited by Hugh Dyer and Maria Julia Trombetta, 423–442. Cheltenham: Edward Elgar.

Bielecki, Janusz. 2002. Energy security: Is the wolf at the door? *The Quarterly Review of Economics and Finance* 42 (2): 235–250.

Boersma, Tim. 2013. *Dealing with energy security in Europe: A comparison of gas market policies in the European Union and the United States.* PhD thesis, Groningen: University of Groningen.

Bohi, Douglas R., and Michael A. Toman. 1996. *The economics of energy security.* Norwell, MA: Kluwer.

Bradley, Paul G. 1973. Increasing scarcity: The case of energy resources. *The American Economic Review* 63 (2): 119–125.

Bridge, Gavin. 2015. Energy (in)security: World-making in an age of scarcity. *The Geographical Journal* 181 (4): 328–339.

Brown, Marilyn A., and Michael Dworking. 2011. The environmental dimension of energy security. In *The Routledge handbook of energy security*, edited by Benjamin K. Sovacool, 176–190. London and New York: Routledge.

Brown, Stephen P. A., and Hillard G. Huntington. 2008. Energy security and climate change protection: Complementarity or trade-off? *Energy Policy* 36 (9): 3510–3513.

Brundtland, Gro Harlem. 1987. *Our common future: Report of the World Commission on Environment and Development.* United Nations.

Buijs, Bram, Henrike Sievers and Luis A. Tercero Espinoza. 2012. Limits to the critical raw materials approach. *Waste and Resource Management* 165 (WR4): 201–208.

Byrne, John, and Noah Toly. 2006. Energy as a social project: Recovering a discourse. In *Transforming power: Energy, environment and society in conflict*, edited by John Byrne, Noah Toly and Leigh Glover, 1–32. New Brunswick, NJ, and London: Transaction.

Carbon Tracker Initiative. 2011. *Unburnable carbon: Are the world's financial markets carrying a carbon bubble?* Available from www.carbontracker.org/wp-content/uploads/2014/09/Unburnable-Carbon-Full-rev2-1.pdf.

Carson, Rachel. 1981. *Silent spring.* Greenwich, CT: Fawcett.

Cherp, Aleh, and Jessica Jewell. 2011. The three perspectives on energy security: Intellectual history, disciplinary roots and the potential for integration. *Current Opinion in Environmental Sustainability* 3 (4): 202–212.

Cherp, Aleh, and Jessica Jewell. 2014. The concept of energy security: Beyond the four As. *Energy Policy* 75: 415–421.

Chester, Lynne. 2010. Conceptualising energy security and making explicit its polysemic nature. *Energy Policy* 38 (2): 887–895.

Ciută, Felix. 2010. Conceptual notes on energy security: Total or banal security? *Security Dialogue* 41 (2): 123–144.

Collier, Stephen J., and Andrew Lakoff. 2008a. Distributed preparedness: The spatial logic of domestic security in the United States. *Environment and Planning D: Society and Space* 26 (1): 7–28.

Collier, Stephen J., and Andrew Lakoff. 2008b. The vulnerability of vital systems: How 'critical infrastructure' became a security problem. In *The politics of securing the homeland: Critical infrastructure, risk and securitisation*, edited by Myriam Dunn Cavelty, 40–62. London and New York: Routledge.

Collier, Stephen J., and Andrew Lakoff. 2015. Vital systems security: Reflexive biopolitics and the government of emergency. *Theory, Culture & Society* 32 (2): 19–51.

Coward, Martin. 2009. Network-centric violence, Critical infrastructure and the urbanization of security. *Security Dialogue* 40 (4–5): 399–418.

Dalby, Simon. 2006. Ecology, security, and change in the Anthropocene. *Brown Journal of World Affairs* 13: 155.

Dalby, Simon. 2014. Rethinking geopolitics: Climate security in the Anthropocene. *Global Policy* 5 (1): 1–9.

Deese, D. A. 1979. Energy: Economics, politics, and security. *International Security* 4 (3): 140–153.

Ehrlich, Paul R. 1970. *The population bomb*. 13th print edition. New York: Sierra Club/ Ballantine.

European Commission. 2000. *Green Paper: Towards a European strategy for the security of energy supply*. COM(2000) 769 final. Brussels: European Commission.

European Commission. 2015. *Energy union package: A framework Strategy for a resilient energy union with a forward-looking climate change policy*. COM(2015) 80 final. Brussels: European Commission.

Farrell, Alexander E., Hisham Zerriffi and Hadi Dowlatabadi. 2004. Energy infrastructure and security. *Annual Review of Environment and Resources* 29 (1): 421–469.

Goldthau, Andreas, and Benjamin K. Sovacool. 2012. The uniqueness of the energy security, justice, and governance problem. *Energy Policy* 41: 232–240.

Gordon, Richard L. 1974. Mythology and reality in energy policy. *Energy Policy* 2 (3): 189–203.

Graham, Stephen, and Nigel Thrift. 2007. Out of order: Understanding repair and maintenance. *Theory, Culture & Society* 24 (3): 1–25.

Greene, D. L. 2010. Measuring energy security: Can the United States achieve oil independence? *Energy Policy* 38 (4): 1614–1621.

Heffron, Raphael J., and Darren McCauley. 2014. Achieving sustainable supply chains through energy justice. *Applied Energy* 123: 435–437.

Hildyard, Nicholas, Larry Lohmann, and Sarah Sexton. 2012. *Energy security: For whom? For what?* London: Corner House.

Hills, John. 2012. *Getting the measure of fuel poverty: Final report of the fuel poverty review*. CASE report. Fuel Poverty Review. London: Centre for Analysis of Social Exclusion, LSE.

Von Hippel, David F., Tatsujiro Suzuki, James H. Williams, Timothy Savage and Peter Hayes. 2011. Evaluating the energy security impacts of energy policies. In *The Routledge handbook of energy security*, edited by Benjamin K. Sovacool, 74–95. London and New York: Routledge.

Hirsch, Fred. 1976. *Social limits to growth*. Cambridge, MA: Twentieth Century Fund.

Homer-Dixon, Thomas F. 1991. On the threshold: Environmental changes as causes of acute conflict. *International Security* 16 (2): 76–116.

Homer-Dixon, Thomas F. 1994. Environmental scarcities and violent conflict: Evidence from cases. *International Security* 19 (1): 5–40.

Hoogeveen, Femke, and Wilbur Perlot. 2005. *Tomorrow's mores: The international system, geopolitical changes and energy*. The Hague: Clingendael International Energy Programme.

Hornborg, Alf. 2013. The fossil interlude: Euro-American power and the return of the physiocrats. In *Cultures of energy: Power, practices, technologies*, edited by Sarah Strauss, Stephanie Rupp and Thomas Love, 41–59. Walnut Creek, CA: Left Coast Press.

Huber, Matthew T. 2009. Energizing historical materialism: Fossil fuels, space and the capitalist mode of production. *Geoforum* 40 (1): 105–115.

Huber, Matthew T. 2011a. Enforcing scarcity: Oil, violence, and the making of the market. *Annals of the Association of American Geographers* 101 (4): 816–826.

Huber, Matthew T. 2011b. Oil, life, and the fetishism of geopolitics. *Capitalism Nature Socialism* 22 (3): 32–48.

Hughes, L. 2009. The four 'R's of energy security. *Energy Policy* 37 (6): 2459–2461.

Hughes, Larry. 2012. A generic framework for the description and analysis of energy security in an energy system. *Energy Policy* 42: 221–231.

IEA. 2007. *Energy security and climate policy: assessing interactions*. Paris: OECD/International Energy Agency.

IEA. 2010a. *World Energy Outlook 2010*. World Energy Outlook. OECD/International Energy Agency.

IEA. 2010b. *Energy poverty: How to make modern energy access universal?* Paris: OECD/International Energy Agency.

IEA. 2015. What is energy security? Available from www.iea.org/topics/energysecurity/subtopics/whatisenergysecurity. Accessed 3 June 2015.

Illich, Ivan. 1974. *Energy and equity*. New York: Harper & Row.

Illich, Ivan. 2009. The social construction of energy. In *New geographies 2: Landscapes of energy*, edited by Rania Ghosn, 11–22. Cambridge, MA: Harvard University Press.

Jansen, Jaap C. 2009. *Energy services security: Concepts and metrics*. Expert paper submitted as input to the ongoing IAEA project: 'Selecting and Defining Integrated Indicators for Nuclear Energy'. Petten: ECN.

Jansen, Jaap C., and Ad J. Seebregts. 2010. Long-term energy services security: What is it and how can it be measured and valued? *Energy Policy* 38 (4): 1654–1664.

Jansen, Jaap C., and Adriaan J. Van der Welle. 2011. The energy services dimension of energy security. In *The Routledge handbook of energy security*, edited by Benjamin K. Sovacool, 239–249. London and New York: Routledge.

Jevons, William Stanley. 1866. *The coal question: An inquiry concerning the progress of the nation, and the probable exhaustion of our coal mines*. 2nd edn. London: Macmillan.

Kaygusuz, K. 2011. Energy services and energy poverty for sustainable rural development. *Renewable and Sustainable Energy Reviews* 15 (2): 936–947.

Kemp, Geoffrey. 1978. Scarcity and strategy. *Foreign Affairs* 56 (2): 396.

Kester, Johannes. 2016. Conducting a smarter grid: Reflecting on the power and security behind smart grids with Foucault. In *Smart grids from a global perspective*, 197–213. Cham: Springer.

Kester, Johannes. 2018. Governing electric vehicles: Mobilizing electricity to secure automobility. *Mobilities* 13 (2): 200–215.

Klare, Michael T. 2008. *Rising powers, shrinking planet: The new geopolitics of energy*. New York: Henry Holt.

Kleber, Drezel. 2009. The US Department of Defense: Valuing energy security. *Journal of Energy Security*.

La Branche, Stephane. 2013. Paradoxes and harmony in the energy-climate governance nexus. In *International handbook of energy security*, edited by Hugh Dyer and Maria Julia Trombetta, 402–422. Cheltenham: Edward Elgar.

Labban, Mazen. 2010. Oil in parallax: Scarcity, markets, and the financialization of accumulation. *Geoforum* 41 (4): 541–552.

Labban, Mazen. 2011. The geopolitics of energy security and the war on terror: The case for market expansion and the militarization of global space. In *Global political ecology*, edited by Richard Peet, Paul Robbins and Michael J. Watts, 325–344. London: Routledge.

Lakoff, Andrew, and Stephen J. Collier. 2010. Infrastructure and event: The political technology of preparedness. In *Political matter: Technoscience, democracy, and public life*, edited by Bruce Braun and Sarah J. Whatmore, 243–266. Minneapolis, MN: University of Minnesota Press.

Levy, W. J. 1973. World oil cooperation or international chaos. *Foreign Affairs* 52: 690.

Lieber, Robert J. 1980. Energy, economics and security in alliance perspective. *International Security* 4 (4): 139–163.

Lovins, Amory B. 1990. The negawatt revolution. *Across the Board* 27 (9): 18–23.

Lovins, Amory B., and L. Hunter Lovins. 1982. *Brittle power*. Androver, MA: Brick House.

Lubell, Harold. 1961. Security of supply and energy policy in Western Europe. *World Politics* 13 (3): 400–422.

Luft, Gal, Anne Korin, and Eshita Gupta. 2011. Energy security and climate change: A tenuous link. In *The Routledge handbook of energy security*, edited by Benjamin K. Sovacool, 43–55. London and New York: Routledge.

Mallaby, Sebastian. 2006. What 'energy security' really means. *Washington Post*, 3 July, A21.

Mayer, Maximilian, and Michele Acuto. 2015. The global governance of large technical systems. *Millennium – Journal of International Studies* 43 (2): 660–683.

Meadows, Donella H., Dennis Meadows, Jorgen Randers and William W. Behrens. 1972. *The Limits to growth: A report for the Club of Rome's project on the predicament of mankind*. New York: Universe.

Mehta, Lyla, ed. 2010. *The limits to scarcity: Contesting the politics of allocation*. Washington, DC: Earthscan.

Metcalf, Gilbert E. 2013. *The economics of energy security*. Working Paper. Cambridge, MA: National Bureau of Economic Research.

Middlemiss, Lucie, and Ross Gillard. 2015. Fuel poverty from the bottom-up: Characterising household energy vulnerability through the lived experience of the fuel poor. *Energy Research & Social Science* 6: 146–154.

Mitchell, John V. 2000. Energy supply security: Changes in concepts. *Royal Institute of International Affairs, Energy and Environment Programme*. London: RIIA.

Mitchell, John V. 2002. *Renewing energy security*. Report. London: Chatham House: Royal Institute of International Affairs.

Mitchell, Timothy. 2013. *Carbon democracy: Political power in the age of oil*. London: Verso.

Moore, R. 2012. Definitions of fuel poverty: Implications for policy. *Energy Policy* 49: 19–26.

Mulder, Machiel, Arie ten Cate and Gijsbert Zwart. 2007. The economics of promoting security of energy supply. *EIB Papers* 12 (2): 38–61.

Mulligan, Shane. 2010. Energy, environment, and security: Critical links in a post-peak world. *Global Environmental Politics* 10 (4): 79–100.

Nye, David E. 2014. The United States and alternative energies since 1980: Technological fix or regime change? *Theory, Culture & Society* 31 (5): 103–125.

Nye, Joseph S. 1981. Energy and Security. In *Report of Harvard's energy and security research project*, edited by D. A. Deese and Joseph S. Nye. Cambridge, MA: Ballinger.

Okereke, Chukwumerije, and Tariya Yusuf. 2013. Low carbon development and energy security in Africa. In *International handbook of energy security*, edited by Hugh Dyer and Maria Julia Trombetta, 462–482. Cheltenham: Edward Elgar.

Pachauri, Shonali. 2011a. The energy poverty dimension of energy security. In *The Routledge handbook of energy security*, edited by Benjamin K. Sovacool, 191–204. London and New York: Routledge.

Pachauri, Shonali. 2011b. Reaching an international consensus on defining modern energy access. *Current Opinion in Environmental Sustainability* 3 (4). Energy Systems: 235–240.

Pagnamenta, R. 2009. France imports UK electricity as plants shut down. *The Times*, 3 July. Available from http://business.timesonline.co.uk/tol/business/industry_sectors/utilities/article6626811.ece. Accessed 26 July 2010.

Parliamentary Debates, Commons. 1913. Navy estimates 1913–1914: Shipbuilding, repairs, maintenance, Etc. *Hansard*: 1474–1477.

Patterson, W. 2008. *Managing energy wrong*. Energy, Environment and Resource Governance Working Paper. Managing Energy: for Climate and Security. London: Chatham House.

Patterson, Walt. 2010. *Managing energy: Rethinking the fundamentals*. Energy, Environment and Resource Governance Working Paper. London: Chatham House.

Pollack, G. A. 1973. Economic consequences of the energy crisis. *Foreign Affairs* 52: 452.

Prasad, Gisela. 2011. Improving access to energy in sub-Saharan Africa. *Current Opinion in Environmental Sustainability* 3 (4): 248–253.

Schumacher, E. F., and G. Kirk. 1977. Schumacher on Energy. In *Speeches and Writings of E. F. Schumacher*, edited by G. Kirk. London: Cape.

Sokona, Youba, Yacob Mulugetta and Haruna Gujba. 2012. Widening energy access in Africa: Towards energy transition. *Energy Policy* 47: 3–10.

Sovacool, Benjamin K. 2011. Introduction: Defining, measuring, and exploring energy security. In *The Routledge handbook of energy security*, edited by Benjamin K. Sovacool, 1–42. London and New York: Routledge.

Sovacool, Benjamin K. 2013. *Energy & ethics: Justice and the global energy challenge*. Basingstoke: Palgrave Macmillan.

Sovacool, Benjamin K., and Marilyn A. Brown. 2010. Competing dimensions of energy security: An international perspective. *Annual Review of Environment and Resources* 35 (1): 77–108.

Sovacool, Benjamin K., and I. Mukherjee. 2011. Conceptualizing and measuring energy security: A synthesized approach. *Energy* 36 (8): 5343–5355.

Sovacool, Benjamin K., Roman V. Sidortsov and Benjamin R. Jones. 2014. *Energy security, equality and justice*. Abingdon: Routledge.

Stern, Paul C., and Elliot Aronson, eds. 1984. *Energy use: The human dimension*. New York: W. H. Freeman.

Stern, Roger. 2006. Oil market power and United States national security. *Proceedings of the National Academy of Sciences* 103 (5): 1650–1655.

Stobaugh, Robert, and Daniel Yergin. 1978. After the second shock: Pragmatic energy strategies. *Foreign Affairs* 57: 836.

UNDP. 1994. *Human development report 1994*. New York and Oxford: Oxford University Press.

Valentine, Scott Victor. 2011. The fuzzy nature of energy security. In *The Routledge handbook of energy security*, edited by Benjamin K. Sovacool, 56–73. London and New York: Routledge.

Verrastro, F., and S. Ladislaw. 2007. Providing energy security in an interdependent world. *Washington Quarterly* 30 (4): 95–104.

Voelkner, Nadine. 2011. Managing pathogenic circulation human security and the migrant health assemblage in Thailand. *Security Dialogue* 42 (3): 239–259.

Voelkner, Nadine. 2012. *Human security assemblages in global politics: The materiality and instability of biopolitical governmentality in Thailand and Vietnam.* PhD thesis, Brighton: University of Sussex.

WEC. 2008. *Europe's vulnerability to energy crises.* London: World Energy Council.

Winzer, Christian. 2012. Conceptualizing energy security. *Energy Policy* 46: 36–48.

Wirth, Timothy E., C. Boyden Gray, and John D. Podesta. 2003. The future of energy policy. *Foreign Affairs* 82 (4): 132–155.

Wright, Philip. 2005. Liberalisation and the security of gas supply in the UK. *Energy Policy* 33 (17): 2272–2290.

Xenos, Nicholas. 1989. *Scarcity & modernity.* London and New York: Routledge.

Yergin, Daniel. 1988. Energy security in the 1990s. *Foreign Affairs* 67 (1): 110–132.

Yergin, Daniel. 1991. *The prize: The epic quest for oil, money & power.* New York: Simon and Shuster.

Yergin, Daniel. 2006. Ensuring energy security. *Foreign Affairs* 85 (2): 69–82.

Yergin, Daniel. 2012. *The quest: Energy, security, and the remaking of the modern world.* New York, NY: Penguin.

3 Analysing energy security

3.1 Introduction

The multiplicity of energy security, its 'slipperiness' or 'multidimensional' character, is well acknowledged within studies on the concept of energy security.[1] With energy as one of the core pillars of modern societies, energy (in)security arguably is everywhere, crossing a wide range of energy sources, actors and positions within the energy supply chains.[2] However, work by both Jarosz and Maxwell on food security shows that this proliferation is not unique to energy security, which confirms the argument in Chapter 2 that the security logic itself could be driving the proliferation instead of an expansion of the referent objects of energy. This is not how the energy security literature sees it.[3] Cherp and Jewell, for example, argue that the proliferation of energy security results from the inherent complexity of the supply of energy, the uncertainties within such a complex energy system, and the conflicting positions that actors have within this system.[4] Another recent overview attributes this proliferation to the difference in 'academic disciplines ... historical contexts ... levels of development ... timeframes ... market dimensions ... value chain ... levels of analysis ... and the primary or transformed fuel in question',[5] in other words all aspects and positions of the energy supply chain as well as its broader economic and historical context, including the different disciplinary reflections on the issue of energy. This chapter turns to this last aspect and discusses how the energy security literature tries to grasp the proliferation and complexity of energy in order to secure it.

There are multiple ways to come to grips with the multiplicity of energy security. Three are worth highlighting and are analysed in this chapter. First, Section 3.2 discusses how both qualitative and quantitative approaches analyse this multiplicity by categorizing and systematizing the wide range of energy security threats. In turn, Section 3.3 looks at the theories that are used to handle the complexity. For energy security, there are three main theoretical lenses: a geopolitical, a neo-liberal and a historic-materialist analysis.[6] Third, Section 3.4 studies the work of several scholars who look more closely how energy security works and try to identify the driving logics behind energy security. Lastly, Section 3.5 builds up to a performative interpretation of energy security and the chapters. Importantly, this chapter does not discuss the emerging use of securitization theory in energy security, but only because this literature is extensively discussed in Section 4.4.[7] For now, this chapter problematizes the mainstream energy security literature, because, without a reflective understanding of how the search for definitions actually shapes human relationships and human relations with nature, the literature misses a core understanding that could move the field out of its current impasse of the constant struggle to tackle the proliferation of energy security and come to a fuller understanding of the practice that is energy security.

3.2 Defining, differentiation and categorization

Qualitative and quantitative research, irrespective of the theoretical background, always starts with some sort of categorization – all research does.[8] For the energy security literature, a well-known categorization is provided by APERC, which tries to order the complexity of energy security through its four As: availability, accessibility, affordability and acceptability.[9] This, however, is nowhere near the only type of categorization available. Quite a number of energy security scholars at some point in their career produce a similar list of their own categories, some resembling the four categories of APERC and others with up to 20 dimensions.[10] In addition, quantitative research takes this categorization a step further by providing a range of indicators for each of the categories, with one study finding up to 320 indicators in total.[11] The previous chapter discussed a range of threats to energy, which are categorized and extended in Figure 3.1. This figure is based on APERC's four As: availability, accessibility, affordability and acceptability. While other categorizations are possible, a simple and descriptive one such as in Figure 3.1 provides for a way to include both security of supply and security of demand perspectives and is indicative of the range of threats, the level of analysis, and the overall complexity of the security dimension of natural resources.

On closer examination, Figure 3.1 shows that threats to natural resources are three-sided. They can be found in the threats *to* a stable and continuous use of natural resources (supply interruption), in the threats that *follow from* an actual disruption in the use of natural resources (economic services, health impact), and in the threats that result *from* a stable and continuous resource use (climate change). In fact, the (in)ability to respond to potential disruptions is nowadays itself seen as a potential threat in relation to natural resources.[12] In such a case, the pre-emptive security logic that drives this (see Section 4.2) makes anything or anybody that hinders the construction of a more resilient energy system circumspect in its own right. In other words, energy and energy systems are often both object of security and subject of security. They are in need of protection while also giving cause for concern.[13]

More indirectly, Figure 3.1 also points towards energy security concerns and how they do not only differ per referent object and the value attached to the referent objects (the resources, the services provided by the resources or the

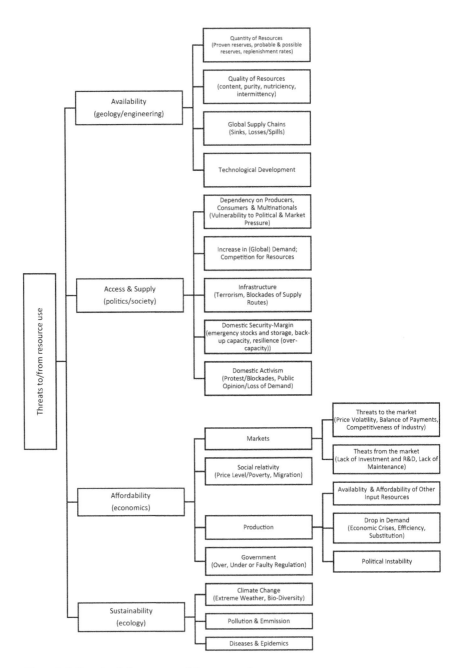

Figure 3.1 Perceived threats to and from natural resources.
Source: author.

workings of the economy as a whole), but how the threats differ in scope as well.[14] For Winzer, these scopes specify how energy security concerns differ not only in magnitude (the *size*) of the possible impact but also on the *speed* of the impact or whether something comes as a shock or not. In addition, he mentions that the duration (the *sustention*) and the scale (the geographic *spread*) of the impact play a role, as does the uniqueness (the *singularity*) of the threat. Lastly, Winzer differs security concerns based on the perceived *sureness* of a possible impact, in other words whether a threat is 'predicted', probable or totally unknown.[15]

Simultaneously, the benefit of Figure 3.1 is limited for a number of reasons. First, any categorization is always inherently incomplete and the political effects of the categorization should not be underestimated. As Cherp and Jewell conclude in a similar discussion on energy security:

> The basis for these classifications is rarely systematically justified: they often seem almost as arbitrary as the lists of energy security concerns which they seek to structure. Moreover, classification is not integration. Placing several concerns in one group does not necessarily help us to understand them better or to develop integrated solutions.[16]

Figure 3.1 is a prime example of this. It is per definition incomplete and its systemization is based on implicit assumptions on the meaning of the four categories in terms of geography and technological prowess, politics and society, economics and ecology. More important, the close connections between the subcategories make the initial differentiation rather arbitrary. Subcategories like government regulation and technology are interwoven in all four categories and could be read as threat and solution at the same time.

Second, the chosen definition of energy security often prestructures the conclusions that can be drawn, as such definitions fixate assumptions on energy, energy security and temporality.[17] To be fair, that is exactly the purpose of simplification. On the other hand, this often leads to an acceptance of a pre-agreed-upon status quo. For instance, the food security literature shows how hunger is often put forward, implicitly, as a supply problem that can only be solved by adding more supply without regard for social entitlements that hinder the distribution of available supplies.[18] It also returns in qualitative energy research where, for example, Von Hippel *et al.* and Valentine show how studies that take a longer time frame often value stability over costs whereas short-time frame studies favour costs above all else.[19] Likewise, Zeniewski, Martinez-Anido and Pearson argue that quantitative approaches regularly favour free market solutions, while qualitative approaches, which are often more socially oriented, prefer regulated energy markets.[20] As they conclude:

> On a practical level, the definition of energy security and its scope conditions will crucially affect how both policymakers and academics identify, order and manage risks and vulnerabilities affecting the energy system, in whatever form it is analysed.[21]

To a certain extent, scholars like Valentine or Zeniewski, Martinez-Anido and Pearson draw attention to the claim of this book that the concepts and theories of energy security help shape the world around us.

This becomes important when one realizes that the definitions and indicators of energy security are, if not defined, then strongly influenced by the IEA, an organization by and for developed countries and their search for secure energy supplies. In other words, modern understandings of energy security build upon definitions written by a small number of capital-intensive consumer countries and their identification of indicators based on their particular experiences.[22] In time, Cherp and Jewell argue, these indicators are exported to other parties who are unable to develop such indicators on their own.[23] To be clear, this does not necessary have to be a bad thing, but it does point to a level of politics often ignored.

Similarly, it is well known that energy security contains both absolute and relative aspects. Chester, in this respect argues that availability and accessibility are absolute aspects of energy security as they are measurable, while affordability and acceptability are relative aspects that depend on weighing and agreement.[24] However, the idea that there are absolute numerical aspects of energy security clearly overlooks the actual politics of energy reserves. A good example is the increase of the officially proven oil and gas reserves between 1982 and 1988 by a number of OPEC members during the run-up to new OPEC production quotas. These increases are circumspect as those countries were not witness to any obvious exploration or technological advancements in that time, while their respective quotas were going to be based on their total reserves.[25] As the 2010 World Energy Outlook stated:

> Definitions of reserves and resources, and the methodologies for estimating them, vary considerably around the world, leading to confusion and inconsistencies. In addition, there is often a lack of transparency in the way reserves are reported: many national oil companies in both OPEC and non-OPEC countries do not use external auditors of reserves and do not publish detailed results.[26]

Another example can be found in Reynolds's analysis of the Canadian decision in 2003, together with the American EIA, to count the Canadian oil sands as fully fledged oil reserves. Reynolds describes how Canada's oil reserves increased from six to almost 174 billion barrels after the political decision to (1) stretch the concept of crude oil to include oil sands bitumen and (2) to decree these oil sands as proven reserves instead of 'remaining established' reserves without physical, technical or economic foundation.[27] In other words, Chester's absolute dimensions of availability and capacity are not as absolute as they seem and are effectively subject to a politics of ontology as well (for more, see Chapter 5).

3.3 Theories of energy security

An alternative to analysing the contents of energy security through categorization is a theoretical reflection on energy security. While a range of theories and disciplines are applicable to energy and offer their own priorities for energy security,[28] like political ecology and its environmental focus, energy security itself, as a field and concept, is primarily discussed by theories that are borrowed from IR and IPE. These include (neo)realist geopolitics with its focus on conflict, neo-liberals focusing on markets and institutions, and more critical theories that study energy as part of a particular economic order.[29] As the latter literature is only marginally used for energy security itself, Aalto *et al.* are right in claiming that the field of energy security lacks theoretical ambition.[30]

First, a neorealist-inspired geopolitics is the study of how geographic factors interact with international relations. It has a long history, but the demand from Asia and the 2008 oil price shock reinvigorated this approach for energy security from 2006 onwards.[31] The geopolitics practised within energy however has less to do with the theory of geopolitics and more with the politics of geographically dispersed natural resources. Actually, not even with the resources themselves, but instead with the politics of control over natural resources and the 'political intentions' behind it.[32] For this, it takes a particular mix between neo-Malthusian ideas about scarce resources and neorealist IR theory. Neorealism within IR assumes an anarchic system with unitary and rational states that are concerned with survival.[33] Combined with (neo-)Malthusian assumptions about finite resources and unlimited demand, it proposes a self-centred zero-sum struggle over the last remaining resources in the world.[34] Problems that are highlighted through this approach are a growing dependency on foreign energy resources, resource nationalism and terrorism.[35] It is a highly state-centric theoretical position that is inherently mistrusting of other actors but also, as Campbell notes, focused 'solely on the supply of oil without interrogating the demand for this resource'.[36] Although the work of geopolitics scholars Criekemans or Scholten and Bosman, for instance, shows that geopolitics can be applied to other energy sources as well, including renewables, demand is indeed hardly ever discussed in this line of reasoning.[37]

Such a pessimistic reading contrasts with a positive neo-liberalist understanding of energy security.[38] A neo-liberalist reading of energy builds on the non-zero-sum logic of neo-liberalism, which is based on the idea that cooperation is possible if there are absolute gains to be made and international institutions structure these international relations in favour of properly functioning energy markets.[39] It perceives markets as the best way to extract, distribute and consume natural resources. Basically, this is the political underpinning of the economic perspective of energy security as described in Chapter 2. For this strand of literature, security, especially the simplistic neorealist geopolitical interpretation, is a danger to the circulation of energy because it has the potential to dislocate energy markets. The main dilemma for all those involved in energy is therefore, according to Van der Linde, 'how to weigh the short-term risks of a serious disruption or undersupply against the longer-term security of more domestically produced (cleaner) energies as long as prices do not reflect all the risks'.[40] This latter observation, that prices should reflect all externalities, is a key economic argument nowadays encountered in climate debates and one that reinforces the importance of markets. Simultaneously, it highlights an aversion of power and the active political manipulation of markets for goals other than profit.[41]

These two strands of literature are often used to analyse energy security debates as they take place in academia and public policy. However, while the last strand of literature is rather small, it does include the modern analyses of energy regimes (Chapter 2), the historical materialist and more discursive analyses of energy security, and the application of securitization theory to energy security (Section 4.4). Each of these theories offers an attempt to break with the dominant policy orientation of neorealist geopolitics and market liberalist perspectives.[42] Each of them questions the power relations behind the respective systems of supply, distribution and consumption. And each of them shares an understanding that theory is part of the reality that is analysed. In other words, the reason why a neorealist geopolitical theoretical analysis seems so applicable is partly because of the theory itself, as policymakers use that theory to justify their decisions and their fears in a self-reinforcing interaction. When theories are used to analyse the world, they come with assumptions and choices about the world that help shape a difference between good/bad, between us/them or between politics and the market.[43] These differences are as arbitrary as the theories, but no less real as they are enacted in the creation and application of these theories. The difficulty to critique neorealist or liberal approaches to energy security however, is that its subject is no longer energy security but the theories and knowledge patterns that are in place about energy security. As such, critical theories have a peculiar position within the overwhelmingly practical policy orientation that is prevalent in the field of energy security.

3.4 Searching for logics of energy security

Besides categorization and theorization, an increasing number of scholars are searching for all-encompassing logics and discourses behind energy security. This section briefly discusses three examples of such work on the logics behind energy security. It starts with the energy trilemma as an example of the relations between energy security and other energy logics, and it subsequently moves to two recent contributions that search for the logics of energy security itself. Lastly, this section reflects on these two sources, among others by offering an alternative logic of energy security, one that identifies three logics that a person/ country can follow in response to the concern of energy dependency. With this brief addition, this section shows that while a search for logics focuses on processes and thus is step closer to a performative reading of energy security; it likewise is not a silver-bullet answer.

A popular way to depict the underlying dynamics of energy policy is the use of the energy trilemma as depicted in Figure 3.2. It depicts energy security, economic equity (access and affordability, often just plain costs) and environmental sustainability concerns (regularly limited to CO_2 emissions alone) as the 'fundamental' policy positions that need to be combined in a trade-off for any reasonable energy policy to work.[44] In doing so, this trilemma shapes the debate on energy, as it sees the different positions as radical opposites that need to meet in the middle. What the middle is differs per actor. Often it includes some form of a sustainable renewable energy system, but whether this system includes nuclear electricity or carbon capture and storage depends on the specific agent. In other words, it can be argued that the trilemma compresses the complexity of energy debates into three distinct positions and flattens it to a single level, while in reality all agents involved have to find their own middle ground on all of these positions before they can even participate in public energy debates. Agents are never purely security-focused, as even the most dedicated energy security scholar defines energy security with economic and ecological aspects in mind. In addition, the trilemma excludes alternative views like social reflections on distribution, a focus on demand reduction or more functional discussions on maintenance.[45] It also discusses energy in terms of private commodities instead of the services or public goods that are to be provided.[46]

Another way to analyse energy security, to find some stable structure within these debates, is to search for the logics behind energy security. Two recent articles by Ciută and by Cherp and Jewell try to find such logics.[47] Interestingly, both articles find precisely three logics or discourses that are present in energy security. First, Cherp and Jewell identify a discourse of *sovereignty*, which refers to military and geopolitical security of supply considerations as put forward by nation states. This comes close to the conflict focused neorealist theory discussed above and is comparable to Ciută's first logic of *war*, by which he refers to political-military conflicts over energy and other resources. Continuing with Ciută, he second identifies a security logic of *subsistence*, where energy is seen as an unavoidable driving force behind biological life. Energy from this perspective needs to be secured because it is a basic need that needs to be fulfilled. Lastly,

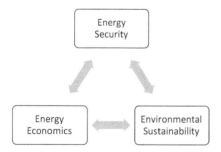

Figure 3.2 Energy trilemma.
Source: author; adapted from WEC 2015.

Ciută identifies what he calls '*total*' energy security. In this reading, energy is a necessity for social life, as there is not one aspect of life that is not in some way enabled by the extraction, distribution and consumption of energy resources.

In contrast to Ciută, who describes the importance and levels of conflict over energy in society, Cherp and Jewell identify the actual logics by which energy systems are secured. Besides a logic of *sovereignty* dealing with the political control over resources, they identify a logic of *robustness* which focuses on the technical vulnerability of the production and transport capacity within a socio-technical energy system. Clearly, this takes an engineering perspective to security and deals with the safety and stability of the physical infrastructure. Lastly, they identify a logic of *resilience*, by which they refer to an alternative meaning of security that focuses on multiple unpredictable complex systemic disruptions to which people need to adapt and mitigate. This includes infra-structure system disruptions, like rolling blackouts, but also instances like price volatility and ecological feedback loops.

Clearly, the logics of Cherp and Jewell are closely connected to the academic disciplines behind them. Sovereignty follows a political science and IR reading of energy security, engineers look at the robustness of the energy infrastructure, and systems analysts, insurers and economists look at the resilience behind energy systems. The question is whether these logics and discourses are not just another way to categorize and prioritize certain phenomena within energy security debates. And, if so, whether that is problematic. Noticeable in this respect is that both articles share a sovereign/war logic and both offer precisely three logics. Why is that? Especially as it is easy to add to them, for example by adding the logics that structure how people deal with energy dependency (the perceived lack of control over the access to a resource).[48] In this respect, briefly, there are three (ironic, right?) extreme logics that a person, country or company can follow in response to the sense of otherness that marks a dependency rela-tionship characterized by fear and addiction.[49] First, an agent can follow an iso-lationist logic and become completely self-sufficient. Second, they could follow an imperialist logic that degrees that one is entitled to the resources no matter what. Third, they can follow a shared fate logic and accept a level of depend-ency knowing that the situation is mutual. In reality, the choice for any of these logics is heavily influenced by neorealist and liberalist readings of international energy relations (reinforcing their political impact). For instance, the isolation-ist logic is excluded based on ideas about economic progress and an addiction to acquired lifestyles. The imperialist logic returns strongly in neorealist approaches to international energy relations. And the shared fate logic is propagated by the (neo-)liberalist understandings of a relationship of interdependency.[50]

On the one hand, such a search for logics definitely helps clarify processes and assumptions behind energy security and thus help explain how energy security works. Yet, the two articles and discussion above show that it is a rather arbitrary process with strong links to categorization and heavily influenced by the theoretical assumptions and disciplines that are said to observe energy security relations. This is probably why, for Ciută, 'energy is not, in this sense, the problem' to explain the proliferation of energy security.[51] The problem originates elsewhere. It derives from the reification of the theories behind energy security and, perhaps for now easier to grasp, it derives from the fact that it is not energy that is secured. What is secured are the infrastructure, the markets, the price agreements, the system and so forth. Energy security in this sense is an empty concept that only 'acquires meaning through a series of assumptions regarding the linkage between growth, sustenance and the environment'.[52] The problem for Ciută therefore 'is that of formulating different concepts of security and creating context where these can acquire legitimacy and political grip'.[53] To be fair, this is exactly what Ciută and Cherp and Jewell do. By simplifying the debates through a search for security logics, they manage to break with a simple understanding of security. That said, neither of these articles fully engages with the full range of insights available within the CSS literature. Furthermore, they still try to define what energy security is and how it works, instead of engaging with the question what energy security does.

3.5 Reflection: unpacking energy security

This chapter discussed how energy security is analysed by the literature on energy security, and specifically how the literature makes sense of the proliferation of the concept. It identified three core strategies: categorization, theorization and a mix of both with the search for underlying logics. In sum, these approaches identify what energy security is and how energy security works, but, in line with this book, not how energy security is used politically in daily life. This becomes important as the chapter above also shows that definitions of energy security always contain two aspects: they define what energy insecurity *is*, as well as what energy security *should be*. A definition of energy security thus closes down a situation by defining it as a form of energy insecurity and simultaneously offers a specific normative alternative orientation as its solution. Defining thus comes with a strong normative judgement on how to secure.

More generally, two other things stand out from the discussion so far. First, the inherent empty nature of energy security and its constant proliferation in terms of ascribed content and scope. Second, the limited critical literature that is available on energy security and the realization that the definitions, categories and theories dealing with energy security are not neutral indicators but help shape what they analyse. The core argument from this book is that the academic discussion on energy security lacks a more abstract theoretical reflection on what the concept and its definitions do besides the deliberations of what they are and how they work. Briefly, what is missing is an understanding that the proliferation of the concept of energy security and its totalizing categorical tendencies hide the multiplicity of energy and the daily political choices that are constantly being made and remade on its behalf.

In other words, while the proliferation of energy security shows the range of choices that can be made regarding the future of energy, it does not detail why those choices have been made available and not others. The conceptual analysis so far does not analyse the politics behind the choices; it only highlights the perceived need for security and a desire for energy. It does not question why certain issues are feared as a security problem and others not. It does not help us understand why people constantly need more energy. These desires and threats are often taken as self-evident in the traditional literature. But are they? And what is behind the constant proliferation of energy security? What are the consequences of state-centrism for energy security? What role does the scientifica-tion of energy security play in the governance of these fields? Why does the literature differ between a security of supply and a security of demand, but not between a security of abundance (protecting what we have) and a security of scarcity (gaining that what we never had), or between a politics of insecurity (the use of security to highlight a new threat) and the politics of security (the use of security to deal with routine threats)? These are all questions that call for a deeper theoretical engagement with security and other aspects of the under-represented humanities literature in the field of energy.[54]

The three chapters that follow take up this call and together problematize any remaining notion that energy security is merely an identifiable problem in need of a solution. The next chapter, Chapter 4, builds on the wider critical security literature to provide a theoretical foundation for the concept of security in order to shed light on the constant proliferation of energy security. This chapter follows a similar line of argumentation as above: it starts by discussing what security is, quickly breaking with any narrow descriptions, and then shifts the focus to how it works and specifically what it does when people use it. In doing so, this chapter provides at least some theoretical grounding to explain the constant proliferation of energy security from a security perspective. Hope-fully, it is clear that this implies that the chapters that follow are no longer about energy security as such but discuss their respective theoretical questions in breath and on their own terms. What's more, as any single theory, method or performative approach simplifies the inherent complexity of each of these topics and hence would inherently break with the contextualization that is of such importance to understand energy security, the coming chapters offer as much breadth as possible for a more complete understanding of the processes at work behind energy security.

Notes

1 Ciută 2010; Sovacool and Brown 2010, 102; Chester 2010; Dyer and Trombetta 2013; Sovacool and Mukherjee 2011; Sovacool 2011a.
2 Ciută 2010, 133.
3 With the exception of Ciută 2010; Bridge 2015.
4 Cherp and Jewell 2011a.
5 Zeniewski, Martinez-Anido and Pearson 2013, 40.
6 There are many more social theories used to analyse energy (transitions). A place to start is Smits 2015, 21, or Rosa, Machlis and Keating 1988.
7 Christou and Adamides 2013; Fischhendler, Boymel and Boykoff 2014; Leung *et al.* 2014; Trombetta 2012; Nyman 2014; Natorski and Herranz Surrallés 2008; Stoddard 2012.

8 Including this book, although here categories are used more loosely (see the shift from definitions to reflection in Chapter 4).
9 APERC 2007.
10 Hughes 2009 (four categories); Sovacool and Mukherjee 2011; APERC 2007; Ang, Choong and Ng 2015; Sovacool and Brown 2010; Vivoda 2010 (11 categories with 44 indicators); Sovacool 2011b (20 dimensions and 320 indicators).
11 Sovacool 2011b; Jansen 2009; Le Coq and Paltseva 2009; IEA 2011.
12 Cherp and Jewell 2014, 418.
13 Johansson 2013.
14 Winzer 2012.
15 Ibid., 37–39.
16 Cherp and Jewell 2011b, 209.
17 Valentine 2011.
18 Sen 1983.
19 Von Hippel *et al.* 2011; Valentine 2011.
20 Zeniewski, Martinez-Anido and Pearson 2013, 41.
21 Ibid.
22 Cherp and Jewell 2011a.
23 Ibid.
24 Chester 2010.
25 Salameh 2004.
26 IEA 2010, 115; Cobb 2012.
27 Reynolds 2005, 55.
28 Smits 2015; Rosa, Machlis and Keating 1988; Aalto *et al.* 2014.
29 Stoddard 2013; Raphael and Stokes 2016.
30 Aalto *et al.* 2014.
31 Correljé and Van der Linde 2006; Bosse and Schmidt-Felzmann 2011; Barnes and Jaffe 2006; Criekemans 2011; Klare 2008; Kropatcheva 2011.
32 Stoddard 2013, 7, quoting Ciută 2010, 130. See also Casier 2011.
33 Waltz 1988.
34 Klare 2001, 2008, 2012; Van der Linde, Perlot and Hoogeveen 2006.
35 Labban 2011, 326.
36 Campbell 2005, 954.
37 Criekemans 2011; Scholten and Bosman 2016.
38 Correljé and Van der Linde 2006.
39 Stoddard 2013; Goldthau and Witte 2009.
40 Van der Linde 2007, 70.
41 Stoddard 2013, 10.
42 On energy regimes see Section 2.6. On discourse analyses see Alcock 2009; Jarosz 2014; Lovell 2008; Scrase and Ockwell 2010. On securitization theory see for example Nyman 2014; Natorski and Herranz Surrallés 2008; Shepherd 2012.
43 Nyman 2014, 47.
44 WEC 2015.
45 Graham and Thrift 2007.
46 Mulligan 2010; Patterson 2008.
47 Cherp and Jewell 2011b; Ciută 2010.
48 Not many scholars describe what dependency means for them. Somebody who does is Le Billon, following Ribot and Peluso, who discusses dependency by separating access from control. Whereas access is '"the ability to derive benefits" using all possible means', control should be seen as 'gaining, controlling or maintaining access'. Hence, 'control can be defined as the ability to enforce the rights to benefit from resources, using all possible means'. See Le Billon 2007, 175–176, who quotes Ribot and Peluso 2003, 173.
49 See Friedrichs 2010.

50 In case of energy, especially oil and gas, this interdependence can even be asymmetrical as the short-term disruptive power of gas suppliers is only balanced on the medium to long term by the income dependency of producers. See Stoddard 2012, 347.
51 Ciută 2010, 139.
52 Ibid., 128.
53 Ibid., 139.
54 Sovacool 2014.

Bibliography

Aalto, Pami, David Dusseault, Michael D. Kennedy and Markku Kivinen. 2014. Russia's energy relations in Europe and the Far East: Towards a social structurationist approach to energy policy formation. *Journal of International Relations and Development* 17 (1): 1–29.

Alcock, Rupert. 2009. *Speaking food: A discourse analytic study of food security*. University of Bristol Working Paper. School of Sociology, Politics and International Studies (SPAIS). Available from www.bris.ac.uk/spais/research/workingpapers/wpspaisfiles/alcock0709.pdf. Accessed 23 January 2013.

Ang, B. W., W. L. Choong and T. S. Ng. 2015. Energy security: Definitions, dimensions and indexes. *Renewable and Sustainable Energy Reviews* 42: 1077–1093.

APERC. 2007. *A quest for energy security in the 21st century: Resources and constraints.* Tokyo: Asia Pacific Energy Research Centre.

Barnes, J., and A. M. Jaffe. 2006. The Persian Gulf and the geopolitics of oil. *Survival* 48 (1): 143–162.

Bosse, Giselle, and Anke Schmidt-Felzmann. 2011. The geopolitics of energy supply in the 'Wider Europe'. *Geopolitics* 16 (3): 479–485.

Bridge, Gavin. 2015. Energy (in)security: World-making in an age of scarcity. *The Geographical Journal* 181 (4): 328–339.

Campbell, David. 2005. The biopolitics of security: Oil, empire, and the sports utility vehicle. *American Quarterly* 57 (3): 943–972.

Casier, Tom. 2011. Russia's energy leverage over the EU: Myth or reality? *Perspectives on European Politics and Society* 12 (4): 493–508.

Cherp, Aleh. 2012. Defining energy security takes more than asking around. *Energy Policy* 48: 841–842.

Cherp, Aleh, and Jessica Jewell. 2011a. Energy Challenges: From local universalism to global contextualism. In *The Routledge handbook of energy security*, edited by Benjamin K. Sovacool, 330–355. London and New York: Routledge.

Cherp, Aleh, and Jessica Jewell. 2011b. The three perspectives on energy security: Intellectual history, disciplinary roots and the potential for integration. *Current Opinion in Environmental Sustainability* 3 (4): 202–212.

Cherp, Aleh, and Jessica Jewell. 2014. The concept of energy security: Beyond the four As. *Energy Policy* 75: 415–421.

Chester, Lynne. 2010. Conceptualising energy security and making explicit its polysemic nature. *Energy Policy* 38 (2): 887–895.

Christou, Odysseas, and Constantinos Adamides. 2013. Energy securitization and desecuritization in the New Middle East. *Security Dialogue* 44 (5–6): 507–522.

Ciută, Felix. 2010. Conceptual notes on energy security: Total or banal security? *Security Dialogue* 41 (2): 123–144.

Cobb, Kurt. 2012. Has OPEC misled us about the size of its oil reserves? Does it matter? *Resource Insights*. Available from http://resourceinsights.blogspot.nl/2012/09/has-opec-misled-us-about-size-of-its.html. Accessed 22 June 2015.

Correljé, Aad, and Coby van der Linde. 2006. Energy supply security and geopolitics: A European perspective. *Energy Policy* 34 (5): 532–543.

Criekemans, David. 2011. The geopolitics of renewable energy: different or similar to the geopolitics of conventional energy? In *Panel 'Geopolitics, Power Transitions, and Energy'*. Montréal, Québec, Canada. Available from www.exploringgeopolitics.org/pdf/Criekemans_David_Geopolitics_Renewable_Energy.pdf. Accessed 9 December 2013.

Dyer, Hugh, and Maria Julia Trombetta. 2013. *International handbook of energy security*. Cheltenham: Edward Elgar.

Fischhendler, Itay, Dror Boymel and Maxwell T. Boykoff. 2014. How competing securitized discourses over land appropriation are constructed: The promotion of solar energy in the Israeli desert. *Environmental Communication* 10 (2): 147–168.

Friedrichs, Jörg. 2010. Global energy crunch: How different parts of the world would react to a peak oil scenario. *Energy Policy* 38 (8): 4562–4569.

Goldthau, Andreas, and Jan Martin Witte. 2009. Back to the future or forward to the past? Strengthening markets and rules for effective global energy governance. *International Affairs* 85 (2): 373–390.

Graham, Stephen, and Nigel Thrift. 2007. Out of order: Understanding repair and maintenance. *Theory, Culture & Society* 24 (3): 1–25.

Von Hippel, David F., T. Suzuki, J. H. Williams, T. Savage and P. Hayes. 2011. Energy security and sustainability in Northeast Asia. *Energy Policy* 39 (11): 6719–6730.

Hughes, L. 2009. The four 'R's of energy security. *Energy Policy* 37 (6): 2459–2461.

IEA. 2010. *World Energy Outlook 2010*. World Energy Outlook. OECD/International Energy Agency.

IEA. 2011. *Measuring short-term energy security*. Paris: OECD/International Energy Agency.

Jansen, Jaap C. 2009. *Energy services security: Concepts and metrics*. Expert paper submitted as input to the ongoing IAEA project: 'Selecting and Defining Integrated Indicators for Nuclear Energy'. Petten: ECN.

Jarosz, Lucy. 2014. Comparing food security and food sovereignty discourses. *Dialogues in Human Geography* 4 (2): 168–181.

Johansson, Bengt. 2013. A broadened typology on energy and security. *Energy* 53: 199–205.

Klare, Michael T. 2001. *Resource wars: The new landscape of global conflict*. New York: Henry Holt.

Klare, Michael T. 2008. *Rising powers, shrinking planet: The new geopolitics of energy*. New York: Henry Holt.

Klare, Michael T. 2012. *The race for what's left: The global scramble for the world's last resources*. New York: Henry Holt.

Kropatcheva, E. 2011. Playing both ends against the middle: Russia's geopolitical energy games with the EU and Ukraine. *Geopolitics* 16 (3): 553–573.

Labban, Mazen. 2011. The geopolitics of energy security and the war on terror: The case for market expansion and the militarization of global space. In *Global political ecology*, edited by Richard Peet, Paul Robbins and Michael J. Watts, 325–344. London: Routledge.

Le Billon, Philippe. 2007. Geographies of war: Perspectives on 'resource wars'. *Geography Compass* 1 (2): 163–182.

Le Coq, C., and E. Paltseva. 2009. Measuring the security of external energy supply in the European Union. *Energy Policy* 37 (11): 4474–4481.

Leung, Guy C. K., Aleh Cherp, Jessica Jewell and Yi-Ming Wei. 2014. Securitization of energy supply chains in China. *Applied Energy* 123: 316–326.

Lovell, Heather. 2008. Discourse and innovation journeys: The case of low energy housing in the UK. *Technology Analysis & Strategic Management* 20 (5): 613–632.

Mulligan, Shane. 2010. Energy, environment, and security: Critical links in a post-peak world. *Global Environmental Politics* 10 (4): 79–100.

Natorski, Michal, and Anna Herranz Surrallés. 2008. Securitizing moves to nowhere? The framing of the European Union's energy policy. *Journal of Contemporary European Research* 4 (2): pp. 70–89.

Nyman, Jonna. 2014. 'Red storm ahead': Securitisation of energy in US–China Relations. *Millennium – Journal of International Studies* 43 (1): 43–65.

Patterson, W. 2008. *Managing energy wrong.* Energy, Environment and Resource Governance Working Paper. Managing Energy: for Climate and Security. London: Chatham House.

Raphael, Sam, and Doug Stokes. 2016. Energy security. In *Contemporary security studies,* edited by Alan Collins, 343–355. Oxford: Oxford University Press.

Reynolds, Douglas B. 2005. The economics of oil definitions: The case of Canada's oil sands. *OPEC review* 29 (1): 51–73.

Ribot, Jesse C., and Nancy Lee Peluso. 2003. A theory of access. *Rural Sociology* 68 (2): 153–181.

Rosa, Eugene A., Gary E. Machlis and Kenneth M. Keating. 1988. Energy and society. *Annual Review of Sociology* 14: 149–172.

Salameh, Mamdouh G. 2004. How realistic are OPEC's proven oil reserves? *Petroleum Review,* August: 26–29.

Scholten, Daniel, and Rick Bosman. 2016. The geopolitics of renewables: Exploring the political implications of renewable energy systems. *Technological Forecasting and Social Change* 103: 273–283.

Scrase, J. Ivan, and David G. Ockwell. 2010. The role of discourse and linguistic framing effects in sustaining high carbon energy policy – An accessible introduction. *Energy Policy* 38 (5): 2225–2233.

Sen, Amartya. 1983. *Poverty and famines.* Oxford: Oxford University Press.

Shepherd, Benjamin. 2012. Thinking critically about food security. *Security Dialogue* 43 (3): 195–212.

Smits, Mattijs. 2015. *Southeast Asian energy transitions: Between modernity and sustainability.* London and New York: Routledge.

Sovacool, Benjamin K., ed. 2011a. *The Routledge handbook of energy security.* London and New York: Routledge.

Sovacool, Benjamin K., ed. 2011b. Evaluating energy security in the Asia pacific: Towards a more comprehensive approach. *Energy Policy* 39 (11). Asian Energy Security: 7472–7479.

Sovacool, Benjamin K., ed. 2014. What are we doing here? Analyzing fifteen years of energy scholarship and proposing a social science research agenda. *Energy Research & Social Science* 1: 1–29.

Sovacool, Benjamin K., and Marilyn A. Brown. 2010. Competing dimensions of energy security: An international perspective. *Annual Review of Environment and Resources* 35 (1): 77–108.

Sovacool, Benjamin K., and I. Mukherjee. 2011. Conceptualizing and measuring energy security: A synthesized approach. *Energy* 36 (8): 5343–5355.

Stoddard, Edward. 2012. A common vision of energy risk? Energy securitisation and company perceptions of risk in the EU. *Journal of Contemporary European Research* 8 (3): 340–366.

Stoddard, Edward. 2013. Reconsidering the ontological foundations of international energy affairs: Realist geopolitics, market liberalism and a politico-economic alternative. *European Security* 22 (4): 437–463.

Trombetta, Maria Julia. 2012. *European energy security discourses and the development of a common energy policy*. Working Paper. Energy Delta Gas Research. Available from www.edgar-program.com/uploads/fckconnector/7acf1f46-7358-4057-86e5-ffee558 13be3. Accessed 6 January 2015.

Valentine, Scott Victor. 2011. The fuzzy nature of energy security. In *The Routledge handbook of energy security*, edited by Benjamin K. Sovacool, 56–73. London and New York: Routledge.

Van der Linde, Coby. 2007. The art of managing energy security risks. *EIB Papers* 12 (1): 50–78.

Van der Linde, Coby, Wilbur Perlot and Femke Hoogeveen. 2006. *Tomorrow's mores: The future geopolitical system and the structure of the international oil market*. The Hague: Clingendael International Energy Programme. Available from www.clingendael energy.com/inc/upload/files/tomorrows_mores_oil.pdf. Accessed 15 January 2014.

Vivoda, Vlado. 2010. Evaluating energy security in the Asia-Pacific region: A novel methodological approach. *Energy Policy* 38 (9): 5258–5263.

Waltz, Kenneth N. 1988. The origins of war in neorealist theory. *The Journal of Interdisciplinary History* 18 (4): 615–628.

WEC. 2015. *Priority actions on climate change and how to balance the trilemma*. World Energy Trilemma. London: World Energy Council & Oliver Wyman.

Winzer, Christian. 2012. Conceptualizing energy security. *Energy Policy* 46: 36–48.

Zeniewski, Peter, Carlo Brancucci Martinez-Anido and Ivan L. G. Pearson. 2013. Framing new threats: The internal security of gas and electricity networks in the European Union. In *International handbook of energy security*, edited by Hugh Dyer and Maria Julia Trombetta, 40–69. Cheltenham: Edward Elgar.

4 Securing undesired (energy) futures

4.1 Introduction

The previous chapters show that energy security is characterized by a constant proliferation, which complicates a study of what it is and how this expansion impacts the inherent prioritization of security. This chapter unpacks this logic of security and finds four characteristics, each of them applicable to energy security.[1] First, (energy) security is not one logic. It consists of multiple forms of insecurity and logics of security, which rely on five different techniques to get to know the future. Many of these logics are inclusionary: there is always another unknown potentially threatening future, just as a failed countermeasure only inspires to do better. Second, (energy) security is highly normative. It is the choice of what to protect and what not to protect, the choice between what to see as a threat and what not to see as a threat. Simultaneously, the urgency of security dispels any thought about the ethical choices inherent to security. Third, (energy) security is something that is made; it does not exist out there but it is called upon or written by politicians, concerned citizens, security experts, insurers etc. Lastly, this chapter will discuss that (energy) security is not only a goal, something that initiates action against a threat, but rather an exercise of power, a way to govern the present based on an imagination of the future.

One of the most elegant descriptions of security is provided by Booth who states that security 'is a powerful political concept; it … energizes opinion and moves material power'.[2] Obviously, this description, in line with the focus of this book, describes what security does instead of providing a definition of what it is. In terms of what security is: often security is simply defined as the absence of threats, in line with Buzan, who sees security as 'being protected from danger, feeling safe, and being free from doubt'.[3] Alternatively, Brauch defines security as something that 'is achieved if there is an absence of objective threats and subjective fears to basic values'.[4] These definitions already show that security has neither a fixed value nor strong boundaries defining its use, and leads to the conclusion that security is an empty logic that carries a multitude of meanings for different people in different times.[5] Security is both a state of being (the end goal of 'feeling secure') and the means towards that end (either repairing threats or avoiding them). Security can be negative (negating threats and dangers) or positive (something to strive for). Definitions range from the individual to the international, from material (food) to symbolic (democracy) forms of security, from internal (rebellion) to external security considerations (invasion), from the security of public goods (air quality) to private services (insurance), and from objective and subjective to intersubjective notions of security (see this chapter).[6]

With security (and energy security) construed as an empty logic, any content driven definition or explanation of what security is comes with strong normative consequences. Chapter 2 on the evolution of the concept of energy security already shows how such definitions not only describe what the insecurities are, but also steer what they ought to be. Any decision on insecurity contains an image of who/what is to be secured, and hence who/what is not part of that security. Following the definition of Booth above, this book moves away from such substantive definitions and instead approaches security *as the mode through which people identify undesirable futures and act upon them in the present*. Such a broad definition might invite the response that it is not a definition, that it is too broad and unworkable because it can include anything that is deemed important,[7] in other words that it makes security into something banal, a critique forwarded earlier in relation to energy security. However, the approach to security proposed above enables a process-driven analysis of what security is said to be, how it comes to be and how it affects current decision-making practices as well as the consequences of such decision-making. In other words, this broad definition enables us to transcend the inherent duality within current understandings of security of friend/enemy or secure/insecure to the politics and origins of security by focusing on how people come to know the future and decide upon its undesirability.

This chapter consists of four sections. Section 4.2 deals with the question of what security is. It provides a detailed and up-to-date examination of security as it lets go of any fixed definition, instead focusing on general processes and how it works: the specific rationalities through which we approach uncertain futures, the techniques used to identify undesired futures, and the security logics that secure these undesirable futures. Together these make up what here is understood as security. Section 4.3 proceeds to discuss the normative dimension of security and goes so far as to argue that security essentially is a form of ethics. This chapter examines the close connection between security decisions and knowledge, the role of fear in relation to security, and the active political (mis)use of security to govern vulnerable populations. The last two sections shift to theories of security and deal with the processes through which undesired futures are turned into a security issue. Section 4.4 looks closely at securitization theory, one of the core theories on security that provides a framework to study how people call upon security (interpreted as exceptional circumstances) in political arenas. Section 4.5 studies the theoretical literature on the security technique of risk calculations (with its focus on routine security practices) and how this helps govern our daily lives. Section 4.6 offers a brief reflection.

4.2 Tackling the unknown

4.2.1 *Security/insecurity and the present future*

While the notion of security is hard to define, whether compared to its conceptual relatives (safety and certainty) or its antagonists (insecurity, uncertainty, risks, threats and dangers), it is one of the dominant values in modern society and often the bottom line when it comes to survival. This has not always been the case. Zedner, for example, contrasts a 'modern' strive for survival with historic notions of security that view it as something to be fearful of. Security, it was believed, would inevitably lead to overconfidence and a person's undoing, because someone who feels totally secure no longer pays attention to life itself.[8] Der Derian forwards a similar argument when he distinguishes three different meanings of security.[9] First, security refers to 'a condition of being protected', in the Hobbesian meaning of security that refers to a secure state of being and an absence of fear. According to Der Derian, this is how security is interpreted within IR. Second, security is used in the 'form of a pledge, a bond, a surety'. This understanding takes up centre position in modern economics under the headers of insurance, law and finance. Lastly, Der Derian identifies a historic interpretation of security when he defines it as 'a condition of false or misplaced confidence' and argues that this historic notion of wrongness or overconfidence seems to have been lost in modern security debates.[10] Recently, this latter interpretation is reintroduced by scholars like Dillon and Lobo-Guerrero, who argue that life itself is radically uncertain and that when one tries to secures life, when one protects and stabilizes it too much, one actually 'kills' life itself (Section 4.5 and Chapter 6).[11]

Besides these three positions on security, two other aspects are central to it. The first is the intricate relationship between security and insecurity. As Dillon phrases it, '[a]ll security, however defined, is consequently a relationship towards insecurity, and *vice versa*. Security and insecurity belong together.'[12] When a situation is framed as a security issue, it is impossible not to think about how it could be organized more securely. Similarly, when a situation is described as secure the first thing that comes to mind is what could break this security. It is impossible to think about one without thinking about the other, irrespective the referent objects and fields of application.

The second aspect relates to the time dimension of security, as it is always the future that is insecure. Even if some historic knowledge is considered threatening, it is in relation to what might happen with it in the future. As Buzan, Wæver and de Wilde explain:

> The impossibility of applying objective standards of securityness relates to a trivial but rarely noticed feature of security arguments: They are about the future, about alternative futures – always hypothetical – and about counterfactuals.[13]

According to Anderson, this future orientation makes security into 'a seemingly paradoxical process whereby a future becomes cause and justification for some form of action in the here and now'.[14] In other words, people act now to foil what they fear might come about, because the moment that a threat realizes it is no longer an imagined future but the present. From such a perspective, security is a form of epistemic uncertainty or a lack of knowledge about the future.[15] The future is interpreted as either too complicated to comprehend in full (inherent incomplete knowledge) or as a constant source of surprise that could in principle be known if only there were enough resources to study them.[16] Then again, while the future is inherently uncertain, many futures are known at the same time. These known futures are often seen as unpredictable and as something to be feared, but are often just as desirable in terms of material gain, political power or social status, and at other times seen as a positive experience that brings fun and enjoyment.[17] The line between desired and undesired futures is hence not fixed: even in those instances where the future is feared, some feared futures are still desired and pursued for the thrill of it (e.g. skydiving), while other people seek generally acknowledged undesirable futures (e.g. suicide).[18]

The beauty of security is that one way or another the future is opened up, reacted to and given shape in doing so. In this process, security offers both cause and justification for its actions. To understand security one therefore needs to 'understand how anticipatory action functions, we must understand the *presence* of the future, that is the ontological and epistemological status of "what has not and may never happen"',[19] a process that Luhmann identifies as 'time-binding'.[20] Seen as a logic it becomes possible to focus on the processual nature behind the manifestation of the future in the present, in particular, the manner in which undesirable futures are identified and subsequently acted on. Hence, (energy) security is here defined as the way people identify and approach undesirable (energy) futures in the present. Starting from this processual logic, the following sections first focus on different types of *in*security by identifying more or less coherent ways of thinking about undesirable futures. The second section deals with several techniques used to identify unwanted futures and the third section deals with security logics or the strategies to counter or relate to the undesirable futures.[21] Together these sections make up Figure 4.1, below.

Figure 4.1 Types, techniques and logics of security.
Source: author.

4.2.2 Types of insecurity

A broader interpretation of security, one that sees security as the politics of knowing undesired futures and acting upon them in the present, shows that there are at least five ways to think about insecurity. These include threats, dangers, catastrophes, uncertainties, risks and safety.[22] These terms are often conflated and used interchangeably, but nonetheless contain individual charac-teristics and particular logics that determine how situations are interpreted and how the future is approached.[23] What makes it especially difficult is the double use of many of these concepts. Threats, uncertainty and risk, for example, are both generic understandings of insecurity that people use in popular language to discuss security generally, but also specific distinguishable rationalities of insecurity.

To start with the conception of *radical uncertainty*. Generically, the future is uncertain and we do not know what the future brings. Still, there are things we fear, outcomes we hope for and things we expect will happen. In other words, there are degrees of uncertainty. Simultaneously, there are those events that truly do surprise, that do not fit the other categories of insecurity. The concept of radical uncertainty covers this final category of surprises.[24] Knight's classic formulation of this problem is based on a distinction between *risks* and *uncer-tainty*. More precisely, Knight sees risks as calculable and measurable whereas uncertainty is seen as something incalculable, often due to the uniqueness of a particular situation.[25] Knight and many current positivists understand uncer-tainty as indeterminacy, as a problem of incomplete information that can and needs to be solved with more and better information. Keynes rejected this formulation and argued that more information is not always enough to over-come uncertainty as people also encounter situations of 'ontic uncertainty'.[26] In these situations, the rules of the game, the event or the setting of the uncertain future itself are unknown and people have to fall back on others and what they believe, not on what they know. Keynes points here to situations where people do not add information but start to reason by analogy.

Kessler and Daase expand upon these insights and distinguish four different forms of uncertainty. They identify *relative frequency* where both game and chance are known (e.g. dice). Second, they identify a form called *logical probability*, where the ontological world is open but assumed to be known and people agree on a distribution of probabilities (e.g. climate change). Third, they identify *subjective probability*, a form of uncertainty where the ontological world is known, but the chance of winning is interpreted subjectively (e.g. stock markets). Lastly, they identify *social probability* by which the authors refer to the epistemic uncertainty of language itself, its open-endedness, double meanings, imprecisions and undefined concepts.[27] This latter category of *social probability* comes close to what is here understood as radical uncertainty. Never-theless, the ambiguity or excess of language is not the only source of radical uncertainty.[28] Above, this chapter briefly referred to the general concept of life, as used by Dillon and Lobo-Guerrero, to denote the openness, potentiality and heterogeneity of the future. Similarly, Latour places his actor-networks against a background of 'plasma' (Section 5.4), Bennett discusses the 'vibrancy of matter' to describe the radical uncertainty which she finds in the plurality and heterogeneity of the assemblage of humans and non-humans (Sections 5.3 and 5.4), and Adorno focuses on his idea of 'non-identity' or that what is not conceptualized but still felt as missing.[29] Whether stemming from linguistic, material or social-material assemblages, this form of radical uncertainty opens the future to change and free will.

This contrasts highly with the concept of *threats* that one often finds in IR and public policy documents. Like uncertainty, threats play a role on two levels. In its generic understanding, threats seem to denote all future instances that people deem undesirable. This use of threats conflates dangers, threats, catastrophes and other forms of insecurity geared towards the prevention of feared futures. What separates the specific notion of threats from other insecurities is the presence of a threatening *other*.[30] Originally, Buzan argued that threats differ based on source, intensity (distance and urgency) and time frame.[31] From a critical perspective, however, the focus shifts to the realization that underneath these differences lies a self–other distinction. In terms of energy security, for example, the EU and its member states see the more recent policy choices by the Russian government once again as a threat to European oil and gas security (Section 4.4). Such a threat rationality, which Wæver calls a war logic, is based on the identification of somebody as being a threat.[32] In that, threats discriminate. Always.[33] Threats create an image of the other by demarcating those who are dangerous as separate from us (the individual or group in need of security). What is more, as will be discussed later in this chapter, in doing so they not only give rise to the other but simultaneously shape the self through the identification and fixation of the referent object (that what needs protection).

Besides the self/other distinction of threats, there are three other ways to think about undesirable futures and they all share their origin in a non-human 'outside world'. In its extreme, the notion of *catastrophe* refers to those events that are expected but cannot be countered in any meaningful way, as they cannot be experienced. The moment one experiences a catastrophic event, the deadly outcome implies that experience is no longer possible, thus leading to a desire to know catastrophes 'without the inconvenience of having to live through the catastrophe itself'.[34] Examples are hard to find as even for an explosion of Yellowstone Park, the impact of an asteroid or a zombie plague there are people adapting, tracking, preparing or moving house in the hope of surviving such imagined catastrophic events. Still, whether based on science or science fiction, the magnitude and inability for proper counteraction prevents such issues to reach the security agendas of policymakers. This is where a catastrophe differs from a *danger*. Contrary to catastrophes, many policies are concerned with worst-case scenarios (more on security techniques below) where people believe that, helpful or not, not acting is not an option. The ability to act makes such issues a *danger* (even when they are presented and dramatized as catastrophes). While some events are more urgent than others, danger refers to those instances where future events are known and counter actions are possible, but which are not predictable as to when they occur. A failed harvest due to bad weather or a fungus fits such a rationality. A last and related form of insecurity is one of *safety*. Here it is not so much a natural occurrence that needs to be countered but a sociotechnical event within a broader engineered system, often framed in terms of quality instead of quantity. Debates about food safety (quality of food) and nuclear safety (malfunctioning reactor) are a case in point as they display sociotechnical failures affecting the safety of human life. Of course, the moment that other *people* are held accountable for these failures the logic shifts to a threat rationality.

That leaves risk, the last type of insecurity. Risk is special in that there are not two but three meanings attached to the concept. First, like uncertainty and threats, risk is used generically to indicate undesired and uncertain futures. Second, risk is one of the main security techniques used to tackle the future, as discussed below. Yet, third, risk also functions as a form of insecurity. What distinguishes risk is that it deals with those possible future events that do not stem from 'the other' or from 'the outside world' but instead result from collective action and decisions within a particular group. Risks follow decisions, or, as Luhmann argues, 'risks are attributed to decisions made, whereas dangers are attributed externally'.[35] According to Luhmann, this means that risks are observer-dependent: the risk that decision makers discuss becomes an externality, danger or threat to the persons subject to the decisions.[36] When the British government decides to construct the Hinkley Point C nuclear power reactor, they decide from a risk rationality. The local residents, however, do not face a risk but the actual decision and thus a threat. These decisions, Luhmann notes, are frequently made by people hidden within a range of different institutions of government and business. This 'allow[s] for the possibility that modern society attributes *too much to decisions, and so where the decision maker (whether an individual or an organization) cannot even be identified*'.[37] In addition, outside observers, like historians looking back at the construction of Hinkley Point C, could decide very differently on the thresholds of the risk that the current government uses to makes its decision.[38] The insecurity behind risk is thus based on the repeated question whether something is the right decision or not.

4.2.3 Knowing the future

The five types of undesired futures are unknown, but people constantly imagine them with the help of a range of security techniques. Here we discuss five of them, including: uncertainty, extrapolation, imagination, risk calculation and simulation. Each of these broadly encompasses a specific way of approaching the future and making it knowable, combining both the above-discussed insecurities and the below-discussed security logics. Not only are the techniques different but they also have multiple uses. This is best exemplified with the three archetypes of future studies, a field that categorizes the use of these techniques in terms of *forecasting*, *foresight* and *backcasting*.[39] Forecasting is about what will happen, often by extrapolating trends within society into the future (expected energy demand). Foresight studies focus on what could happen by picturing a range of possible futures (IEA scenarios). Lastly, backcasting identifies one particular desired future and looks backward from that particular future to identify the requirements and actions necessary to reach it (reducing CO_2 to remain under two degrees of global warming). The techniques discussed below can thus be used for multiple purposes, but we will discuss the techniques themselves instead of their broader use.

Out of the five techniques, *uncertainty* might be the most difficult to describe as it is not a technique per se. Contra the other techniques, which all aim to gain knowledge over the future, the technique of uncertainty is the residual category that describes all those instances when people act in relation to the future without knowing precisely why. This includes moments of intuition, fate, luck or, as some see them, moments of divine intervention. These are all post hoc explanations of course, but still moments when something does not feel right and people decide to wait for the next train or to eat something different. They have no way of knowing the future but in hindsight have acted as if they did. This also includes moments when judgement is sought from experts about situations that could go either way. Situations where none of the instruments below provide a decisive course of action and it is left to the 'expert' to decide whether it is the right *moment* for action and to choose from a range of alternatives on the right *course* of action. If arranged systematically, for example through the Delphi method, the use of expert opinion becomes a way to imagine the future that is more closely related to scenario planning.[40]

Scenario planning, in turn, is a technique that tries to *imagine* the future by offering multiple alternative futures. The idea of imaging multiple futures has a long history and lies at the core of military planning and games like draughts and chess. The development of scenarios sped up during World War II and continued in the 1960s.[41] Nevertheless, the use of scenarios outside the military only gained traction when Shell responded surprisingly fast and favourably to the 1973 oil crisis. This response was accredited to previous in-house scenarios to which its management was exposed in 1972 and which had forced the board to imagine just such a possibility and the responses to it.[42] For Shell:

> Scenarios are not projections, predictions or preferences. Rather they are coherent and credible stories, describing different paths that lead to alternative futures. The process of producing and using scenarios is as important as the scenario stories themselves.[43]

The importance of the process itself follows from the main function of scenarios, which is to order all possible imaginable futures into coherent stories. It is this ordering process and its socializing effect that helps participants to understand the scenarios they are working with.[44] After Shell's success, the use of scenarios quickly spread across society.[45] The main issue with scenarios is that, irrespective of (or due to) their broad application, they are often developed by experts instead of executive decision makers. This leads to situations where, in hindsight, the future is almost always imagined by someone somewhere, but that this does not guarantee that they are acted upon or favoured by the decision makers.[46] Salter, for example, notes how the terrorist attacks of 9/11 were not a failure of imagination or scenario planning but that the failure corresponds to the fact that the imageries in this case failed to convince the policymakers in charge.[47] This practice of using imagination and scenarios by policy and the media to identify as many possible futures as possible has also been called premediation.[48]

The third technique is *extrapolation*. This is a quantitative way of forecasting the future by estimating the future value of a variable through an extension of the historic trend into the future. In the case of natural resources, extrapolation can be traced to Malthus's argument about the arithmetic versus geometric change of respectively food production and population growth.[49] More sophisticated approaches gained traction, in particular during the first half of the twentieth century in relation to industrial development and, in particular, in relation to the military during World War II.[50] However, extrapolation techniques really took off with the development of information technology that allowed for the handling of more complex trend analyses over larger data sets. One of the main examples remains the original *Limits to Growth* report, which reinforced (neo-)Malthusian concerns on the environmental consequences of economic growth. Similarly, the price expectations in relation to natural resource commodities are partly based on trend analyses. An example would be the oil price expectations in 2008. At that time, a report by Goldman and Sachs stated that the oil price, at that moment hovering around 120 dollars a barrel, would continue to rise to 150 or 200 dollars per barrel (the price peaked at 147 dollars).[51] These days, extrapolation is often combined with scenarios wherein particular variables are altered to offer bandwidths of most likely trends.

The fourth technique is *risk calculation*. Where extrapolation deals with the identification of the future, '[c]alculation … renders complex future geographies actionable through the numericalization of a reality to come – numbers that may thereafter circulate, be reflected on and take on an affective charge'.[52] In other words, calculation focuses on the likely impacts and the chance of an event occurring. The technique of risk calculation thus centres on the statistical probability of well-known events with known variables.[53] Accordingly, and unlike the previous security techniques, risk calculation does not identify the future but instead categorizes multiple futures. This leads some scholars to argue that risk should be seen 'as a governance framework [which] seeks to focus scarce resources on risks that are ranked according to frequency and impact'.[54] The reason that risk calculation is interpreted as a security technique is because risk assessments are used to identify a set of futures that are not per definition undesirable or desirable. Risks display both possible costs and potential benefits and it is up to the individual to decide whether to take the risk or not. This subsequently points towards the politics behind risk calculation, as quantitative models do not explain the 'disaster threshold' or that point in time when people decide that the risks are no longer acceptable.[55] Recent work by Amoore, among others, shows the importance of this, as risk calculation seems to be shifting from the statistical probability of imagined futures and their underlying variables to calculations that try to prevent events through a method that uses risk calculation to search for statistical correlations of non-related variables in extremely large databases (see Section 4.5.5) in order to identify terrorists before the actual act by the (not related and non-criminal) acts that they have in common.[56]

A last security technique is *simulation* (performance or acting). This technique too does not primarily discover new futures but instead enables people to experience a particular future. For Anderson, performance involves that 'futures are … made present through practices that stage an interval between the here and now and a specific future through some form of acting, role-play, gaming or pretending'.[57] By simulating a future, participants emotionally and affectively experience that future as they play it out in the present, leading to a better understanding of that particular possible future and one's potential response. The best-known examples are fire drills (e.g. on oil and gas platforms), the Cold War-style war games, large-scale disaster management exercises and the stress testing of oil and gas systems by the IEA.[58] On a more individual level, the performance technique is of course the corner stone behind many training programmes. Pilots, soldiers, physicians and managers are all trained with simulators and real-life exercises. In these exercises, people act in the present based on imagined and experienced futures. They get to know particular futures, and the skills to handle them, by experiencing these futures.

4.2.4 Logics of security

These security techniques do not stand on their own but identify the undesired futures and thereby bridge the forms of insecurity with the logics of security that tackle them. Indeed, it is possible to detect eight security logics divided in three categories. The logics of prevention and deterrence deal with knowable undesired futures, the logics of pre-emption and precaution tackle unknowable futures, whereas the logics of preparedness and resilience counter unavoidable undesired futures. In relation to these security logics, there is a remaining category as well. While the logics below are all aimed at identifying and countering undesired futures, there are undesirable futures where no action is taken at all. In line with Rumsfeld's 'unknown unknowns', these are the 'unknown knowns': those things that are forgotten, misplaced or actively ignored.[59] Daase and Kessler identify this category, which they call ignorance, for those instances where nothing is done to counter undesirable futures, except perhaps to actively forget them.[60]

In turn, when the undesirable future can be attributed with a degree of certainty to a particular cause, it is possible to approach such futures through either a logic of prevention or a logic of deterrence. In a *logic of prevention*, one tries to prevent the undesired future from occurring, whereas in a *logic of deterrence* prevention has failed as the other has gained the potential to act and one tries instead to discourage that from occurring. For Massumi the difference between prevention and deterrence can be found in their internal justification. He argues that in a logic of prevention an undesired future stems from an externally given object or event with strong cause–effect relationships for which the moment and force of impacts is unsure.[61] Sharing the same epistemological knowable but undesired future, a logic of deterrence does not result from an external object but from the knowledge itself that something is going to happen soon and needs to be stopped before it happens. Deterrence misses the flexibility of prevention and replaces it with a certainty and total sense of urgency. To Massumi, this urgency and the lack of an exogenous foundation marks deterrence as a self-referential process:

> The only way to have the kind of epistemological immediacy necessary for deterrence is for its process to *have its own cause* and to hold it fast within itself. The quickest and most direct way for a process to acquire its own cause is for it to *produce* one. The easiest way to do this is to take the *imminence* of the very threat prevention has failed to neutralize and make it the foundation of a new process.[62]

In this new process, the perceived urgency of the undesired future loses all doubt; it becomes the justification for the urgency itself and makes the undesired future a reality in the present. In other words, the undesired future is known because it is acted upon as if it were real. It is performed.

Then there are also undesirable futures that are 'not yet fully formed'.[63] These undesirable futures are both epistemological and ontological uncertain: they cannot be known because the ontic nature of the future is not fully known.[64] In other words, there is some idea about what the undesirable future is, but not where or how it will come about. A *logic of pre-emption* was originally coined in relation to pre-emptive wars: wars that break the peace in the face of an attack of the threatening other (contra preventive wars, in which one attacks without immediate threat of attack). Pre-emption thus tries to halt a threat from coming into existence and hence does not deal with possibilities (risks) but with potentialities (scenarios), a constant flux of self-referential new potentialities.[65] Similar to deterrence, the logic of pre-emption deals with these imagined undesirable futures by believing them to happen at any moment and with drastic impacts.[66] Massumi sees pre-emption therefore as a logic that works affectively instead of causally, as it needs to create its own 'otherness' based on a constant regeneration of the fear of new potential threats.[67] The best way to counter such fears is by acting upon them as if they are real. In doing so, pre-emption realizes the potential undesired future in the present. When you fear your neighbour and treat him as a threat, everything the neighbour does potentially is threatening and thereby reinforces your fear and further justifies the actions you take to 'keep him in check'. Consequently, such an affective realization of an undesirable future cannot be proven wrong.[68] When acting upon pre-emptive fear, there is no objective ground to reflect on your actions and subsequently no ground for proportionality to your actions. Whether the undesired future ensues or not, countering the fear was the right thing to do.

Comparable to a logic of pre-emption, a *logic of precaution* also works on and through potentially undesirable futures. Contrary to pre-emption, however, precaution does not 'unleash ... transformative events in order to avoid a rupture in a valued life' but instead cautions against any actions that could potentially lead to undesired futures.[69] This logic is best known through the precautionary principle, a principle that states that 'when human activities may lead to morally unacceptable harm that is scientifically plausible but uncertain, actions shall be taken to avoid or diminish that harm'.[70] Often precaution leads to demands for more scientific knowledge, although it is just as often a justification to prevent undesirable actions completely.[71] In other words, the precautionary logic contains strong debates on the proportionality of activities, weighing the potentiality of a decision to commence those activities against their potential impacts (in contrast to deterrence and pre-emption). Precaution is thus a logic that focuses primarily on the potential impacts of one's own actions and one's own decisions instead of something exogenous. In this it closely resembles Luhmann's analyses of a risk rationality, although it misses the ability to calculate the impact of an action or decision as the potential future itself is still uncertain.[72]

Besides avoiding undesired futures, some logics work to reduce the impacts of those undesired futures that are deemed unavoidable. A *logic of preparedness*, for example, focuses on a reduction of impacts. It has preventive qualities in that it deals with what you as an individual or social group can do to keep your current way of life.[73] When analysing natural resource use and critical infrastructure, preparedness includes well-known measures like the construction of reserves, redundancy, interconnections and back-up capacity, but also includes instruments like insurance and contract law. In the case of insurance, risk calculation is used to reduce the impact of certain undesired futures by spreading the costs for rebuilding over a group of people. In the case of contract law, the uncertainty of decision-making is reduced by agreeing to keep each other accountable and to discuss responsibilities and cost distribution in case of impacts. Preparedness (or mitigation) contrasts in this case with a *logic of resilience*. Resilience (or adaptation) is discussed a bit more in Section 4.5 and Chapter 6, but for now can be described as a prudential way to tackle the future by taking a more proactive approach, in line with pre-emption, in actively adapting towards undesirable futures.[74] These two differ because a logic of resilience does not actualize a particular undesired future like pre-emption. Instead, it makes agents see themselves as vulnerable and forces them to be aware and constantly open to undesirable futures. In other words, a resilience logic does not try to prepare for the impacts of possible undesirable futures (as in a logic of preparedness) but forces the agent to adapt by changing *himself* instead of his surroundings.

In sum, the above forms of insecurity, techniques and logics of security quickly dispel any remaining illusion or hope for a clear definition of what (energy) security is. Security is all of those and more. First, security relates to different types of insecurity following rationalities of threats, dangers, cata-strophes, uncertainties, risks and safety. Second, security is the range of tech-niques used to gain knowledge over the future, whether through uncertainty, extrapolation, imagination, risk calculation or simulation. Lastly, security is the combination of logics that aim to counter undesired futures, whether known through the logics of prevention and deterrence, unknown through pre-emption and precaution or unavoidable via preparedness and resilience. This multiplicity of logics and techniques reinforces the richness that lies behind the emptiness of security and energy security while focusing our attention away from energy to the range of rationalities, techniques and logics that we use to get to know and prioritize undesired (energy) futures.

4.3 The ethics of security

4.3.1 Security as ethics

Interestingly, the (critical) security literature has been able to identify these techniques and logics by broadening its own scope of security. Initially, the the-ories of security evolved in response to the end of the Cold War by increasing the attention to topics that were considered low politics, like energy and climate security. In turn, the theoretical debate on security shifted from realist under-standings of security towards strong ethical critiques and a focus on individual human security.[75] In addition, it started to discuss the role of risk in society.[76] The field also benefited greatly from the idea that security could be approached as a political argument, as something that people call upon in political debates (see Section 4.4).[77] This claim in turn has been criticized and extended by approaches that interpreted security as routine practices and a form of govern-ance.[78] In other words, it is possible to trace a constant broadening and theoret-ical deepening of the idea of security on an academic level as well. In broadening its scope, the literature progressively builds on a critical under-standing that points towards the ethical implications of security. This will be taken up below together with a subsequent discussion on fear, or how people are motivated to decide and act upon undesired futures.

To start, it seems this attention to the ethics and normativity of security practices coincides with the increasing use of more open – e.g. epistemic and ontic uncertain – security logics and techniques that deal with multiple poten-tial futures, like pre-emption and imagination. In line with Massumi, it is pos-sible to argue that we have entered a period wherein the manner used to approach the future is best characterized as a situation where the 'absence makes the threat loom larger' instead of smaller.[79] It no longer matters whether an undesirable future has happened, is about to happen or is imagined to happen somewhere in the distant future. It no longer matters, because, as Massumi con-tinues, the current generic 'threat is self-organizing, self-amplifying, indiscrimi-nate and indiscriminable, tirelessly agitating as a background condition, potentially ready to irrupt'.[80] The generic idea captured by concepts like threat, risk or uncertainty is everywhere and is constantly pressing for attention, which makes decisions on undesired futures as risky as the futures themselves.[81] They are risky because they have no easy identifiable origin and their '"cause" [is] complex and non-local' and often self-referential.[82] Yet, with the help of Massumi it becomes possible to describe security as the 'pragmatic and provisional' 'ascriptions' of a notion of undesirability to certain futures, each 'relative to a particular systemic take on the event',[83] in other words as the mode through which people identify undesirable futures and act upon them in the present.

Besides being highly relative and context-bound, the function of these generic insecurities as a background condition means that 'the potential of [the] threat is already, in the waiting, an incipient systemic disruption'.[84] In highlighting that an ascription stems from and only works in relation to an existing system while simultaneously changing this system because of it, Massumi hints at the close connection between the identification of an undesired future and the consequential impact of that identification in the present. Campbell describes this more explicitly by showing how the identification of an undesired future 'objectifies events, disciplines relations, and sequesters an ideal of the identity of the people said to be at risk'.[85] In other words, security *does* things, or, as Dillon pushes this point:

> By being secured something becomes something that it previously was not. The act of securing both invents and changes whatever is so secured.... In short, for something to be secured it must be acted upon and changed, forced to undergo some transformation through the very act of securing itself. *Securing something therefore violates the very thing which security claims to have preserved as it is.* Securing an object is only possible on the condition that the integrity of the original thing is destroyed.[86]

The moment something is identified as undesirable, the referent object and our relation to the referent object are changed, irrespective whether action has been taken or not. For Dillon the question therefore is not what security is, or who or what is threatening or in need of protection, but instead:

> What does a representation of danger make of 'us' and of those who are not 'us'? Not by asking who or what is threatened, or what is doing the threatening? But by asking how does the specification of threat and its discourse of danger determine 'who', the 'we', and the 'what' that is said one the one hand to be endangered, and on the other to be doing the endangering? ... And, finally, not by asking how to secure security? But, by enquiring about what is lost and forgotten, and who or what pays the inevitable price, for the way that 'we' are thus habited in fear?[87]

This gets to the core of the critical position on security. Rejecting the assumptions that it is possible to separate theory from reality, facts from values and self from others, a critical security perspective questions and problematizes the taken-for-granted nature of security as something easily identified, with clear consequences and equally clear countermeasures. Instead, it focuses on the politics of security: the hard work that is needed to make something into a security issue, for example by highlighting the American diplomatic efforts to find support for the 2003 Iraq War. In addition, a critical perspective also focuses on the consequences of the security distinctions that are forwarded in these political debates, and studies the effects that result from the countermeasures which both reinforce previous situations and materialize their own cause for concern.

From such a critical security position, it is possible to derive an understanding of security as a highly normative process, if not a form of ethics in itself. Burgess makes this argument when he states that:

> The unknown in its essence, by virtue of being unknown, is the foundation of ethics. This is the space where ethics 'happens'; between necessity and randomness. Ethics, from a certain point of view, is nothing other than making decisions in the absence of certainty.[88]

The close connection between security and ethics can be witnessed in the multiple ethical positions on energy security. Chapter 2 concludes that current definitions of energy security contain an equality principle when they support the right of all humankind to energy. On the one hand, such a position can be pushed further by arguing along Kantian lines that it should be forbidden to actively cause harm. This would imply that we take action against those who actively withhold energy from those without, but it could also include all those benefiting from a system that methodically excludes sections of the global population. On the other hand, a utilitarian would claim that the benefit of most precedes the harm done to some and that an unequal system does not automatically imply an unethical system. Of course, contrary to both, it is also possible to argue in favour of a primary biological imperative to feed and protect oneself and one's children first (the few over the many). Such a self-centred position clearly conflicts with the others' ethical positions, and is generally frowned upon, but lies at the heart of security.

Within CSS, the ethical dimension of security and the normativity of security choices are interpreted both positively, neutrally and negatively. First, a more positive form of security can be found in Booth's theory of emancipatory security.[89] Booth argues that true security can only come about if people are free of 'the life-determining conditions of insecurity', which for him cannot come to pass without their equality and emancipation.[90] In his work, Booth explicitly studies security in terms of *what should be*. Not in terms of a utilitarian end goal, as the future cannot be known precisely, but as an egalitarian process that constantly strives for a more equal and inclusionary humanitarian world. For Booth, a critique of current security practices alone is not enough; those practices need to be improved. To do this he accepts the exclusionary nature of security, but only because he explicitly starts from those who are least secure in life. As Booth makes clear:

Like health and status, security is a condition that is not difficult to define; in each case, the starting-point should begin in the experiences, imaginings, analyses, and fears of those living with insecurity, ill-health, or low status.[91]

If security is the drawing of boundaries, then Booth's position is to shift its moral entry point to those who are less secure and put the burden and responsibility on to those who are more secure.

Second, Booth's explicit positive interpretation of security contrasts with the interpretation of scholars like Dillon and Massumi for whom security is neither positive nor negative. For them, and other scholars following the insights from Foucault, security is the process through which society is organized and governed (see Chapter 6).[92] They study how security is used to govern society but refrain from normative judgements on whether the governing is good or bad. They do not focus on the objects in need of security but on the process of security by studying for example how freedom and equality are used instrumentally as a form of governance.

Lastly, Booth's positive reading of security also contrasts with those who see security negatively. This is, for example, the position of scholars working from securitization theory.[93] This theory analyses how agents use security arguments to justify extraordinary measures that ignore normal decision-making procedures. It poses security as a temporary state of affairs, as a moment to deal with an undesirable future and then to be returned to normal.[94] Security is something you need, but is not preferable. Another example, one even stronger driven by a negative understanding of security, can be found in the work of the Foucauldian- and Marxist-inspired scholar Neocleous, who equates security with oppression.[95] For Neocleous, security is and has been actively (mis)used to structure society in such a way that it is beneficial for the elites and capital rich. Among other things, he discusses the close connection between capital/business and security in the security industry, where security is transformed into a commodity to be sold and bought at will (creation of demand/insecurity) while, simultaneously, capital, business and finance are deemed in need of protection themselves as well from attempts to alter/transform them. With this last point Neocleous pushes the business–security linkage a step further than, for example Leander, who studies the 'commodification of violence' by focusing solely on the role of private security companies and how their supply of security creates the actual demand for it.[96]

While these positions within CSS differ in respect to the role that security plays in the governing of the state and the political economy, they do highlight the importance of a reflection on the hidden normativity of one's view on security in general and the security choices one makes in particular. Unfortunately, any such normative reflections on security are dispelled by the inherent logic(s) of security that overrule any ethical reflection with the urgency of the threat.

4.3.2 Fear and undesirable futures

The above-mentioned logics and techniques describe how futures are characterized as undesired and as something in need of prevention, adaptation or mitigation. However, they do not explain why a future is deemed undesirable. The intricate relationship between ethics and security has already offered a glimpse of the origin of insecurity by showing that security is something that can be actively used and called upon. This section enquires further into these processes by analysing how fear works and is mobilized collectively to make some futures feared and others desired (to be clear, fear is only one motivational force; others include anger, grief, profit and power).[97] In general, people desire and fear to lose three things. First, a conservation or improvement of the status quo (goods, relations, needs). Second, a solution to the threat or object that they fear. Third, knowledge itself, in particular the ontological certainty derived from a knowledge of the future.[98] These three together indicate that fear and desire are not one-on-one related. Hence, it should come as no surprise that the processes behind fear and a desire for security are as context-bound and relative as security itself. Some people desire an emotion of fear (adrenaline junkies), while others fear their desires (addicts). Similarly, emotions like fear and desire on their own do not explain *why* some futures are feared or desired, nor which referent objects are so desired that they need security. Fear is an emotion, but also a mechanism of security. Below, we will discuss, respectively, the cause and identification of fear, the active (mis)use of fear, how fear is changing as it is shifting from fear alone to a fear of fear itself, and how this latter shift affects society.

First, the cause and identification of fear. In brief, the literature suggests that fear results from desire and simultaneously enables desire to act upon that particular fear. 'In fear we are met by something outside ourselves, and what we meet is a negation of what we want'.[99] We fear a rejection of our desires, but at the same time fear also spurs a desire for action. As Svendsen continues, fear is an emotion 'through which we consider the world', a 'contagious' emotion that 'seek[s] to conserve' and simultaneously spurs 'creativity' to counter itself.[100] Fear is not just an emotion but, as Frost argues, a 'passion' that is always applied towards an object.[101] This includes obvious objects, like forms and quantities of energy, but also a fear for the unknown – where the unknown becomes the object to be feared. The presence of an object is important because, contrary to fear, anxiety and panic miss such an object.[102] Anxiety for example is a pure emotion that disperses itself to other people through mimesis.[103] Where fear offers 'the illusion of individual autonomous agency', anxiety has no (un)desirable external object and thus cannot be countered.[104] Fear thus differs from anxiety and notions like resilience with its sense of vulnerability, as the desire to counter a fear provides it with an object that leads to the ability to act upon it. In other words, fear empowers the individual, while anxiety and the inescapable vulnerability of resilience undermine such empowerment.

Second, this brings us to the active (mis)use of fear. Building on this distinction between fear and (objectless) anxiety or panic, Robin distinguishes

private fears from two forms of public fears. Under private fears Robin categorizes phobias for spiders and so on. Under public fears Robin includes those fears
which are shared across groups of people and which originate either exoge-
nously or endogenously. Exogeneous fears are defined by political elites and,
through a politics of fear and self–other distinctions, come to determine the
political agenda. On the other hand, endogenous fears are based on the inherent inequalities within society.[105] In this case, fear, through security practices,
not only helps identify the self in relation to a threatening other but also
fixates the socio-economic and political hierarchies within society. For Robin,
endogenous fear is not just about survival or physical harm, but about something that he describes '[as] an apprehension of harm, and because harm is the
deprivation of some good to the individual, wielders of power can arouse fear
merely by threatening the individual's enjoyment of that good'.[106] This form of
fear deals not with fear in the sense of explicit threats to life and limb but with
the fear of losing employment, liberty or education, in other words the 'quite
fears' or the 'low-grade fears' to livelihoods.[107] Interestingly, Robin sees these
public low-key political fears often actively translated as depoliticized private
fears and terrors. For Robin, it is the active conflation of private and public
fears that leads to 'a separation of fears from morality and politics' as public
fears are no longer seen to originate from politics and thereby reinforce the
underlying social order.[108]

Third, while Robin analyses the institutionalized depoliticization of fear,
others conflate Robin's public fear with the understanding of anxiety proposed
by Svendsen and Frost. Scholars like Massumi, Dillon or Furedi, for example,
argue that fears are feared not because of the object to which fear is attached,
nor because of the active manipulation of fear, but because of the fear for fear
itself.[109] Fearing fear itself or the 'objectification' of fear can be linked, according
to Furedi, to the idea of constant vulnerability and risk, which gained momentum in the late 1980s.[110] The idea behind vulnerability is one of victimhood, for
'to be a victim is to be relieved of responsibility for the situation in which one
finds oneself'.[111] Such a sense of vulnerability leads to a constant attentiveness
to ones surroundings, an attentiveness that starts to blur underlying causes and
objects, away from a person's direct experiences with the object and towards the
fear itself. This fear for fear itself and how it motivates or 'activates' people, is
something Massumi elsewhere describes in relation to the colour-coded terror
warning systems.[112] These yellow, orange and red coded schemes indicate threat
levels and are aimed to change people's routines without sharing the information or evidence behind the indicated threat level. According to Massumi, such
a coding scheme works on the future present 'pre-effect of fear', by which he
refers to the unconscious effects of fear:

> As William James famously argued, fear strikes the body and compels it to
> action before it registers consciously. When it registers, it is as a realization
> growing from the bodily action already under way: we don't run because we
> feel afraid, we feel afraid because we run.[113]

The body acts even before we are consciously aware of it. Only when we realize that our body responds, whether via fight, flight or freeze reactions, do we feel afraid. This private feeling then continues to drive us. Massumi describes how people start to reflect on their bodily reaction, trying to find the object or source of what has become their fear.[114] In rationalizing the moment and source of fear, the fear becomes an affective emotion. Moreover, when we recount that fear and its rationalized origin to others in a later step, the fear becomes an object itself, an object that is anticipated by the people who have heard of it and forces their bodies to react *without* the initial unconscious bodily response.[115] As an emotion, fear 'becomes its own virtual cause'.[116] When the colour shifts from yellow to red, the collective calls upon the embodied private fear, without ever experiencing the original object 'that we have become fearful in response to'.[117] Fearing the fear itself thus has two effects: it decouples the social from the material (the body) while simultaneously linking the individual to the collective.[118]

Fourth, such a publicly shared sense of private fear affects society as it has many forms and can be found everywhere, to be called upon and experienced together and alone. Whereas Robin and Neocleous focus on elites using this public fear for their benefit, Furedi shows how extensive the use of this public fear is across government, business, media and NGOs. Basically he points to everyone who is trying to generate 'awareness' and influence people's individual lives based on the urgency of a particular cause (or a reduction of the urgency of other causes).[119] 'When we witness the autonomisation of fear,' Furedi states, 'then the question becomes not simply what is causing fear, but what are the potential negative consequences of fear'.[120] The main consequence for Furedi is that the existence of such an objectified fear has led to a society characterized by a 'culture of fear' that is constantly 'at risk',[121] in other words a society that sees individuals as passive and vulnerable.[122] And, because it *sees* individuals as vulnerable, it treats them as vulnerable. According to Furedi, this leads to a situation where (1) everybody else is deemed governable by those who know best on a particular issue; (2) fear, not vision, is seen as something positive within politics as it helps govern those who are vulnerable, passive and unknowing; (3) those who know best are often so convinced of their cause that they are not afraid of using half-truths and 'good lie[s for] the greater truth'; and (4) with new issues constantly emerging everyone can become an expert – thereby reinforcing the culture of public fear as nobody can 'know' everything.[123] Elsewhere, Burgess describes this inability to understand all the security concerns that are affecting us in terms of the 'fundamental asymmetry of security politics'.[124]

When we follow Massumi and Furedi, the cause of fear is of little importance anymore. The autonomous existence of political fear implies that it cannot be proven wrong. While it only works when called upon, the above makes clear that almost everybody does so. What is more, contrary to an individual's private experience of fear, where the undesired future and desired future are identified simultaneously in response to bodily reactions, in the case of public fear there is a more intentional logic at work as the particular desired futures are identified *before* their current state is publicized as undesirable and something to be feared. This brings this chapter back to where it started, with security as a way to govern the present based on an imagination of the future. Even a primal emotion like fear turns out to be open to (mis)use based on political choices over which futures are desirable or not.

Unfortunately, the discussion about fear has not helped us to understand why some futures are feared or desired, only how they become so. Perhaps it should be concluded that this is not necessarily a bad thing, as the contextual nature of security makes any answer to such a question a relative answer anyway. This chapter instead highlighted the institutionalized and intentional social use of public fear, as one way to explain how security acts as a form of ethics. In fact, the above showed that there are multiple ethical positions towards security, also within the literature itself, and choosing one of them is already a normative act that shapes a particular world. What is more, this normativity is often dispelled from awareness through the urgency and necessity that is inherent in the exercise of security itself. When one is trying to secure an object, or minimize the actions of another, that security process and logic trumps any reflection on one's own position and actions. Taking all of this into account means that the challenge becomes to 'explore the meaning attached to fear and the rules and customs that govern the way in which fear is experienced and expressed',[125] in other words to look even further into how security works. Fortunately, CSS has two theoretical approaches that do this: on the one hand, securitization theory, focusing mainly on the manner in which public fears are called upon, and, on the other, the Foucauldian governmentality approach to risk that studies how vulnerability is translated into routine and everyday risks and thereby governs society.

4.4 Securing exceptional threats

4.4.1 Securitization theory

As hinted at above, one way of studying the meaning, experience and expressions of fear is through an analysis of 'the "security" label [, which] conveys urgency, public attention, and resources'.[126] A theory that deals with such a shift from normal politics to security, to that heightened sense of urgency and a justification to spend resources on it is securitization theory. This theory is part of the framework for analysis of the Copenhagen School introduced by Buzan, Wæver and de Wilde in *Security: A new framework for analysis*.[127] The theory focuses on existential threats and the way these are perceived and constituted by agents through speech acts. Instead of focusing on the objects of fear or the subjective feeling of fear, the Copenhagen School focuses on the perception of threats (in the generic sense). For the Copenhagen School, threats are intersubjective, meaning that they originate socially in-between actors, instead of objective (e.g. that the threat is real and unavoidable) or subjective (that the threat originates in the fears of one or more persons). This implies that the theory excludes the material content of threats, as it claims that the importance and meaning of a threat – or public fears – are primarily provided by its social context.[128] Basically, the theory posits that, until the actual explosion of a natural gas well the fears for such a possible explosion do not originate from the reality of an explosion but from a shared imagination that it might explode (e.g. a security concern). The following chapters will discuss this theory further, respectively, by introducing its main theoretical claims; by discussing four points of critique; by offering an illustration on EU–Russia gas relations; and, lastly, by following more recent literature that moves beyond the claim of exceptionality.

First, the theory divides issues on a shifting non-political, political and security scale. Based on these three distinct scales, the theory argues that issues can shift from one level to another. Non-issues can become political, just as political issues can become security issues, and vice versa. The last move, from the political to security, is of particular interest for the theory as it focuses on a decision of exceptionality depending on whether the agents deem a certain issue existentially threatening or not. The focus is thus on those issues that are so important that they overrule all regular political considerations, in terms of (legal) rules, time and resources.[129] In line with Carl Schmitt's claim that 'the sovereign is he who decides upon the exception', this decision is often made by traditional sovereign institutions like the government, although the theory explicitly states that this does not have to be the case.[130] Instead, Schmitt's claim is interpreted more broadly and includes all who are able to reframe a non-political or political issue into a security issue.

Second, these 'securitizing actors', the agents who are able to reframe an issue, make this move through the use of speech acts: moments in time when speaking about a certain topic, in a certain time, in a certain manner implies a (call to) action and not just the mouthing of the words.[131] The frequently used example is saying 'I do' during a wedding ceremony, when you do not just say the words but 'act' in making a promise for life and engage in a contract. In instances like these, speaking is more than just mouthing the words. For the theory, arguing that something is a threat and in need of a security solution is an act itself, because it shifts the issue from a political debate into a security issue and thereby is able to overrule normal (democratic) political procedures. Buzan, Wæver and de Wilde refer to this act when they argue that securitization is 'the processes of constructing a shared understanding of what is to be considered and collectively responded to as a threat'.[132] More crudely, securitization theory concentrates a scholar's analysis on those agents that are most persuasive in voicing their concern on a particular situation and accompanying referent object (that what is secured).

Third, such a *securitization move* needs to be accepted by the intended *audience* for the securitizing actor to be able to introduce overriding measures that exceed regular political procedures. For the theory, 'a successful speech act is a combination of language and society, of both intrinsic features of speech and the group that authorizes and recognizes that speech'.[133] Just as the speech actor can be anybody, so too the audience is not pregiven. It could be the parliament if a minister is speaking, or the media if an environmentalist is campaigning, but it could also be the prime minister when parliament is voicing its concern or a whole neighbourhood when the fire department orders them to stay indoors after a gas leak. Not only do the audiences shift per issue; frequently there are multiple audiences crossing formal government institutions, informal communities or media organizations.[134] Important, however, is that it is only after the audience acceptance of a securitization move and the inherent need to protect the referent object that the theory claims that there is a case of successful *securitization*.[135] All other speech acts that call on the logic of security are, theoretically, unsuccessful securitizing moves, and hence instances of *politicization*.[136]

4.4.2 Critique on securitization theory

The theory that emerges from these three points offers an easy-to-grasp and original alternative to the study of security but is not without its shortcomings. The theory has faced much debate on four aspects in particular. These include the relation between the political and exceptionality, the role of the context of security, the normative position of the theory and the analytics of the theory.

First, the discussion of multiple audiences above already indicates a certain inflexibility within the theory. By offering the criteria of exceptionality as the benchmark for success, the theory is inherently driven to one act, one speaker and one audience. However, not only are there multiple audiences, there are also multiple actors who either speak on the same topic or in favour of other topics, climate change to name but one, which means that often the same audience has to weigh a multitude of differing, sometimes contrasting securitizing moves, making security first and foremost a political contestation. This brings security back to something akin to Furedi's *culture of fear*, namely that security is all around us always, instead of an exception.

The divergence between these two security notions results from the theory's main assumption that successful securitization only happens when truly extraordinary measures have been taken. Moments when the law and normal political procedures are put aside to quickly counter the undesirable future.[137] However, the exceptionality and the conditions behind it are not explained further, making it hard to sketch the successfulness of a securitization move. To further complicate this, there is little guidance on whether it is the speech actor or the observing scholar who is defining the success of a securitizing move and its subsequent measures as securitization. In addition, this focus on the exception contrasts with Furedi's and Ciută's earlier assumption that the exception has become the routine, that fear and a desire for security are totalizing. According to Booth, this focus and its resulting 'inflexibility' results from the theory's primary definition of security in terms of survival, which keeps up with a traditional threat logic dating back to its initial opposition of the then-dominant military security notions. In his own work, Booth also understands security in terms of exceptionality. However, whereas securitization theory assumes security as having no choice, Booth instead defines security as 'the choice that comes from (relative) freedom from existential threats'.[138] This leads him to argue that 'the more an individual's life is determined by insecurity, the more the space for choice, and acting effectively, is closed down'.[139] As mentioned, Booth regards security positively, because to be secure for him means that a person has already conquered questions of survival and has a predefined plan ('a prior political programme') on how to increase security further.[140]

Securitization theory, on the other hand, considers security negatively.[141] This follows from the inherent claim behind speech acts that there is no choice except to act and instantiate extraordinary measures, which would not have been possible otherwise. Security breaks with the normal state of affairs when it shifts to a 'logic of war' mode.[142] Within this logic, security orders society in a particular way, geared towards the protection of us, through 'fast-track' 'practices [which] buttress institutional arrangements and legitimize forms of domination and exclusion'.[143] Interpreting security in such a manner implies that security always excludes. Buzan, Wæver and de Wilde are aware of this and argue as such, for example, when stating that 'national security should not be idealized. It works to silence opposition'.[144] The theory notes how security silences politics when dictators decide on threats but also, especially, in democracies, where, for example, advocates of privacy are silenced during the implementation of the extraordinary security measures against terrorism. This leads them to argue that 'basically, security should be seen as a negative, as a failure to deal with issues as normal politics'.[145]

Simultaneously, these extraordinary measures are always aimed towards 'the optimal outcome', namely a negation of the threat.[146] The moment when somebody says '"we are safe now; security has been achieved" – a speech act echoing a past threat'.[147] In other words, counter to the political decision to shift to a security logic (of war) stands a logic of *desecuritization*: the counter move that proposes that actors should strive for truly securitized topics to be politicized once more. To bring the exception back into the routine of politics. Elsewhere, de Wilde highlights four ways through which issues can be desecuritized: one can successfully counter the undesirable future, accept the undesirable future and adapt, find other more pressing concerns, or fail to do anything and succumb to the undesired future.[148] In contrast to their earlier work that saw security negatively, de Wilde argues that desecuritization is not automatically positive, but that like securitization it is a logic that on its own 'is not right or wrong; it simply happens or not'.[149] What makes the logics of securitization and desecuritization morally acceptable or not is their context. It is this folding into context that makes Wæver assert that 'desecuritization is preferable in the abstract, but concrete situations might call for securitization'.[150]

More critically, Hansen claims that the initial military survivalist and thus realist origin of securitization also influences *de*securitization by preventing a critical stance towards both the manner in which agents themselves desecuritize events and how observers implicitly assume that a security issue will become political.[151] Hansen gives the example of female soldiers in post-conflict situations who are simply forgotten after the conflict and shows how issues like these are overlooked by both the local agents and observers as they are not considered important enough or do not fit the 'normal' discourse of security and its focus on male soldiers.[152] Subsequently, these and comparable issues are transformed from security to the non-political and skip the political contestation level altogether. Hansen's critique highlights how the theory is only equipped to study speech acts, moments when people are able to voice their concerns, not silences or other (accepted) dominant power structures.

Furthermore, Huysmans raises the reflexive implication that observers cannot write about a certain security issue or a securitizing move without further securitizing those issues themselves.[153] It is impossible to write about the security or insecurity of an issue without drawing attention to the dialectic other, which returns the debate towards the question of ethics, as acknowledged by Wæver:

> The securitization approach points to the inherently political nature of any designation of security issues and thus it puts an ethical question at the feet of analysts, decision-makers and activists alike: why do you call this a security issue? What are the implications of doing this – or of not doing it?[154]

Besides this ethical implication, we are also left with a methodological hermeneutic critique: that between a strict observer who observes what actors themselves see as a security practice and a more judgemental observer who decides when something truly is a successful security speech act – in this case, when extraordinary measures are adopted.[155] This is a split which, according to Ciută, originates from a double definition of the term security in the original theory, where security is defined simultaneously intersubjectively in-between the agents themselves and by the security analyst in terms of survival, extraordinarity and existentialism.[156] This complicates the theory and combined with its notion of success makes it turn from a theory and method into a model, a static one that could blind scholars to the other logics of security at work in their case studies.[157]

4.4.3 EU–Russian gas relations

Irrespective these critical comments on exception, context, normativity and analytical consequences, it is hard not to notice how applicable this theory is to read energy security debates. In these debates, often energy security specialists or other proponents (the securitizing actors) try to convince IGOs, governments or specific key individuals (the audience) that energy security needs additional attention based on the claim that international developments are threatening the future delivery of energy supplies, which in turn threatens the well-being of the economy (the referent object). And quite simply we can identify other energy-related referent objects or securitizing actors like companies, government departments and consumer organizations. Interestingly, although energy is not one of the core sectors of the theory, it does link all five of the sectors that Buzan, Wæver and de Wilde discuss in their work.[158]

This has not gone unnoticed and a number of studies have tried to use securitization theory to analyse energy security. For example, Nyman uses it to problematize the increasing securitization of US–China energy relations as a hindrance to potential cooperation and highlight how such a representation impacts the range of policies open to both countries.[159] Leung *et al.* similarly use the theory to analyse the energy supply chains of China, arguing that historic events and certain institutional agents have an interest in securing oil supplies, but not the rest of the energy system.[160] Christou and Adamides use it to analyse the newly discovered natural gas reserves in the Mediterranean against the backdrop of the social changes after the Arab Spring.[161] And Judge and Maltby use it to compare types of energy security concerns by looking at securitization and riskification of Polish and British gas security.[162] Likewise, a growing number of authors have used it to study the security relations between European countries and Russia on natural gas supplies (the working paper by Trombetta deserves close reading especially).[163] The rest of this section offers an example in line with this last branch of literature to show how securitization theory could be applied to energy security.

Within the studies that focus on the Russia–Ukraine gas crises in 2006, 2007, 2009 and 2014, it is possible to differ between studies with a historic attitude and those that have a future-oriented perspective. The latter highlight the increasing insecurity that follows from a dependency of European countries on Russian gas. They note how Russian gas averages 30 per cent of European imports (in 2014), down from almost 40 per cent in 2006, and how some Eastern European countries are completely dependent on Russian gas.[164] In this argument these numbers are aggravated by the position of transit countries, Ukraine in particular, and an increasing (re)politicization of Russian oil and gas exports by the Russian government. This contrast with the historically oriented perspectives that, on the one hand, weaken this insecurity frame by pointing towards the historic role of the Soviet Union as a steady supplier during the Cold War.[165] However, they also describe how post-Cold War Russia has used its oil and gas exports to influence former Soviet republics, through price differentiation and supply regulation. McGowan for example traces four cases of active, albeit circumstantial, exertion of influence ranging from a reduction in exports to the Baltic states in 1992–1993, to the disruptions in both Georgia and Lithuania in the 1990s and 2006, and, lastly, the 2009 cut offs to Ukraine after a price disagreement that coincided with the stationing of the Black Fleet.[166]

These and the more recent repeated price conflicts over Ukraine's gas prices, including the 2009 reduction in supplies that left a number of Balkan countries without gas supplies in the middle of winter, have fuelled the perception of dependency and insecurity within Europe. Both Russia and the transit countries are perceived to be threatening the European economy and the health of its inhabitants. Whether Europe and the EU really are (inter)dependent on Russia, as well as the question whether this dependency should be seen in terms of an asymmetrical dependency (short-term gas supplies versus medium-term gas income) is of course of no concern to securitization theory, which only deals with the perception of threat as voiced by a range of differing speech actors – including the European Council, the European Commission, think tanks and the European Parliament.[167] Neither the lack of direct evidence for the four cases of active political involvement nor the strong market-oriented discourse wherein the Russian–Ukraine conflicts are placed negate the perceived uncertainty so much as reinforce it. This is, for example, visible in the way the European Commission introduced the 2014 European Energy Security Strategy:

> The EU's energy dependence is of course not new. But it did gain an added dimension in the light of recent geopolitical events, i.e. the crisis in Ukraine. Temporary disruptions of gas supplies in the winters of 2006 and 2009 already provided a wake-up call for the EU, underlining the need of infrastructure development, increased cooperation and of a common European energy policy.[168]

Or by former European Commission president Barroso, who stated at a conference in the run-up to this strategy that:

> With the events in Ukraine, Europe is facing a threat to its peace, stability and security the likes of which we have not seen since the fall of the Iron Curtain. The 'Great Game' of geopolitics has made an unwelcome return and this is being particularly felt in the area of energy.... In fact the Ukraine crisis once again shows that for Europe energy independence is crucial.[169]

In both cases, the Ukraine crises are clearly used by speech actors. But they are not used to securitize a new issue. They are not even put forward as new threats. Instead they are voiced as self-evident, as threats for which the audience acceptance is taken for granted. In these high-level notifications, the crises are used to reinforce the existing securitized issue of energy dependency and to legitimize existing and new political and institutional arrangements dealing with that. As Barroso argued:

> There were many times in which we … were pleading for a truly European energy policy. The reality is that because there were probably other priorities at the time … minds were not sufficiently focused on the urgency of a real energy policy for the EU. But because of these recent developments, I believe now minds are focused and we could now make more progress than in the years before.[170]

In line with the strict perspective on speech acts in securitization theory, this form of bureaucratic agenda setting can be regarded as a securitizing move (as it lacks the extraordinarity of securitization). This is similar to earlier conclusions by other scholars on the applicability of the theory to the 2006 and 2009 Ukraine–Russia gas crises,[171] simply because they cannot confirm whether the measures enacted in response are truly exceptional. More integration, back-up capacity, strategic reserves, or a diversification of suppliers and resources are not exceptional because these measures have been in place even before Churchill's famous statement in 1913 that 'safety and certainty in oil lie in variety and variety alone'.[172] The events and their interpretations therefore do not break with the already-accepted routine security measures. They are integrated into an existing perception of insecurity and subsequently used to reinforce the underlying social and material dynamics of a fossil fuel system and the community that lies at its core – in this case a European community as favoured by the European Commission.[173]

At the same time, such wake-up calls do enable additional institutional and financial measures that might not have been possible otherwise. In the words of Barroso, minds are focused once more, and the urgency of insecurity pushes other items from the agenda, opens up additional budget and enables a stretching of the original mandate. In response to the 2006 and 2009 interruptions, the EU pushed for preventive action plans, further integration of the EU internal gas and energy markets and introduced the Third Energy Package, which includes a clause that inhibits international parties (read Gazprom) from buying into European upstream markets without reciprocity on its own markets. The first two measures in particular, through which the European Commission encroached on the energy security mandate of the member states, had little institutional backing before these interruptions.[174] These initiatives were followed by an extensive EU programme on infrastructure priorities and added the concept of energy solidarity to the Lisbon Treaty (nowadays extended to an overall European Energy Union). Similarly, in response to the early 2014 Russia–Ukraine conflict the European Council tasked the Commission to come up with a revised European Energy Security Strategy before June 2014. For Trombetta, this request and the time pressure behind it enabled the Commission to put forward its own community building project, as it combined the specific supply risks with broader environmental and socio-economic concerns and thereby strengthened the Commission's claim for a stronger mandate on European energy policy.[175] Then again, Natorski and Surrallés disagree and have argued that this initial communitarian call on security in effect undermines the Commissions position, because a successful framing of the events in a particular neorealist geopolitical security frame reinforces the intergovernmental mandate of the member states themselves.[176]

The tension between, on the one hand, a neorealist geopolitical security perspective on energy supplies and, on the other hand, the depoliticized measures proposed to deal with energy security threats fits well with the theory's normative position that securitized issues should be approached from a desecuritization logic. The problem being that securitization is only helpful in analysing (and thereby reifying) these and other geopolitical aspects of security and not the wide range of uncertainties found elsewhere in energy politics. Theoretically, only these explicit threats allow for successful securitization based on extraordinary measures, whereas for oil and gas it is so far only possible to conclude that 'threats are successfully constructed, that construction has been accepted by a relevant audience and often policy changes have followed'.[177] Hardly ever are these policy changes extraordinary. Is it extraordinary that the gas pipeline from Ukraine to Slovakia is refitted for two-way transport, enabling the supply of gas to Ukraine from Europe if needed? One can argue that without the perception of supply risks this investment would not have been made as the market would not have made it. On the other hand, it is a technical solution to resolve the Ukraine plight temporarily by increasing the flexibility of the grid; it does not tackle the root cause – dependency on and political intervention from Russia – at all.

A last aspect of the use of securitization theory to explain EU–Russian natural gas relations has to do with the 'other' and the referent object. The 'other' in the case above, for many is self-evident. But is it? At first glance, the idea of supply disruption due to Russia's political control of its gas exports merits seeing Russian political elites as the other. However, such a perspective excludes the role played by the Ukrainian government, which decided to tap its share from European deliveries. It also excludes the role played by European member states, for example Germany, and their bilateral agreements with Russia. In other words, the 'other' *is made* to be Russia. In addition, while the above is written from the idea of a securitizing move on supply disruptions, from the implicit undesired future of scarcity, Trombetta argues that, while important, this was not the main referent object in the securitizing move for the European Commission. For the Commission, '[t]he threat was posed not directly by Russia or by the scarcity issue but by what Russia represented and by the reaction to the possibility of a return of geopolitics'.[178] The threat for the Commission, besides the supply disruptions, relates to Russia's geopolitical realist approach to international relations, which contrasts with the European Union's neo-liberal faith in trade and international institutions. From this argument, it is a threat to both what we *need* and *who we are*. If one pushes this point, then the claim would be that without the geopolitical realist policies of Russia the Commission has no 'other' to justify a 'self' (on this issue at least).[179]

This brief reflection on EU–Russia natural gas relations through the lens of securitization theory highlights its workings as well as its strengths and weaknesses. On the one hand, the EU–Russia gas illustration shows why securitization theory is considered elitist, realist and statist.[180] It is most easily applicable to cases like traditional energy security of supply concerns, where the debate is structured and organized on a national level by governments and with a clearly identifiable 'other'. Similarly, the above clearly shows the difficulties in categorizing the counter measures in terms of exceptionality, especially as the proposed countermeasures are market-oriented and hence non-political, thereby desecuritizing the issue the moment it is securitized. On the other hand, the theory

helps pinpoint at least part of the politics of security, including the active production of security issues and the analysis and definition of the threat in line
with the history and language it builds on by naming the other, while fixating
the referent object and reinforcing the self.

4.4.4 Moving beyond the exception

The example of EU–Russia natural gas relations, a most likely case if ever there
were one, opens up securitization theory away from exceptionality towards a
politics of security focusing on agenda setting and the routine of threats and
countermeasures. Even if one took a broad definition of speech acts – one that
moves away from a static event to processes over time and one that would
include the acts of *not acting* (e.g. silence) – the theory offers few tools to analyse
these routines, nor does it provide for ways to include the broader intersubjective historical and social context in which these speech acts find their relevance.[181] This last part in particular, the lack of contextualization, is problematic.
Butler is most succinct when she writes that the 'realities brought into being
depend upon a speech act, but the speech act is a reiterated form of discourse, so
we would be mistaken *to overvalue the subject who speaks*'.[182] Neal, in turn, posits
that securitization theory seems to forget that any theory that builds upon
understandings of 'urgency, extraordinary circumstances and exceptional measures' inherently takes on board the 'structural, institutional and ethic-political
implications' that 'are already implicit' in these concepts.[183] Similarly, Patomäki
goes so far as to argue that in the absence of any political and economic contextualization, '[securitization theory] is no more than an ideal-typical model of a
limited-scale social mechanism'.[184] In short, securitization theory explains how
security comes to be, but only for a few very limited cases of truly exceptional
circumstances. It neglects the large range of security debates that are political in
orientation and discussed on a daily basis.

   This is also the position advocated by scholars like Bigo and Balzacq, who are
working on alternative theory of security that is based on *practice theory*.[185] The
main insight of this alternative is that security practitioners, like border guards
or terrorism and energy security experts, in their daily routines 'enact a governmentality of fear and unease' by constantly reminding others and themselves of
the undesirable future that needs to be countered, in addition to interpreting
and approaching new events through the routines that have helped them in the
past.[186] First, Bigo assumes that securitization explains these routines 'ex post
facto', as for him securitization is not the act of asking for new extraordinary
measures but a justification to extend the measures that are already in place.[187]
Balzacq therefore shifts the focus to the agents themselves and to the routine
daily acts performed by these agents. He does so because he believes that successful securitization depends not only on the logics of securitization but on the
strategic connections to an external reality that can be witnessed in the acts of
the agents. When analysing agents, Balzacq looks at their relative power positions and their shared social identity, but above all he looks at the capacity and

nature of the audience(s), including the enemy and other actors involved, for example whether an audience provides formal or moral support. Within his practice theory he analyses the acts from both an illocutionary threat text level (the logic or grammar of securitization) and from a contextual level, where the attentions shifts to the *strategic* (perlocutionary or performative) use of language in persuading the audience.[188]

Besides practice theories, there have been other attempts to build upon securitization theory. Promising is the work of Vuori, who broadens the application of security speech acts by showing that security speech acts, with their inherent claims and warnings, are not only aimed at gaining legitimation for certain exceptional measures (we need to do this because…) but could also include agenda setting (this is more important than…), declarations of deterrence (if you do this then I will…), a struggle for control (this is mine) or the reproduction of previous securitizations (we are not safe yet).[189] In phrasing speech acts like this, Vuori comes closer to theories of agenda setting and framing, in other words to how the speech act logic is not only used to shift something outside the political but also to shift topics within the political through a dramatization of sorts. However, while Vuori on the one hand broadens security speech acts by opening them to other purposes besides an upfront legitimation of the exception, he simultaneously narrows the theory by seeing security speech acts as the political use of the threat logic only. Vuori thus opens the door by offering multiple classifications of speech acts but then closes it again by limiting these classifications to a single security logic.

Whereas Vuori opens the speech acts themselves to other effects, Huysmans and Stritzel take an alternative linguistic approach. Like Vuori, Huysmans also returned to the speech act literature itself, but he champions an even broader interpretation of speech acts, one where the actual 'act' comes from people who 'politically invest' in 'creat[ing] a scene in which actors and things are brought into a relation that challenges a given way of doing things'.[190] For Huysmans, security is an open-ended form of politics that follows the meaning of security within the daily language of the agents themselves. In such a daily language use, each new iteration is signified by the creation of a rupture and the assembly of a new set of relations based on claims for urgency. With such an understanding, Huysmans opens the speech act to other logics besides the strict (realist, statist and elitist) war logic of securitization theory. Elsewhere, Stritzel takes a similar linguistic avenue by comparing the idea of speech acts with the sociological concept of translation.[191] Instead of deepening our understanding of securitization in more detail, this approach 'suggests an understanding of security that is historical, local, non-essentialist, empirical-reconstructive and reflectivist'.[192] It builds on the understanding that in each situation the meaning of security is translated *locally* through a rupture from a specific old historic meaning into a new open-ended meaning. Stritzel here is close to Huysmans's notion of politics, although he approaches the issue from knowledge production in general instead of security. While this implies a total contextualization and thus a break with any form of predicative theorizing, it opens up security by allowing for situation where a new meaning of security can conflict with older global notions of security. In the words of Neal:

> When one describes 'exceptionalism', the aim should not be to describe a special category, but to describe a dispersed regularity, an assemblage of practices, an already existing archive of statements, an array of competing subject positions, a body of tactics and strategies, a formation of historical conditions of possibility, the limits of which can never be distilled and formalized, only problematized.[193]

Such a linguistic contextualized understanding helps explain why the same illocutionary speech act can have different perlocutionary consequences for different audiences.[194] It explains for example why the US security claims for the most recent Iraq War were interpreted differently in the US and in parts of Europe. The exception in these cases is always local and relative, a form of politics that plays out at the same time, in different places for different people. Both Huysmans's rupture and Stritzel's translation will be taken up in the next chapters when discussing the materiality of energy and the ontological politics around it.

To sum up, securitization theory offers an analysis of how security works as a social mechanism through the speech act of moving something out of the regular political debate into the exceptionality of security. The theory is questioned from two directions: first, in terms of the meaning of exceptionality (vs politics) and the absence of any contextualization and, second, in relation to the theory's double methodological positions and the normativity of these positions and assumptions. By taking on the same questions that securitization theory has introduced and has been openly struggling with, Huysmans, Vuori, Stritzel and Balzacq offer interesting additions and alternatives to the speech act theory that opens the focus of the theory to broader social contexts and to comparable logics that do not depend on the word security as such. This broader approach fits the field of energy security better, as energy security sees a lot of securitizing moves but hardly any strict securitization in terms of exceptionality. It is hard to find exceptionality, because there are very few crises in energy (and other fields) that, one way or another, have not seen any preparation. These preparations, which are based on imaginations and an abstraction of scarcity and shortages, lead to a politics of energy security. Security in energy, or energy security, is not just the moment of crisis itself but the routine prevention of the next crisis. This makes it a form of politics where security arguments are used to dramatize an issue to justify investments for one course of action over another.

Nevertheless, if we ignore the focus on successfulness, securitization theory remains one of the more interesting perspectives on security owing to its focus on the securitizing moves and the speech acts behind those moves. Speech acts are an interesting method to highlight how, within the political domain, actors are dramatizing issues through a call on security logics by which they claim scarce resources and the time to tackle their preferred issue. It bears reminding that, although the theory helps to explain how security comes to be, it does not provide reasons why it does. It only shows the politics of security, the construction of a (self-evident) need to counter an undesirable future. Simultaneously, by using insights from securitization theory it becomes possible to analyse both routine practices and moments of rupture. And, instead of putting one before the other, Bourbeau is correct when he argues that 'the social world we live in is a world of feedback', where speech acts and routine security practices are acting together 'in a complex and wider range of ways'.[195] The next section therefore will take up a theory that looks at a more routine security practice named risk.

4.5 Risk as a security instrument

4.5.1 Risk as an ordering principle

Continuing the move away from a focus on the exception to more routine security practices, a second CSS theory discusses the practice and logic of risk. Unfortunately, while risk is a core CSS theory, it has seen little uptake in relation to energy and energy security besides the more traditional risk analyses behind company investments.[196] In line with the problems inherent to securitization theory, this is unfortunate as much of the energy security practices seem to fit more routine risk decisions that are just as performative of society as the explicit threat logics that lie at the heart of securitization theory. This section will therefore introduce the literature on risk. It starts with a brief overview of the concept of risk as a performative knowledge practice, it then takes a step back and looks at the uncertainty and unknowability that risks try to make knowledgeable. After describing what risks are, the section focuses on the way risks are 'written' (e.g. performed) and how this is changing. It does so by looking at the accountability and political decision-making processes that are hidden behind a calculable risk rationality. Then it will highlight a number of trends within the use of risk. And, lastly, it will reflect on how a zero-risk approach and increasing computation power are transforming the logics of risk itself from a calculative into a correlation logic. As all of this it is quite theoretical, Chapter 7 will offer an empirical example which draws on securitization and risk to analyse an energy security case. Also, while the discussion below is written from the risk literature that is present in CSS, the insights originally derive from the French philosopher Foucault and his thoughts on security as a form of governmentality (which is taken up in Chapter 6).[197]

Traditionally, when people consider risk they often think in terms of a future threat that is estimated in terms of likelihood and its possible impact, leading to a decision to act upon this risk or not.[198] Within CSS, however, risk instead is seen as an ordering principle that is based on (statistical) calculative principles. It is 'a means of making an uncertain and unknowable future amenable to intervention and management',[199] in other words as a way to translate dangers and threats into probabilities and, subsequently, into financial losses and profits.[200]

Seeing risk as an ordering instrument used to govern populations has at least six implications on how risk is defined.

First, as Ewald has put it, 'Nothing is a risk in itself; there is no risk in reality. But on the other hand, anything can be a risk; it all depends on how one analyses the danger, considers the event'.[201] Second, following the notion that nothing is a risk in itself, risks need to be seen as performative: in the process of naming them, they constitute their effects.[202] In other words, when people have identified something in terms of risk they already behave differently towards it; it is impossible to think of a risk without also thinking about ways of levelling it. Third, it follows that risks should not be seen as pregiven entities to be studied independently. Instead, Amoore and De Goede highlight Foucault's attention towards '"differential risks," "risk zones", [and] "different curves of normality"'.[203] What they refer to is Foucault's insight that there are no absolute risks. Risk assessments differentiate between and within populations on a continuum that ranges from higher to lower risks, with the goal to 'normalize' the abnormal high-risk individuals within a population through identification and targeted policies.[204] This often means that individuals are 'broken up', compared and excluded based on one aspect of their behaviour, but which one differs as the 'measurable risk factors' are constantly shifting.[205] Risks are thus mobile, and as a result, fourth, the idea of actually 'securing' these risks is a utopia: while individuals can take action to minimize risks and insure against them, the population as a whole will always remain at risk.[206] From a Foucauldian perspective, therefore, 'what matters instead is that the appearance of securability and manageability is sustained'.[207] Risk does this quite effectively, as its numerical expression gives an appearance of control. Fifth, Foucauldian-inspired scholars argue that to really understand risk one should move away from the risks themselves towards the 'forms of knowledge that make [them] thinkable', by which they mean the practices in those sectors and techniques that 'make the incalculable calculable'.[208] Finally, sixth, one of the most important aspects of risk is the fact that once the uncertain has become calculable it becomes tradable as well.[209] Insurance schemes make it possible for risks to be bought and sold, thereby spreading the possible costs of risky decisions, activities or events while making a profit doing so.

Most of the insights on risk and insurance derive from Ewald's seminal article 'Insurance and risk'.[210] It is in this article that Ewald concludes that insurance has no 'special field of operations' but that it should be seen as a 'general principle for the objectification of things, people, and their relations'.[211] Because risk, like security for securitization theory, has no object to which it can be attached, 'new elements are constantly drawn into its concern'.[212] Ewald therefore focuses on the practice of risk and its main characteristics, which he identifies as calculability, collectivism and financialization.[213] Risk is calculable, because it combines a statistical defined 'regularity of events' with subsequent probability calculations. This implies a radical shift away from more legal discourses on faults and responsibilities: inside a rationality of risk, accidents happen, no matter who is to blame.[214] Risk is thus collective, and it calculates the regularity of events for a certain population statistically. In fact, it makes individuals part of a population, as it ascribes a shared identity or norm to a group of people (and excludes those not part of this population). Moreover, it judges whether individuals fit high- or low-risk profiles in relation towards this shared acceptable group norm. Lastly, Ewald sees risk also as a form of capital as it covers the monetary losses and damages after an event, never the actual life or limb that is lost. It cannot, because the insurer writes such financial compensations beforehand based on group statistics and thus never in relation to a specific event.

These characteristics lead Ewald to conclude that risk is not just an economic and financial technique but also a moral technique that forces individuals to take up responsibility for their own future, and a governing technique for 'administering justice' by spreading out the costs for damages and loss from the individual over the population. He concludes, in the words of Dean, that insurance is 'a political technology in that it is a way of combining and using social forces in a specific fashion, one in which the possibility of the optimization of individual responsibility is combined with a maximization of social solidarity'.[215] In short, with Ewald's analysis of insurance we can see risk as an ordering principle by which people are routinely governed in their daily life.

4.5.2 *The commodification of contingent events*

So, risk is a form of knowledge that translates uncertainty into contingency. But what is this uncertainty that risk translates into tradable monetary products? To be clear, the risk identified is not the identification of the uncertainty, as Section 4.2 shows it is only one of many forms of taming the future.[216] In fact, theoretically, the uncertainty itself cannot be identified or known at all. It cannot be known, because every attempt to understand uncertain futures uses pregiven forms of knowledge.[217] Lobo-Guerrero argues that even to think in terms of *uncertainty* itself already implies that one relies up on a specific understanding of the world that is *certain*. However, what exactly *is* certain often 'relates to centuries-long discussions on the determination of what is from what is not, what is to become the matter of the empirical, the observable and thinkable phenomena'.[218] Discussions on certainty and uncertainty thus highlight the politics of ontology or *ontopolitics* where 'risk management [and other forms of security become] then a continuous problematization of the order of being in the world, a problematization that makes the political a contingent matter'.[219] In other words, what enables thinking in terms of uncertainty is a shift from 'traditional security discourses' like danger (live with it) or the will of the gods (divine intervention) towards perceiving life in terms of a sequence of contingent events.[220]

This interpretation is not unproblematic, as a discussion of ontopolitics in terms of an event or number of events can be problematized from both a historic and philosophical perspective. 'The event' is often defined by 'the surprise' or that which 'disrupts the knowledge resources and expertise available to practices of governance'.[221] Foucault, when thinking on a procedure of 'eventualization', describes this as 'a breach of self-evidence [which] means making visible a singularity at places where there is a temptation to invoke a historical constant'.[222] Yet Foucault also notes how immediately after witnessing the surprise of an event this singularity is 'rediscovered' as being part of a whole, deemed 'self-evident, universal and necessary'.[223] Alternatively, Lundborg follows the work of Deleuze when he differentiates such an historical event from a pure event.[224] The Foucauldian historical event is based on a separation of 'before' and 'after', which Lundborg sees simultaneously as a result (and assumption) of a temporal delineation of boundaries between events. However, as delineations are always decided upon by someone in authority (including historians), the process of producing a historical chronology of separate events implies a particular political practice. In contrast, a pure event does not have ascribed boundaries but builds on the idea of paradoxical processes of becoming (instead of being), meaning that without a clear referent object pure events can only be studied by focusing on the paradoxes that they create. In a way, Foucault's first aspect, the surprise, might be said to relate to the pure event or that part of an event that cannot be pinned down. His second aspect, of a historical constant, relates more to a process that Deleuze calls the actualization of a pure event and which Lundborg describes as a political practice of historical eventualization; as writing history as we know it.[225]

No matter how we describe the event itself, risk presupposes a sequence of such events and approaches such a sequence through an epistemology based on a *commodification of contingency*. It uses mathematical techniques to calculate the chance and impact of separate events and in doing so steers how our reality is defined.[226] It is a practice of ontopolitics that works by making the contingency calculable, or rephrased, by giving 'presence to that which is nevertheless only probable'.[227] That what is unknown is imagined and subsequently calculated and visualized, 'made real', repeated in speeches and used as an argument in decision-making processes for people to act on, and so on. The contingency thus becomes real but only as part of a sequence.

This process of riskification comes with its own normative considerations. For example, such an eventual thinking contains assumptions about biological life. Risk sees life primarily in terms of protection through 'strategies of resilience, self-repair and regeneration' and the 'instigation [of] new life forms'.[228] It understands life as something in need of change and emergence.[229] Contingency therefore needs to be monitored and softened but should never be 'killed' by closing the possibility for new events, for example through over-regulation. This contrasts with processes of security, which often try to fixate and hold on to the way life is governed at a particular moment. Where security fixates, the (bio)politics of risk let live (see Chapter 6). This assumption, in all its innocence, defines the Foucauldian shift from fixed referent objects to the fluid referent processes of circulation (of goods, energy, people etc.) that enable life and particular lifestyles.[230] As Foucault describes it, risk is a security instrument that helps 'organiz[e] circulation, eliminating its dangerous elements, making a division between good and bad circulation, and maximizing the good circulation by diminishing the bad'.[231]

4.5.3 *Writing risks and unaccountable power*

Risk is thus an instrument to govern populations, but official public authorities do not always write them. Instead, risks are composed by underwriters. Underwriters are persons who produce risks by seeing individuals as part of a population: those who identify the risk by imagining it and who calculate and commodify such a risk by weighing the likelihood of an event with the impact it might have, but also those who decide on the level of financial compensation and put that down in contractual agreements with predefined categories and profiles of individuals, and those who trade those contractual insurance agreements with others as a risk itself. These underwriters are frequently situated in financial institutions but could also include a system operator analysing the chance of a blackout or a dietician calling for a better diet. Amoore and Butler respectively describe these underwriters in terms of 'proxy sovereignty' or 'petty sovereigns'.[232] Thereby referring to what Dean calls 'a government without a centre, a form of administration in which there is no longer a centrally directing intelligence',[233] in other words a form of governmentality without direct accountability.

With risk being decided upon in the back offices of large financial institutions, the question is whether this is problematic. On the one hand, this lack of accountability and the technicality of risk is something that is actively used in politics to avoid accountable decision-making on topics ranging from ethical questions to climate change. The use of the technical nature of risk to postpone difficult political decisions is something Amoore observes in respect to the increasing use of consultation practices by policymakers. She argues, following Derrida, that this is not a political choice but a 'redeploy[ment of] calculative practices' and therefore 'a decision that is not a decision', just the application of pre-decided upon rules of calculation.[234] There is no decision being made when something is subjected to a risk calculation, because the algorithm already contains the decisions on the weight of the variables involved. In other words, risk in this sense is neutral. It is politically useful and it hides a level of accountability. On the other hand, a risk does not exist by the grace of the insurer alone. Like securitization, risk exists by the grace of the population that is its target.[235] Ewald, for example, argues that the reason why some risks become accepted depends 'on the shared values of the threatened group'.[236] This implies that what is deemed an acceptable risk does not automatically follow from the level of danger or the level of certainty involved. Whatever the material reality behind risks, it depends on the shared values of the population whether a risk is accepted. Amoore's example of the accountants in the UK during World War II and how they wrote the norms around food supplies (discussed in Section 6.4) argues that they did not invent these norms out of thin air; they based them on earlier small-scale practices and understandings of what was deemed appropriate behaviour. Similarly, an explosion of Yellowstone Park is a real material possibility but one that people try to forget, while GMOs are an accepted risk for the US and other countries that introduce them in their agriculture but not for most European countries that oppose them fervently.

The security instrument of risk is thus political in three ways. First, risk is political because insurers and accountants take upon themselves some of the sovereignty of security that was originally only granted to heads of state, diplomats and the military.[237] Second, risk is also political in the sense that a risk needs to be accepted for it to exist. This in turn makes 'the political a contingent matter'.[238] Lastly, risk is political in the sense that risks can be used politically. Dean argues that this is an overlooked but fundamental aspect of Foucault's argument that risk is a security instrument and as such can be attached to different political programmes and strategies.[239] Indeed Dean shows that there are multiple forms of risk assessments and that an epidemiological risk, which studies rates of morbidity and health, is more preventive than a form of risk inspired on insurance and capital, while both are more quantitatively oriented compared to what Dean calls individual 'case-management risk', which also uses qualitative tools like expert diagnostics and interviews to decide on the risk posed by an individual.[240] Choosing what risk assessment to take is a political choice as well.

4.5.5 Broadening the use of risk calculation

The politics of risk becomes obvious when looking at the history of risk and insurance. From dangers to individual risk, insurance and other actuarial tools have helped transform risk into a collective phenomenon, which slowly developed into the collective welfare states of the twentieth century.[241] During this time, risks were socialized as the collective increasingly covered the misfortune of individuals. Three trends are drastically turning this twentieth-century collectivism around. These include individualization, an extension to include systems and a scientific move from extrapolation to correlation.

First, the collectivism of insurance is reversed with the withdrawal of the state in line with privatization and individualization. As Dean concludes, 'risk has been to some extent desocialized, privatized and individualized'.[242] Aradau and Van Munster agree and highlight an important aspect of this trend, namely how insurance is slowly transformed from its early industrial society conception, where it was seen as a positive force to counter some of the 'latent side-effects of industrialization', into a more negative conception that focuses mainly on 'the prevention of "bad's"'.[243] Today's events and risks are seen as a fact of life and it is again partly the case that it is the responsibility of an individual to organize proper insurance. In that sense, risk has increasingly been interpreted in terms of risk minimization – to get the insurance an individual has to change their behaviour or environment to minimize their vulnerability. Together with the shift from collective insurance to practices of risk profiling, this means that risk has become an instrument of governance that is increasingly focused on the identification and exclusion of possible future bads (behaviour, events or ideas).[244]

Second, it is possible to see an extension in risk analysis from accidents and individual (mis)behaviour towards the security of critical infrastructure and climate systems. This trend, identified for example by Collier and Lakoff, combines the modern reflexive focus towards potential future events with a shift away from individuals and populations towards 'vital systems security'.[245] Collier and Lakoff describe how this shift from persons to systems started after World War II in relation to the threat of nuclear attacks. Exercises, mapping and scenarios quickly showed the growing importance of a wide range of infrastructure systems (electricity, communications and transport) and their material components to protect the people and their way of life.[246] The focus shifted when analysts started to think in terms of and gathered data on systems, their material and human components and the interdependencies between systems. Besides the human–material interaction, another important consequence of a systems perspective is the evolution and introduction of complex systems theory and the idea of resilience.

Third, Amoore and De Goede reflect on the changing role of scientific knowledge in relation to insurance and risk.[247] They follow Ewald, who notes the growing time spent by risk assessments on 'the infinitely small-scale' and the 'infinitely large-scale'.[248] While Beck at some point claimed that these are not insurable, in reality they are, although with more complex financial products, higher risk premiums and more stringent insurance terms and conditions.[249] More important, from a risk calculation perspective, is the fact that the analyses are not able to provide a level of 'certainty' for the 'infinitely large-scale' disasters like climate change and nuclear war. They have never happened and are therefore not based on historic events but on intellectual imaginations. This shifts risk analysis from statistical extrapolation, which needs at least some fixed parameters, to practices of (capital market) speculation grounded on a monetary translation of the expectations of the markets.[250] The scientific uncertainty of such precautionary issues coupled with a need to anticipate future risks leads to forms of 'objective' knowledge that include 'emotional, affective, and speculative domains'.[251]

4.5.6 From calculable to derivative risk

Following these trends, it is possible to identify three approaches to risk that play a role in modern-day security policies. Besides the management of known risks through *insurance* and *prevention*, the trends highlight the management of unknown risks through practices of *precaution*. Insurance is still one of the main instruments to minimize the costs of an undesired future. In turn, prevention is a form of risk minimization that limits as much of the consequences as possible of a known course of action, for example through contingency planning and training.[252] The earlier discussed logic of precaution, however, tackles the unknowability of risks itself, by assuming a worst-case scenario and pushing for (in)action even if the risks are only virtual.[253] For Amoore and De Goede, the first two deal with 'known knowns' (insurance) and 'known unknowns' (prevention), while precaution instead deals with 'unknown unknowns' and touches upon those instances where statistics and computation alone cannot provide an answer.[254] As a consequence, any decision made to counter a worst-case scenario has to assume this particular future as real and in so doing makes this unknown future an actual reality. However, these futures *cannot* actually be known and, because we cannot know the future, it becomes very hard to account for the decisions that are made on its behalf.[255] Aradau and Van Munster elsewhere call for 'precautions against precautionary politics' as they argue we are witnessing 'arbitrary sovereign decision[s]' at 'the limit of knowledge' based on '"objective" socio-economic configurations' that make it very hard to challenge these decisions.[256]

The extent and practical consequences of such an approach to risk only become clear when considering the role that the precautionary logic plays in relation to the War on Terror. Here pre-emptive strikes and precautionary measures are witnessed in the continuous drawing of boundaries and the hidden decisions on:

> The arrest and detention of travellers at the border, the freezing of financial transactions, the pre-emptive disruption of plots and indictment of suspects, the stopping and searching of young Muslim men in the city subway, the entry of a name onto a selectee list [or the kill orders for a drone attack] – all advance an invisible political violence, taking unaccountable and often unchallengeable decisions.[257]

Moreover, these decisions are made by connecting as many databases as possible, ranging from financial data to telecommunications, travel, biometrics, health, judicial, educational, Internet and consumption data. These are linked for 'scenario planning, risk profiling, algorithmic modelling, information integration, and data analysis' and are used not so much to find evidence of previous unwanted behaviour but to find associations and other signs of imagined unwanted behaviour in the future.[258] In these cases of 'derivative risk', Amoore convincingly argues that what is sought are not 'risk *probabilities*' but 'risk *possibilities*'.[259] Risk analyses no longer focus on the *chance* that a risk might occur based upon particular historical patterns but increasingly focus on multiple *possible* risky futures and how to identify them before they occur. To prevent these possible futures, big data is used to find clues for possible feared events by associating pieces of information that are not related themselves but nonetheless offer a certain 'precision as a basis for decision'.[260] In this risk logic, decisions are made irrespective of the fact that the information is not causally related and reported in such a way that the increasingly 'obscure' and complicated algorithms and assumptions behind these connections are hidden behind simple 'objective' visual representations (e.g. a green or red light).[261] In the move from probabilities to possibilities, it has become even harder to question the decisions and assumptions behind risk.

A precautionary risk logic based on possibility instead of probability highlights two aspects that add a troubling note towards the unaccountability of power discussed above. First, it highlights the mobility of the norms behind those who are (or behind what is) deemed a risk factor. Research on practices initiated in counterterrorism show that what is considered to be normal behaviour, or, vice versa, what is seen as unwanted behaviour, is not based on a clearly defined norm. Instead, such considerations are derived from a norm that is mobile over place and time.[262] By behaving correctly today, one can still be found lacking at a later moment in time. This clearly collides with criminal law, where one cannot be punished for an action that was not against the law at the time that it was committed. Second, Amoore shows how the use of fully automatic analysis of big data means that public authorities increasingly need to rely on outside commercial expert knowledge (for ICT and mathematics) in order to identify, imagine and measure possible future threats, not to mention that these experts play a vital role in helping to interpret and explain the crises that have occurred. This influential position should be considered carefully as these same experts and consultancies have a vested economic interest in offering ways to counter these threats, advising on surveillance equipment, data algorithms and protocols etc.[263] For such experts and companies, risk is truly a way to commodify and capitalize on insecurity.

In short, it is possible to summarize risk as a performative practice that identifies and problematizes contingency based on mobile norms that cannot be overcome but can only be managed and traded. To understand risks and the different risk logics, this section followed the focus of the literature on the knowledge practices that lie behind risk calculations. More specifically, it showed that the translation from uncertainty to contingency is always based on existing systems of knowledge, which are reified by each articulation and calculation of risk. For risk logics to work, one needs to be able to think in terms of certainty and uncertainty, to separate and identify events as particulars and to understand life as something to be kept 'open'. Based on these underlying assumptions, risk works through its statistical methods to make the unknown real by imagining a particular future and then calculate and visualize it. These commodified 'facts' are then repeated in speeches and used as an argument in decision-making processes, to be acted upon through insurance and prevention schemes and to be traded for profit.

Simultaneously, this section problematizes risk by questioning the unaccountable power distribution that results when those who define the past and imagine the future are just as important as official sovereign decision makers, in particular as the role of these underwriters and other commercial security experts is growing as they decide increasingly on the importance of variables and the connections between variables, thereby identifying what we should fear, how bad the situation is and what should be done to make it better. Through risk and financial insurance schemes aimed at risk minimization, these underwriters actively shape how individuals organize and live their lives. Moreover, it is their way of seeing the world that is coded in the risk logics and algorithms themselves, making an apolitical technical instrument suddenly quite political. Most troubling in this respect is the shift from probable risk to possible risk, to the desire to act on multiple possible futures instead of the most probable future, based on only indirectly associated data points from everyday life connected through increasingly complex algorithms which paradoxically are translated in ever-simpler binary outcomes.

4.6 Reflection

The goal of this chapter was threefold. First, to give a potential explanation for the proliferation of energy security concerns. Second, to unpack the notion of security in order to problematize its use in the field of energy security. And, third, closely related, to introduce and provide an overview of the recent insights from critical security studies as a basis to push energy security analyses beyond its realist, liberalist and securitization applications. The subsequent sections offered insights into the multiple logics of security, the ethics of security, the manner in which security is called upon, and the exercise of power inherent to the calculation of risk. Together these sections present security as a form of governing the present based on an imagination of undesired futures.

In pushing the recent literature on security, this chapter started by approaching security in its broadest sense as dealing with and deciding upon undesired futures. A logical consequence of such a broad definition is the possibility to observe a more extensive range of different insecurities or undesirable futures, the techniques used to imagine and decide on that undesirability and the logics of security that drive the application of these techniques and search for countermeasures. Together, these techniques and logics help make sense of the future and make people act performatively in the here and now. The security logics are both inclusionary and exclusionary. They are inclusionary as there is always another unknown potentially threatening future, just as failed countermeasures only inspire to do better. While these logics are inclusionary and help make sense of events, they do not define the issues at stake. Instead, interpretations shift and depend on the agent's position and relation to the referent object. Hence, security is exclusionary as the identification of an undesired future always builds on a politics that excludes those not part of the security arrangement. Such normative judgements create ruptures, which are reinforced by the countermeasures that are enacted. Security was reasoned to be a form of ethics itself, shaping and reinforcing the interpretation of an event, the image of the other, the referent object and oneself. The security of undesirable futures is thus not only epistemological but strongly ontological as well. It is the choice of what to protect and what not to protect, or, more importantly, the choice between what to see as a threat and what not to see as a threat.

Security is something that is made; it does not exist out there but is called upon or written by politicians, concerned citizens, security experts, insurers etc. To understand the identification of undesired futures, this chapter focused on the emotion of fear (and desire) as well as the explicit use of fear in political contexts. Through a separation of private and public fears, it becomes possible to see the emotive and political use of fear, more specifically how public fears build upon a depoliticized idea of private fear by linking the individual to the collective, while decoupling the private experience of fear from the social call upon fear. Together with an increasing epistemic and ontic uncertainty that triggers an autopoietic fear for fear itself, this leads to a situation where the existence of political fears cannot be proven wrong. Besides, while it only works when called upon, the above makes clear that almost everybody calls on security and thus engages or is subject to to security practices. Clearly, not all calls are successful, but in today's culture of fear that seems to be of less importance as the calls always already succeed in reinforcing the desire for more security. Moreover, contrary to an individual private experience of fear, where the undesirable future and its opposite (the desired future) are identified in response to a bodily reaction, in the case of public fear there is a more intentional logic at work where particular desired futures are identified *before* their current state is publicized as undesirable and something to be feared.

The call upon security was analysed more closely through a study of the insights provided by securitization theory and its singular focus on the exceptionality of security over normal politics. With the concepts of speech acts, securitizing moves and securitization, this theory helps to understand and study how people call on security. While the theory highlights the process of how something becomes a security issue, it does not provide the reasons why particular issues are called on and hence should not be used as such. More generally, there are questions on the conflation of the theory and methodology of securitization, its normativity and its focus on exceptionality and lack of context. Still, the theory, as well as its different critiques, highlight the politics behind security instead of the outcome of such processes. Behind the self-evident threats lies the active politics of multiple audiences, multiple speech actors and multiple issues that are securitized. In addition, besides showing the activity that goes into making something a security issue, the theory also opens up the relationality behind the self–other distinction.

While securitization has proven useful to analyse energy security, it struggles with the routine nature of energy security. Energy definitely has extraordinary moments, but most of the time it is characterized by practices that try to secure the daily functioning of its sources and systems. The reflection on risk with its focus on routine security practices and its underlying risk calculations offered an alternative theory. Risk was described as a performative practice that identifies and problematizes uncertainty as contingency following mobile norms of security that can only be managed, not overcome. Through its statistical methods, risk makes the unknown real as it imagines, calculates and visualizes the future. These commodified 'facts' are repeated in speeches and used as arguments in decision-making processes. Financial insurance schemes aimed at risk minimization thus actively shape how individuals organize their daily lives: what they buy, say and do. The use of risk calculation was problematized by highlighting the growing political role of risk underwriters and ICT experts and the shifting accountability following recent changes in risk calculation from probable to possible risks.

Both theories discuss a particular logic of security, respectively a threat rationality and a logic and technique of risk, but both agree that security is an exercise of power that is called upon by people who decide on its boundaries. Yet, where the risk logic accepts an increasing level of contingency, a threat logic actively resists such contingency. At the same time, the risk literature can only ascribe probability to an already-identified undesired future but cannot explain how something becomes a threat nor how particular thresholds of risk are set. In turn, the speech act-inspired security literature is unable to move away from the exceptional threat to the routine of everyday security and safety practices that are also inherent to these threats. Clearly, we need to understand the normative and instrumental characteristics of security and risk, as both security and risk 'do ... things rather than merely name things'.[264] Equally importantly, they both approach events from a *how* question, with neither offering reasons or generalized conclusions that can be used predictively.

What this chapter means for energy security is manifold. At the beginning, this chapter stated that it is very well possible to read this chapter by just adding the word energy whenever it spoke of security. While that might push it, this chapter makes a clear case for moving away from a 'simple' goal-oriented definition of energy security to an understanding of energy security that is called upon every time it is used. This chapter thus supports the initial reflections in the chapters on energy security to move beyond the search for a better understanding of the content of energy security, to the actual political work that is done to get particular forms of energy security accepted as a security concern. Energy security is made to be, by elites, (insurance) companies, academia (including observing energy security scholars) and the public. It is not some natural state of affairs. Many of the issues raised in the first two chapters, on the proliferation of the concept, the geopolitical and state-centric focus, and the uncritical theorization, can be placed in context now. At the same time, this chapter also shows that energy security does exist. In line with Ciută (energy) security is not a banal process; it is very much the opposite. While everything is constantly performed, there are concerns, like Russian gas, that can be called on much easier and with a much larger backing and audience than others, because they fit historical insecurities or because they are materialized in such a way that they could affect many. The difference between traditional theories of energy security and the theories on security that were discussed in this chapter is that the latter acknowledge that they themselves play a role in the process of securing energy while analysing these processes and the conditions behind them. In this way, they introduce an understanding of energy security that is socially performed and never the same, yet made to be so, while functioning as an exercise of power with strong normative consequences.

Notes

1 This chapter discusses security, not energy security. However, as a logic it is possible to read this chapter almost from the beginning to end and just add the word energy before the word security to make it into a discussion on energy security.
2 Booth 2005, 23, as quoted by C.A.S.E. Collective 2006, 456.
3 Buzan 1983, 19.
4 Brauch 2011, 99.
5 Booth 2007, 95–101.
6 Zedner 2003; Booth 2007, 105–106.
7 Such a debate about what is acceptable or real, points to a ontopolitics of (in)security.
8 Zedner 2003, 157, quoting *Macbeth*, Act III.
9 Der Derian 1995, 28–29.
10 Ibid.
11 Dillon and Lobo-Guerrero 2008.
12 Dillon 1996, 33 (emphasis in original); also Neocleous 2008, 28.
13 Buzan, Wæver and de Wilde 1998, 32.
14 Anderson 2010b, 779. Also Anderson 2010a; Massumi 2007.
15 Burgess 2011, 26.
16 Anderson 2010b, 781.
17 Anderson and Adey 2011.
18 Booth 2007, 104; Svendsen 2008.
19 Anderson 2010a, 778 (emphasis in original), quoting Massumi 2007, n.p.
20 Luhmann 1993.
21 See Anderson 2010a.
22 Alternatively, Daase and Kessler 2007 argue for a categorization of uncertainty built upon four categories of knowledge. In their article these authors differentiate between *known knowns* (meaning actual threats that provide a clear basis for action), *known unknowns* (risks where the ontic structure is blurred but methods exist to diminish these unknowns), *unknown unknowns* (dangers in the form of uncertainty) and *unknown knowns* (ignored or forgotten actual threats). Daase and Kessler thus approach the concepts of risk, uncertainty, danger and threat from a systemic perspective by showing the ontic and epistemic differences between these categories.
23 Anderson 2010a, 789.
24 On surprise and the politics of events, see Section 4.5.
25 Knight 1921; Best 2008; Kessler 2012.
26 Keynes 1921. Compare with Barad in Section 5.5.
27 Kessler and Daase 2008.
28 Best 2008, 356. Best argues that linguistic ambiguity has three functions: it could actually help govern forms of epistemic uncertainty, it could also be used as an instrument to govern through, and, lastly, it poses a limit to the actual governance that can take place.
29 Latour 2005, 244; Bennett 2010; Adorno 1973. For a discussion on Latour's plasma, see Harman 2009, 132–134.
30 Rasmussen 2004, 393. See also: Luhmann 1993, 21–22; Beck 2002, 41; Corry 2012.
31 Buzan 1983, 83–84.
32 Wæver 1995.
33 Massumi 2009, 162.
34 Burgess 2011, 61.
35 Luhmann 1993, 107.
36 Ibid., 109.
37 Ibid., 119 (emphasis in original).

38 Ibid., 68.
39 Vergragt and Quist 2011.
40 Linstone and Turoff 2002; Mullen 2003.
41 Mietzner and Reger 2005.
42 Davis 2002.
43 Ibid., 1.
44 De Goede and Randalls 2009, 869.
45 For an overview of different types of scenarios: Mietzner and Reger 2005, 225–227.
46 Salter 2008a, 233.
47 Ibid., 235–236.
48 Grusin 2004; De Goede 2008a.
49 Malthus 1798.
50 Linstone 2011.
51 Subrahmaniyan 2008. Other expectations predicted prices of $300 a barrel in ten to fifteen years: Korosec 2009, 2011.
52 Anderson 2010a, 784.
53 Amoore 2013, 73.
54 Salter 2008a, 233.
55 Luhmann 1993, 2.
56 Amoore 2013, 73.
57 Anderson 2010a, 786.
58 IEA 2014.
59 Rumsfeld 2002; Daase and Kessler 2007.
60 Daase and Kessler 2007.
61 Massumi 2007.
62 Ibid., para. 7 (emphasis in original).
63 Ibid., 13.
64 Ibid.
65 Also Amoore 2013; Amoore and De Goede 2008c; De Goede 2008b, 2008c, 2011; De Goede and Randalls 2009; Anderson 2010a, 791.
66 Anderson 2010a, 791.
67 Massumi 2007, note 9.
68 Ibid., paras 17–20; Anderson 2010a, 791.
69 Anderson 2010a, 791; Commission of the European Communities 2000.
70 UNESCO World Commission on the Ethics of Scientific Knowledge and Technology 2005, 14.
71 Bigo 2010, 11; Ravetz 2004.
72 See also Anderson 2010a, 791.
73 Ibid., 792; Collier and Lakoff 2015, 2008b.
74 Evans and Reid 2013.
75 Booth 1991; UNDP 1994.
76 Beck 1992, 2002.
77 Buzan, Wæver and de Wilde 1998.
78 Bigo 2002; Balzacq *et al.* 2010; Dillon 1996; Huysmans 2011; Dillon and Lobo-Guerrero 2008; Amoore and De Goede 2008b; De Goede 2012; Amoore 2013.
79 Massumi 2009, 161.
80 Ibid.
81 Luhmann 1993.
82 Massumi 2009, 162.
83 Ibid.
84 Ibid., 161.
85 Campbell 1998, 3.
86 Dillon 1996, 122. Italics added.
87 Ibid., 35.

88 Burgess 2011, 4. See also Browning and McDonald 2013.
89 Booth 1991, 2007.
90 Booth 2007, 256, 348–392.
91 Ibid., 98.
92 Foucault 2007.
93 Buzan, Wæver and de Wilde 1998.
94 Ibid.; Wæver 1995.
95 Neocleous 2008.
96 Leander 2003; Leander 2005. See also C.A.S.E. Collective 2006, 464.
97 See also Åhäll and Gregory 2013.
98 On ontological security, see Wendt 1999, 131.
99 Svendsen 2008, 12.
100 Ibid., 13–16, 71.
101 Frost 2010, 160.
102 Ibid., 167–170; Svendsen 2008, 35–37.
103 Frost 2010, 169.
104 Ibid., 160.
105 Robin 2004, 16–18.
106 Ibid., 19.
107 Furedi 2007.
108 Robin 2004, 6, 9.
109 Furedi 2007.
110 Ibid.
111 Svendsen 2008, 52–53.
112 Massumi 2005, 36.
113 Ibid. quotes William, James. 1950. *Principles of Psychology*, vol. 2. New York: Dover, 449–450, 467.
114 Ibid., 38.
115 Ibid., 40.
116 Ibid., 41.
117 Furedi 2007.
118 Massumi 2005, 45–46.
119 Furedi 2005, chap. 7.
120 Furedi 2007.
121 Ibid.
122 Furedi 2008, 2005, 2007.
123 Furedi 2005, chap. 7, in particular 137 and 139.
124 Burgess 2011, 62.
125 Furedi 2007.
126 Booth 2007, 325.
127 Buzan, Wæver and de Wilde 1998. The securitization framework also contains a level of analysis focus, a sectorial focus and regional security theory.
128 This argument on materiality will be taken up in Chapter 5.
129 See also: Latour 2004.
130 Schmitt 1985, 5; see also Neal 2006.
131 Austin 1975. Austin differentiates within a speech act between: locutionary acts that are the utterances; illocutionary acts or that what is done in saying (shifting discourse to exceptionality); and perlocutionary acts or that what is done by saying (effects on target audience). Balzacq 2005, 175, quotes Habermas: 'To say something, to act in saying something, to bring about something through acting in saying something'.
132 Buzan, Wæver and de Wilde 1998, 27.
133 Ibid., 32.
134 Roe 2008; Vuori 2008; Balzacq 2005.

135 Besides the securitizing actors, referent objects and the audiences that accept the securitization move, the theory also mentions functional agents, actors not actively involved in the securitization process but profoundly influencing the issue nevertheless.

136 Compare with Latour 2004 on matters of fact (non-political) and matters of concern (political/security).

137 On speed and silence, see Roe 2012. However, see the earlier discussion on Neocleous 2008.

138 Booth 2007, 106.

139 Ibid., 107. Compare with recent work on scarcity and abundance that defines abundance as the ability to choose wrongly, see Mullainathan and Shafir 2013.

140 Wæver 2011, 467.

141 Buzan, Wæver and de Wilde 1998, 29; Roe 2012; de Wilde 2012.

142 Wæver 1995, 54. Compare with Ciută 2009.

143 Aradau 2008, 72.

144 Buzan, Wæver and de Wilde 1998, 29.

145 Ibid.

146 de Wilde 2012, 213, 2008.

147 de Wilde 2012, 213.

148 Ibid.

149 Ibid.

150 Wæver 2011, 469; Buzan, Wæver and de Wilde 1998, 29.

151 Hansen 2000, 2012.

152 Hansen 2012. She actually identifies four options of desecuritization: stabilization, replacement, rearticulation and silencing.

153 Huysmans 1998b.

154 Wæver 1999, 334.

155 Roe 2008; Salter 2008b; Stritzel 2007.

156 Ciută 2009; Buzan, Wæver and de Wilde 1998, 27.

157 Huysmans 1998b, 501; Wæver 2011, 469.

158 Buzan, Wæver and de Wilde 1998.

159 Nyman 2014.

160 Leung *et al.* 2014.

161 Christou and Adamides 2013.

162 Judge and Maltby 2017.

163 For specific applications of securitization theory on the Russian and European energy relationship, see: Natorski and Herranz Surrallés 2008; Stoddard 2012; Khrushcheva 2011; Radoman 2007; Boersma 2013; McGowan 2011; Trombetta 2012. For more general energy security reflections on Russia and the European Union, see: Aalto 2008; Aalto and Korkmaz Temel 2014; Casier 2011; Goldthau 2008; Högselius 2012; Stern 2006. And for good use of the theory in relation to other countries, see: Nyman 2014; Christou and Adamides 2013; Leung *et al.* 2014; Nyman and Zeng 2016; Judge and Maltby 2017; Judge, Maltby and Szulecki 2018; Cox 2016; Aglaya Snetkov 2017; Fischhendler and Nathan 2014.

164 Stern 2006.

165 Smith Stegen 2011; McGowan 2011; Boersma 2013; European Commission 2000.

166 McGowan 2011.

167 Stoddard 2012.

168 European Commission 2014.

169 Barroso 2014.

170 Ibid.

171 Boersma 2013, 37; McGowan 2011, 488; Trombetta 2012, 22.

172 Yergin 1991.

173 Trombetta 2012.

174 Ibid., 16.
175 Trombetta 2012; for the theoretical argument, see Huysmans 1998a.
176 Natorski and Herranz Surrallés 2008, 84.
177 Trombetta 2012, 9.
178 Ibid., 21.
179 Huysmans 1998b, 239.
180 Ciută 2009; McDonald 2008; Stritzel 2007; Balzacq 2005.
181 Ciută 2009.
182 Butler 2010, 149 (emphasis added).
183 Neal 2006, 34.
184 Patomäki 2015, 133.
185 Balzacq 2005, 178–179. Interestingly, in this article Balzacq also argues, with numerous disclaimers, that there are non-social, 'brute' threats that affect humans 'regardless of the use of language' (181). He argues that these external effects/threats should stand central in any constructivist analysis of security (181) as these are used by the audience as evidence in weighing securitization claims thereby reducing the importance of the speaker (191, 193); Bigo 2002, 2014.
186 Bigo 2014, 211; Bourbeau 2014, 196.
187 Bigo 2014.
188 See note 131 on Austin and Habermas.
189 Vuori 2008, 76; Stritzel 2012.
190 Huysmans 2011, 372, 373; Isin 2008.
191 Stritzel 2011.
192 Ibid., 346.
193 Neal 2006, 44.
194 Stritzel 2011, 350.
195 Bourbeau 2014, 197.
196 A recent exception includes Judge and Maltby 2017.
197 Foucault 2007, 2008; Luhmann 1993, 13; C.A.S.E. Collective 2006, 468.
198 Salter 2008a, 233 explicitly mentions scarce resource management: 'Risk management as a governance framework seeks to focus scarce resources on risks that are ranked according to frequency and impact'.
199 Amoore and De Goede 2008a, 9. Dean 2010, 206–207 argues, contra Beck, that because risks is about making future threats calculable, there is no such thing as incalculable risks. If something is incalculable it cannot be a risk.
200 Ewald 1991, 199.
201 Ibid.
202 Butler 2010; Amoore and De Goede 2008a, 9.
203 Amoore and De Goede 2008a, 11, quoting Foucault 2007, 68 and 91.
204 See also Ewald 1993, 221.
205 Amoore and De Goede 2008a, 9, quoting Valverde, M., and M. Mopas. 2004. Insecurity and the dream of targeted governance. In *Global governmentality: Governing international spaces*, edited by W. Larner and W. Walters, 233–250. London: Routledge; De Goede 2012.
206 As Dean argues: 'Risk is a continuum rather than a clear break. Risk, in this sense, never completely evaporates. It can be minimized, localized and avoided, but never dissipated'. 2010, 195.
207 Amoore and De Goede 2008a, 9.
208 Dean 2010, 206–207.
209 Lobo-Guerrero 2012, 10.
210 Ewald 1991. Also Ewald 1993, 2002, 2012.
211 Ewald 1991, 206.
212 Dillon and Lobo-Guerrero 2008, 281.
213 Ewald 1991, 201–205.

214 Ibid., 202.
215 Dean 2010, 214.
216 Amoore and De Goede 2008a, 25–26.
217 Dillon 2007, 45.
218 Lobo-Guerrero 2012, 128–129.
219 Ibid., 18.
220 Dillon 2008, 327; Foucault 2007, 20.
221 Lobo-Guerrero 2012, 128; Nancy 2000.
222 Foucault 1991, 76.
223 Ibid.
224 Lundborg 2012, 1–7.
225 Ibid., 7.
226 Dillon and Lobo-Guerrero 2008, 280–281; Dillon 2008, 320.
227 Ewald 1993, 227.
228 Dillon and Lobo-Guerrero 2008, 287. Elsewhere, Dillon describes how biopolitical security builds upon biological complex systems theories, à la Kauffman, to describe life as being about circulation (autocatalysis), connectivity (radical relationality) and complexity (non-linearity). See Dillon 2008, 312.
229 Dillon 2008, 314–315, 2007; Dillon and Lobo-Guerrero 2008, 280 and 283.
230 Dillon and Lobo-Guerrero 2008, 268; Lobo-Guerrero 2012, 18.
231 Foucault 2007, 18.
232 Butler 2004; Amoore 2013, 6. As also discussed in De Goede 2008b, 101. Compare with Shannon 2014, 252.
233 Dean 2010, 259.
234 Amoore 2013, 6–7, 17–18.
235 Ewald 1993, 225.
236 Ibid.
237 Lobo-Guerrero 2012, 18.
238 Ibid.
239 Dean 2010, 220.
240 Ibid., 218–219.
241 See for example Lobo-Guerrero 2012.
242 Dean 2010, 221.
243 Aradau and Van Munster 2007, 92.
244 Rose 2001, 11; Amoore and De Goede 2008a, 27.
245 Collier and Lakoff 2015, 2008b, 2008a.
246 Kester 2018.
247 Amoore and De Goede 2008a, 27–28.
248 Ewald 1993, 222; Amoore and De Goede 2008a, 27.
249 Beck 1992.
250 Aradau and Van Munster 2007, 106–107.
251 Amoore 2013, 9–10. In respect to information, Amoore (p. 85) also discusses how risk analyses, for example during border control, increasingly reject people based on information that would not have been acceptable in court, thereby effectively judging people outside the law.
252 Prevention is acting without imminent threat (in conflict a preventive war is legally deemed an act of aggression). Pre-emption is acting before an imminent threat materializes and as such is seen as the more justifiable tactic. See also Massumi 2009, 168.
253 Aradau and Van Munster 2007, 103; Amoore 2013, 9.
254 Amoore and De Goede 2008a, 29.
255 Aradau and Van Munster 2008, 35.
256 Aradau and Van Munster 2007, 109.
257 Amoore and De Goede 2008a, 14.

258 Amoore 2013, 9; Amoore and De Goede 2008b; Aradau and Van Munster 2007,
2008; De Goede 2008b.
259 Amoore 2013, 67–68 (emphasis in original).
260 Ibid.
261 Ibid., 69–70, 103.
262 Ibid., 17.
263 Ibid., 20–21.
264 Dillon 1996, 34.

Bibliography

Aalto, Pami. 2008. *The EU-Russian energy dialogue: Europe's future energy security*. Aldershot: Ashgate.

Aalto, Pami, and Dicle Korkmaz Temel. 2014. European energy security: Natural gas and the integration process. *Journal of Common Market Studies* 52 (4): 758–774.

Adorno, Theodor W. 1973. *Negative dialectics*, translated by E. B. Ashton. London: Routledge.

Aglaya Snetkov. 2017. Theories, methods and practices – a longitudinal spatial analysis of the (de)securitization of the insurgency threat in Russia. *Security Dialogue* 48 (3): 259–275.

Åhäll, Linda, and Thomas A. Gregory. 2013. Security, emotions, affect. *Critical Studies on Security* 1 (1): 117–120.

Amoore, Louise. 2013. *The politics of possibility: Risk and security beyond probability*. Durham, NC, and London: Duke University Press.

Amoore, Louise, and Marieke de Goede. 2008a. Introduction: Governing by risk in the war on terror. In *Risk and the war on terror*, edited by Louise Amoore and Marieke de Goede, 5–20. London and New York: Routledge.

Amoore, Louise, and Marieke de Goede. 2008b. *Risk and the war on terror*. London and New York: Routledge.

Amoore, Louise, and Marieke de Goede. 2008c. Transactions after 9/11: The banal face of the preemptive strike. *Transactions of the Institute of British Geographers* 33 (2): 173–185.

Anderson, Ben. 2010a. Preemption, precaution, preparedness: Anticipatory action and future geographies. *Progress in Human Geography* 34 (6): 777–798.

Anderson, Ben. 2010b. Security and the future: Anticipating the event of terror. *Geoforum* 41 (2): 227–235.

Anderson, Ben, and Peter Adey. 2011. Affect and security: Exercising emergency in 'UK civil contingencies'. *Environment and Planning D: Society and Space* 29 (6): 1092–1109.

Aradau, Claudia. 2008. *Rethinking trafficking in women: Politics out of security*. New York: Palgrave Macmillan.

Aradau, Claudia, and Rens van Munster. 2007. Governing terrorism through risk: Taking precautions, (un)knowing the future. *European Journal of International Relations* 13 (1): 89–115.

Aradau, Claudia, and Rens van Munster. 2008. Taming the future: The dispositif of risk in the war on terror. In *Risk and the war on terror*, edited by Louise Amoore and Marieke de Goede, 23–40. London and New York: Routledge.

Austin, J. L. 1975. *How to do things with words: J. L. Austin*, edited by J. O. Urmson and M. Sbisá. 2nd edn. Cambridge, MA: Harvard University Press.

Balzacq, Thierry. 2005. The three faces of securitization: Political agency, audience and context. *European Journal of International Relations* 11 (2): 171–201.

Balzacq, Thierry, Tugba Basaran, Didier Bigo, Emmanuel-Pierre Guittet and Christian Olsson. 2010. Security practices. In *International Studies Encyclopedia Online*, edited by Robert A. Denemark. Oxford: Blackwell. Available from www.blackwellreference. com/public/book.html?id=g9781444336597_9781444336597.

Barroso, Jose Manuel Durao. 2014. *Speech by President Barroso at the conference 'Paving the way for a European energy security strategy'*. Speech. Brussels: European Commission.

Beck, Ulrich. 1992. *Risk society: Towards a new modernity*. London: SAGE.

Beck, Ulrich. 2002. The Terrorist Threat: World Risk Society Revisited. *Theory, Culture & Society* 19 (4): 39–55.

Bennett, Jane. 2010. *Vibrant matter: A political ecology of things*. Durham, NC, and London: Duke University Press.

Best, Jacqueline. 2008. Ambiguity, uncertainty, and risk: Rethinking indeterminacy. *International Political Sociology* 2 (4): 355–374.

Bigo, Didier. 2002. Security and immigration: Toward a critique of the governmentality of unease. *Alternatives: Global, Local, Political* 27 (special issue): 63–92.

Bigo, Didier. 2010. The future perfect of (in)security (P8): Pre-crime strategy, proactivity, preemption, prevention, precaution, profiling, prediction, & privacy. Interdisciplines. Available from www.interdisciplines.org/paper.php?paperID=342. Accessed 2 November 2014.

Bigo, Didier. 2014. The (in)securitization practices of the three universes of EU border control: Military/Navy – border guards/police – database analysts. *Security Dialogue* 45 (3): 209–225.

Boersma, Tim. 2013. *Dealing with energy security in Europe: A comparison of gas market policies in the European Union and the United States*. PhD thesis, Groningen: University of Groningen.

Booth, Ken. 1991. Security and emancipation. *Review of International Studies* 17 (4): 313–326.

Booth, Ken. 2005. Security. In *Critical security studies and world politics*, edited by Ken Booth, 21–25. London: Lynne Rienner.

Booth, Ken. 2007. *Theory of world security*. Cambridge and New York: Cambridge University Press.

Bourbeau, Philippe. 2014. Moving forward together: Logics of the securitisation process. *Millennium – Journal of International Studies* 43 (1): 187–206.

Brauch, Hans Günter. 2011. Concepts of security threats, challenges, vulnerabilities and risks. In *Coping with global environmental change, disasters and security*, edited by Hans Günter Brauch, Úrsula Oswald Spring, Czeslaw Mesjasz, John Grin, Patricia Kameri-Mbote, Béchir Chourou, Pál Dunay and Jörn Birkmann, 61–106. Berlin and Heidelberg: Springer.

Browning, Christopher S., and Matt McDonald. 2013. The future of critical security studies: Ethics and the politics of security. *European Journal of International Relations* 19 (2): 235–255.

Burgess, J. Peter. 2011. *The ethical subject of security: Geopolitical reason and the threat against Europe*. London and New York: Routledge.

Butler, Judith. 2004. *Precarious life: The powers of mourning and violence*. London and New York: Verso.

Butler, Judith. 2010. Performative agency. *Journal of Cultural Economy* 3 (2): 147–161.

Buzan, Barry. 1983. *People, states, and fear: The national security problem in international relations*. Brighton: Wheatsheaf.

Buzan, Barry, Ole Wæver and Jaap H. de Wilde. 1998. *Security: A new framework for analysis*. Boulder, CO: Lynne Rienner.

Campbell, David. 1998. *Writing security: United States foreign policy and the politics of identity*. Revised edition. Manchester: University of Manchester Press.

C.A.S.E Collective. 2006. Critical approaches to security in Europe: A networked manifesto. *Security Dialogue* 37 (4): 443–487.

Casier, Tom. 2011. The rise of energy to the top of the EU–Russia agenda: From interdependence to dependence? *Geopolitics* 16 (3): 536–552.

Christou, Odysseas, and Constantinos Adamides. 2013. Energy securitization and desecuritization in the New Middle East. *Security Dialogue* 44 (5–6): 507–522.

Ciută, Felix. 2009. Security and the problem of context: A hermeneutical critique of securitisation theory. *Review of International Studies* 35 (2): 301–26.

Collier, Stephen J., and Andrew Lakoff. 2008a. Distributed preparedness: The spatial logic of domestic security in the United States. *Environment and Planning D: Society and Space* 26 (1): 7–28.

Collier, Stephen J., and Andrew Lakoff. 2008b. The vulnerability of vital systems: How 'critical infrastructure' became a security problem. In *The politics of securing the homeland: Critical infrastructure, risk and securitisation*, edited by Myriam Dunn Cavelty, 40–62. London and New York: Routledge.

Collier, Stephen J., and Andrew Lakoff. 2015. Vital systems security: Reflexive biopolitics and the government of emergency. *Theory, Culture & Society* 32 (2): 19–51.

Commission of the European Communities. 2000. *Communication from the Commission: on the precautionary principle*. Brussels.

Corry, Olaf. 2012. Securitisation and 'riskification': Second-order security and the politics of climate change. *Millennium – Journal of International Studies* 40 (2): 235–258.

Cox, Emily. 2016. Opening the black box of energy security: A study of conceptions of electricity security in the United Kingdom. *Energy Research & Social Science* 21 (Supplement C): 1–11.

Daase, Christopher, and Oliver Kessler. 2007. Knowns and unknowns in the war on terror: Uncertainty and the political construction of danger. *Security Dialogue* 38 (4): 411–434.

Davis, Ged. 2002. *Scenarios as a tool for the 21st century*. Strathclyde University. Available from www.pik-potsdam.de/news/public-events/archiv/alter-net/former-ss/2006/programme/31-08.2006/leemans/literature/davis_how_does_shell_do_scenarios.pdf. Accessed 6 November 2014.

De Goede, Marieke. 2008a. Beyond risk: Premediation and the post-9/11 security imagination. *Security Dialogue* 39 (2–3): 155–176.

De Goede, Marieke. 2008b. Risk, preemption and exception in the war on terrorist financing. In *Risk and the war on terror*, edited by Louise Amoore and Marieke de Goede, 97–111. London and New York: Routledge.

De Goede, Marieke. 2008c. The politics of preemption and the war on terror in Europe. *European Journal of International Relations* 14 (1): 161–185.

De Goede, Marieke. 2011. *European security culture: Preemption and precaution in European security*. Amsterdam: Amsterdam University Press.

De Goede, Marieke. 2012. *Speculative security: The politics of pursuing terrorist monies*. Minneapolis, MN: University of Minnesota Press.

De Goede, Marieke, and Samuel Randalls. 2009. Precaution, preemption: Arts and technologies of the actionable future. *Environment and Planning D: Society and Space* 27 (5): 859–878.

de Wilde, Jaap H. 2008. Environmental security deconstructed. In *Globalization and environmental challenges*, edited by Hans Günter Brauch, Úrsula Oswald Spring, Habil Czeslaw Mesjasz, John Grin, Pál Dunay, Navnita Chadha Behera, Béchir Chourou, Patricia Kameri-Mbote and P. H. Liotta, 595–602. Hexagon series on human and environmental security and peace 3. Berlin and Heidelberg: Springer.

de Wilde, Jaap H. 2012. Security and the environment: Securitisation theory and US environmental security policy. By Rita Floyd. New York: Cambridge University Press, 2010. *Perspectives on Politics* 10 (1): 213–214.

Dean, Mitchell. 2010. *Governmentality: Power and rule in modern society*. 2nd edn. London: SAGE.

Der Derian, James. 1995. The value of security: Hobbes, Marx, Nietzsche, and Baudrillard. In *On security*, edited by Ronnie D. Lipschutz, 24–45. New York: Columbia University Press.

Dillon, Michael. 1996. *Politics of security: Towards a political philosophy of continental thought*. London and New York: Routledge.

Dillon, Michael. 2007. Governing through contingency: The security of biopolitical governance. *Political Geography* 26 (1): 41–47.

Dillon, Michael. 2008. Underwriting security. *Security Dialogue* 39 (2–3): 309–332.

Dillon, Michael, and Luis Lobo-Guerrero. 2008. Biopolitics of security in the 21st century: An introduction. *Review of International Studies* 34 (02): 265–292.

European Commission. 2000. *Green Paper: Towards a European strategy for the security of energy supply*. COM(2000) 769 final. Brussels: European Commission.

European Commission. 2014. *Questions and answers on security of energy supply in the EU*. Memo.

Evans, Brad, and Julian Reid. 2013. Dangerously exposed: The life and death of the resilient subject. *Resilience* 1 (2): 83–98.

Ewald, François. 1991. Insurance and risk. In *The Foucault effect: Studies in governmentality*, edited by Graham Burchell, Colin Gordon and Peter Miller, 197–210. London: Harvester Wheatsheaf.

Ewald, François. 1993. Two infinities of risk. In *The politics of everyday fear*, edited by Brian Massumi, 221–8. Minneapolis, MN: University of Minnesota Press.

Ewald, François. 2002. The return of Descartes's malicious demon: An outline of a philosophy of precaution. In *Embracing risk: The changing culture of insurance and responsibility*, edited by Tom Baker and Jonathan Simon, translated by Stephen Utz, 273–301. Chicago, IL: University of Chicago Press.

Ewald, François. 2012. *The future of risk – François Ewald 'After Risk'*. Available from http://vimeo.com/48164425. Accessed 2 April 2014.

Fischhendler, Itay, and Daniel Nathan. 2014. In the name of energy security: The struggle over the exportation of Israeli natural gas. *Energy Policy* 70: 152–162.

Foucault, Michel. 1991. Questions of method. In *The Foucault effect: Studies in governmentality*, edited by Graham Burchell, Colin Gordon and Peter Miller, 73–86. Chicago, IL: University of Chicago Press.

Foucault, Michel. 2007. *Security, territory, population: Lectures at the Collège de France 1977–1978*, edited by Michel Senellart, translated by Graham Burchell. New York: Palgrave Macmillan.

Foucault, Michel. 2008. *The birth of biopolitics: Lectures at the Collège de France 1978–79*, edited by Michel Senellart, translated by Graham Burchell. New York: Palgrave Macmillan.

Frost, Samantha. 2010. Fear and the illusion of autonomy. In *New materialisms: Ontology, agency, and politics*, edited by Diana Coole and Samantha Frost, 158–177. Durham, NC, and London: Duke University Press.

Furedi, Frank. 2005. *Politics of fear: Beyond left and right*. London: Continuum.

Furedi, Frank. 2007. The only thing we have to fear is the 'culture of fear' itself. *Spiked*. Available from www.spiked-online.com/newsite/article/3053#.VHSP-YuG98E. Accessed 25 November 2014.

Furedi, Frank. 2008. Fear and security: A vulnerability-led policy response. *Social Policy & Administration* 42 (6): 645–661.

Goldthau, Andreas. 2008. Rhetoric versus reality: Russian threats to European energy supply. *Energy Policy* 36 (2): 686–692.

Grusin, Richard A. 2004. Premediation. *Criticism* 46 (1): 17–39.

Hansen, Lene. 2000. The little mermaid's silent security dilemma and the absence of gender in the Copenhagen School. *Millennium – Journal of International Studies* 29 (2): 285–306.

Hansen, Lene. 2012. Reconstructing desecuritisation: the normative-political in the Copenhagen School and directions for how to apply it. *Review of International Studies* 38 (03): 525–546.

Harman, Graham. 2009. *Prince of networks: Bruno Latour and metaphysics*. Melbourne: re.press.

Högselius, Per. 2012. *Red gas: Russia and the origins of European energy dependence*. New York: Palgrave Macmillan.

Huysmans, Jef. 1998a. Security! What do you mean?: From concept to thick signifier. *European Journal of International Relations* 4 (2): 226–255.

Huysmans, Jef. 1998b. Revisiting Copenhagen: Or, on the creative development of a security studies agenda in Europe. *European Journal of International Relations* 4 (4): 479–505.

Huysmans, Jef. 2011. What's in an act? On security speech acts and little security nothings. *Security Dialogue* 42 (4–5): 371–383.

IEA. 2014. *Energy supply security: Emergency response of IEA countries 2014*. Paris: OECD/International Energy Agency.

Isin, Engin F. 2008. Theorizing acts of citizenship. In *Acts of citizenship*, edited by Greg Marc Nielsen, 15–43. London and New York: Zed. Available from http://enginfisin.eu/assets/2008d.pdf. Accessed 10 December 2014.

Judge, Andrew, and Tomas Maltby. 2017. European Energy Union? Caught between securitisation and 'riskification'. *European Journal of International Security* 2 (2): 179–202.

Judge, Andrew, Tomas Maltby and Kacper Szulecki. 2018. Energy securitisation: Avenues for future research. In *Energy security in Europe*, edited by Kacper Szulecki, 149–173. Cham: Palgrave Macmillan. Available from https://link.springer.com/chapter/10.1007/978-3-319-64964-1_6. Accessed 4 January 2018.

Kessler, Oliver. 2012. Sleeping with the enemy? On Hayek, constructivist thought, and the current economic crisis. *Review of International Studies* 38 (2): 275–299.

Kessler, Oliver, and Christopher Daase. 2008. From insecurity to uncertainty: Risk and the paradox of security politics. *Alternatives: Global, Local, Political* 33 (2): 211–232.

Kester, Johannes. 2018. Governing electric vehicles: Mobilizing electricity to secure automobility. *Mobilities* 13 (2): 200–215.

Keynes, John Maynard. 1921. *A treatise on probability*. London: Macmillan.

Khrushcheva, Olga. 2011. The creation of an energy security society as a way to decrease securitization levels between the European Union and Russia in energy trade. *Journal of Contemporary European Research* 7 (2): 216–230.

Knight, Frank H. 1921. *Risk, uncertainty, and profit.* Boston, MA: Houghton Mifflin. Available from http://oll.libertyfund.org/title/306.

Korosec, Kirsten. 2009. Pickens: $300 oil is still on its way. Available from www.cbsnews.com/news/pickens-300-oil-is-still-on-its-way. Accessed 15 January 2015.

Korosec, Kirsten. 2011. Another $300 oil prediction – and why this one matters. Available from www.cbsnews.com/news/another-300-oil-prediction-and-why-this-one-matters. Accessed 15 January 2015.

Latour, Bruno. 2004. Why has critique run out of steam? From matters of fact to matters of concern. *Critical inquiry* 30 (2): 225–248.

Latour, Bruno. 2005. *Reassembling the social: An introduction to actor-network-theory.* Oxford: Oxford University Press.

Leander, Anna. 2003. The commodification of violence, private military companies, and African states. Copenhagen: Danish Institute for International Studies, DIIS.

Leander, Anna. 2005. The power to construct international security: On the significance of private military companies. *Millennium – Journal of International Studies* 33 (3): 803–825.

Leung, Guy C. K., Aleh Cherp, Jessica Jewell and Yi-Ming Wei. 2014. Securitization of energy supply chains in China. *Applied Energy* 123: 316–326.

Linstone, Harold A. 2011. Three eras of technology foresight. *Technovation* 31 (2–3): 69–76.

Linstone, Harold A., and Murray Turoff, eds. 2002. *The Delphi method: Techniques and applications.* Online reprint by New Jersey Institute of Technology. Available from https://web.njit.edu/~turoff/pubs/delphibook/index.html. Accessed 5 November 2014.

Lobo-Guerrero, Luis. 2012. *Insuring war: Sovereignty, security and risk.* London and New York: Routledge.

Luhmann, Niklas. 1993. *Risk: A sociological theory.* Berlin and New York: Walter de Gruyter.

Lundborg, Tom. 2012. *Politics of the event: Time, movement, becoming.* London and New York: Routledge.

Malthus, Thomas. 1798. *An essay on the principle of population, as it affects the future improvement of society with remarks on the speculations of Mr. Godwin, M. Condorcet, and other writers.* Project Gutenberg Ebook 4239. London: J. Johnson.

Massumi, Brian. 2005. Fear (the spectrum said). *Positions: East Asia Cultures Critique* 13 (1): 31–48.

Massumi, Brian. 2007. Potential politics and the primacy of preemption. *Theory & Event* 10 (2): n.p.

Massumi, Brian. 2009. National enterprise emergency steps toward an ecology of powers. *Theory, Culture & Society* 26 (6): 153–185.

McDonald, Matt. 2008. Securitization and the construction of security. *European Journal of International Relations* 14 (4): 563–587.

McGowan, Francis. 2011. Putting energy insecurity into historical context: European responses to the energy crises of the 1970s and 2000s. *Geopolitics* 16 (3): 486–511.

Mietzner, Dana, and Guido Reger. 2005. Advantages and disadvantages of scenario approaches for strategic foresight. *International Journal of Technology Intelligence and Planning* 1 (2): 220–239.

Mullainathan, Sendhil, and Eldar Shafir. 2013. *Scarcity: Why having too little means so much.* New York: Times.

Mullen, Penelope M. 2003. Delphi: Myths and reality. *Journal of Health Organization and Management* 17 (1): 37–52.

Nancy, Jean-Luc. 2000. *Being singular plural: The surprise of the event*, translated by Robert D. Richardson and Anne E. O'Byrne. Stanford, CA: Stanford University Press.

Natorski, Michal, and Anna Herranz Surrallés. 2008. Securitizing moves to nowhere? The framing of the European Union's energy policy. *Journal of Contemporary European Research* 4 (2): pp. 70–89.

Neal, Andrew W. 2006. Foucault in Guantánamo: Towards an archaeology of the exception. *Security Dialogue* 37 (1): 31–46.

Neocleous, Mark. 2008. *Critique of security*. Edinburgh: Edinburgh University Press.

Nyman, Jonna. 2014. 'Red storm ahead': Securitisation of energy in US–China Relations. *Millennium – Journal of International Studies* 43 (1): 43–65.

Nyman, Jonna, and Jinghan Zeng. 2016. Securitization in Chinese climate and energy politics. *Wiley Interdisciplinary Reviews: Climate Change* 7 (2): 301–313.

Patomäki, Heikki. 2015. Absenting the absence of future dangers and structural transformations in securitization theory. *International Relations* 29 (1): 128–136.

Radoman, J. 2007. Securitization of energy as a prelude to energy security dilemma. *Western Balkans Security Observer-English Edition* (4): 36.

Rasmussen, Mikkel Vedby. 2004. It sounds like a riddle: Security studies, the war on terror and risk. *Millennium – Journal of International Studies* 33 (2): 381–395.

Ravetz, Jerry. 2004. The post-normal science of precaution. *Futures* 36 (3): 347–357.

Robin, Corey. 2004. *Fear: The history of a political idea*. Oxford: Oxford University Press.

Roe, Paul. 2008. Actor, audience (s) and emergency measures: Securitization and the UK's decision to invade Iraq. *Security Dialogue* 39 (6): 615–635.

Roe, Paul. 2012. Is securitization a 'negative' concept? Revisiting the normative debate over normal versus extraordinary politics. *Security Dialogue* 43 (3): 249–266.

Rose, Nikolas. 2001. The politics of life itself. *Theory, Culture & Society* 18 (6): 1–30.

Rumsfeld, Donald. 2002. Defense.gov transcript: DoD news briefing – Secretary Rumsfeld and Gen. Myers. Available from www.defense.gov/transcripts/transcript.aspx?transcriptid=2636. Accessed 15 January 2015.

Salter, Mark B. 2008a. Conclusion: Risk and imagination in the war on terror. In *Risk and the war on terror*, edited by Louise Amoore and Marieke de Goede, 233–246. London and New York: Routledge.

Salter, Mark B. 2008b. Securitization and desecuritization: A dramaturgical analysis of the Canadian Air Transport Security Authority. *Journal of International Relations and Development* 11 (4): 321–349.

Schmitt, Carl. 1985. *Political theology: Four chapters on the concept of sovereignty*, translated by George Schwab. Cambridge, MA: MIT Press.

Shannon, Jerry. 2014. Food deserts: Governing obesity in the neoliberal city. *Progress in Human Geography* 38 (2): 248–266.

Smith Stegen, Karen. 2011. Deconstructing the 'energy weapon': Russia's threat to Europe as case study. *Energy Policy* 39 (10): 6505–6513.

Stern, J. 2006. The Russian-Ukrainian gas crisis of January 2006. *Oxford Institute for Energy Studies* 16: 5–12.

Stoddard, Edward. 2012. A common vision of energy risk? Energy securitisation and company perceptions of risk in the EU. *Journal of Contemporary European Research* 8 (3): 340–366.

Stritzel, Holger. 2007. Towards a theory of securitization: Copenhagen and beyond. *European Journal of International Relations* 13 (3): 357–383.

Stritzel, Holger. 2011. Security as translation: Threats, discourse, and the politics of localisation. *Review of International Studies* 1 (1): 1–27.

Stritzel, Holger. 2012. Securitization, power, intertextuality: Discourse theory and the translations of organized crime. *Security Dialogue* 43 (6): 549–567.

Subrahmaniyan, Nesa. 2008. Goldman's Murti says oil 'likely' to reach $150–$200 (update 5) – Bloomberg. Available from www.bloomberg.com/apps/news?pid=news archive&sid=ayxRKcAZi630. Accessed 15 January 2015.

Svendsen, Lars Fr H. 2008. *A philosophy of fear*, translated by John Francis Irons. London: Reaktion.

Trombetta, Maria Julia. 2012. *European energy security discourses and the development of a common energy policy*. Working Paper. Energy Delta Gas Research. Available from www.edgar-program.com/uploads/fckconnector/7acf1f46-7358-4057-86e5-ffee558 13be3. Accessed 6 January 2015.

UNDP. 1994. *Human development report 1994*. Oxford: Oxford University Press

UNESCO World Commission on the Ethics of Scientific Knowledge and Technology. 2005. *The Precautionary Principle*. Paris: United Nations Educational, Scientific and Cultural Organization.

Vergragt, Philip J., and Jaco Quist. 2011. Backcasting for sustainability: Introduction to the special issue. *Technological Forecasting and Social Change* 78 (5): 747–755.

Vuori, Juha A. 2008. Illocutionary logic and strands of securitization: Applying the theory of securitization to the study of non-democratic political orders. *European Journal of International Relations* 14 (1): 65–99.

Wæver, Ole. 1995. Securitization and desecuritization. In *On security*, edited by R. D. Lipschutz, 46–86. New York: Columbia University Press.

Wæver, Ole. 1999. Securitizing sectors? Reply to Eriksson. *Cooperation and Conflict* 34 (3): 334–340.

Wæver, Ole. 2011. Politics, security, theory. *Security Dialogue* 42 (4–5): 465–480.

Wendt, Alexander E. 1999. *Social theory of international politics*. Cambridge and New York: Cambridge University Press.

Yergin, Daniel. 1991. *The prize: The epic quest for oil, money & power*. New York: Simon and Shuster.

Zedner, Lucia. 2003. The concept of security: An agenda for comparative analysis. *Legal Studies* 23 (1): 153–175.

5 The materialization of energy security

5.1 Introduction

The discussion on energy security and security so far hints at a primarily social and linguistically oriented understanding of energy security. What seems to be ignored are the different material aspects underlying the questions of energy security. This includes the actual supplies of energy that dissuade security concerns as well as the shortages that are still prevalent, and it includes the rigid and durable material infrastructure that handles the production, transport and consumption of different forms of energy. In the case of oil, for example, this infrastructure ranges from the sulphur and nitrogen content to the overall quality of the resources, the depth of the wells, the size of the reserves, the distance to the markets, the infrastructure in place to refine and transport it and so on.[1]

This chapter focuses on the social literature that discusses the relationship between knowledge (over energy systems) and materiality (of energy systems), and it asks three questions: (1) how do the social and material relate in line of dominant social interpretations that characterize security, (2) how do these new materialist theories view our ontology (e.g. how do their theories approach social-material relations and objects) and (3) how do they approach surprising events or change/uncertainty (e.g. their ontological politics)?

The chapter subsequently does not argue that either the material or the social explanations are better, but it tries to understand their relationship. Based on a discussion of both the critical constructivist literature and an analysis of different 'new' materialist theories, this chapter puts forward four arguments. First, that the dialectical representation of matter and thought (mind/body or nature/society) is an artificial understanding that is simultaneously overblown in theoretical discussions on poststructural and constructivist research, yet still a necessary distinction to better understand processes of becoming (the performative identification, ascription of meaning, reactive politics and the assemblage that closes the events). Second, when the material and social are able to perform each other, they are open to a virtuality and eventfulness (e.g. surprising events) on both sides. Such an eventfulness calls for a politics of ontology: the politics dealing with the identification of what the event is (like security).

Based on the epistemological argument that it is impossible to know what is 'out there', this calls for a relational or phenomenological ontology devoid of substance and objects except for those that are created relationally and best described as *materialdiscursive*. Third, such a relational identification is based on distinctions. With these distinctions come exclusions and the subsequent need to be aware of the ethics of observation. In short, fourth, while new materialist theories argue for additional attention to matter, they ultimately also discuss knowledge gathering practices albeit in terms of durability and materialization. In other words, they offer an account based on the materialization of potentiality, but have to concede that this only matters because of human-driven politics.

Unfortunately, this means that the already-abstract discussion on energy security will turn even more abstract as discussions on materialism and discourse cannot be separated from commentaries on, for example, different forms of agency or the dualisms between object/subject and nature/culture. The easiest way to introduce these theoretical discussions is by categorizing them into three distinct positions: between positivist scholars, postpositivist scholars and new materialist or posthumanist scholars. Where *positivist*-inspired research includes realist and liberalist theories with their assumption of a material world out there that can be studied objectively, *postpositivism* consists of a range of poststructuralist and constructivist theories that disagree with this and favour the (structured) social knowledge people have *of* the world. Lastly, recent 'new materialist' theoretical developments outside IR introduce a *posthumanist* view that originates from fields as diverse as sociology with actor-network theory (ANT), feminism with agential realism, philosophy with object-oriented ontology (OOO), anthropology and history (e.g. material culture).[2] This is a perspective that focuses on the material world in its becoming, instead of an exclusive focus on human social interaction or the explanation of a world that already is. Within IR, a small but growing number of articles is taking up these insights.[3]

This chapter is constructed as follows. Section 5.2 will analyse the postpositivist rejection of positivism. It will briefly describe the main epistemological argument and discuss the differences of opinion between critical realists and radical constructivists on the role of scientific knowledge within such an epistemological position. It closes with a brief discussion of two highly abstract linguistic and social structural scholars to see whether these really do reject the material world as argued by some new materialist scholars. Section 5.3 moves to the new materialist critique on postpositivist theories and discusses why new materialist believe a focus on the material is important, what matter is, and how this can be approached with a performative understanding that observes a materialdiscursive world. Section 5.4 delves into the new materialist theories by introducing the relational ontology of ANT. It then reflects on this ontology by following the critique on ANT, in particular its difficulty to discuss the origin of the virtuality (change) of its relations. This abstract discussion is subsequently simplified by discussing the vibrancy of the material in terms of a politics of ontology that focuses on the event and how observations and subsequent actions are folded together to close these events. Section 5.5 continuous on the politics behind observation as it introduces the work of Barad on agential realism to discuss the ethics behind knowledge practices. The reflection summarizes and reflects on the theoretical debates by setting the stage for the next chapter.

5.2 How do we know of the world?

5.2.1 Observing 'the world'

Discussions on the role of the material are often phrased in terms of the ability of people to know the outside material world. While this is self-evident for positivist scholars, there is more to it for postpositivist scholars. This section explores how the social/material divide is discussed within IR theory as a preamble to the subsequent sections on new materialism. It will subsequently introduce the postpositivist argument on the importance of the role of language (including knowledge and discourses) in structuring the behaviour and actions of social agents, as it introduces the epistemological argument that it is impossible to gain neutral knowledge over the outside world as all knowledge is mediated by previous historic decisions on what constitutes 'good' knowledge. Third, after briefly describing the differences between positivism and postpositivism and the underlying Cartesian dualist dilemma, this section contrasts the two main postpositivist positions within IR theory, namely critical realism and radical constructivism. By contrasting these two positions, and by pushing the radical constructivists' position through a short discussion of Wittgenstein's language games and Luhmann's communicative systems, it becomes possible to question the social essentialism that new materialist scholars accuse radical constructivists of.

Still, it is important to note that even to ask the question how the material world can be known implies that one already has to presuppose ontologically that there is a distinction between knowledge and matter. In other words, the question itself is not neutral and presupposes a specific *dualist* world where matter is separated from knowledge. This dualism is most famously known as the Cartesian mind/body dualism. It is based on the epistemological insight that we can know, for certain, that we are able to think and thus that our mind exists, but we cannot know whether our bodies exists.[4] To be fair, the Cartesian ontological dualist position is not the only possible position that one can take, but it is one that is very common in everyday language use. Importantly, it leads to the question of causality between the mind and the body, as (1) the mind could be an independent non-bodily phenomenon, (2) the mind and body could be causally linked (either through minds or through bodies) or (3) the physical could be an independent causally closed phenomenon. All three options are plausible, but the Bieri trilemma states that only two can ever be consistent with one another.[5]

In this respect the philosopher Searle argues for a form of physicalism (a combination of (2) and (3)), which is based on an ontological differentiation between 'brute facts' and social 'institutional facts'.[6] Where the rocks and pebbles on the ground are brute material facts, he argues that 'there are portions of the real world, objective facts in the world, which are only facts by human agreement. In a sense there are things that exist only because we believe them to exist.'[7] Both the money in your wallet or the government people pay taxes to are a fact of life, but only because we all agree on them. If, for some reason, people stop believing in these social facts, they cease to exist.[8] Between brute and social facts, Searle identifies four mixed categories based on the relative importance they attach to the collective assignment of function, in other words to what extent humans create the facts. There are (1) natural and biological systems that continue whether humans interpret them correctly or not; and (2) material products or artefacts that are 'real' but need human interpretation to function, for example, chairs and hammers. Besides these brute facts there are institutional facts, facts that do not exist without human interpretation. Searle divides these into (3) non-linguistic facts like money and (4) linguistic facts based on written or spoken language, for example business contracts.[9] According-ing to Searle, these brute and social facts are erected iteratively on top of each other, meaning that all institutional facts can be traced to some brute factual origin. He describes this in terms of the formula X counts as Y in C: every insti-tutional fact Y is built in a certain context C on a previous social fact X, which in turn is built on another previous social fact Y-1 in context C-1, all the way down to some brute fact X.[10]

Within the social sciences the question whether people are able to observe the outside world returns in debates between positivist and postpositivist approaches to research. Positivism and postpositivism are based on different epistemological positions (e.g. 'how do we know') that also inherently come with ontological assumptions (e.g. on 'what exists'). On the one hand, the posit-ivism of realist and liberalist theories (Chapter 3) is often presented in combi-nation with the ontological belief of naturalism. The belief that there is a given physical reality that can be experienced and explained through the senses of an observer who is clearly separated from the observed object.[11] This epistemologi-cal claim – that it is possible to study the outside world by creating a true repres-entation based upon humankind's experiences – is called empiricism.[12] The latter should not be confused with positivism itself, which calls for a scientific method consisting of law-like generalizations and causal facts to analyse these experiences. Positivism hence rest on a clear dualist ontology that assumes that the mind can learn about and in time mirror the material world that it observes. On the other hand, postpositivist scholars reject this dualist epistemological position as they question the separation between observers and observed. Scholars from constructivist, critical, feminist and poststructuralist approaches all argue that reality (which they do not reject), or, to be precise, the experi-ences of reality, can only be witnessed by interpreting events with the know-ledge that we already have. These scholars view knowledge, in other words, as something that is inherently social (not an individual or factual experience) and can only be shared through language in describing, defining and categorizing the world around us. This implies that all new knowledge is filtered by that what we already know. New knowledge is therefore not an actual representation of the world 'out there' but a consequence of historically developed and socially agreed constructions of what the world is and how it should look like. From this, it logically follows that no research is value-free and that researchers should focus on the consequences of these linguistic structures and their constant performativity.

5.2.2 Critical realism

Cox famously describes the distinction between positivist and postpositivist theories as a distinction between (positivist) problem-solving theories and (postpositivist) critical theories.[13] Where the former accepts the world as a given and tries to improve it, the latter 'attempts to stand outside the framework of analysis or action it is exploring and seeks to appraise it in terms of its origins, development, institutions, and its potentiality for change'.[14] In fact, within postpositivist IR research, there are currently two meta-philosophical positions that struggle with the above ontic-epistemological questions. However, while both critical realism and radical constructivism agree epistemologically on the intersubjectivity of knowledge and the role of linguistic structures, they disagree on the consequences of such a position and the role that scientific knowledge plays in this. The rest of this section discusses critical realism while the next section turns to radical constructivism.

Critical realism draws on a metaphilosophy originally developed by Bhaskar, which resembles the ontology of Searle to a certain extent.[15] In the last decade it has been reinvigorated in IR with contributions from Wight and Patomäki, among others.[16] Critical realists hold that, while a true representation of the world (e.g. empiricism and the so-called correspondence theory of truth) is indeed impossible, it is possible to use a scientific method to study objectively the experiences people have of the world, simply because they believe that scholars should at least try to improve the theories they have. And, for them, falsification and verification are still the best methods to gain knowledge, ask questions and reject less plausible answers. They support this argument with two claims: first they highlight the 'practical success of scientific knowledge', which is demonstrated when scientists manipulate otherwise unobservable entities.[17] Second, they build on an 'ordinary language use' argument, as 'scientific practice itself assumes a depth to reality that it investigates in order to provide explanations of empirical phenomena'.[18] By combining these arguments with the epistemological lesson that 'knowledge itself is a social product' and 'dynamically produced by means of prior knowledge', Wight claims that knowledge is an 'inherently fallibilist enterprise' that is based on 'rational choices between competing knowledge claims'.[19] In other words, critical realists believe that it is in the nature of human beings to constantly strive for better theories and descriptions through a method of trial and error following observations and rational assessments.

This focus on *ontological realism* (a reality that can be experienced independently of the mind), *epistemological relativism* (that this reality can only be described with 'potentially fallible socially produced beliefs) and *judgemental rationalism* instead of empiricism (that it *is* possible to judge between social theories) also more or less describes the position taken by social constructivists in IR.[20] Based on the metaphilosophy of critical realism, (thin) social constructivism is an IR theory that Adler once described as taking the 'middle ground' between positivist and postpositivist research.[21] There are many authors working on social constructivism, but the theory most attentive to the material world and nearest to Searle's brute and social facts is the one proposed by Wendt.[22] With his concept of 'rump materialism', Wendt is one of the few IR scholars who explicitly tries to take both the material *and* the social into account.[23] For Wendt's social constructivist theory, the material plays a role following bodily differences, technological differences and geographical and natural characteristics.[24] More specifically, Wendt's rump materialism rests on a distinction between two different needs: on the one hand, biologically prescribed needs for food, water, shelter etc. and, on the other hand, socially induced interests.[25] Yet, even with all this attention to the material, Wendt still prioritizes the social when he states that '(1) the structures of human association are determined primarily by shared ideas rather than material forces, and (2) that the identities and interests of purposive actors are constructed by these shared ideas rather than given by nature'.[26] Thus, while Wendt's social constructivism shifts the attention away from the use of language towards the relationship between ideas and (material) interests, he too places the social over the material by claiming that the meaning objects have for people are more important than the objects themselves.[27]

While critical realism and (thin) social constructivism seem coherent theories at first, Jackson, in a recent article, argues that many of these critical realists, while adhering to the epistemological logic that it is impossible to have an objective representation of the world, actually only pay lip service to it and betray this logic at a later stage in their argument, as Jackson argues, not because they secretly refer to some form of representationalism between the social and the natural but because these scholars with their focus on hypothesis testing and the constraining effects of the 'outside' world reinstall a dualism between an object and observer.[28] They artificially create a distance to fulfil their desire to observe objectively.

5.2.3 Radical constructivism

Postpositivism rejects this object/observer distinction and the resulting scientific method because it claims that the social cannot be explained by it in any meaningful way. To postpositive scholars, the social world consists of intersubjective knowledge (whether called social facts, language, discourses, practices, fields or a similar concept) and does not have the same characteristics as the natural world. The staunchest proponents of this position even go so far as to argue that, while reality might exist, we can never know about it and as such should forgo the search for this holy grail and instead focus on the use and misuse of knowledge.[29] A linguistic-oriented postpositivist scholar would argue that there is no role at a linguistic level for the inclusion of a changing material world, because it is not important whether it is nature or society that 'acts'. This is not because radical constructivists reject the surprising event itself but because they deem it more important who interprets these events, at what moment and for what reasons. When a volcano erupts in the South Pacific or in northern Italy the last is interpreted as more important because it endangers human life. A similar volcanic eruption on Iceland would matter less in terms of human life were it not that all air traffic across the Atlantic can be hindered by it.[30] People interpret events with the knowledge that they have and with a degree of urgency that follows from the hopes and fears they have for the future.

This position is favoured by radical constructivists as well as poststructuralists, and, to a lesser extent, critical theorists.[31] It is a position that finds its origin in the Frankfurter Schule and the work of French poststructuralists.[32] Below this section will reflect on the importance of language by briefly discussing two other strongly linguistic-oriented scholars (neither of them part of the above traditions). After discussing Wittgenstein's language games and Luhmann's communicative social systems, this section moves back to IR and the response of Kratochwil and other radical constructivist IR scholars to the critique of critical realism. In short, through these two discussions this section highlights how meaning is ascribed, how observations should be seen as the production of distinctions, and how these two arguments together make all judgements ultimately value judgements and a matter of politics.

First, the role and importance of knowledge. To understand how meaning is ascribed to events based on the knowledge that people possess, it is helpful to turn to the later writings of Wittgenstein on language games and his understanding of the grammar that enables the interactive and iterative *meaning as use*.[33] Simplistically, people describe the world using concepts and words. The meaning of these concepts stems from its use and its (family) relationship with other concepts within a shared 'grammar' or set of rules that clarify acceptable combinations. These combinations and their shared grammar mark different language games. For example, the concept of energy is different for a physicist (joules), a consumer (light/heat) or an oil trader (demand/supply) as each of these take place within a particular language game: natural science, bodily experience/survival and economic markets. Consequently, it is only in their constant use and with repeated reference to other words that concepts gain and are able to keep a particular meaning.[34] Even when people object to a meaning, they still use that concept and thereby reinforce the overarching language game. Language games thus presume *multiplicity*, a world where a concept means different things, for different people, within different contexts. As long as they are continuously interpreted in their ongoing use, these worlds are never entirely defined and cannot be closed off from other agents. In fact, agents constantly participate in multiple, sometimes even contrasting worlds. A physicist working on energy is also a consumer of energy at home. It follows that agents are able to reflect on and compare between language games. However, they can only observe themselves from within a third language game, another set of rules, never from within the primary language game itself.

An even more radical argument about social observation can be found in Luhmann's *systems theory*.[35] Luhmann offers a theory that perceives the world to be divided into physical systems, psychic systems and social systems. Of these three, Luhmann has written most extensively on social systems, in particular on the role of communication in and between social systems.[36] According to Luhmann, all communication between two humans, or, more precisely, between two egos (psychic systems of cognition), takes place within social systems made up of modes of communication. Luhmann sees social systems as self-regulating entities that are based on a distinction between the system (inside) and the environment (outside). These distinctions are autopoietic: each system is based on a self-referential distinction that (re)produces or constitutes the meaning that a system attaches to itself and its environment.[37] Each system closes itself off from its complex environment by constantly (re)drawing its boundaries through a reconfiguration of its own specific identity (designed to reduce the outside complexity). From this ontology it follows that all communication between systems should, according to Luhmann, be seen as an internal debate *within* a particular system over the interpretation of the stimulus witnessed in its environment. Because language 'stores' meaning, new communications between systems can only be incorporated in a system if it fits or builds on the already existing autopoietic constituted distinction (what Luhmann calls operational closure).[38] For Luhmann, observation is thus a constant process of producing and reproducing distinctions. This can be compared with a map – whatever map you use or make, whether it is a topographic map, a satellite image or a street map – different distinctions show different aspects of the world depending on what the observer *needs*. To be able to make such a claim Luhmann identifies two levels of observation. Luhmann separates first-order observations, where time plays no role for decision makers as everything is happening simultaneously and people are in the moment, from second-order observations, where the observer is able to actually reflect on an event. In reflecting on an event, a second-order observer also makes multiple distinctions on, for example, before and after, good and bad, etc.[39]

Radical constructivists share this concern over observers and their objects with Wittgenstein and Luhmann. In fact, it is a concern that returns as well in other important concepts in the literature. For example, in line with the iterative linguistic idea of *meaning as use*, the concept of a *hermeneutic circle* deals with the continuous theoretical and contextually enforced interpretation of texts by observers: that all knowledge is always already situated in other knowledge. Likewise, debates on *agents and structures* and their mutual interaction deal with the position of the individual (agent) in relation to society (structure) and that neither can be seen as separate from the other.[40] If one accepts this epistemological argument, then these concepts draw attention towards the equal impossibility to separate facts and values.[41] And from this it follows that those who are able to claim which facts exist actually engage in a political struggle over the shared knowledge that defines what is normal and what is considered to exist outside of language.

This in turn is the main argument of radical constructivists in IR against critical realism, especially with the latter's focus on rationality and the scientific method.[42] Kratochwil argues that the epistemological argument about the socio-historical mediation of observation should not be solved by putting ontology first, as critical realists do when they start from the material impact of scientific knowledge, but instead should be bracketed by 'pragmatically' focusing on methodology and methods to 'provid[e] the necessary warrants' against claims of voluntarity and 'anything goes' arguments.[43] More specifically, Kratochwil argues for a pragmatic social objectivity that is achieved through a consensus 'courtroom ethics' (e.g. a consensus theory of truth).[44] When all matter and social relations are interpreted through language and social knowledge, the only truth available is a social one, and this implies that meaning can only be achieved by social agreement. Wight replied to this by asking why these scholars offer an alternative explanation of current phenomena in the first place, if not because they believe them – in whatever sense – to be better.[45] In fact, it is not so much that radical constructivists reject the scientific logic Wight criticizes them to be following as well (they do indeed) but that they question, on a higher abstraction level, the scientific logic itself as being one of many logics or discourse that can be used to find the 'truth'.[46] In other words, these scholars take fault with the meaning of the term 'better' as they consider this a value judgement.[47] For these scholars, what should be asked instead is the critical question of 'better for whom?'. Whose interests are aided by proclaiming something as 'better' or 'progress'?

5.2.3 Social essentialism

There are two popular arguments against the postpositivist approaches discussed so far. Both of these are strongly influenced by decontextualized quotations from, on the one hand, the early Wittgenstein, who once wrote that 'the limits of my language mean the limits of my world', and, on the other, Derrida's famous 'there is no outside-text'.[48] The first argument is made by positivists who misread the positions above and succumb to a 'fear of relativism'.[49] This is the anything goes argument, which states that if all that exists is based on language and communication, why not just speak and think differently to change the world? In a sense, this argument is correct. Language and knowledge are pliable to an extent that matter is not. However, the above already indicates the force and stability of social practices, thought patterns (discourses) and communicative structures: while they change, people constantly and with each iteration work hard to preserve and stabilize them. Moreover, as discussed below, people act on them and in doing so *materialize* the social structures and norms.

A second argument represents the basic assumption behind a relatively new strand of literature called 'new materialism'. It is an assumption that builds on claims like Patomäki and Wight's argument that 'for positivists, sense-experience is real; for postpositivists, discourses or intersubjectivity is real'.[50] The problem for many new materialists is that, if this is the case, if language is all that we can study, as for example argued in securitization theory, would that not imply that one has simply shifted a representation of the world towards a representation of linguistic structures instead?[51] As Dolphijn and Van der Tuin quote De Landa:

> General categories do not refer to anything in the real world and ... to believe they do (i.e. to reify them) leads directly to essentialism. Social constructivism is supposed to be an antidote to this, in the sense that by showing that general categories are mere stereotypes it blocks the move towards their reification. But by coupling the idea that perception is intrinsically linguistic with the ontological assumption that only the contents of experience really exist, this position leads directly to a form of social essentialism.[52]

Following a similar line of thought, Barad argues:

> Language has been granted too much power. The linguistic turn, the semiotic turn, the interpretative turn, the cultural turn: it seems that at every turn lately every 'thing' – even materiality – is turned into a matter of language or some other form of cultural representation.[53]

Where De Landa and Barad focus on the ontological and epistemological preposition of language over materiality in these quotes, Latour questions the categorical use of the 'social' as distinct from the natural. For Latour, what happens when people designate something as social is that they are diverting attention away from the process of actual *association* between the different elements of such a phenomenon.[54] In other words, he focuses on the act of defining something as social and sees this as a form of politics that performs a closure of an ongoing process of association between different elements that exist and originate in the space in-between humans (e.g. Section 4.4 on the speech act literature).

De Landa, Barad and Latour all find fault with many postpositivists, who, according to them, have simply shifted their representational position within the material/social dichotomy from the material towards the social. The core of their critique thus focuses on the idea that postpositivist scholars still uphold a Cartesian dualistic worldview, based on the observer who a priori assumes that language and the world are separated to begin with.[55] It is only in a Cartesian dualism where mind and body can represent each other that the above critique makes sense. This, however, might be phrased too strongly. On the one hand, yes, it is easy to over-essentialize language in postpositivist theories, as highlighted by the quotes of Wittgenstein and Derrida above. Then again, most of the postpositivist work, including the work of Wittgenstein and Luhmann, acknowledges objects and materiality. As Hekman (herself working on materiality) reflects on Wittgenstein: 'His discussion of language games as activities, of general facts of nature, form of life, and many other concepts suggests an interactive understanding of the relationship between the discursive and the material'.[56] Similarly, Derrida's quote on text above, which points to the understanding that all knowledge is 'always already' situated in other knowledge, is quite easily reinterpreted in a broader sense of 'ongoing historicity'.[57] A narrow theoretical focus on linguistic structures therefore does not automatically imply that scholars claim that language is all that exist.[58]

In short, it can be argued that the Cartesian dualism that separates matter and discourse permeates much of contemporary IR research. However, this section shows that a dualist worldview leads to tensions on both a metaphilosophical, theoretical and methodological level, especially for those who accept the epistemological insight that all knowledge is mediated through discourse and other linguistic structures. For such postpositivist scholars, all that we know are the discourses and the concepts that derive their meaning through the differentiation from other concepts. These differences have a history that is based on previous understandings and distinctions. This makes it impossible to see or experience something new without first being structured by the rules of society hidden in an intersubjective understanding of the world and the linguistic structures that enable (or inhibit) possible routes of thought and action. Each of these understandings and distinctions is based on a judgement made by an observer on an object of study. This translates facts into shared distinctions, which are based on shared values of judgement. It is here that we see a difference between critical realists, for whom the better argument is always based on something because we can act on things (we cannot know the world, but it exists), and radical constructivists, who instead argue for a pragmatic argument (we agree that the world exists). Nevertheless, both share that the material world exists and that it cannot be understood independently of shared social understandings.

5.3 Moving beyond humans and language

5.3.1 New materialism

To be fair, the broader ontological context of postpositivist studies with its focus on language, knowledge and social structures does limit the research parameters of postpositivism, if only for the pragmatic reason that it is hard to study everything. The subsequent inattention to matter is something that sits ill with a rising number of scholars in IR and the wider social sciences, driven in part by the complexity and (perceived) urgency to understand phenomena like climate change, genetically modified food and nanotechnology. This discomfort is often illustrated with an argument along the lines of Pickering's claim that one way or the other the world actively resists and accommodates human activity.[59] Whatever meaning we attach to the world, the world is believed to be able to act of itself and on itself, and is therefore capable of surprising humans by altering the conditions of possibility. What these scholars question is the predominantly human-centred approach in current social theories, from both positivist and postpositivist theoretical perspectives. As an alternative, they argue in favour of a *posthumanist* metatheory, a metatheory that shifts the scholarly focus away from the overwhelming attention on human agency towards an entangled material *and* human agency (hence posthuman and not anti-human).[60] In this way, instead of entering the matter/social discussion from the side by way of a postpositivist focus on shared language, a positivist focus on representation or a focus on materialism, these authors tackle the debate head-on by questioning how matter and the social interact or, some would say, intra-act.[61] As Dolphijn and Van der Tuin describe this intra-action, 'the material and the discursive are only taken apart in the authoritative gesture of the scholar or by the common-sensical thinker; while in the event, in life itself, the two seeming layers are by all means indiscernible'.[62]

New materialist scholars thus argue that what is missing is an approach that tries 'to provide an account of how both materiality and language matter'.[63] What is missing is what Jackson elsewhere has called a 'monist' approach, by which he refers to a way of thinking that studies the practices that create both thought and things.[64] A key concept in such a monist approach is *entanglement*, which states that the mind/body, society/nature, matter/social and object/subject distinctions are all posterior distinctions made by human observers while in reality the world itself is not as clear-cut.[65] The next sections will therefore build on several new materialist insights to offer an entangled *materialdiscursive* ontology instead of a dualist material *and* discursive ontology.[66] An ontology that still forwards the postpositivist epistemological insights about the importance of linguistic structures, observation and meaning ascription, but links this with a constantly changing materiality. This section will introduce the shared premises of new materialism, it will discuss materiality in terms of what it is and how it is analysed, and it will introduce Butler's ideas on performativity as a general approach to mitigate the dialectic understanding of matter and discourse.

The question of how to approach an entangled and active materiality is studied by an agglomeration of scholars working from a range of different disciplines, including philosophy, feminist studies, geography, science and technology studies (STS), performance studies, history and IR. For convenience's sake, these are all branded as 'new materialist' even though none of the scholars seems to support this label.[67] As broad as the underlying disciplines are, so are the perspectives on how to answer the question posted above wide-ranging. Below, this chapter's main influences are Latour and other STS scholars working on ANT, Harman and Bryant on object-oriented philosophy, and Bennett and Barad on the phenomena of entangled agency and the ethics behind materiality.

While these theories differ in their ontology and all approach this entanglement from very different angles, these authors do share a range of understandings. First, they share an understanding of the non-human world 'out there' that is severely influenced by the natural sciences, in particular by the insights gained from particle physics, chaos theory and complex systems theories.[68] They take from particle physics the instability of objects, as all objects consist of smaller entities all the way to subatomic particles and smaller, and they take that all objects are in a constant state of flux in response to the movement of like entities. In addition, these theories draw on chaos and complexity theories, which depict the world as a constant dynamic process of 'an intricate filigree of relationships' that is described as self-organizing (with both positive/reinforcing and negative/adapting feedback mechanisms), intersectional, multiscalar and, in the case of chaos theory, nonlinear.[69] Basically, new materialism moves past 'fixed' material objects to constantly interacting, shifting and mobile objects and their relative durability.

Second, they all share a move from epistemology to ontology and the question of how things *become*.[70] The focus lies not on matter itself but on *how* things materialize. New materialists approach this by assuming that materialization takes place through self-organization, in a pluripotential, multiscalar and multidimensional form of actual and virtual agency.[71] Third, this 'more-than-human mode of enquiry' rejects any totalizing 'overly theoretical, formal approaches'.[72] For new materialist everything is local. Hence, they not only question radical constructivist theories, with their focus on social structures, norms and rules, but also deterministic positivist research, like statistics, where everything is subsumed under the logics of theory and methodology.[73] Fourth, to study such an ontology these scholars shift their epistemology from a focus on discourse and material objects towards practices and relational affects in order to highlight the relationality between more-than-human entities.[74] They position themselves thus in-between discourse and material objects by studying the practices and relations that enable the existence of both. To repeat, these shifts together do not mean that new materialism scholars reject the main critique of constructivists on positivist materialist studies.[75] On the contrary, fifth, they actually build on it, through something that Whatmore calls the shift from a 'politics of identity to a politics of knowledge'[76] and Mol introduced as 'ontological politics', which she describes by arguing that:

> If the term 'ontology' is combined with that of 'politics' then this suggests that the conditions of possibility are not given. That reality does not precede the mundane practices in which we interact with it, but is rather shaped within these practices. So the term politics works to underline this active mode, this process of shaping, and the fact that its character is both open and contested.[77]

This fifth move draws attention to the idea that in a more-than-human world the questions what something *is* and who exactly acts (and through what) become two very political questions with strong ethical connotations as they touch upon notions of responsibility and accountability. When every explanation (knowledge) of an event is seen as a potential closure that fixates particular material and social subjectivities, structures and power relations, they are constantly open to critique.

New materialism is not the only theoretical work that sees the world as an open and dynamic system devoid of inert objects. For example, the chapter on security already described risk and resilience with their sense of vulnerability. In addition, much of the literature on natural resources has shifted towards system approaches (e.g. energy systems or food systems) based on infrastructure, logistics or (political) ecological understandings of anthropocentrism. In a time when humankind dominates its environment, many of these theories highlight its smallness and note that humans are only a part of the total system. Dillon and Reid describe this posthuman position as a shift from a world that is complicated to a world that is complex: where complicated worlds can be 'reduced' and 'simplified', complex worlds can only be 'embraced' and 'orchestrated'.[78] Moreover, in such a complex relational perspective, agency and causality are dispersed, mediated and thus no longer as predictable as once imagined.[79]

5.3.2 When matter matters

Before discussing the relational ontology of new materialism, it is useful to take a closer look at what we mean by matter or the material, not because it will miraculously solve these long-standing debates but, as Dolphijn and Van der Tuin make clear above, because the nature/culture dualism itself is something that is formed in and through people's everyday use.[80] Consequently, we should be aware of how the use of a term like materiality actually constitutes such differences. This is taken up below through three different readings of the meaning of matter, which range from a negative definition, via a substantive meaning of matter, to an interpretation of matter as a verb, and ends with a brief reflection on the instrumentalist and deterministic approaches to artefacts.

First, an easy way to circumvent any discussion on the precise meaning of matter is to turn the question around and define the material by claiming that it is everything non-social. But then, is there anything like that? And what precisely is meant by the social? Dolwick, a maritime archaeologist, clearly struggled with similar questions on the relations between matter (in particular human-constructed artefacts) and the social, and approached them from sociology. In his overview of social theories, Dolwick starts with a brief description of three broad, inherently limited and heavily contested categories of 'the social'.[81] The first and broadest definition describes the social as *associations* between relational objects (e.g. ANT's heterogeneous networks of relations; Pickering's mangles of practice; Barad's materialdiscursive entanglements). More limited is the definition of the social seen purely as 'humans-among-themselves', thus entering the Cartesian dualism with its agent structure debates and focus on the creation of meaning. Lastly, and most narrow, is a definition focused on *social structures* or *social facts*. In this definition, the social is bereft of agency (a position most often taken in empirical postpositivist IR research).[82] What becomes clear from Dolwick's overview is that the distinction is not natural and basically that a negative definition does not work. These different explanations of the 'social' indicate that it is up to the observer to define what is social and what is not social, thus reinforcing the epistemological argument of the linguistic turn. It also confirms that only an interpretation of the social in terms of associations allows new materialist to escape this fallacy.

Second, a similar discussion on the concept of matter leads to a differentiation between a substantive definition of matter and a socially engaged value judgement about what matters. The substantive definition of matter builds on a difference between the interchangeably used terms matter, the material, materiality and materialization. *Matter* can be defined as something that occupies space and consists out of mass (atoms, particles, energy). The *material* is a term used to describe something made out of matter, when matter is reworked in different substances or elements. In turn, *materialization* describes the process of turning, shaping, enacting or creating material objects from social practices and ideas. Lastly, the concept of *materiality* stands for the theoretical and ontological position that claims that matter exists outside of human sensory observation. These different aspects of matter clearly show the complexity of matter, one that is further confused by the shifting links between materiality and terms like foundationalism (e.g. unquestioned basic beliefs that justify other beliefs, whether defined as brute material facts or social facts), essentialism (that all entities, social or material, contain a specific set of attributes) or naturalism (that everything can be explained in terms of natural causes and laws).[83]

Third, in addition to these meanings of matter, what matters as well is an understanding of *mattering*: the value judgement that some things are more important. Of course, mattering can be explained anthropocentrically, when for instance things matter because people desire them (scarce resources) or because they give cause for concern and are undesired (security). However, such a social explanation only tells half of the story. It neglects whether the material matters because it cannot be influenced as it exists independently and lies outside of 'us humans' (a Cartesian argument) or whether it matters because the material is more durable, because it is too hard to change (a relational or relative argument). New materialists combine exactly these two points, for example when Ahmed describes matter by arguing that 'what matters is itself an effect of proximities: we are touched by what comes near, just as what comes near is affected by directions we have already taken'.[84] New materialist scholars thus study the things that matter based on a combination of the matter outside of humans and how it matters relationally for the object in question, how it inhibits and structures action, threatens one's existence or contains desirable qualities worth obtaining. More than that, with the attention to nearness new materialist scholars argue in line with Deleuze that what matters 'is always a practical problem, never a universal problem mattering for everybody'.[85] For new materialists everything is local, *always*.

A last aspect worth mentioning in this respect is the role of technology and artefacts as the materialized bridge between the social and matter. As a bridge, Winner described technology or artefacts already in the 1980s as being 'by their very nature political in a specific way'.[86] Winner was one of the first to write about the active politics of artefacts (including infrastructure), which he described in two ways: either artefacts matter because of the explicit political effects of technology, or artefacts matter owing to the particular ingrained political organization that is necessary for the technology in question to come into existence. Winner highlighted the explicit political effects of technology with the example of the bridges to Long Island, New York.[87] Designed at a specific height and width, these bridges prevented buses from reaching the island. With personal automobile ownership and use prevalent for whites, these bridges, through their design in that socio-economic context, prevented non-whites from reaching the island. The design and construction thus had a political effect. Other examples discussed by Winner include the neglected access to transport and other facilities for people with a disability or the deliberate construction of labour replacing machinery to limit the influence of labour unions. As he summarizes:

> Consciously or not, deliberately or inadvertently, societies choose structures for technologies that influence how people are going to work, communicate, travel, consume, and so forth over a very long time.[88]

While these examples rest on a (conscious) political choice at the initiation of the technology, Winner also touches on the ingrained political organization of artefacts by highlighting the prerequired political and social relations necessary for the technology to exist in the first place. He explains, for example, how nuclear energy requires a knowledgeable and capital-intensive elite as well as an administrative hierarchy to be able to build and steer a nuclear infrastructure in the first place. Of course, once constructed, the existence of the infrastructure reinforces the positions of these elites.

In contrast to Winner's argument, technology today is mainly discussed in non-political terms as either substantive (deterministic) or instrumental.[89] Of these two perspectives, Bourne argues that the instrumental view on technology 'predominate[s] in western political and social thought', where it is seen as a 'neutral tool'.[90] As a tool, its use and social impact is determined not by the technology itself but by the people that use it within their social relations. A deterministic perspective disagrees with this instrumentality and views technology as the determining independent factor that shapes social relations and sets the context of human action.[91] On its own a deterministic argument is clearly overstated, as technology is designed and thus political. However, for McCarthy a small nuance makes technological determinism more viable than instrumentalism because for him they are relative as he argues that 'it is not that technology develops outside of human agency, but that it develops outside of *some* humans' agencies'.[92] What McCarthy argues is that technological determinism exist the moment one looks at the relations between societies spread over time and space.[93] The European use of gunpowder and navigation techniques are an obvious example, just as drone warfare is both an American political choice on the use of an instrumental technique and a determining factor in the life of many in Central Asia.

5.3.3 Towards the performativity of new materialism

The deterministic perspective is not only viable based on the plain technological dominance of one group over another. McCarthy also discusses the social and institutional norms that come with such a material dominance and discusses these as a major source of power that determine the life of those distanced from the technological innovation and its decision-making process itself.[94] With gunpowder and navigation came perceptions and norms on mathematics, accounting and investment, just as the American drones are accompanied with rules about proper civil behaviour and (debatable) ideas of justice and security.

It is possible to (re)turn from the discussion on technology to the politics of matter with the help of Butler, who makes a similar claim as McCarthy on a very individual and bodily level when she writes:

> Of course, persons use technological instruments, but instruments surely also use persons (position them, endow them with perspective, establish the trajectory of their action); they frame and form anyone who enters into the visual or audible field, and, accordingly, those who do not.[95]

In a way, both McCarthy and Butler highlight that it is not a neutral affair to describe technology in terms of determinism or instrumentalism. Any analysis starting from these positions becomes pre-structured and directs the focus of the scholar involved. Importantly, these predetermined positions close off any potential analysis of the actual interaction of matter and social.[96] This is a similar point to the general criticism of Barad on positivist and postpositivist studies, when she argues that 'the nature/culture dualism foreclose[s] the understanding of how "nature" and "culture" are formed' in the first place.[97] In other words, for Barad the driving question is not so much whether the social *or* the material matter – in fact, not even whether the social *and* the material matter – but 'how matter *comes* to matter'.[98]

This question opens the analysis to both sides of the mind/body dialectic. It studies how matter changes and sediments social understandings, but it also studies how language plays a role in making sense of matter. Simultaneously, it moves away from postpositivist understandings of deconstruction and construction. For new materialists the goal is not to deconstruct issues and open them to critique and reconstruction.[99] Instead, they move the speech act literature back to its original starting point on acts (in line with Section 4.4) and thereby include not only explicit and exceptional speech acts but also the distinctions and delimitations implicit in ordinary language use.[100] In addition, the act is extended to include things not speech-related, like human behaviour, bodily actions and cause and effect relationships. The concept developed by Butler to describe this is *performativity*.

Importantly, in Butler's original introduction to performativity in 1993, the concept is not taken to include non-linguistic acts. For Butler, performativity 'must be understood not as a singular or deliberate "act," but, rather, as the reiterative and citational practice by which discourse produces the effects that it names'.[101] The act that Butler describes is one based on discourse that produces an ontological effect as it materializes and brings into reality the social effects that follow from the discursive delimitations behind the repetition and reiteration of previous practices; it 'decides, as it were, what will and will not be the stuff of the object to which we then refer'.[102] Performativity is the '*process of materialization that stabilizes over time to produce the effect of boundary, fixity, and surface we call matter*'.[103] For Butler, performativity highlights what discourse does to the non-discursive. At the same time, its constant reiteration unlocks the potential failure that is inherent to performativity by highlighting a contextualized process where things only exist in the moment. Performativity is inherently incomplete, even when materialized or codified (in contrast to theoretical explanations of society).[104] Part of this incompleteness stems from the materiality itself, as bodies and matter resist the ascription of discourse.[105] A body is never shaped by discourse but it is normalized by it and forms itself in line with its historical social and material evolution. This productive normalization is something Butler takes from Foucault and leads her to define materiality as 'designat[ing] a certain effect of power or, rather, [as] power in its formative or constituting effects'.[106]

Where Butler remains focused on discourse and the materialization it initiates, others, including Latour and his colleagues from ANT as well as Barad, broaden this idea of performativity. These scholars try to move away from a human-centred approach by opening up their ontology to the actions of matter itself. They do so by building on the relationality that is inherent in Butler's (and Foucault's) performativity. Contrary to Butler, however, these authors push the argument by officially moving away from a preference of discourse to the entangled relationships that shape objects. These relations include the relation between humans and between minds and bodies (discourse/non-discursive), but also the interactions or cause–effect relationships between material elements. In allowing for interaction outside and in addition to discourse, these new materialists claim to move beyond Butler's understanding of performativity.

An interesting performative example that details such a relational understanding is Bennett's analysis of the August 2003 north-east American electricity blackout.[107] Her discussion of this massive blackout that affected over fifty million people highlights not only a – quite literal – relational analysis, but also discusses the manageability of such assemblages and the ingrained ethical questions that such an approach calls for. Bennett herself describes the blackout as 'the end point of a cascade—of voltage collapses, self-protective withdrawals from the grid, and human decisions and omissions'.[108] While she concludes that the investigators tasked with studying the blackout had no idea what stopped the cascade,[109] she analyses in detail their conclusions on the accumulation of (unrelated) factors that contributed to it. As Bennett summarizes the official report:

> The U.S.–Canada Task Force report was more confident about how the cascade began, insisting that there were a variety of agential loci. These include electricity, with its internal differentiation into 'active' and 'reactive' power ...; the power plants, which are understaffed by humans but overprotective in their mechanisms; the wires of transmission lines, which tolerate only so much heat before they refuse to transmit the electron flow; the brush fire in Ohio underneath a transmission line; FirstEnergy and other energy-trading corporations, who, by legal and illegal means, had been milking the grid without maintaining its infrastructure; consumers, whose demand for electricity is encouraged to grow without concern for consequences; and the Federal Energy Regulatory Commission, whose Energy Policy Act of 1992 deregulated the grid, separated the generation of electricity from its transmission and distribution, and advanced the privatization of electricity.[110]

This assemblage of factors led to a situation where the stress on the grid increased in a matter of minutes and kept increasing with each of the power plants that withdrew from the grid, as each of them added to the strain and in turn activated the alarms of other power plants. At the end of the cascade, more than 100 power plants had initiated their automatic safety and shutdown procedures.

Most interesting for Bennett about this cascade is the fact that it is impossible to account it to human agency alone. This is not to say that humans played no role at all. In fact, Bennett is quite adamant that humans most definitely played a role in the blackout through their capitalist behaviour in the – in hindsight – faulty regulated and liberalized electricity markets. However, in addition to the automatic safety systems, Bennett also highlights the agentic capacity of the electricity flow itself, a flow which spontaneously shifted its direction after several transmission lines broke down and thereby strained the grid in ways it had not experienced before.[111] For Bennett, such a distributed agency calls for an equally distributed accountability, and hence for an ethics that is 'detached from moralism' and a 'politics of blame' as both of these are human-focused.[112] In fact, Bennett argues that responsibility and accountability in events like the blackout should be approached in terms of a choice. Pending the political or social need, it becomes a judgement to either acknowledge a distributed accountability or hold only humans accountable.

In sum, in the rejection of a sole focus on language and discourse, new materialist scholars are trying to study the actual relationship between the social and the material, by moving away from human-centred analyses and asking how matter comes to matter. For this, they use a local and relational ontology that allows them to study the materialization of relationships between humans, matter, discourse and so forth. They study the becoming or enactment of new sets of relationships, by taking a performative approach that looks at these relationships irrespective whether their origin is social or material. In other words, they place the material on an equal footing with the discursive, as in Bennett's example. Interestingly, they still separate the material and social analytically, and they are unable to study these ontological politics without referring to knowledge and language. In addition, as discussed below, while new materialism has the tools to describe and observe new relationships from both sides of the materialdiscursive assemblage, that is all it can do. It is an approach that does not hypothesize the reasons why people and objects do things and it has trouble explaining change as it can only describe what the relationships do and how they do it.

5.4 Relational ontologies and the question of change

5.4.1 The relational ontology of actor-networks

Building on that, three elements of Bennett's example touch on the question where change comes from. These include the relationality of the different interacting nodes of the electricity grid, the surprise of unintended material effects and the ethics behind the question of accountability. This first section will introduce a Latourian version of ANT to further study the ontological relationality of new materialism. The second section discusses the critique that is levied against ANT in relation to the source of change and the last section will translate this back to the broader new materialist literature by focusing on the unintended material effects.

Actor-network theory stems from the work of Latour, Law, Callon and Mol within STS.[113] ANT is arguably the most popular of the new materialist approaches within the social sciences owing to its highly empirical framework around a network metaphor that studies the relations and traces between the nodes in that network, while offering explanations for its durability and inherent political effects. The core reason behind ANT's rejection of a sole focus on language rests upon the broadly shared observation that the material is vital as an ordering principle for society, in other words that it is the material that helps order societies. Latour gives the example of a group of chimpanzees that is constantly touching, fleaing and performing other niceties, not because they like it but because they lack the use of materials and, as a result, are constantly in need to (re)constitute their 'decaying' society and its hierarchical relations.[114]

The materialization of social effects in durable material artefacts is not unique to ANT. Miller, working from a (historic) anthropologic orientation on the theory of material culture, combines precisely this insight of sedimentation with a 'humility of things' and what Latour describes as 'black boxing', namely the argument that artefacts constantly shift in and out of focus and that the most *unobserved* artefact is, in fact, the one that influences humans the most.[115]

However, before things can shift in and out of focus, Miller claims that these objects (and subjects) should have gone through a process of 'objectification'.[116] This is based on Hegel's insight that, in the words of Miller, 'everything that we are and do arises out of the reflection upon ourselves given by the mirror image of the process by which we create form and are created by this same process'.[117] Rephrased, he argues that humans can only know themselves when they look in the 'material mirror' of 'the historical world created by those who lived before us'.[118] A mirror that comes to us in the form of material culture. For Miller, historical ideas and intentions (social agency) are sedimented through an objectification in the material, after which the material object shifts in and out of focus and through its connections with other objects is able to extend a limited agency of its own.[119] While Latour agrees with Miller that the social is inscribed into the material and that ideas need materialization, he questions the assumption of material culture that only humans can be agents. Because then 'objects … would be simply connected to *one another* so as to form a homogeneous layer, a configuration that is even less likely than one which imagines humans linked to one another by nothing else than social ties'.[120] Instead, Latour sees people witnessing a wide range of *hybrid quasi-objects*, objects that are material, social, human and non-human and that do things which are often overlooked and fluctuating depending on the phenomena in question.[121]

This realization, that scholars will never really know 'who or what' is acting if they do not first question this explicitly, is the basic premise of ANT.[122] Latour argues in this respect that:

> The task of defining and ordering the social should be left to the actors themselves, not taken up by the analyst. This is why, to regain some sense of order, the best solution is to *trace connections between the controversies themselves* rather than try to decide how to settle any given controversy.[123]

In order to trace the connections, ANT envisions (1) a relational network of nodes that exhibits heterogeneous and rhizomatic qualities.[124] Each of these nodes are actor-networks in themselves and consist of subsequent nodes and relations, which in turn are networks of shifting associations, and so on. To be able to study these sets of actor-networks without any a priori assumptions on how the relations look like ANT (2) assumes them to be irreducible and flat.[125] All actor-networks are irreducible (different) from any other actor-network. And because the nodes can never be explained by something larger (because then they would be vertically reducible), the ontology of these networks is flat in Whitehead's sense that all entities have an identical (horizontal) ontological standing, which in practice means that the smallest atom can be as important as the largest set of human economic relations.[126]

While ANT talks about actor-networks, it does not envision these nodes as human actors but instead (3) prefers the posthuman term 'actants'. For ANT, the term actor is not only too human, but it also hides the real set of relations that make the action possible in the first place.[127] An actor never acts alone, or, as Tuana describes it, 'agency in all these instances emerges out of such inter-actions; it is not antecedent to them'.[128] To get behind the figurehead of the actor and get to the action itself, ANT introduces the term actants, which 'are simply different ways to make actors *do* things' irrespective of whether they are social or material, human or non-human, micro or macro.[129] An actant does not need motivation, willpower or rationality (which differentiates humans from animals) and it is neither object nor subject; instead, an actant 'is that which does something, has sufficient coherence to perform actions, produce effects, and alter situations'.[130] Like the overall network, each actant in turn is an assemblage of a range of associations in itself. These assemblages are constantly shifting, one moment closing old relations and the next entering into new ones. While ANT sees actants as irreducible and flat to begin with, it does allow for differences in power: the more associations an actant has, the stronger it can affect its surroundings and the more real it appears.[131]

However, an observer can only witness the effects and strength of an actant if (4) the actant accounts for itself by leaving a mark or trace upon another actor-network. Here ANT (5) differentiates between mediators and intermedi-aries. On the one hand, an intermediary is an actant who offers a highly predict-able causal relation as it 'transports meaning or force without transformation'.[132] For example, writing a paper depends on many factors, most of which the author is not aware as these factors (6) have withdrawn from sight and are black boxed. These intermediaries do not make a difference. That is, *until* they break down, as all heterogeneous networks inherently fail at some point. Then suddenly an unobserved object becomes a thing: the computer could break down owing to a power surge, a software glitch or a corrupt hard drive, or the author could develop RSI as the result from a cheap office chair etc. In each case, the 'black box' of the intermediary normally working components are opened up and *matters of fact* become *matters of concern*.[133] For ANT, all intermediaries can transform into mediators, which 'transform, translate, distort, and modify the meaning or the elements they are supposed to carry'.[134] At that moment of translation from input to output, mediators leave a trace. More importantly, they shape reality as 'they make each other *be*'.[135] However, mediators can only transform into intermediaries when they are transformed or translated by the effects of other mediators. Humans are no different. As actants (e.g. based upon both human and non-human relations), they often use specific mediators (tools of observation, like a microscope) to get intermediaries (viruses) 'to talk'.[136] ANT searches for these translations, as these, no matter how big or small, hint at the actual associations and agency that make up our world.[137]

In an early reflection on ANT, Law summarized these traces into three different strategies. The first strategy deals with ordering through *time* with prac-tices of inscription and sedimentation (durability). The second strategy deals with ordering through *space* by enabling action and communication at a dis-tance (ANT's 'immutable mobiles' – letters, ships etc.). Third, Law discusses a strategy of *translation* based on practices of anticipation, an anticipation of future relations, which he primarily describes in terms of calculative practices (compare with Chapters 4 and 6).[138] For ANT, all these traces are material. Even knowledge is considered a collection of material traces because 'it comes as talk, or conference presentations. Or it appears in papers, preprints or patents. Or again, it appears in the form of skills embodied in scientists and technicians'[139] Simultaneously, Latour enforces that all ANT scholarly work comes as a textual account of a set of relations of a heterogeneous network.[140] Where ANT differs from other theoretical explanatory accounts in the social sciences with its descriptive tracing of relationships is in the accuracy it provides. But to do so it has to accept a greater level of uncertainty:

> An account which accepts to be 'just a story' is an account that has lost its main source of uncertainty: it does not fret any longer at being accurate, faithful, interesting, or objective.... In a bad text only a handful of actors will be designated as the causes of all the others.[141]

Latour refers here to the idea of capitalism. He does not deny that capitalism exists but argues that one can only truly study it by tracing its local relations, which in this case means starting with the Wall Street trading rooms and household budgets decided on at kitchen tables.[142]

In other words, for ANT scholars, the idea of society or social explanations like norms, social facts or a concept as scarcity or energy security do more harm than good because they close off an understanding of what is really going on. Latour is quite strong on this and criticizes social scientists, who, instead of providing 'powerful explanations', are engaging in the politics of the situation they describe by freezing 'the entities already mobilized to render asymmetries longer lasting'.[143] Instead, ANT scholars argue in favour of a better examination of the construction of social events, one that acknowledges that things can always fail.[144] Because when everything is based on inherently fragile heterogeneous networks and their mediators, 'the dichotomy between the real and the constructed is, like all dichotomies, a false one'.[145] Instead, the question becomes one of stability or *how well* things are constructed and performed.[146]

5.4.2 The missing virtuality in ANT

One of the most interesting and thorough arguments against this Latourian version of ANT is made by the philosopher Harman in his argument for an object-oriented philosophy (OOP), which basically states that ANT is unable to explain the origin of change.[147] By placing ANT in perspective with other posthumanist philosophers, Harman identifies a renewed attention to the classic problem of 'isolation and interbleeding of individual things'.[148] In particular, he questions Latour's paradoxical claim of 'action at a distance': that actants are simultaneously irreducible to other actants, both large and small, but nonetheless able to act and affect each other. For Harman, to be irreducible is to have distance, while to affect something requires a sense of nearness, a connection of sorts.[149] As described above, Latour and ANT offer translation (by mediators) and abstraction (black boxing) as an answer to this dilemma. According to Harman, however, such a networked position results in actants who are always present, and as they are always visible they cannot hide and thus have no essence.[150]

By denying actants any form of essence, ANT faces 'an infinite regress of actors' as each network consists of actants, consisting of networks, consisting of actants etc.[151] In this respect, Fine questions the observational arbitrariness behind what counts as part of a heterogeneous network. If there is always a larger or smaller network, then the observer actively takes position when they decide to stop studying the rest of the network.[152] In turn, for Harman this lack of essence means that ANT only studies *actual* states of affairs and that Latour theoretically is unable to account for change as he rejects any form of potentiality: all relations that can take place do take place.[153] Latour is unable to account for that moment when an actant's 'alliances shift', because at that same moment 'by *definition* the actor has changed'.[154] One consequence of such an actuality is a tendency within ANT and other network approaches to favour those relations that can be observed and measured most easily and thereby offer an illusion of manageability.[155] In line with this, Harman argues that Latour is unable to explain the reality of 'buffered causation', that not all relations are entered the moment that they can be made.[156]

To counter the infinite regress in ANT, Harman proposes a perspective that builds on 'an absolute distinction between the domestic relations that a thing needs in order to exist, and the external alliances that it does not need. But the actor itself cannot be identified with either'.[157] When matter is depicted as something firm and hard, people do not refer to an essential characteristic of the object but to its relational qualities: something is hard or intelligent only in relation to that which is not. In Harman's view, most of his points could be answered by taking Latour's metaphysics of actor-networks and adding the distinction between internal relations and external relational qualities to the insight that actants are able to enter a relation through the core of a mediator.[158]

The precise argumentation of Herman is dense and will not be reproduced here. Of interest here is the fact that in his more recent work Latour accepts Harman's argument and steps away from his earlier claims of irreduction, that no actant is reducible to another, while admitting that ANT has no way to study trajectories.[159] Before that, Latour offered his view of networks against a background of unarticulated plasma as a way to explain change in ANT.[160] This plasma represented the potentiality of the network and filled the empty spaces between the nodes and the connections. Farías criticizes this move in a similar fashion as Latour criticizes social sciences: in shifting to a base plasma of virtuality that is 'interrupted' by the actual relations that take effect, Latour creates an a priori asymmetry that only explains where change comes from and not how the virtual becomes actual.[161] Interestingly, this brings this section back to the beginning of the chapter as Farías and Bryant below offer an alternative interpretation of change (the actualization of virtuality) and return to Luhmann and Derrida and their focus on differences.

On the one hand, Farías turns to Luhmann's systems of communication, which he describes as irreducible par excellence and thus comparable to Latour's actor-networks.[162] What Farías likes in particular is the self-referentiality of Luhmann's systems and how they make sense of their own environment (their virtuality according to Farías) and subsequently differentiate themselves from that environment and make themselves actual. He sees each node (actant) as a system of relations (actant-networks) that observes the other nodes (actant-networks) and differentiates itself from it.

Alternatively the philosopher Bryant proposes an ontic principle that states that 'there is no difference that does not make a difference' and that 'to be is to make or produce differences'.[163] This has some major consequences, because if everything results from difference, than nothing can be traced back to a pure origin and you can only be sure of your knowledge if you actively engage with the differences.[164] Similarly to ANT, Bryant argues that such an ontic position leads to a posthuman (all beings differ), irreducible (because beings differ they are irreducible) and flat ontology (all beings differ and are thus equal) where scholars have to trace translations (that relations are actively made) and need to be careful in providing 'hegemonic' explanations (that one difference explains all).[165] Contrary to ANT, however, Bryant agrees with Harman as he too observes that 'objects persist through time while nonetheless undergoing change at the level of their qualities'.[166] Hence, he too separates the endogenous relations of an object from its exogenous relations. In contrast to Harman, however, Bryant looks at topologies of inter-ontic relations that constrain individual actants.[167] By this Bryant refers to the observation that beings often share endogenous relations, independent of any actual relations between the objects. These inter-ontic relations are forced on objects by a larger topology (Bryant gives the example of gravity, which creates a shared need for skeletons). For Bryant, the possibility for change, the virtual, is limited to the space between these inter-ontic topologies and the capacity to act or be acted upon, as only the latter actualizes a virtual relationship. Change, in Bryant's work, stems from the idea that not all effects are always actualized nor that all actualizations bring new effects, but that the material conditions of possibility are pre-structured by the virtual and actual relations of actants and their topologies.

The discussion in this section, with Latour, Harman and Bryant, is dense, highly abstract and hard to summarize. The reason why it is included in this book on energy security is twofold. First, the above shows that the question of stability and change – already difficult when looking only at the material or the linguistic – becomes even harder when change can come from everywhere and one loses the stability of a clear dominant social or material explanation. In other words, in line with the proliferation of energy security, it offers a potential way to approach energy security when the latter is taken as a truly empty concept, without favouring the material or the linguistic elements of energy and energy security. And, second, it clearly links to another aspect within the chapter on security, namely the discussion of the event, where the event was interpreted with terms like the surprise and contingency, both terms denoting change and stability and the ontological politics that interpret and shape these events. The next section continues this discussion in a form that is less abstract and more focused on the event itself.

5.4.3 An eventful folding

The virtual ontology that the performative theories above try to describe with their metatheoretical discussions about networks of relations is more generally known in new materialism as the 'vibrancy of matter':[168]

> Materiality is always something more than 'mere' matter: an excess, force, vitality, relationality, or difference that renders matter active, self-creative, productive, unpredictable.[169]

Neither mechanistic nor reducible, this vibrant materialism envisions a world of becoming.[170] In a relational ontology this points to the 'uncertain exchanges between stabilized formations and mobile forces that subsist within and below them'.[171] This vibrancy is something that a more traditional Cartesian understanding of matter would never be able to tackle. Matter in a Cartesian dualist worldview is, according to Coole, 'sheer exteriority' and as such 'devoid of interiority or ontological depth. It is without qualities like color or smell … without dark recesses, crevices, or hollows … unaffected by time or negativity…. It is inert stuff emptied of all immanent vitality.'[172] Cartesian matter is observable in its causality as it 'tends to determination; it gives itself up to calculation, precision, and spatialization'.[173] But the above shows that matter does not behave like that, as it constantly changes and stabilizes.

Furthermore, matter and 'things are not just simultaneously material and meaningful; they are also *eventful*'.[174] New materialists interpret the event as that what interrupts the habits and routines that make up subjects as well as the withdrawal of objects from its active relations.[175] An event is the break with habit (Chapter 4). That what starts mattering, not because of any a priori socially provided interests but because:

> it gives to that something a power it does not generally possess: the power to cause us to think, feel and wonder, the power to have us wondering how practically to relate to it, how to pose relevant questions about it.[176]

Events actually can be perceived in two ways. First, an event is the surprise (e.g. something in need of interpretation). Connolly describes an event in this respect as something that:

> Happens rather rapidly; it throws some regular institutions and role definitions into turmoil or disarray; its antecedents often seem insufficient to explain its emergence and amplifications; its settlement, when under way, is uncertain; and it makes a real difference in the world, for good or ill.[177]

As a surprise, an event often emerges as a failure or a breakdown that transforms a matter of fact into a matter of concern.[178] Barry, for example, is interested in the manner in which the corrosion of the metals of an oil pipeline ignites a political debate, sometimes even constituting a public that was not there before.[179] Second, Latour also talks about the event in terms of an achievement. In this interpretation, events are seen as successful practices of observation, as the achievement to observe and ascribe meaning to a phenomenon that has never been observed before.[180] For Latour, this is an event because it achieves to connect two previously unlinked objects, thereby creating 'new possibilities and new questions for the concerned parties'.[181] Defining events in terms of surprise and achievement thus very much depends on one's perspective. For instance, the breakdown of a pipeline through corrosion is an achievement of the elements involved but a surprise for the people who depend on the pipeline.

Another way to indicate both the surprise and the achievement is by describing objects, including (post)humans, as folded entities. A fold (or assemblage) refers to the manner in which an object bridges moments in space and time as well as opening up additional actions for the user. Latour, when not discussing the withdrawal or black boxing of objects, uses the example of a hammer to show how such an object folds time (the history of iron, wood, production, transport, use), space (mines, forests, factories, markets, homes) and the 'flux of possibilities' that the hammer offers to its wielder (construction, weapon, ornament).[182] These folds are never static and always hide their own negation, simply because something that can be folded can also be stretched, broken and opened up. [183] The surprise of the inherent failure is countered by the achievement of the folding itself. Brassett and Vaughan-Williams draw on Butler when they describe this as 'the performative *politics* of ... *attempted* closures, which are nevertheless already in excess of their own logic and give rise to unexpected, unforeseen, and disruptive effects'.[184] This separates new materialism once more from strict constructivist approaches. According to new materialism, the habitual and repetitive folding of sets of relations is based on fragile practices and not on social norms or rules, as the latter do not allow for their own negation and have to be resisted from the outside by another norm.[185] Furthermore, these practices enact or perform the actual reality of the folding itself, they 'co-constitut[e] "subjects", "objects" and "environments"'[186] This means that folds, and the practices that create them, cannot be studied from a distance as any observation is an act itself and affects the folded object.[187]

In short, this section offered an example of a new materialist, posthuman and relational theory by introducing Latour's ANT and how it deals with change and stability. While discussing this theory and its assumptions, two things became clear. First, specifically in relation to this theory, that the flat ontology and irreducibility of actor-networks prevent the theory from explaining change and instead leave it open to a constant regress of actants. This follows, in part because the theory is biased towards observable relations and provides no guidance for observers on where to limit their research. The work of Farías and Bryant offered an alternative, with their focus on differences as the answer to the question of virtuality. Both argue that these differences are performatively given shape in and by the relations themselves, as these relationships observe their own distinctions – either as a surprise or an achievement – in something that the last section introduced as a practice of eventful folding. Second, more generally, that all of this (1) extends the discussion on the surprising event in the security chapter, (2) offers a materialdiscursive ontology that adds and contrasts to the socially oriented performative security theories, and (3) starts to point to a more general shared performative notion of ontological politics and the close connection between events, observation and assemblages. This is taken up further in the next section.

5.5 The politics of observing *with* things

While the analysis above of a relational ontology paints a very technocratic and descriptive picture of relations being entered and disrupted, such a perspective runs the risk of forgetting the politics behind such disruptions, especially when humans are involved.[188] As soon as humans are involved, either as affected or affecting party, 'a host of ethical and political issues' opens up. [189] A good example of a situation of ontological uncertainty and the collapse of observation and practice can be found in the many necessary real-life experimentations when introducing or transforming infrastructures and other technologies.[190] The environmental impact of wind turbines or the social effects of smart meters, let alone the optimal configuration of a smart grid, can only be analysed when they are build and utilized on scale. Meaning that people need to use them for others to get to know them. On the one hand, this implies that to analyse the materialdiscursive consequences of an artefact in its totality, it is necessary to take the *risk* to use it in its environmental and social context. And, on the other hand, such an experimentation not only deflates any social/material dualistic understanding but also deflates the distinction between experts and laypersons, as those who use the technology are as much experts as those who are experts in name.[191] In other words, the excess potentiality of the materialdiscursive collapses the distinction between observation and objects and opens up to a politics of ontology, which deals with 'the conditions of possibility [as] enacted'.[192]

Someone who explicitly studies ontological politics is Barry in his work on the BTC pipeline in the Caucasus.[193] He focuses in particular on the knowledge disputes surrounding the construction, maintenance and possible (environmental) effects of this pipeline. While highlighting the materiality of the pipeline, its metal construction, landscape, route and environmental impacts, Barry argues for a better understanding of the public knowledge controversies that 'make things political'.[194] He clearly agrees with the earlier claim of Barad that it is not about matter, but about materialization and that what makes the material matter. While acknowledging the instability of matter (its vibrancy) and its 'informational enrichment' in case of alloys and metallurgy, matter is analysed by Barry as something that enables and hinders, something that is represented, debated and made public or not by and for humans.[195] In other words, for Barry matter is ultimately subject to human fears and desires.

Then again, contra Barry's gas pipeline, it is possible to find ontological politics at work in cases without direct human involvement. For instance, Brassett and Vaughan-Williams analyse a posthuman informational-enriched materiality by analysing self-learning sensors that are used in the protection of critical infrastructure, in their case, natural fresh water filtration areas.[196] With the self-correcting and improving accuracy of the database behind the motion and audio sensors, Brassett and Vaughan-Williams argue that in this case it is the infrastructure itself (the sensors, databases, cables etc.) that is performing its own – and our – security. The database raises the alarm, not after an activation of the sensors but on whether the activity that is measured falls outside the scope of its own historic irregular activities. It then adds that same measurement to the database to be used next time that the sensors are activated. The database and sensors act politically, based on the politics that is written into the program by its designers who allow the program to define its own normality curve (Section 4.5.5).

An alternative theory that allows for an active role of artefacts in relation to knowledge is the agential realist theory of the physicist and feminist philosopher Barad.[197] What is remarkable regarding the theoretical perspectives so far, when looking at ANT and OOO, is that in their choice for objects and relations they all seem to start from continental philosophy. Barad, however, builds her argument on insights gained from quantum theory, especially the work of Niels Bohr. Based on her combination of Bohr and postpositivist philosophy, Barad's theory starts from an ontology of phenomena in contrast to the relational ontologies discussed so far. This helps her to open the definition of materiality to a politics of materialization and to argue for an extension of postmodern concerns on the inseparability of ontology, epistemology and ethics.[198] By addressing ethics and arguing for an inseparability of these three concepts, Barad, first, introduces a politics of materialization, and, second, by linking ethics to the practices of observation introduces a radical different view on knowledge. In contrast to ANT and other new materialist offerings, Barad sees objects playing an important role in informing and determining what humans are capable of knowing in the first place. She thus argues in favour of a theory of performativity that includes how discourse moderates the non-discursive but also how matter itself helps perform knowledge in a particular way.

Barad's work leans heavily on Bohr's insights concerning the so-called measurement problem in quantum theory. Physicists, after having shown that subatomic particles can behave both as a wave (showing diffraction patterns) and as a particle (taking up a particular position in space), concluded that it is impossible for an observer to study both at the same time.[199] The focus of the observer, even retrospectively according to recent research as described by Barad, determines whether they are witness to particle- or wave-like behaviour. The example used by Barad (and Bohr) to clarify this deals with the study of momentum and position: to study momentum (speed and direction) the observer has to use a movable camera, while if an observer wants to study the position of an object they can only do so from a fixed position. Momentum and position are thus mutually exclusive phenomena; it is impossible to study them both at the exact same time.[200] Often this is described as Heisenberg's uncertainty principle, which sees the measurement problem as epistemological uncertainty: it is impossible to know whether something is a wave or a particle. Barad, however, shares Bohr's understanding of the measurement problem in terms of ontological indeterminacy. For Bohr, the measurement problem does not result from epistemological uncertainty but from an ontological complementarity: the world is ontologically inseparable, and that it is the observation and the theories behind the observation that determine which properties in fact exist in the world.[201] Both wave and particle exist and we are simultaneously moving and in position, only the observer dictates what exactly we are. From this follows the main message that Barad tries to convene, that is to say Bohr's lesson that 'we are part of that nature that we seek to understand'.[202]

Barad rephrases this Bohrian insight by arguing that the practice of observation should therefore be seen as an agential cut, a becoming of reality. While the previous theories offered a range of core concepts like materialism, social structures, language, systems of communication, hybrid forms or actor-networks of relations, Barad offers an ontology of phenomena as a way to include all possible realities that are delineated by this agential cut. In fact, Barad argues that it is not so much the observer who makes the cut but that the materialdiscursive practices themselves make the cut. The cut originates from the intra-action between all the 'agencies of observation': the observer, but also the tools, the social structures and so on.[203] Simultaneously, it creates its own *agential separability*, a separation between the 'object' and 'agencies of observation'.[204] In the practice of observation, a causal relationship is enacted between the object (a cause) and the effect or traces left on the agencies of observation (the subjects), which in turn enables a logic of objectivity resembling scientific realism.[205] The origin of the cut is not a conscious choice but the result of a constant intra-acting between mutually constituting entangled agencies. (Barad prefers the concept of intra-acting to the concept of interacting, as the latter implies a relationship between two separate entities, while intra-acting refers to two entities within the same phenomena). These agencies are ongoing enactments and only become distinct on a relational level: they never are and never will become individual entities (owing to their ontological inseparability).[206] Barad, however, does distinguish between different intra-actions that result in different phenomena, just as she sees that a phenomenon can be part of other, larger phenomena.

For Barad, these phenomena are real; what is more, she argues that they are physical.[207] She comes to this through her argument that 'knowing does not come from standing at a distance and representing but rather from *a direct material engagement with the world*'.[208] Claiming that either the discursive or the material comes prior to the other is nonsensical, because the ontological inseparability makes these concepts, like space and time, products of observation (à la

Latour). Instead the world is entangled and 'the material and the discursive are mutually implicated in the dynamics of intra-activity'.[209] At this point Barad redefines what we understand as the discursive and material. In line with post-positivist scholars, she sees discourse losing its meaning without ongoing use. However, contra those scholars she reinterprets discursive practices in line with Butler and Bryant as 'material (re)configurings of the world through which the determination of boundaries, properties, and meanings is differentially enacted'.[210] Simultaneously, she argues that 'matter does not refer to a fixed substance; rather, matter is substance in its intra-active becoming – not a thing but a doing a congealing of agency.... "[M]atter" refers to phenomena in their ongoing materialization.'[211] For Barad, discourse is thus material, but matter does not exist 'out there' and instead comes into being through its relations and observations. Clearly, this latter position, on coming to matter by hiding the cut, resembles the black boxing of ANT and the 'humility of things' form material culture. This ontological inseparability of materialdiscursive practices leads Barad to a world of entangled phenomena. A world open to both sides of the ontological indeterminacy, where an iterative and intra-acting process of agential cuts enact particular materialdiscursive practices based on agential separability.

Barad, like Luhmann and Bryant, thus searches for differences.[212] To highlight the agential cuts or the boundaries created through differentiation, she proposes a method called *diffractive reading*. This method builds on diffraction (patterns), a term used in the natural sciences to explain the effects of the interaction between waves, to show how differences create difference.[213] For example, when analysing energy security this would mean that one reads it through both new materialist and security theories and in doing so find differences and new insights at the crossing of both approaches. Another important implication of her theory of entanglement relates to the inherent ethical consequences of observational cuts:

> what is on the other side of the agential cut is not separate from us – agential separability is not individuation. Ethics is therefore not about right response to a radically exterior/ized other, but about responsibility and accountability for the lively relationalities of becoming of which we are a part.[214]

With her example of the brittle star, a sea creature not to be confused with the more popular sea star (brittle stars have snakelike arms), Barad clarifies both the entanglement and ethics of observational 'cuts'.[215] First, there is the observation that a brittle star does not have eyes, nor does it have a brain. As such it does not have the capacity for language, nor can its body be separated from its mind (it has none). That said, a brittle star still reacts to differences in light intensity and, above all, it can flee from its predators. Instead of eyes, brittle stars have an extensive nerve system that makes their entire body act as one big eye. Theoretically, this means that a brittle star is constantly intra-acting with its environment: it does not separate between what it sees or what it thinks; it just is. 'For a brittle star, being and knowing, materiality and intelligibility, substance and form, entail one another.'[216] In other words, a brittle star does not face the Cartesian dualism intuitively ascribed to humans and (most other) animals. A second interesting lesson from the brittle star is that it can break off one of its arms when it is cornered by a predator. In terms of Barad's theory, the moment a brittle star observes a predator it is thus able to *discursively* redraw the *material* boundary between itself and its environment. Sometimes these arms still wriggle, an event that is often interpreted by human observers as a survival technique. For Barad, such an interpretation would mean that the main body and arm are still part of the same phenomenon, e.g. the original brittle star. However, she argues that one could also see the arm as becoming an autonomous living thing itself, especially in light of the observation that some brittle stars reproduce by cloning their arms. As Barad concludes, in the end, '*it's all a matter of where we place the cut*' that defines 'what matters and what is excluded from mattering'.[217]

In other words, through the act of observation differences emerge, phenomena are enacted 'and knowledge is produced about "subjects" and "objects" (and "environments")'.[218] First, these cuts are never definitive. Any observation, like ANT's settlement of relations, is a simplification of a messy reality and is temporary as it incorporates its own demise.[219] Second, these cuts are not only human-made. Barad in particular highlights the role instruments play when humans gain knowledge, as when she discusses the piezoelectric transducer, a scanning device used in ultrasonography.[220] These and other observational devices often measure only one thing (e.g. sound, light etc.) and a such play an active role in deciding what is observed or not, especially when they stutter or break down. What is more, people need particular skills to use them.[221] Tools and tool use are both part of the agential cut that is made. So, while all theoretical insights from new materialism highlight their attentiveness to a vibrant material world, Barad, in ascribing this role to observational tools, is most explicit in stating how tools and objects *actively* influence not only other objects but our practices of knowledge gathering as well. Third, in line with Bryant, these cuts are ontological and not epistemological.[222] They shape the world(s) in which people and things live, because they engage and perform, not because they imagine.

Together, these three observations about cuts create a theoretical approach that calls for a certain humility and perhaps even a sense of vulnerability of humans. For if everything is both affected and affecting, then, as Butler states, 'one's life is always in some sense in the hands of the other'.[223] Together with Butler, Latour and other new materialists, Barad argues that we are responsible for each other. Not in the sense of a responsibility towards the other, as in a typical security relation, but in the sense of a responsibility for us both.[224] Such an encompassing responsibility thus explicitly includes, according to Tuana, a responsibility for those 'practices that account for *not* knowing', those actively '*ignored or rationalized*' accounts of issues like food insecurity or energy poverty.[225] As Latour writes on the morality behind technology:

Between the gesture of switching on my computer and what I write on the screen, I can either ignore the nuclear industry which enables me to work this morning, or find myself immersed in the uncertain destiny of that same industry which forces me to take account of the burial in deep silos of the waste from its stations that the French do not support.[226]

To deal with this, Hekman offers the concept of *disclosure* to approach these settlements (e.g. cuts, actants or assemblages). Based on a Baradian ontology and a critical realist perspective on scientific research, Hekman proposes that the concept of disclosure can 'bring to light' a variety of aspects and perspectives of those settled phenomena/folds/assemblages that hide the differentiation and cuts underneath them. None of these disclosed messy realities is more truthful than the other, but, in a critical realist sense, Hekman does see them as materially braced and hence comparable on objective grounds.[227] Alternatively, Bellacasa introduces the ethical and more critical transformative duty for *matters of care*, after Latour's matters of fact and matters of concern.[228] As she would have it, to explain matters of fact or Barad's agential cuts, one needs to explain them with *care* by respecting all those involved in the observational cut and by giving those who are silenced a voice – even if that means that in each instance observers actively have to choose for whom to care more (in line with Booth's positive security). Scholars are not only part of what they study but also play a critical transformative role in a world of becoming.[229]

In closing, Hekman argues that Barad's agential realism shows promise as it is grounded in local experiences, collapses the material/social dichotomy, focuses on boundaries and boundary drawing practices, and draws ethical conclusions from practices of observation.[230] This chapter can only confirm Hekman's summary but adds that Barad, in pushing for a materialdiscursive entanglement, argues for an understanding of the politics of 'materialisation and dematerialisation'.[231] In other words, while it is impossible to separate the material from the discursive and to observe without acting (humans and non-humans), Barad calls attention to the fact that it is mainly politics, broadly understood, that deals with the virtuality of matter. Here we touch on a slightly paradoxical claim in her argument, because, while she acknowledges the activity of tools to an extent not seen elsewhere, she too discusses these politics overwhelmingly in terms of observing scientists, as in the example of the brittle star. In the end, it seems that Barad too refers back to humans, although no longer masters of the universe, as the core subjects wilfully reflecting and shaping the materialdiscursive in their image.

5.6 Reflection

In response to the mostly sociolinguistic understandings of (energy) security presented in the earlier chapters, this chapter drew attention to the materiality of energy systems and subsequently examined the role and importance of matter in relation to knowledge. At the heart of this chapter were three questions:

(1) how the social and material relate in line of dominant social interpretations that characterize security, (2) how these new materialist theories view our ontology (e.g. how their theories approach social-material relations and objects) and (3) how they approach surprising events or change/uncertainty (e.g. their ontological politics)?

The chapter started with a discussion on the Cartesian mind/body duality within IR by opposing critical realism and radical constructivism. This debate highlighted a strong theoretically induced epistemological argument against representational knowledge as favoured by positivism, in other words that it is impossible to know what we observe objectively and truthfully. For many this is not a new argument, and in fact it lies at the core of the critical theoretical understandings of security. Still, Section 5.2 discussed a matter of contention between these strands of theory, in particular whether the pursuit for scientific knowledge is valid on its own or whether it is a pragmatic social activity. While this debate is ongoing in IR, Section 5.2 ended with the new materialists, who questioned the absence of the non-discursive world in the radical constructivist theories dealing with meaning and discourse. Without matter, new materialists claim, one neglects alternative sources of change and order that drastically influence human life.[232] That said, the section concluded that the new materialist critique of an absence of anything material in critical and radical social theories was phrased a bit too strongly, as original postpositivist theorists were acutely aware of the interplay between knowledge and matter but made the choice to focus on that interaction through a deeper understanding of the social.[233] On the other hand, it could be argued that the many one-sided attempts to translate these linguistic insights into empirical research do eschew anything material and hence validate part of the new materialist claim.

In turn, the new materialist alternative seemed to have proceeded in two phases. The first phase was mainly focused on showing the relevance of the material world against linguistic-oriented postpositivist theories. Section 5.3 in this respect put forward the shared assumptions of new materialism, including its adherence to the epistemological critique of postpositivists, its trust in a world outside of humans, its focus on local assemblages, and the ethical consequences inherent to it. This chapter also offered a partial reprise of the ways in which the material is used and spoken about. Besides the many meanings and different terms used to describe 'the world out there', the material was discussed as something non-social, as objects outside of human influence or as objects with relational qualities (durable, hard, colourful and so forth), with a special reference for those technological artefacts that are made by humans. Based on the latter category, questions were raised towards the traditional separation of matter as something passive or active and as something instrumental or deterministic. The section ended with a core approach that most new materialists use, namely an extended understanding of Butler's performativity or the reiterative acts of materialization. Bennett's example of the north-east American blackout subsequently exemplified this and simultaneously introduced the core aspects of how new materialist view the world: the relationality of the different interacting nodes of the electricity grid, the surprise of unintended and unanticipated material effects, and the ethical consequences of the decision on accountability within such a relationality.

Section 5.4 took these up as it offered a network-inspired relational ontology based on ANT. In analysing the ontological assumptions of ANT, what emerged was an empirical-oriented methodology that assumes a network of relations or actants (actor-networks), which are posthuman and irreducible, stand on equal footing in a flat ontology, and which relate to each other through traceable translation. However, just as social theories are questioned, these networks too are vulnerable. In particular to an infinite regress argument, meaning that there is no end to one's observation while scholars simultaneously only observe fixed traceable relations, relations that are already actualized.

The story of new materialism as described in this chapter hence moved to a second phase and the discussion on how to incorporate the virtual in already-actualized networks of relations, in other words how to explain the transformation of beings while also allowing for independent objects. This virtuality was later described in terms of the condition of possibility of the materialdiscursive assemblages, or, simply, as the vibrancy of matter. This vibrancy in turn was described as eventful, with the event acting both as a surprise and as an achievement. Here new materialist theories move beyond security theories that only focus on the surprise. However, new materialism shows that the insecurity or surprise for one person could very well be the achievement or security of another (e.g. security dilemma). With events interpreted as either surprises or achievements, the virtual and actual were subsequently placed and found in the performative folding of practices. Earlier described as a withdrawal or black boxing of agentic capacities, a fold was seen as the closure of a phenomenon (like a security measure), but a closure that is always incomplete and incoherent (also like a security measure).

Another element was the performative remark that part of the folding is completed with the practice of observation, both outward and inward. By defining observations as achievements, observations become an activity and thus a political act based on differentiation, and as such observation is a core element of ontological politics.[234] Section 5.5 took this up and discussed the politics that ensues from such a materialdiscursive interpretation of life. Following the phenomenological agential realist approach offered by Barad, this chapter argued for a closer attention towards the 'agential cut' when observing and singling out a phenomena, object, practice or event. In connecting ontology, epistemology and ethics, these cuts, whether enacted by humans or non-humans, affect the observed event itself (thereby offering the only truly non-human active theory in new materialism). They create difference. And, as difference, these cuts call for a political awareness and ethical reflection on the cuts and where to place them.

Barad and new materialist scholars therefore call for an ethics of responsibility and care for the relations that are observed. Once observation is seen as the creation of difference, the practice of observation by an assembly of humans and non-humans becomes performative of its own reality as it defines what comes to matter and what does not. As such, observation has long-lasting ethical consequences for that what is not observed: that excess or negation within the assemblage that will ultimately undermine it. Knowing this, new materialist scholars argue for an ethical awareness towards the broader 'us' and to support those who do not matter (e.g. like Booth's positive security). Basically, what new materialist theories add is a materialdiscursive understanding of the vibrancy and order of life and the ontopolitics of difference that shapes it. This enables an understanding of creativity, durability and adaptability, while it disrupts and discloses most dualistic understandings that we know, like the mind/body, social/material, past/future, or expertise/laypersons.

In the end, the link between energy and this chapter is strong but not directly crystalized. Energy security is a discourse that defines the limits of how people properly secure energy, but it is also a knowledge practice through which meaning is ascribed to certain events, and it is a materialdiscursive phenomenon or actor-network where earlier energy security observations and knowledge practices have generated differences and subsequently achieved to gather and materialize an infrastructure like the electricity grid in response to that observation. New events subsequently are influenced by these materialized materialdiscursive relationships/phenomena through their scope, scale, historicity, durability, time-binding and mediation of the observation of events. The implies that the claim from securitization theory that the material does not matter might be epistemologically correct, but misses that observations are not purely social; they are materialdiscursive as well and mediated by the tools used to observe and imagine events. Furthermore, while security is often seen as a technique to define events/provide closure, another insight from a relational or phenomenological materialdiscursive ontology is that every observation of energy security is inherently incomplete and thus itself a potential 'threat' in need of disclosure.

In this sense, new materialism helps to explain the underlying dynamics of the postpositivist argument in security debates. It offers a fuller account of performativity, one that pushes even the practice theories within the security literature. They also help turn the focus towards the politics of ontology and, especially, the role of observation and knowledge in achieving closure. Moreover, they lead to a drastic ethical rereading of practices of observation and the role that knowledge gathering plays in shaping the world. In other words, they deflate the distinction between ontology and epistemology, between a politics of ontology and a politics of knowledge. In general, this chapter describes the potentiality and virtuality of the endless set of relations of matter and the social as life itself. However, to acknowledge a more-than-human world while keeping up with the epistemological critique of postpositivist scholars is a challenge all on its own. With Barad's materialized discursivity and a substance-less materiality, the chapter returned to the same questions of radical social constructivists: how to account for the actuality and virtuality that can be found in-between the discursive and non-discursive. In the end, while new materialist scholars offer an account based on the materialization of potentiality, they also acknowledge that this only matters because of politics. The next chapter will therefore focus on how humans *govern* their world through a materialdiscursive environment.

Notes

1 Bridge 2008.
2 For actor-network theory, see Latour 2005; Law 1992, 2007. For agential realism, see Barad 2003, 2007. On object-oriented ontology, see Harman 2009; Bryant, Srnicek and Harman 2011. And on material culture, see Miller 2005. Other more general work includes: Coole and Frost 2010b; Braun and Whatmore 2010a; Cudworth and Hobden 2011; Bennett 2010. Specifically, these authors depart from the old definition of 'materialism', a term used to describe a theoretical framework that depicts the world to exist from matter, energy and material interactions, and where all social interactions can be explained by material processes. Also note that there is quite some resistance against the use of the term of a 'material turn', as it is claimed that the material has never left and as such cannot return. Interestingly, a similar argument can be made in favour of the 'linguistic turn', although that term is well established.
3 Aradau 2010; Schouten 2014; Cudworth and Hobden 2011; Voelkner 2011; See also the special issue in *Millennium*: Srnicek, Fotou and Arghand 2013; including the article by Connolly 2013. Recent articles in IR with an explicit but more traditional focus on 'the material' include: Sorensen 2008; Aradau 2010; Meyer and Strickmann 2011; McCarthy 2011, 2013.
4 Robinson 2012.
5 Kessler 2007; Bieri 1981. For example, when combining (1) and (2) one enters a classic dualist position described as interactionism where mind and body can interact freely; similarly, a combination of (2) and (3) is described as physicalism and stands for an approach where the mind is seen as part of the body but not reducible to it; and, lastly, a combination of (1) and (3) results in epiphenomenalism, where the mental is seen as a by-product of the physical without any causal effects at all.
6 Searle 1995, 2, 7.
7 Ibid., 1.
8 Ibid., 2.
9 Ibid., 121.
10 Ibid., 55–56.
11 Patomäki and Wight 2000, 216–218. Naturalism is sometimes also described as realism, which, in turn, should not be confused with materialism.
12 Jackson 2008, 132–133 describes this position as 'classical objectivity', meaning before quantum mechanics, before post-structuralism and before the linguistic turn.
13 Cox 1981.
14 Booth 2005, 11.
15 Bhaskar 2005.
16 Wight 2007b, 2007a, 2012; Patomäki and Wight 2000; Joseph and Wight 2010.
17 Wight 2007b, 383.
18 Ibid.
19 Ibid., 386.
20 The italic terms are from Patomäki and Wight 2000, 224; compare with Jackson 2008. Other scholars working from this position include Wendt 1999; Adler 2002; Wight 2007b.

21 Adler 1997.
22 Wendt 1999.
23 Ibid., 111. 'Real' does not imply materiality, as explained above.
24 Ibid., 110; Sorensen 2008, 10.
25 Wendt 1999, 110–113, 130–136.
26 Ibid., 1.
27 Wendt 1999. Sorensen 2008, 10. Wendt is not alone on this; see: Hopf 1998; Tannenwald 2005; Guzzini 2000; Adler 2002; Checkel 1998; Reus-Smit 1996.
28 Jackson 2008, 134–135, 139.
29 See for example the illustrative, slightly ironic, subtitle of Kessler 2012b.
30 Adey, Anderson and Lobo-Guerrero 2011.
31 Kratochwil 2000, 2007b; Kessler 2012b; Fierke 2002; Milliken 1999.
32 Derrida 2005; Foucault 1977; Adorno 1973; Habermas 1984.
33 Wittgenstein 1958.
34 See for instance Derrida 2005.
35 Luhmann 1993, 1995, 2006. Also, Arnoldi 2001; Guzzini 2001; Kessler 2009, 2012a.
36 Luhmann defines communication broadly: language, writing, art, silence, gestures etc., everything that has or contains meaning for the entities using it to communicate.
37 In the act of observing or constituting a distinction, a system thus creates an observer (e.g. subject/object distinction).
38 In addition, he identifies a number of social subsystems based on the recursively used, and therefore structured or 'codified' processing of meaning that leads to functional differentiation between subsystems. The economic subsystem, for example, has as a code payment/non-payment and uses money as a communication medium. Other subsystems include politics, the judiciary, art, media, ecology, society etc. In switching to these social systems of communication, Luhmann tries to move away from the Cartesian dualism by excluding the human and the material as a primary focus of analysis and by placing the agency, as such, on a different level altogether (that of systems of communication).
39 Luhmann 1993, 34–35.
40 Giddens 1986; Wendt 1987; Sewell 1992; Carlsnaes 1992; Doty 1997.
41 Foucault 1977, 27.
42 Kratochwil 2000. See also: Der Derian and Shapiro 1989; Ashley and Walker 1990; Der Derian 2009; Onuf 2013.
43 Kratochwil 2000, 73. See Herborth 2012 on the 'quest for certainty'.
44 Kratochwil 2000, 2007a, 2007b.
45 Wight 2007a. See also Wight 2000 or more abstract Suganami 2013.
46 Compare with Wittgenstein's language games. God/religion is another logic.
47 See the discussion in Jackson 2008, 136–142.
48 Wittgenstein 1922, para. 5.6; Derrida 1976, 158–159.
49 Jackson 2012.
50 Patomäki and Wight 2000, 218.
51 Wight 2007a, as well as Jackson 2008; Jackson 2010.
52 Dolphijn and Van der Tuin 2012, 98 quote De Landa's 2006 book *A New Philosophy of Society* (pp. 45–46) [original emphasis]; Compare with Lemke 2002, 61, who argues that scholars:

> should prevent … a very serious flaw that dominates much contemporary critique: the 'essentialization of the critique of essentialism.' What do I mean by this? When social and political scientists increasingly claim the importance of categories like 'invention,' 'fiction,' and 'construction' for their work, they often double the theoretical attitude they initially set out to criticize: they hold that the 'poststructuralist' or 'anti-essentialist' stance they adopt does signal a 'right' or 'true' knowledge.

53 Barad 2007, 132, 2003, 801.
54 Latour 2005.
55 Jackson 2008, 2010.
56 Hekman 2010, 32.
57 Van der Tuin 2011, 285–287, quoting Barad 2003, 821 on 'ongoing historicity'.
58 See also Hekman 2010, 30–31 or the discussion in Lundborg and Vaughan-Williams 2015. Luhmann 1995 of course starts from three systems, only one of which is the social system of communication. Similarly, Cheah 2008 discusses the nondialectical materialism that is present in Derrida's focus on 'text'.
59 Pickering 1993; Pickering 1999.
60 Coole and Frost 2010a, 27.
61 For the term intra-action, see the explanation of Barad below in Section 5.5.
62 Dolphijn and Van der Tuin 2012, 92–93. Likewise, Latour states that 'There exists no relation whatsoever between "the material" and "the social world", because it is this very division which is a complete artefact'. Latour 2005, 75–76.
63 Aradau 2010, 497.
64 Jackson 2010.
65 Jackson 2002; Barad 2007.
66 Barad 2007.
67 Whatmore 2006.
68 Coole and Frost 2010a, 11–14.
69 Ibid.
70 Hekman 2010, 68.
71 Coole 2013.
72 Whatmore 2006; Coole 2013, 454.
73 Coole 2013, 454.
74 Whatmore 2006.
75 Walters 2014, 103; Coole and Frost 2010a, 26; Bourne 2012, 155.
76 Whatmore 2006, 604.
77 Mol 1999, 75.
78 Dillon and Reid 2001, 46–47.
79 Bryant 2014, 4.
80 See Dolphijn and Van der Tuin 2012, 92–93, as well as Barad 2003, 828.
81 Dolwick 2009.
82 Pouliot 2004, 329 discusses this in terms of essentialization:

> acts of essentialization … are commonplace in social life. They lie at the foundation of the social construction of reality…. Repeated acts of essentialization result in the generation of 'social facts', the portions of the world that are treated as if they were real by social agents…. Once reified, social facts confront agents' everyday life as 'objective' facts that cannot be ignored.

83 Elsewhere, Harman 2009, 74 and 141–143, notes that Latour sees materialism actually as a covert form of idealism because it shifts the attention away from actors and agency towards the physical world (instead of the social) to explain everything.
84 Ahmed 2010, 234.
85 Stengers 2010, 28.
86 Winner 1980, 124, 129.
87 Ibid., 123–126.
88 Ibid., 127.
89 McCarthy 2013; Bourne 2012.
90 Bourne 2012, 142; McCarthy 2013, 473–474.
91 Bourne 2012, 143; McCarthy 2013, 472–473.
92 McCarthy 2013, 476.

93   Ibid., 478–479, 481.
94   Ibid., 488.
95   Butler 2009, xii. Also in Holmqvist 2013, 545.
96   Bourne 2012, 143.
97   Barad 2003, 828.
98   Barad 2003, 2007. See also Latour 2004, 2005.
99   Bialasiewicz *et al.* 2007; De Goede 2012, 32.
100   Butler 2010.
101   Butler 1993, 2.
102   Butler 2010, 1993, 11.
103   Butler 1993, 9 (emphasis in original).
104   Ibid., 2; Butler 2010, 153.
105   Loxley 2007, 135.
106   Butler 1993, 34.
107   Bennett 2005.
108   Ibid., 448.
109   Thereby acknowledging Grove's point on the incapability of network-inspired analyses like ANT to analyse creativity, or in this case non-existing agentic traces. See
Grove 2014 and Section 5.4.2.
110   Bennett 2005, 449.
111   Ibid., 451.
112   Ibid., 464.
113   Latour 2005; Law 1992; Law and Mol 1995; Callon 1986; Mol 1999.
114   Latour 2005, 70, 198. See also Law 1992, 3 on 'material durability' or Pels, Hetherington and Vandenberghe 2002, 11, who claim that: 'Objects need symbolic fram-
ings, storylines and human spokespersons in order to acquire social lives; social
relationships and practices in turn need to be materially grounded in order to gain
temporal and spatial endurance'.
115   Miller 2005, 2–8, esp. 3. Material culture is particularly interested in the relation
between the material and the anti-material, for example, when it comes to religion,
or, more recently, the current economic society based upon consumption.
116   Latour 2005.
117   Miller 2005, 4.
118   Ibid., 5.
119   Ibid., 17–18. This material culture perspective questions the bivalent logic of reification (the material framing of social relations) or fetishism (the symbolic framing
of material objects) as it does both. See also Le Billon 2007, 176 on commodification versus fetishization.
120   Latour 2005, 84–85 (emphasis in original). See also: Bourne 2012, 161.
121   Latour 2005, 72 argues, for example, that 'there might exist many metaphysical
shades between full causality and sheer inexistence'. On pages 84–85 he identifies
four: historical materialism (a material infrastructure like Marx's that determines
social relations); a material world that 'mirrors' the social distinctions (Bourdieu
and other more critical oriented theories); and the material as a stage for human
interaction (instrumentalist perspective); and, lastly, those who put a heterogene-
ously layer atop the material and social (material culture).
122   Latour 2005; Law 1992; Law and Mol 1995; Callon 1986.
123   Latour 2005, 23 (emphasis added).
124   On rhizomatic networks, see Deleuze and Guattari 1987.
125   Bourne 2012, 154. Of course, this goes both ways. While it might be perceived as
more real, in fact all actants are real. They only differ in the number/strength of
their associations, see Fine 2005, 96.
126   Harman 2009, 773; Bourne 2012, 154. For a more critical discussion, see Fine 2005.
127   Latour 2005, 46.

128 Tuana 2008, 9; Dolphijn and Van der Tuin 2012, 54.
129 Latour 2005, 55. Bennett 2005, 446–447 discusses actants as both coherent entities (e.g. a tree) and forces (e.g. gravity or mineralization), depending on how they appear to us humans.
130 Bennett 2004, 355. In general, Bennett refers to this with her concept of 'thing-power'.
131 Latour 2005, 180.
132 Ibid., 39.
133 Latour 2004. Things are continuously (re)produced relata, a continuous 'gathering' of relations as fact or concern, while Latour describes objects as failed 'things', as taken-for-granted end-products of observation.
134 Latour 2005, 39.
135 Dolwick 2009, 45 (emphasis in original).
136 Latour 2005, 79.
137 Hence 'flattening the social' and 'localizing the global' – i.e. the social does not stand above the material, and the macro is not more important than the micro/local, thereby removing the level of analyses problem. See ibid., 165.
138 Law 1992, 6–7.
139 Ibid., 2.
140 Latour 2005, 122–130.
141 Ibid., 127, 130.
142 Ibid., 178–179, 192. For similar arguments on security and economic markets see: Schouten 2014, 27 and Caliskan and Callon 2010.
143 Latour 2005, 5, 8, 23, 68, 85, 260.
144 Ibid., 249.
145 Hekman 2010, 110.
146 Mol 2002, 7; Hekman 2010, 110; Latour 2005, 89–90.
147 Harman 2009.
148 Ibid., 6, also 99–107.
149 Ibid., 34–35.
150 Ibid., 72 and 75.
151 Ibid., 106.
152 Fine 2005, 96. However, compare Bennett 2012, 228.
153 Harman 2009, 130–134. See also Grove 2014.
154 Harman 2009, 105.
155 Grove 2011, 1–2, 6.
156 Harman 2009, 147. However, Latour does mention overflow. See Latour 2005, 166.
157 Harman 2009, 135.
158 Ibid., 145–146 To read his specific treatise: pp. 151–228, in particular pp. 207–211, but also p. 187: 'The potential can only mean a potential for future relations, and the actual can only mean what is in and of itself actual apart from any relations'.
159 Farías 2014, 28–29; Latour, Harman and Erdelyi 2011.
160 Latour 2005, 244.
161 Farías 2014, 28–29.
162 Ibid., 31.
163 Bryant 2011, 271, 272.
164 Ibid., 272–273.
165 Bryant 2011.
166 Ibid., 279.
167 Ibid., 280–282.
168 Bennett 2010.
169 Coole and Frost 2010a, 9.
170 Connolly 2010.
171 Ibid., 179.

172 Coole 2010, 94.
173 Grosz 2010, 150.
174 Braun and Whatmore 2010b, xxi (emphasis added). Later in the chapter they also call it 'originary' (xvii).
175 Braidotti 2010, 213; Stengers 2010, 27; Latour 2002, 251.
176 Stengers 2011, 374; Deleuze 1994; Grove 2014, 366; Bennett 2005, 457–458.
177 Connolly 2013, 404.
178 Latour 2004.
179 Barry 2013a; Marres 2005.
180 Stengers 2010, 12.
181 Ibid., 25.
182 Latour 2002, 249–250.
183 Coole 2010, 107. Compare with Adorno 1973, who discusses this in terms of a 'non-identity': the difference between concept and thing, with something in the 'thing' always resisting the concept. For a discussion, see Bennett 2004, 349, 361–362.
184 Brassett and Vaughan-Williams 2015, 4; Butler 2010. On closure, see Luhmann 2006.
185 Stengers 2010, 16; Connolly 2013, 404–405.
186 Squire 2015, 153. The term enactment is introduced by Mol 2002.
187 Mol 2002, 5–6.
188 Walters 2014, 103; Squire 2015, 151.
189 Coole and Frost 2010a, 19.
190 Whatmore 2006, 607; Callon, Lascoumes and Barthe 2009; Mitchell 2013, 240–242.
191 Callon, Lascoumes and Barthe 2009.
192 Hekman 2010, 82; Mol 2002. Braun and Whatmore 2010b, xxiii.
193 Barry 2013a; Barry 2013b. For another new materialist discussion on the politics of ontology (identifying the event, debating its solution), see Schouten 2014 for a discussion on the role of the body scanner at airports from a security perspective.
194 Barry 2013b, 7.
195 Ibid., 12–13. Star 1999 actually discusses nine characteristics of infrastructure: (1) its embeddedness in other (infra)structures; (2) its transparency (once build it is there in the open); (3) its temporal and spatial effects; (4) its effects on users, through skills; (5) its effects on social practices; (6) its embodiment of standards; (7) its fixation of (capital) investments and interests; (8) its modular qualities; and (9) its withdrawal or black boxing effects.
196 Brassett and Vaughan-Williams 2015, 39–42.
197 Barad 2007, 2003, 1996, 1998, 2011.
198 Barad 1996, 2003, 2007.
199 However, see the very recent work of Rozema *et al.* 2012 and Piazza *et al.* 2015, which state that it is possible to observe both without influencing them. While this places question marks behind Barad's indeterminacy argument, it simultaneously reinforces her argument about the role that matter plays in observing matter (as we could not confirm this with older equipment), and thus the boundaries that objects enact.
200 Barad 2007, 111–113. Another example given by Bohr (as described by Barad) is when a person holds a stick: you either feel the stick, or you feel through the stick, but never simultaneously. Compare to Heidegger's tool-in-use.
201 Barad 2003, 2007, 2011.
202 Barad 2007, 26, 117–118 (emphasis in original).
203 Ibid., 31.
204 Ibid., 140.
205 Ibid., 120. Both Barad and Latour seem to agree that linguistic/semiotic interpretation can only occur if based on such a trace or mark.

206 Ibid., 33, 141.
207 Opening her argument to claims that she is a naturalist, which she is, but not in the normal sense of the term. See Rouse 2004.
208 Barad 2007, 49, also 55–56 and 180–181 (emphasis in original); Barad 2003, 829.
209 Barad 2007, 152.
210 Ibid., 151, 335. On boundaries, see 154–156.
211 Ibid., 151, 336; Barad 2003, 828.
212 One of the main implications of Barad's framework is that one can only study a phenomenon by comparing two complementary phenomena from within a third phenomenon. Comparable to Luhmann, it is not possible to study a system from within that system.
213 Barad 2007, 71–72.
214 Ibid., 393.
215 Ibid., 369–384.
216 Ibid., 375.
217 Ibid., 348 and 394 (emphasis in original).
218 Squire 2015, 156.
219 Ibid., 157.
220 Barad 2007, 201–222; Aradau 2010, 499.
221 Preda 1999, 350–356. The skills people need to use these machineries result from the intra-action between the machine and the observer and hence are a folding of both.
222 Vint 2008, 316–317.
223 Butler 2009, 14; as quoted by Holmqvist 2013, 549; Braun and Whatmore 2010b, xxv.
224 Dolphijn and Van der Tuin 2012, 69.
225 Tuana 2008, 19 (emphasis in original).
226 Latour 2002, 255.
227 Hekman 2010, 91–93, 127.
228 Bellacasa 2011.
229 Ibid., 100. Booth 2005.
230 Hekman 2010, 73.
231 Squire 2015, 151.
232 Sources of durability, resistance, sedimentation, triggers etc.
233 See also Lemke 2015.
234 Mol 2002, 5.

Bibliography

Adey, Peter, Ben Anderson and Luis Lobo-Guerrero. 2011. An ash cloud, airspace and environmental threat. *Transactions of the Institute of British Geographers* 36 (3): 338–343.

Adler, Emanuel. 1997. Seizing the middle ground: Constructivism in world politics. *European Journal of International Relations* 3 (3): 319–363.

Adler, Emanuel. 2002. Constructivism and international relations. In *Handbook of international relations*, edited by Walter Carlsnaes, Thomas Risse and Beth A. Simmons, 95–119. London: SAGE.

Adorno, Theodor W. 1973. *Negative dialectics*, translated by E. B. Ashton. London: Routledge.

Ahmed, Sara. 2010. Orientations matter. In *New materialisms: Ontology, agency, and politics*, edited by Diana Coole and Samantha Frost, 234–257. Durham, NC, and London: Duke University Press.

Aradau, Claudia. 2010. Security that matters: Critical infrastructure and objects of protection. *Security Dialogue* 41 (5): 491–514.

Arnoldi, Jakob. 2001. Niklas Luhmann: An introduction. *Theory, Culture & Society* 18 (1): 1–13.

Ashley, Richard K., and R. B. J. Walker. 1990. Introduction: Speaking the language of exile: Dissident thought in international studies. *International Studies Quarterly* 34 (3): 259–268.

Barad, Karen. 1996. Meeting the universe halfway: Realism and social constructivism without contradiction. In *Feminism, science, and the philosophy of science*, edited by L. H. Nelson and J. Nelson, 161–194. London: Kluwer.

Barad, Karen. 1998. Getting real: Technoscientific practices and the materialization of reality. *Differences: A Journal of Feminist Cultural Studies* 10 (2): 87–128.

Barad, Karen. 2003. Posthumanist performativity: Toward an understanding of how matter comes to matter. *Signs* 28 (3): 801–831.

Barad, Karen. 2007. *Meeting the universe halfway: Quantum physics and the entanglement of matter and meaning*. Durham, NC, and London: Duke University Press.

Barad, Karen. 2011. Erasers and erasures: Pinch's unfortunate 'uncertainty principle'. *Social Studies of Science* 41 (3): 443–454.

Barry, Andrew. 2013a. Pipelines. In *Globalization in practice*, edited by N. Thrift, Nick Tickell and Steve Woolgar. Oxford: Oxford University Press.

Barry, Andrew. 2013b. *Material politics: Disputes along the pipeline*. Chichester: Wiley Blackwell.

Bellacasa, Maria Puig de la. 2011. Matters of care in technoscience: Assembling neglected things. *Social Studies of Science* 41 (1): 85–106.

Bennett, Jane. 2004. The force of things: Steps toward an ecology of matter. *Political Theory* 32 (3): 347–372.

Bennett, Jane. 2005. The agency of assemblages and the North American blackout. *Public Culture* 17 (3): 445–65.

Bennett, Jane. 2010. *Vibrant matter: A political ecology of things*. Durham, NC, and London: Duke University Press.

Bennett, Jane. 2012. Systems and things: A response to Graham Harman and Timothy Morton. *New Literary History* 43 (2): 225–233.

Bhaskar, Roy. 2005. *A possibility of naturalism: A philosophical critique of the contemporary human sciences*. Third edition. London: Routledge.

Bialasiewicz, Luiza, David Campbell, Stuart Elden, Stephen Graham, Alex Jeffrey, and Alison J. Williams. 2007. Performing security: The imaginative geographies of current US strategy. *Political Geography* 26 (4): 405–422.

Bieri, Peter. 1981. Generelle Einfurung. In *Analytische Philosophie des Geistes*, edited by Peter Bieri, 1–28. Konigstein: Hain.

Booth, Ken. 2005. Security. In *Critical security studies and world politics*, edited by Ken Booth, 21–25. London: Lynne Rienner.

Bourne, Mike. 2012. Guns don't kill people, cyborgs do: A Latourian provocation for transformatory arms control and disarmament. *Global Change, Peace & Security* 24 (1): 141–163.

Braidotti, Rosi. 2010. The politics of 'life itself' and new ways of dying. In *New materialisms: Ontology, agency, and politics*, edited by Diana Coole and Samantha Frost, 201–220. Durham, NC, and London: Duke University Press.

Brassett, James, and Nick Vaughan-Williams. 2015. Security and the performative politics of resilience: Critical infrastructure protection and humanitarian emergency preparedness. *Security Dialogue* 46 (1): 32–50.

Braun, Bruce, and Sarah Whatmore. 2010a. *Political matter: Technoscience, democracy, and public life*. Minneapolis, MN: University of Minnesota Press.

Braun, Bruce, and Sarah Whatmore. 2010b. The stuff of politics: An introduction. In *Political matter: Technoscience, democracy, and public life*, ix–xl. Minneapolis, MN: University of Minnesota Press.

Bridge, Gavin. 2008. Global production networks and the extractive sector: Governing resource-based development. *Journal of Economic Geography* 8 (3): 389–419.

Bryant, Levi R. 2011. The ontic principle: Outline of an object-oriented ontology. In *The speculative turn: Continental materialism and realism*, edited by Levi R. Bryant, Nick Srnicek and Graham Harman, 261–278. Melbourne: re.press.

Bryant, Levi R. 2014. *Onto-cartography: An ontology of machines and media*. Speculative realism. Edinburgh: Edinburgh University Press.

Bryant, Levi R., Nick Srnicek and Graham Harman. 2011. *The speculative turn: Continental materialism and realism*. Melbourne: re.press.

Butler, Judith. 1993. *Bodies that matter: On the discursive limits of 'sex'*. New York: Routledge.

Butler, Judith. 2009. *Frames of war: When is life grievable*. London and New York: Verso.

Butler, Judith. 2010. Performative agency. *Journal of Cultural Economy* 3 (2): 147–161.

Caliskan, Koray, and Michel Callon. 2010. Economization, part 2: A research programme for the study of markets. *Economy and Society* 39 (1): 1–32.

Callon, Michel. 1986. The sociology of an actor-network: The case of the electric vehicle. In *Mapping the dynamics of science and technology*, edited by Michel Callon, John Law and Arie Rip, 19–34. Basingstoke: Macmillan.

Callon, Michel, Pierre Lascoumes and Yannick Barthe. 2009. *Acting in an uncertain world: An essay on technical democracy*, translated by Graham Burchell. London: MIT Press.

Carlsnaes, Walter. 1992. The agency-structure problem in foreign policy analysis. *International Studies Quarterly* 36 (3): 245–270.

Cheah, Pheng. 2008. Nondialectical materialism. *Diacritics* 38 (1–2): 143–157.

Checkel, Jeffrey T. 1998. The constructivist turn in international relations theory. *World Politics* 50 (2): 324–348.

Connolly, William E. 2010. Materialities of experience. In *New materialisms: Ontology, agency, and politics*, edited by Diana Coole and Samantha Frost, 178–200. Durham, NC, and London: Duke University Press.

Connolly, William E. 2013. The 'new materialism' and the fragility of things. *Millennium – Journal of International Studies* 41 (3): 399–412.

Coole, Diana. 2010. The inertia of matter and the generativity of flesh. In *New materialisms: Ontology, agency, and politics*, edited by Diana Coole and Samantha Frost, 92–115. Durham, NC, and London: Duke University Press.

Coole, Diana. 2013. Agentic capacities and capacious historical materialism: Thinking with new materialisms in the political sciences. *Millennium – Journal of International Studies* 41 (3): 451–469.

Coole, Diana, and Samantha Frost. 2010a. Introducing the new materialisms. In *New materialisms: Ontology, agency, and politics*, edited by Diana Coole and Samantha Frost, 1–46. Durham, NC, and London: Duke University Press.

Coole, Diana, and Samantha Frost. eds. 2010b. *New materialisms: Ontology, agency, and politics*. Durham, NC, and London: Duke University Press.

Cox, Robert W. 1981. Social forces, states and world orders: Beyond international relations theory. *Millennium – Journal of International Studies* 10 (2): 126–155.

Cudworth, Erika, and Stephen Hobden. 2011. *Posthuman international relations: Complexity, ecologism and global politics.* London: Zed.

De Goede, Marieke. 2012. *Speculative security: The politics of pursuing terrorist monies.* Minneapolis, MN: University of Minnesota Press.

Deleuze, Gilles. 1994. *Difference and repetition,* translated by Paul Patton. New York: Columbia University Press.

Deleuze, Gilles, and Félix Guattari. 1987. *A thousand plateaus: Capitalism and schizophrenia,* translated by Brian Massumi. Minneapolis, MN: University of Minnesota Press.

Der Derian, James. 2009. *Critical practices in international theory: Selected essays.* London and New York: Routledge.

Der Derian, James, and Michael J. Shapiro, eds. 1989. *International/intertextual relations: Postmodern readings of world politics.* New York: Lexington.

Derrida, Jacques. 1976. *Of grammatology.* Baltimore, MD: Johns Hopkins University Press.

Derrida, Jacques. 2005. *Writing and difference,* translated by Alan Bass. London and New York: Routledge.

Dillon, Michael, and Julian Reid. 2001. Global liberal governance: Biopolitics, security and war. *Millennium – Journal of International Studies* 30 (1): 41–66.

Dolphijn, Rick, and Iris Van der Tuin. 2012. *New materialism: Interviews & cartographies.* Ann Arbor, MI: Open Humanities Press. Available from http://hdl.handle.net/2027/spo.11515701.0001.001. Accessed 12 June 2013.

Dolwick, Jim S. 2009. 'The social' and beyond: Introducing actor-network theory. *Journal of Maritime Archaeology* 4 (1): 21–49.

Doty, Roxanne Lynn. 1997. Aporia: A critical exploration of the agent-structure problematique in international relations theory. *European Journal of International Relations* 3 (3): 365–392.

Farías, Ignacio. 2014. Virtual attractors, actual assemblages: How Luhmann's theory of communication complements actor-network theory. *European Journal of Social Theory* 17 (1): 24–41.

Fierke, K. M. 2002. Links across the abyss: Language and logic in international relations. *International Studies Quarterly* 46 (3): 331–354.

Fine, Ben. 2005. From actor-network theory to political economy. *Capitalism Nature Socialism* 16 (4): 91–108.

Foucault, Michel. 1977. *Discipline and punish: The birth of the prison,* translated by Alan Sheridan. New York: Vintage.

Giddens, Anthony. 1986. *The constitution of society: Outline of the theory of structuration.* Berkeley and Los Angeles, CA: University of California Press.

Grosz, Elizabeth A. 2010. Feminism, materialism, and freedom. In *New materialisms: Ontology, agency, and politics,* edited by Diana Coole and Samantha Frost, 139–157. Durham, NC, and London: Duke University Press.

Grove, Jairus Victor. 2011. *Becoming war: Ecology, ethics, and the globalization of violence.* PhD thesis, Baltimore, MD: Johns Hopkins University.

Grove, Jairus Victor. 2014. Ecology as critical security method. *Critical Studies on Security* 2 (3): 366–369.

Guzzini, Stefano. 2000. A reconstruction of constructivism in international relations. *European Journal of International Relations* 6 (2): 147–182.

Guzzini, Stefano. 2001. *Another sociology for IR? An analysis of Niklas Luhmann's conceptualisation of power.* Paper prepared for the 42nd Annual convention of the International Studies Association in Chicago.

Habermas, Jürgen. 1984. *The theory of communicative action: Volume 1: Reason and the rationalization of society*. Boston, MA: Beacon Press.

Harman, Graham. 2009. *Prince of networks: Bruno Latour and metaphysics*. Melbourne: re.press.

Hekman, Susan J. 2010. *The material of knowledge feminist disclosures*. Bloomington, IN: Indiana University Press.

Herborth, Benjamin. 2012. Theorising theorising: Critical realism and the quest for certainty. *Review of International Studies* 38 (01): 235–251.

Holmqvist, Caroline. 2013. Undoing war: War ontologies and the materiality of drone warfare. *Millennium – Journal of International Studies* 41 (3): 535–552.

Hopf, Ted. 1998. The promise of constructivism in international relations theory. *International Security* 23 (1): 171–200.

Jackson, Patrick Thaddeus. 2002. Rethinking Weber: Towards a non-individualist sociology of world politics. *International Review of Sociology* 12 (3): 439–468.

Jackson, Patrick Thaddeus. 2008. Foregrounding ontology: Dualism, monism, and IR theory. *Review of International Studies* 34 (01): 129–153.

Jackson, Patrick Thaddeus. 2010. *The conduct of inquiry in international relations: Philosophy of science and its implications for the study of world politics*. London and New York: Routledge.

Jackson, Patrick Thaddeus. 2012. *Fear of relativism*. 2. Vol. 2. Working Paper. The Duck of Minerva.

Joseph, Jonathan, and Colin Wight, eds. 2010. *Scientific realism and international relations*. Basingstoke and New York: Palgrave Macmillan.

Kessler, Oliver. 2007. From agents and structures to minds and bodies: Of supervenience, quantum, and the linguistic turn. *Journal of International Relations and Development* 10 (3): 243–271.

Kessler, Oliver. 2009. Toward a logic of social systems? *International Political Sociology* 3 (1): 132–136.

Kessler, Oliver. 2012a. World society, social differentiation and time. *International Political Sociology* 6 (1): 77–94.

Kessler, Oliver. 2012b. On logic, intersubjectivity, and meaning: Is reality an assumption we just don't need? *Review of International Studies* 38 (01): 253–265.

Kratochwil, Friedrich. 2000. Constructing a new orthodoxy? Wendt's 'social theory of international politics' and the constructivist challenge. *Millennium – Journal of International Studies* 29 (1): 73–101.

Kratochwil, Friedrich. 2007a. Of communities, gangs, historicity and the problem of Santa Claus: Replies to my critics. *Journal of International Relations and Development* 10 (1): 57–78.

Kratochwil, Friedrich. 2007b. Of false promises and good bets: A plea for a pragmatic approach to theory building (the Tartu lecture). *Journal of International Relations and Development* 10 (1): 1–15.

Latour, Bruno. 2002. Morality and technology: The end of the means. Translated by C. Venn. *Theory, Culture & Society* 19 (5–6): 247–260.

Latour, Bruno. 2004. Why has critique run out of steam? From matters of fact to matters of concern. *Critical inquiry* 30 (2): 225–248.

Latour, Bruno. 2005. *Reassembling the social: An introduction to actor-network-theory*. Oxford: Oxford University Press.

Latour, Bruno, Graham Harman, and P. Erdelyi. 2011. *The prince and the wolf: Latour and Harman at the LSE*. Alresford: Zero.

Law, John. 1992. Notes on the theory of the actor-network: Ordering, strategy, and heterogeneity. *Systemic Practice and Action Research* 5 (4): 379–393.

Law, John. 2007. Actor network theory and material semiotics. Available from www.heterogeneities.net/publications/Law2007ANTandMaterialSemiotics.pdf. Accessed 7 January 2013.

Law, John, and Annemarie Mol. 1995. Notes on materiality and sociality. *The Sociological Review* 43 (2): 274–294.

Le Billon, Philippe. 2007. Geographies of war: Perspectives on 'resource wars'. *Geography Compass* 1 (2): 163–182.

Lemke, Thomas. 2002. Foucault, governmentality, and critique. *Rethinking Marxism* 14 (3): 49–64.

Lemke, Thomas. 2015. New materialisms: Foucault and the 'government of things'. *Theory, Culture & Society* 32 (4): 3–25.

Loxley, James. 2007. *Performativity*. London and New York: Routledge.

Luhmann, Niklas. 1993. *Risk: A sociological theory*. Berlin and New York: Walter de Gruyter.

Luhmann, Niklas. 1995. *Social systems*, translated by John Jr. Bednarz and Dirk Baecker. Stanford, CA: Stanford University Press.

Luhmann, Niklas. 2006. System as difference. *Organization* 13 (1): 37–57.

Lundborg, Tom, and Nick Vaughan-Williams. 2015. New Materialisms, discourse analysis, and international relations: A radical intertextual approach. *Review of International Studies* 41 (1): 3–25.

Marres, Noortje. 2005. *No issue, no public: Democratic deficits after the displacement of politics*. PhD thesis, Amsterdam: University of Amsterdam.

McCarthy, Daniel R. 2011. The meaning of materiality: Reconsidering the materialism of Gramscian IR. *Review of International Studies* 37 (03): 1215–1234.

McCarthy, Daniel R. 2013. Technology and 'the international' or: How I learned to stop worrying and love determinism. *Millennium – Journal of International Studies* 41 (3): 470–490.

Meyer, Christoph O., and Eva Strickmann. 2011. Solidifying constructivism: How material and ideational factors interact in European defence. *JCMS: Journal of Common Market Studies* 49 (1): 61–81.

Miller, Daniel. 2005. Materiality: An introduction. In *Materiality*, edited by Daniel Miller, 1–50. Durham, NC, and London: Duke University Press.

Milliken, Jennifer. 1999. The study of discourse in international relations: A critique of research and methods. *European journal of international relations* 5 (2): 225–254.

Mitchell, Timothy. 2013. *Carbon democracy: Political power in the age of oil*. London: Verso.

Mol, Annemarie. 1999. Ontological politics. A word and some questions. *The Sociological Review* 47 (S1): 74–89.

Mol, Annemarie. 2002. *The body multiple: Ontology in medical practice*. Durham, NC, and London: Duke University Press.

Onuf, Nicholas Greenwood. 2013. *World of our making: Rules and rule in social theory and international relations*. Reissue. New York: Routledge.

Patomäki, Heikki, and Colin Wight. 2000. After postpositivism? The promises of critical realism. *International Studies Quarterly* 44 (2): 213–237.

Pels, Dick, Kevin Hetherington and Frédéric Vandenberghe. 2002. The status of the object: Performances, mediations, and techniques. *Theory, Culture & Society* 19 (5–6): 1–21.

Piazza, L., T. T. A. Lummen, E. Quiñonez, Y. Murooka, B. W. Reed, B. Barwick and F. Carbone. 2015. Simultaneous observation of the quantization and the interference pattern of a plasmonic near-field. *Nature Communications* 6 (7407).

Pickering, Andrew. 1993. The mangle of practice: Agency and emergence in the sociology of science. *American Journal of Sociology* 99 (3): 559–589.

Pickering, Andrew. 1999. Explanation and the mangle: A response to my critics. *Studies in History and Philosophy of Science Part A* 30 (1): 167–171.

Pouliot, Vincent. 2004. The essence of constructivism. *Journal of International Relations and Development* 7 (3): 319–336.

Preda, Alex. 1999. The turn to things: Arguments for a sociological theory of things. *The Sociological Quarterly* 40 (2): 347–366.

Reus-Smit, Christian. 1996. *The constructivist turn: critical theory after the Cold War*. Working Paper. Canberra: National Library of Australia.

Robinson, Howard. 2012. Dualism. In *The Stanford encyclopedia of philosophy*, edited by Edward N. Zalta. Available from http://plato.stanford.edu/archives/win2012/entries/dualism. Accessed 13 February 2015.

Rouse, Joseph. 2004. Barad's feminist naturalism. *Hypatia* 19 (1): 142–161.

Rozema, Lee A., Ardavan Darabi, Dylan H. Mahler, Alex Hayat, Yasaman Soudagar and Aephraim M. Steinberg. 2012. Violation of Heisenberg's measurement-disturbance relationship by weak measurements. *Physical Review Letters* 109 (10): 100404.

Schouten, Peer. 2014. Security as controversy: Reassembling security at Amsterdam Airport. *Security Dialogue* 45 (1): 23–42.

Searle, John R. 1995. *The construction of social reality*. New York: Simon and Schuster.

Sewell, William H. 1992. A theory of structure: Duality, agency, and transformation. *American Journal of Sociology* 98 (1): 1–29.

Sorensen, George. 2008. The case for combining material forces and ideas in the study of IR. *European Journal of International Relations* 14 (1): 5–32.

Squire, Vicki. 2015. Reshaping critical geopolitics? The materialist challenge. *Review of International Studies* 41 (01): 139–159.

Srnicek, Nick, Maria Fotou, and Edmund Arghand. 2013. Introduction: Materialism and world politics. *Millennium – Journal of International Studies* 41 (3): 397–397.

Star, Susan Leigh. 1999. The ethnography of infrastructure. *American Behavioral Scientist* 43 (3): 377–391.

Stengers, Isabelle. 2010. Including nonhumans in political theory: Opening Pandoras box? In *Political matter: Technoscience, democracy, and public life*, edited by Bruce Braun and Sarah Whatmore, 3–34. Minneapolis, MN: University of Minnesota Press.

Stengers, Isabelle. 2011. Wondering about materialism. In *The speculative turn: Continental materialism and realism*, edited by Levi R. Bryant, Nick Srnicek and Graham Harman, 368–380. Melbourne: re.press.

Suganami, Hidemi. 2013. Causation-in-the-world: A contribution to meta-theory of IR. *Millennium – Journal of International Studies* 41 (3): 623–643.

Tannenwald, Nina. 2005. Stigmatizing the bomb: Origins of the nuclear taboo. *International Security* 29 (4): 5–49.

Tuana, Nancy. 2008. Witnessing Katrina: Re/cognizing nature for socially responsible science. In *Material feminisms*, edited by Stacy Alaimo, 188–213. Bloomington, IN: Indiana University Press.

Van der Tuin, Iris. 2011. The new materialist 'always already': On an a-human humanities. *NORA – Nordic Journal of Feminist and Gender Research* 19 (4): 285–290.

Vint, Sherryl. 2008. Entangled posthumanism. *Science Fiction Studies* 35 (2): 313–319.

Voelkner, Nadine. 2011. Managing pathogenic circulation human security and the migrant health assemblage in Thailand. *Security Dialogue* 42 (3): 239–259.

Walters, William. 2014. Drone strikes, dingpolitik and beyond: Furthering the debate on materiality and security. *Security Dialogue* 45 (2): 101–118.

Wendt, Alexander E. 1987. The agent-structure problem in international relations theory. *International Organization* 41 (3): 335–370.

Wendt, Alexander E. 1999. *Social theory of international politics*. Cambridge and New York: Cambridge University Press.

Whatmore, Sarah. 2006. Materialist returns: Practising cultural geography in and for a more-than-human world. *Cultural Geographies* 13 (4): 600–609.

Wight, Colin. 2000. Interpretation all the way down?: A reply to Roxanne Lynn Doty. *European Journal of International Relations* 6 (3): 423–430.

Wight, Colin. 2007a. Inside the epistemological cave all bets are off. *Journal of International Relations and Development* 10 (1): 40–56.

Wight, Colin. 2007b. A manifesto for scientific realism in IR: Assuming the can-opener won't work! *Millennium – Journal of International Studies* 35 (2): 379–398.

Wight, Colin. 2012. Critical realism: Some responses. *Review of International Studies* 38 (01): 267–274.

Winner, Langdon. 1980. Do artifacts have politics? *Daedalus* 109 (1): 121–136.

Wittgenstein, Ludwig. 1922. *Tractatus logico-philosophicus*, translated by C. K. Ogden. London: Kegan Paul, Trechn, Trubner.

Wittgenstein, Ludwig. 1958. *Philosophical investigations*, translated by G. E. M. Anscombe. 2nd edn. Oxford: Basil Blackwell.

6 Governing with and through energy security

6.1 Introduction

Whereas previous chapters described security and materialization, this chapter tries to combine many of the insights that are gathered there by introducing the work of an author who seems to have written on all of them, yet is underutilized in relation to energy security.[1] In the security chapter, the risk literature discussed calculative metrics applied to populations to define the norm of acceptable behaviour. In turn, the materiality chapter discussed materialization, the performative politics through which reiterative discursive acts become material (and vice versa), and the role that knowledge gathering practices play within this materialization. Both of these insights are based on the work of the French philosopher Michel Foucault, who developed a theoretical framework to understand the power politics and knowledge structures that govern our lives.[2] For Foucault, the relation between security, materiality and knowledge needs to be seen in close connection to power. He draws attention to the power/knowledge nexus that enables discourse to materialize and security to act as a governance technique that makes this happen. In short, with Foucault's understanding of governmentality it becomes possible to analyse the role of security by studying the techniques and social structures (the mentalities and rationalities) that are used to exercise power over a population within a political economic knowledge base to organize, regulate and order the circulation behind human reality.[3] While this is a mouthful, this chapter will explain each element in turn.

In fact, this chapter draws four arguments from the work of Foucault. First, it explicitly understands security as a productive form of power. Productive security implies a performative understanding of security, meaning that ideas about (energy) security help govern and produce a specific way of life (e.g. high-energy consumption) through the creation of subjects, markets and the materialization of its concerns. Second, it is not possible to secure something, through risk or other security practices, when people do not know what it is that needs securing. Security, earlier interpreted broadly as undesired futures, hence is a prime example of ontic politics: the identification of that what needs to be secured and the politics of knowledge and observation that guide it. Third, security works as it performs bodies, minds, objects and the material world around us. More specific, security works increasingly in one of two ways. Either by governing the milieu of the humans or objects that need governing or else by letting the people involved govern themselves based on shared understandings of normal and acceptable behaviour. Fourth, based on Foucault's theory, this chapter examines how security functions in relation to society, governments, the economy and nature, and how the boundaries between these fields are constantly performed and redefined through the rearticulation of these concepts, logics and modes of reasoning.

This chapter proceeds by introducing the concept of *governmentality* in Section 6.2 as part of the theoretical framework behind Foucault's notion of security and risk. To introduce governmentality, this chapter delves deeply into Foucault's understanding of the *conduct of conduct*, his understanding of *power* and his concept of *biopolitics*. Following the identification of *biopower* as a new form of power in the early eighteenth century, and the active use of this form of power under the header of biopolitics, Section 6.3 will continue the discussion of governmentality by studying the relation between government, markets and society. A particular form of governmentality that is discussed here is neo-liberalism: how freedom is organized through security and how neo-liberalism actively works to separate economics from politics and society. Section 6.4 will bring the different notions together, by focusing respectively on the relations between materiality and governmentality, between knowledge and materiality and between security and materiality. This chapter ends with a brief summary and reflection.

6.2 Foucault on security, power and politics

6.2.1 Conduct of conduct

To guide the reader through the rest of this chapter, five initial remarks can be made on Foucault's overarching concept of governmentality. First, governmentality is said to link the French words *gouverner* and *mentalité*.[4] By including the French term for governing, the concept of governmentality seems to refer to a modern definition of governing, as in the 'management by the state or the administration'.[5] Foucault, however, uses governing more broadly by referring to its classical Greek use, where it meant both the management of *the household* (*oeconomia*), one's soul and oneself.[6] As will become clear below, for Foucault, governmentality or:

> the art of government ... is essentially concerned with answering the question of how to introduce economy – that is to say, the correct manner of managing individuals, goods and wealth ... and of making the family fortunes prosper – how to introduce this meticulous attention of the father towards his family into the management of the state.[7]

Second, Foucault captures this triple understanding of government with his *conduct of conduct*, a concept that he explains as the 'activity of conducting' and by which he refers to both the directing of someone and the 'way in which one conducts oneself [and] lets oneself be conducted'.[8] In his reflection on governmentality, Dean actually presents three forms of conduct that are captured with this concept. Dean separates the verb 'to conduct', which describes the act of conducting, from the noun 'conduct' describing bad and proper behaviour, and a third form of conduct that describes the ethical self-reflection of how one conducts oneself.[9] In other words, governmentality is not just about a form of governing from above, by the state or someone in authority, but it is as much a form of governing by people themselves through a reflection on what they think is 'appropriate'. Good examples of governing oneself are dieting or working out: whether for health or aesthetic reasons, people practise them because they are constantly confronted by pictures of beautiful models and warnings about unhealthy lifestyles: messages that structure how people think about themselves and thus how they behave in relation to their body, to the food they buy and to others.

Third, directing this reflexive behaviour, this bombarding or nudging of people in a certain direction is where the latter half of the term governmentality, namely *mentalité*, comes in. Better translated in its plural as *rationalities of government*, a mentality is described by Gordon as a 'system of thinking about the nature of the practice of government (who can govern; what governing is; what or who is governed), capable of making some form of that activity thinkable and practicable both to its practitioners and to those upon whom it was practised'.[10] It is only by questioning and becoming aware of these invisible and hidden forms of power that one can study them.[11] Fourth, for Foucault the connection between these two forms of governing, from above and from the self, is his main object of study. It is at this intersection where one can see resistance brewing, questions being asked, and uncertainty being made certain again. Not as something tangible, because there is no physical place where these forms of power meet, but as a balance of forces that no person or organization can escape.[12]

Fifth, Foucault shunned polemics and deliberately focused on *how* questions.[13] His thinking on governmentality, therefore, does not provide guidance for future decisions, nor does it provide a map to follow if you have a desire for power. His main argument not to do so is epistemological, namely that reasons are always provided ex post facto, after the event, and thus originate from within a system of thought and consequentially are always already polemic. Arguing that something is 'good' means that one has already drawn a boundary that excludes the 'bad'. Defining the good and bad thus depends on the rationality to which one adheres. For an economist, a core priority is often the organization of free markets to reduce overall transaction costs and improve efficiency and profits, but that is clearly not the priority for somebody who identifies primarily as a climate activist. These five points will be explained more extensively in the rest of chapter, but already it is possible to see how Foucault focuses on techniques of power and modes of thought to govern people, how the relationship between economics and politics is enacted, and, as we will see, what role security and risk play within this notion of governmentality.

6.2.2 Power

It is not just the concept of governing that Foucault sees differently. Another, closely related, concept is power.

> Foucault teaches that power is less a commodity that can be held than a force which comes into circulation when human beings – who he considers to be free beings – come into relation with one another. To be crude, power as a force that circulates is more like electricity than it is like a lever or a sword.[14]

Power, for Foucault, is thus not something tangible nor is it intentional. It is not the light switch but everything that lies behind one's ability and desire to pull the switch. It has no source and no end, but it shifts and transforms. It is 'located and exercised at the level of life' and as such seems to resemble life.[15] Moreover, because it resembles life, Foucault argues that power is not only restrictive but productive as well. It produces subjects: individuals behaving within and conform a particular system of thought (a rationality of government).[16] That said, while it is impossible to touch power, it is still possible to analyse it, something that Foucault manages by differentiating between multiple forms of power, namely sovereignty, discipline and biopower.

The first form of power is sovereign power or the power of the prince. An often-quoted description that captures Foucault's understanding of sovereign power is 'the right to take life or let live'.[17] In the endorsed ability to order a death, the sovereign is able to govern life. As a form of power, sovereign power is aimed at the good of the prince against both internal and external opposition (other princes). The survival or 'good' of the sovereign was seen in terms of the strength of arms, which consequently was translated in the number and well-being of the population within his territory,[18] in other words on the number and wealth of his *subjects*.[19] Sovereign power works through both judicial instruments (laws, degrees) and instruments of control (punishment). Such a feudal form of sovereign power is no longer applicable and Foucault noticed how, within a modern state, power is actually dispersed over state officials, mothers, teachers, bosses, generals etc. In other words, lots of individuals and institutes have some form of sovereign power. This 'plurality of forms of government' or 'the multiplicity and immanence of these activities distinguishes them radically from the transcendent singularity of Machiavelli's prince'.[20]

A second form of power identified by Foucault is discipline. Foucault's insight regarding discipline is that the training and conditioning of individuals in schools or armies, while being applied *on* the individual is in reality concentrated on the group as a whole.[21] People are disciplined towards what is considered to be useful knowledge or correct behaviour. 'Discipline, of course, analyzes and breaks down; it breaks down individuals, places, time, movements, actions, and operations. It breaks them down into components such that they can be seen, on the one hand, and modified on the other.'[22] In other words, discipline separates those that 'behave' from those that do not and exercises itself on the latter. It does so by exercising its power on a micro level, meaning the individual body, by correcting towards a norm that applies to the whole group.[23] Foucault for that reason argued in a later work that discipline is not just about 'normalization' or the correction of the bad, but about 'normation' or the diffusion of the norm itself.[24] As a form of power, discipline is of interest for Foucault because it shifts the focus from the prince and his subject to an individual body as part of a particular population.[25]

Foucault's third form of power is what he sometimes discusses as security but initially identified as biopower. Biopower, according to Foucault, is a form of power that combines aspects of both disciplinary and sovereign power, but is more than just a combination of the two. From discipline, it takes the focus on populations and the role of individuals. From sovereign power, it takes the focus on life and well-being. Importantly, however, is that in relation to life and well-being the focus of biopower shifts from 'taking lives' to 'making live and letting die'.[26] In other words, it differs from both as biopower is mostly a productive form of power. Literally *productive*, as it deals with biological 'matters of life and death' and thus 'with birth and propagation, with health and illness … and with the processes that sustain or retard the optimization of the life of a population'.[27] Biopower is the power to increase life and decrease death through policies that are based on birth and mortality rates and explicitly aimed at influencing those rates. This is what Dean calls 'the administration of life' or what Foucault in his earlier work described as 'regulation' and later called 'biopolitics' (a concept that is taken up below).[28]

These three forms of power differ. Discipline and biopower differ on the level at which their power is effected, with discipline focusing on the individual body while biopower concentrates on the level of populations.[29] They differ as well in that biopower, by focusing on biological life, works on 'a number of material givens', while discipline instead first 'determines a segment' of the overall population by 'isolat[ing] a space' for itself to work on – those that are in need of disciplining.[30] As a form of power, discipline only works within this site, but once set 'allows nothing to escape'.[31] In contrast, biopower has no boundaries and constantly expands to new areas and spaces, depending on what is known about life and deemed necessary to enhance that life. Most of all, the forms of power differ on the level of the individual. Whereas discipline makes a normative judgement on the behaviour of the individual and sovereignty subjugates the individual to the will of the sovereign, biopower instead takes the behaviour of individuals for granted and acts only on those effects that are considered consequential for the population as a whole.[32] While they differ, Foucault is explicit in arguing that they do not exclude one another and always return in specific combinations.[33] And, through these combinations, these three forms of power make up particular forms of governmentality.

6.2.3 Biopolitics

As a form of power, biopower quickly conflates with biopolitics: the actual administration of life, or, as the concept implies, the *politics* or strategies of biopower. While biopolitics is about the politics of life, it is neither a form of power nor a mode of governmentality. Instead, Foucault sees it as a technology of power, Collier describes it as a 'problem space to be analyzed' (as does Foucault), while Dillon and Lobo-Guerrero argue that 'there is no biopolitics which is not simultaneously also a security apparatus. There is no biopolitics of this, or a biopolitics of that. When one says biopolitics one says security, albeit in a certain way.'[34] Biopolitics is all that because it administers biological life, not through the individual as with discipline but by influencing the conditions or the milieu of individuals based on the knowledge it has gathered over the population that needs to be secured. Instead of feeding the hungry, biopolitics is about setting up the conditions for people to feed themselves by enabling and supporting a circulation of food. Ultimately, biopolitics tries to bring out the full potential of individuals, a 'potential [which] is sought to be promoted, enhanced and, in the process, protected'.[35] This full potential needs to be *protected* against the 'random element inherent in a population of living beings'.[36] Accidents happen and they are highly uncertain for individuals. Yet, accidents happen all the time, so statistically on the level of the population they are far from uncertain (e.g. insurance). In other words, to administer life and protect the well-being of a population, what is needed are security apparatuses or techniques and mechanisms aimed at the 'objects' of 'species life' by gathering and acting upon the assessed numbers available on a population.[37]

Even in this brief description of biopolitics, a number of terms stand out and call for further inquiry; these are population and statistics, prosperity and potential, things and the milieu, and security. First, biopolitics is geared towards populations. Foucault identifies the advent of biopolitics in the shift when wars were no longer fought in 'the defense of the sovereign' but instead were aimed 'to secur[e] the existence of a population'.[38] Before the idea and ability to think in terms of populations, government was aimed either at the level of the sovereign, as the head of the state, or at the level of the family, as the Greek did when describing the *oeconomia* as the management of the family. Combining both levels only became possible with the invention of statistics, through which it became possible to gain knowledge at the level of the population.[39] When Malthus advanced his food scarcity dilemma, it was based on his insight about the 'bio-economic problem' of a limited area for food production and a faster-growing *population*.[40]

Statistics, in Foucault's argument, developed along two tracks: on the one hand, with the organization of the police and, on the other, with the evolution of mercantilism.[41] Police, as a form of government that is internal to the state, is said by Foucault to be aimed at securing and increasing the domestic output of the state. It is concerned with the protection of active life, especially those activities that relate to the state. This implies that the number and safety of the population, their basic needs, their health and their productivity are all subject to this form of government. Importantly, before the police can secure all of this, it needs to know what to secure.[42] In other words, to protect life it is necessary to know life. Foucault argues in this respect that 'police makes statistics necessary, but police also makes statistics possible'.[43]

The biopolitical use of statistics, second, is thus aimed at the well-being of the state.[44] In this modern form of power the goal is no longer the well-being of the prince and his tax revenue but the conditions for the well-being and potential of the population. This well-being and 'making life proliferate' has been interpreted, from the Greek household *oeconomia* onwards and especially since the sixteenth-century physiocrats, as being first and foremost about 'good economic government'.[45] A good example of this can be found in Foucault's discussion of scarcity and how the main idea behind the government of scarce food supplies shifted from mercantilism to liberalism.[46] Foucault describes how food shortages in France were originally seen as either an unlucky event caused by bad weather or as a consequence of 'man's evil nature' (his never-ending desire and unwillingness to share).[47] The reigning mercantilists countered scarcity through an 'anti-scarcity system' that tried to control all economic and trade related aspects of it through price controls, hoarding prohibitions, export restrictions, import diversification and the stockpiling of reserves.[48] In other words, mercantilism tried to govern scarce food supplies by introducing 'laws, decrees, regulations: that is to say, the traditional weapons of sovereignty'.[49] As it fixed prices and organized distribution, it also stifled incentives to increase food production during periods of scarcity and thereby prolonged the shortage periods.[50] Foucault noted how a strand of scholars called the physiocrats hence argued for what now would be seen as a more liberal programme: one that moved away from 'the obsessive fear of scarcity' to 'the reality of grain' and trusted the markets to minimize scarcity by letting prices fluctuate and goods circulate in order to provide individuals incentives to counter a shortage.[51] Basically, as Dean remarks, 'the discovery of the ontological reality of scarcity … mean[t] that the administration of life must take into account the means of production for the subsistence of that life'.[52] However, as these means cannot be controlled by the state directly, the government had to find a way to let go and let the market handle it (while indirectly governing people by managing the undesired elements of these markets).

Third, the discovery of the 'reality of scarcity' and the 'means of production' implies that what is governed through biopolitics are things, not people alone. Whereas sovereignty exercises its power on a particular territory, biopolitics exercises its power on the conditions that enable people to live freely; in other words, on the things they relate to. Foucault takes a broad perspective on these 'things'. He sees them as material, that is, things like resources or the weather. He also sees them as 'men in their relationships with things', by which he focuses on the 'customs, habits, ways of acting and thinking' through which men and things relate.[53] Finally, Foucault describes these things as uncertain events, events like 'accidents, misfortunes, famine, epidemics and death' that result from 'men in their relationship with things',[54] in other words the uncertainty inherent in life, which is discussed as undesired futures in Chapter 4 and as surprising events in Chapter 5. Biopolitics works on these things: it 'disposes' of them using different forms of power to achieve the desired goal of an affluent population.[55]

Fourth, not only is biopolitics a governing of individuals through the things they relate to, it is also a form of governing based on a certain 'naturalness'.[56] Since the physiocrats, the well-being of a population has been based on the laws of the market. While these laws are not part of nature as such – they stem from the interaction between people – they are seen as natural, as a given. This naturalness results, according to Foucault, in a separation of the state and the economy.[57] Gordon in fact describes this 'naturalized' way of thinking in terms of a 'transformation in the relationship between knowledge and government'.[58] He sees it as an internalization at the side of the government of the liberal argument that it can never know the economy completely and therefore can never govern it completely.[59]

Fifth, just as the category *population* combines the state with the household, it also bridges the individual and his environment, a point Foucault takes from Darwin and his focus on the survival and evolution of the species within a particular *milieu*.[60] The milieu for Foucault is both a medium and an element. The milieu is a medium as it 'is needed to account for action at a distance of one body on another', while it is simultaneously the 'element in which it circulates'.[61] As both medium and element, the milieu offers a circular reasoning of cause and effect between those parts of the milieu that affect and those that are affected.[62] In more general terms, the milieu, for Foucault, is 'a certain number of combined, overall effects' of the above-mentioned people in their relationship with things and each other. In recent commentaries, the milieu is often translated in terms of a flat network analogy, where everything is connected in constant circulation across time and space.[63] Through such a relational analogy, discussed in Chapter 5, the milieu bridges the social environment of people with their material environment.

To govern such a milieu, filled with men, things, mentalities and uncertainties, biopolitics aims to administer the conditions of life while remaining open to life itself, in other words to deal with the complexity and uncertainty inherent in the relations that make up life itself.[64] Foucault describes biopolitics consequentially as a *security apparatus* (also security dispotif or mechanism). Such a security apparatus tries to manage the constant uncertainty of life by 'plan[ning] a milieu in terms of events or series of events or [its] possible elements'.[65] Biopolitics does not govern humans directly but focuses on their conduct by:

> structuring the desires, proprieties and possibilities that shape the operation of life working on and through subjective freedoms, governmental rationalities typically develop around specific problematics, such as those of health, wealth, security, poverty, esteem, culture, sexuality or migration.[66]

Alternatively, as Renzi and Elmer state it:

> At the same time, government is no longer exercised directly on the subjects but through interventions that both safeguard and actively produce the conditions for free exchange, circulation and competition, while expanding and intensifying mechanisms of social control and surveillance.[67]

While firmly driven by security considerations, biopolitics thus has a clear economic focus, a focus that does not influence people by controlling their (economic) freedom through laws but by nudging what they desire and by what they see as possible; in other words, by administering the freedom that individuals experience.[68] Freedom in this perspective is something that is constantly constructed through the particular ways that we understand a problem and what we see as appropriate behaviour. As Amoore concludes, connecting the statements above, 'in contrast to a world in which biopolitics eclipses sovereign and disciplinary power, we see a security apparatus that mobilizes specific techniques for deploying the norm to govern uncertain and unfolding populations'.[69]

6.3 Governing people, markets and the milieu

6.3.1 *Governmentality*

Whereas biopolitics (security), sovereign power and discipline are techniques of power, Foucault sees governmentality simultaneously as a technique and as something more than a technique. Foucault writes that he sees governmentality in three ways: as an ensemble, as a mode of power (equating it with biopower), and as a process. Governmentality refers to the *ensemble* of 'institutions, procedures, analyses and reflections, calculations, and tactics' that exercises itself as a form of power.[70] In turn, as a form of *power* governmentality has overshadowed other types of power (sovereignty, discipline), which are now only active under governmentality. This follows the creation of the modern state based on the development of an evolving administrative *process* from the Middle Ages onward, which is the third meaning of governmentality. To be clear, the state itself is not driving this process. On the contrary: the state is an outcome, a tactic according to Lemke, of governmentality.[71] Governmentality is 'the tactics of government that allow the continual definition of what should or should not fall within the state's domain, what is public and what private, what is and is not within the state's competence, and so on'.[72] Within this constant judging of its domain, Dean remarks how a failure to govern has the peculiar effect of reinforcing the actual governmentality process.[73] In line with the discussion on how failed security leads to more security, governmentality as a mode of power continues even when its programmes have failed.

Governmentality stems from what Foucault has identified as the *pastoral* mentalité and the mentalité of raison d'état. The pastoral mentalité, the Christian understanding of a shepherd herding a flock, is explained by Foucault as 'a subtle economy of merit and fault' where power is not applied on individuals but through them.[74] It is a teleological economy that creates obedient subjects or people who see themselves as sheep needing to be saved and are situated within a certain system of knowledge based on a particular truth, in this case the word of God that can be found in scripture. Within this rationality, the merits and faults of the individual are analysed by the pastor, atonements are transferred and penance is offered for the individual to reach salvation. A pastoral mentalité is thus guiding, instead of forcing, individuals as part of the population for the good of the individual, instead of the state or the sovereign.[75]

A more modern form of pastoral power can be found, according to Foucault, in the above-discussed 'police government' as this has a similar economy of merit and faults.[76] Of course, the economy of a police government is not driven by salvation and obedience to God but by raison d'état or the survival of the state itself. Based on statistics and calculation, the state, by way of its authoritative subjects (police officers and other representatives of the state), learns of itself and acts on itself through its population. Ultimately, it tries to produce happy individuals by protecting processes of circulation (of people, goods, ideas) and by separating good from bad circulation, for the simple reason that happy citizens are also economically active and useful citizens who strengthen the state, especially in comparison to other states and their populations.[77]

In building on both the pastoral economy of merits and faults and the calculation and statistics of raison d'état, governmentality introduces an even larger focus on economic reasoning and thereby increases the separation of economics and society.[78] In each of the mentalités discussed so far, individuals are subjectivized as part of a population within a particular system of knowledge containing a particular truth. Foucault even argues that 'to become individual one must become subject'.[79] In other words, while Western citizens consider themselves free individuals, they are only free because they have become subjects. Whether that is to a technology of the self (self-reflection), a form of discipline, or a technology of the market (promoted circulation) is irrelevant. People are free because they are made to think and act as if they were free. They are only free, as Hayek argues, owing 'to restraints of freedom'.[80] In other words, as stated before, the only freedom people have is the freedom that is provided, organized and secured.

This hints at the wider relations between the state, economy and society.[81] Governmentality builds on a Marxist-inspired separation of political and non-political spheres, with society and the economy as clear examples. By accepting the reality of grain, the early physiocrats worked hard to make the economy into a non-political sphere as they separated it from sovereign forms of control based on, first, the unknowability of the total economic process (ungovernable) and, second, the 'naturalness' of the economic relations between men (e.g. Smith's invisible hand).[82] Because the sovereign or government cannot know all the processes related to the economic circulation of men and things, it cannot act upon them. A liberal organized economy, according to Foucault, therefore always assumes that 'one always governs too much' and in reaction tries to organize government as cost-effectively as possible.[83] In Foucauldian terms, the market (e.g. the naturalness of economic processes that cumulate in and are visualized by prices) becomes 'a standard of truth' that is used to judge 'governmental practices'.[84] Still, while government can only act indirectly (as described above), this does not mean that economics is the 'science of government' or that it is the 'governmental rationality itself'.[85]

One reason for this is because society plays a role as well. What nowadays is known as society is explained by Foucault as 'the juridical structure (économie juridique) of a governmentality pegged to the economic structure (économie économique)'.[86] He sees (civil) society as a wider and mainly judicial, sphere of government, which, on the one hand, offers the economic relations a space to be played out and, on the other hand, limits the government by offering another moment of self-reflection by asking the fundamental question 'why must one govern' in the first place?[87] Besides limiting the government, society also interacts with the economy. This too is a double-edged relationship as markets are part of society and thus reinforce it, but at the same time undermine the communitarian relations of society with their focus on self-interest.[88] Foucault describes this interaction by referring to his earlier food scarcity example:

> When the economic subject sees that he can make a profit by buying wheat in Canada, for example, and selling it in England, he will do so. He does it because it is to his advantage, and furthermore it will benefit everyone. However, the bonds of civil society mean that one prefers to stay in one's community, even if one finds abundance and security elsewhere.[89]

What this quote highlights is that neither the economic nor the security rationalities are total. In other words, there are options that 'free' individuals are able to take which do not follow the forceful logics of either the market or security. In a sense, this is what Dean means when he argues that 'while government gives *shape* to freedom, it is not constitutive *of* freedom'.[90] Instead, Dean sees freedom as originating in the acting and thinking of both those who are being governed and those who are governing.[91] Freedom is thus enacted or performed by all those involved and, as such, is open to change.

Nevertheless, the resulting uncertainty inherent to life that follows from this openness is a form of freedom that is constantly secured. The desire to secure against the unexpected is something that Dillon and Lobo-Guerrero have identified as the 'fundamental paradox [behind] biopolitics'.[92] To secure the living, life needs to be fixed. However, once secured it is no longer true life, as true life thrives on transformation and unfulfilled potential. 'In order for a living thing … to be secured it has to be allowed – indeed encouraged – to pass out of phase with itself and become something other than what it was in order to continue to live'.[93] Foucault's freedom, therefore, is not a freedom in terms of 'exemptions and privileges' but it is a particular 'freedom of circulation' of goods, people and ideas, and it is this freedom of circulation that he sees secured in everyday practices.[94] The consequence of such a practice is that it is not an actual threat that needs to be contained but that the attention shifts to those parts of life that *might become* dangerous, in other words the virtual of Chapter 5.[95] By shifting to the virtual, every fear and imagination can become a source for action. Everything can become dangerous and undesired, but Foucault argues that this all-embracing stance is limited by the liberal cost–benefit analyses to which security is subject as well. Instead of prohibiting *all* soft drugs, there is an increasing number of countries where it is regulated or tolerated, only to be acted upon when thresholds are crossed and the costs incurred by its usage warrant the cost of governmental intervention.[96]

To be clear, the goal of governmentality or biopolitics is neither security nor freedom, especially not liberal (democratic) freedom. In fact, Foucault argues that a liberal governmentality, as it builds on biopower, is and needs to be inherently *racist* in the sense that it constantly creates distinctions (in line with the focus on differentiation in Chapter 5).[97] It needs to be, because how else to identify and act on those parts of the population that weaken it? How else to decide 'between what must live and what must die'.[98] Moving this argument to its extreme, Dean argues that this is another aspect where sovereign power and biopower differ: contrary to sovereign power, biopolitics does not have a constraint on 'the right to kill'.[99] For the sovereign prince the ultimate exercise of power was to kill, but this would have left him one fewer person to govern. However, biopolitics, in order to strengthen the population as a whole has no such limitations and instead contains a Darwinian need to weed out the weak. An additional violation identified by Dean is found within the subjects themselves, who, in the constant biopolitical struggle to behave in a 'mature and responsible' way, in effect repress any alternative desires to behave otherwise.[100] Security, in short, draws a boundary between forms of life that are valued and forms of life that are not.

These boundaries are akin to power, which in line with Foucault is a good thing. The reason being that a person can resist, however little, a form of power that is exercised over him or her. If a person *cannot* resist, if they cannot even think or whisper, then what is exercised according to Foucault is not power but brute force.[101] Whereas brute force is applied on objects, power is meant to guide individuals as subjects and can therefore be resisted. This resistance against the current conduct, whether by thinking, acting or speaking, is something Foucault named *counter-conduct*.[102] With this term, Foucault refers not to opposition, dissidence or revolt. Each of these terms originates from within a system of biopolitics and is used to exclude those involved, to differentiate us from them. Indeed, active opposition to a particular system of thought and practices often reinforces that system, as direct opposition is simultaneously an indirect form of acknowledgement. A system can reject and ridicule such opposition, for example in the case of Occupy Wall Street, but it can also incorporate the concerns. Liberalism is so prevalent because it incorporates sociocultural concerns on natural resource use, climate change or privacy concerns within its own system of thought by translating them from externalities to commodities (carbon markets).[103] In short, counter-conduct is not a direct act against a particular mentalité but refers to the desire to behave 'well' from within *another* rationality, one that counters some of the core assumptions of the former. In this sense, Evans and Reid as well as Lundborg and Vaughan-Williams question the recent interest in the concept of resilience. They see resilience as a concept which, instead of offering *a way out*, is a solution that constantly reinforces the virtual uncertainty and vulnerability that is inherent in liberal systems.[104] For Evans and Reid such resilient subjects are passive subjects: they no longer actively secure or change the world around them, they only *adapt* to 'a series of dangerous events'.[105] This in turn, as Foucault teaches, reinforces the initial assumption behind society, namely that individuals and their freedom are vulnerable and need to be governed.

6.3.2 (Neo-)liberalism

Another aspect to mention in respect to the broader line of Foucault's work is the already-touched-upon link between governmentality, biopolitics and (neo-)liberalism.[106] The organization and role of markets and economic relations is of principal importance in Foucault's understanding of forms of governance. Burchell explains how, for Foucault, liberalism is not a 'theoretical doctrine' but a 'rationalizing governmental practice'.[107] It is a rationalizing governmental practice because it is 'a political project that endeavors to create a social reality that it suggests already exists' (comparable to Barroso's securitization in Chapter 4).[108] In turn, while it is a political project, it is not *only* a political project. Collier rightly remarks that it is first and foremost a *system of thought* that promotes its own mentalité and practices while it criticizes other modes of thinking. It is something that is pushed by certain thinkers in a certain time.[109] In other words, 'liberalism is a version of biopolitics', as well as a limit on the biopolitics of governmentality due to its dominance and principles.[110]

That liberalism limits sovereign power based on both the unknowability of the total system and the naturalness of the economic relations has already been discussed. However, liberalism also limits governmentality by building 'on the rational behaviour of those who are governed', which it does by presupposing free and rational individuals who uphold a liberal calculative rationality instead of envisioning individuals with juridical rights and responsibilities.[111] In shaping these rational individuals and the responding rational theories, a liberal governmentality is thus reliant on free individuals who also have the ability to resist that same liberal governmentality.[112] There is, consequently, a certain restraint on liberal governmentality and the state. Yet, at the same time, the restraint supports the view of rational individuals and thereby upholds the liberal governmentality. In this respect, Lemke sees the shifting boundaries between state, society and markets 'as element and effect' of a neo-liberal-inspired governmentality.[113] As he argues, 'the so-called retreat of the state is in fact a prolongation of government: neoliberalism is not the end but a transformation'.[114]

This free individual is not only considered free and rational; they are also considered to be driven by desire. By translating desire into personal interests and by assuming that these personal interests, when given 'free play' on the market, become the collective interest, it is desire that links the individual to the population in liberal economic thought. Foucault argues that in this transformation to collective interests one can witness 'both the naturalness of population and the possible artificiality of the means one adopts to manage it'.[115] This implies that desire is something that is and can be managed, which makes it a technology of power.[116] In other words, liberalism governs through the calculation of a population's collective interests, which it secures by identifying the conflicting individual desires and personal interests that endanger the population.[117] It then works on these individual desires by manipulating the *milieu*, but to do so it needs to assume that individual desires are rational (cost-effective) and thus governable based on the conduct of conduct. (If these personal interests are deemed irrational, it is hard to act upon them through the market itself and liberalism needs to fall back on the state and more traditional forms of power by actively intervening in the freedom of the individuals.) As Foucault summarizes this liberal line of thought from the perspective of security and governmentality:

> The problem of security is the protection of the collective interest against individual interests. Conversely, individual interests have to be protected against everything that could be seen as an encroachment of the collective interest.... The game of freedom and security is at the very heart of this new governmental reason.[118]

The market and all of society are built around this game between freedom and security: between the protection from dangers *to* the game and the protection against dangers that stem *from* within the game itself.[119]

The description of liberalism so far should not be interpreted as if there is *a* liberalism, as if it is a closed, totalized system. It is not. Foucault's main approach was to open up the naturalness of such central characteristics by showing how certain ideas have developed over time. In the case of liberal thought, Foucault differentiates for instance between classic liberals and two types of neo-liberals, including German ordo-liberals and American liberals. Disregarding all his nuances, early liberals can be said to have introduced the 'naturalness' of the market through the principle of exchange and to have introduced the separation of market and state. Ordo-liberals shifted the focus to the principle of competition and consequently looked at the twin organization of the state and the market, while striving for the optimum conditions for individuals to be able to live up to their potential. American liberals, in turn, exported the economic perspective of rational individuals to other social areas, introducing a broader economized society as a check on government action.[120] Again, and following Dean, these forms of liberalism support the initial position of Foucault that one should not judge these liberal rationalities but instead be mindful of their different effects and implications.[121] Dean, however, contradicts his own state-ment by concluding that both classic and neo-liberalism are 'naïve' as they reduce the role of the state and thereby open the door to a return of sovereign power, but this time applied by the markets themselves: he gives the example of forced work projects for the unemployed.[122]

Of course, this does not mean that scholars using Foucault's ideas cannot be critical. Nally, for example, is highly critical when he discusses the influence of a liberal rationality on hunger from a food systems perspective.[123] His main con-clusion is that the continuous struggle against hunger is not a 'failure of the modern food regime' as such but instead a 'logical expression of [the food sys-tem's] central paradoxes, particularly its reliance on over-production in some places and under-production in others'.[124] These paradoxes, Nally concludes, are a result of 'the neoliberal truth regime [which] presents global markets, agrarian biotechnologies and multinational corporate initiatives as the structural precon-ditions for alleviating world hunger'.[125] Nally shows how hunger in Europe steadily decreased with an increase in colonization, not because the problem of hunger was solved but because the problem was displaced from the poor in Europe to the people in the colonies, where 'the destruction of pre-existing anti-scarcity programmes was rapid and severe as market mechanisms were frequently permitted to operate unchecked and with devastating consequences'.[126] Pro-duced food was shipped to those who could afford it: creating abundance where there was scarcity and scarcity where there was abundance. By using a Foucauldian-inspired critical approach to disclose these paradoxes, it becomes possible to argue that current solutions (often technical fixes or claims for more free markets) are 'empirically shaky and ideologically driven' as they inherently disregard other alternative explanations, like Sen's argument that the entitle-ments to food are more important than the actual amount of food.[127]

6.3.3 The environment and risk

Nally's example also highlights that (neo-)liberalism not only has an effect on humans and how they are governed. As a biopolitical rationality geared towards 'men in their relation with things' it governs through the *milieu*, implying that it also effects *the* milieu. For this reason, Massumi interprets governmentality as an 'ecological theory of power', which transforms nature, real physical nature, increasingly into a *cultured* nature.[128] Nature becomes the:

> 'environment' of the capitalist system [wherein] previously untapped areas are being opened in the interest of capitalization and chances for commer-cial exploitation. Nature and life itself are being drawn into the economic [and technocratic] discourse of efficient resource management.[129]

Nature thus becomes part of a capitalist system, which, like liberalism, is also not a 'fixed' or 'completed' way of doing things.[130] Instead, Nitzan and Bichler describe it as a 'forward-looking' and 'commodified' mode of power.[131] The financialization of nature, of the milieu itself, offers a search for and commodification of knowledge about the future. In other words, in the commodification of the milieu, 'enterprising' capitalists turn towards the practices of risk calculation to make sense of a 'permanently uncertain environment', not to fight it, but, as Massumi claims, to 'ride' it.[132]

Risk calculation is discussed extensively in Section 4.5, but in terms of neo-liberalism and governmentality there are some additional remarks to be made. First, in terms of its historic development, it is possible to say that modern risk has its origins in the collective insurance schemes installed with the organization of the early shipping expeditions to the Eastern and Western hemispheres. These schemes transformed individual risks into collective risk and ultimately evolved with and into the West European welfare states, which took responsibility for social risks such as health and unemployment on a national level. More recently, with the 'withdrawal of the state', risk is once more turning into an individual responsibility, something the individual is *expected* to buy into (or not) depending on the individual's personal risk analysis.[133] Expected, first, because it is deemed cost-ineffective for governments to organize totalizing social insurance programmes, and, second, because, as Lemke argues, a neo-liberal rationality 'aspires to construct responsible subjects whose moral quality is based on the fact that they rationally assess the costs and benefits of a certain act as opposed to other alternative acts'.[134] Making a risk analysis, making the right risk analysis and behaving in line with the countermeasures to minimize risks become moral qualities for people to uphold and on which they are judged and judge themselves.[135] Risk thus works through the technologies of the market towards the state (and governmentality) and as a moral quality on the level of the self.

Not only is the meaning of risk changing over time; its contents are shifting as well. From the possibility of insuring oneself against well-known but uncertain events (natural disasters, sickness, investments), neo-liberal risk is increasingly focusing on *the virtual*. It is no longer enough to deal with events that most likely will happen, but these days everything needs to be analysed and secured, from the infinitely small impact and high-likelihood events to the infinitely large impact but low-chance calamities.[136] A neo-liberal future is therefore described as 'radically uncertain' and it is in this uncertainty that security and economy meet.[137] In this respect, Dillon concludes that:

> 'the aleatory' [the radical uncertainty or contingency], arises for Foucault as one of those factical elements or 'natural' processes to which liberal governmentality must attend, with which it must deal and in relation to which it has to regulate and evaluate its own performance and effectiveness in its ambition to exercise power over life.[138]

He continues by concluding that this contingency, which a (neo-)liberal governmentality takes as given, is actually a double contingency. It is the contingency of emergent life itself, as described above, but also the contingency of decision-making, on what is appropriate and the right course of action in relation to future developments.[139] Whatever the form of uncertainty, in dealing with the unknown, security and economics meet through risk and are played out in the milieu to govern the strategies behind conduct of conduct. In the search for profit and the need for security, both seek to know the radical uncertain future the best they can. The practice of risk is what binds them and makes it possible that 'at the level of ontology, forms of economy offer forms of sovereignty a means to harness the productivity of possible futures and the capacity to reconcile openness, freedom, and mobility with the pursuit of security'.[140]

6.4 Governing and materialization

6.4.1 *Governing through a milieu*

The insights from Foucault clearly resonate with the other theoretical chapters. Although the brief discussion above does not do justice to his nuanced and extensive work, three aspects in particular deserve closer attention in line with those chapters. These include the governing of things through the milieu, the power/knowledge nexus and its relation to the materialization of calculation, and lastly the material security of circulation.

Before moving on to discuss the governing of things through the milieu, it is interesting to note that all three of these aspects involve the relation between discourse and the material. Foucault himself, purposely, was never clear in distinguishing them, just as he never clearly defined what he meant by discourse or the non-discursive.[141] On the one hand, Foucault describes discourse as based on statements and the 'rule of repeatable materiality that characterizes these statements' and simultaneously 'as practices that systematically form the objects of which they speak'.[142] On the other hand, he offers the concept of the non-discursive as a 'field of practices, appropriation, interests, and desires' covering domains that include 'institutions, political events, economic practices and processes'.[143] Clearly, he sees them as different yet both focused on acts and practices, as well as on the materialization of thought through language. Switching from discourse to materiality itself, Foucault argues that materiality acts 'as an instrument and vector of power', in fact, elsewhere he argues that 'nothing is more material, physical, corporeal than the exercise of power'.[144] It is this definition of the material (together with the reiterative nature of statements) and the realization that all the matter that people see is always in some way materialized *and* subjected to forms of power, that Butler uses to build her case for a performative approach.[145] Together, these 'definitions' from Foucault lead Hardy and Thomas to conclude, in line with the new materialist authors in Chapter 5, that Foucault might differentiate epistemologically between discourse and the non-discursive, but ontologically he 'collapses the Cartesian dualism of mind/body' and sees them as highly interconnected and made to be differently per context.[146]

More implicitly, Foucault described his position on materiality in his later work with the help of La Perriere's 1567 definition of government as 'the right disposition of things arranged so as to lead to a suitable end'.[147] From the same text by La Perriere, Foucault takes his broad definition of things as described earlier in this chapter (material things, men in their relationship with discursive things, and men in their relationship with uncertain event like things). The main lesson Foucault takes from this text, Lemke argues, is the intricate relationship between humans and things, and how this relationship is *made* to be political:

> The art of government determines what is defined as subject and object, as human and non-human. It establishes and enacts the boundaries between socially relevant and politically recognized existence and 'pure matter', something that does not possess legal-moral protection and is 'reduced' to 'things'.[148]

Human-like things and thing-like humans (e.g. ANT's hybrid human/things) are made to be subjects with discursive and non-discursive practices that are enacted through their milieus. Above it was already discussed that the milieu offers both the instrument to act on a distance and the element within which it is possible to do so. This enables Foucault to collapse the distinctions between the material/social and between the social/environmental milieus. In his original manuscript, Foucault actually describes the milieu as the relations between multiple humans and things 'that act on them and on which they act in turn'.[149] From this quote, Lemke rightly remarks that what today is described as agency is not something that thing's *also* have (contra Bennett), but something that follows from the actual relations and boundaries between humans and things (in line with ANT and Barad).[150]

A good example of this complexity between humans and things, and how they interrelate and shape each other, can again be found in the politics of food. Shannon, for instance, discusses the conduct of conduct of food on a local municipal level, where 'the choice between a fried chicken and fruit salad is never simply a matter of nutrition'.[151] In describing how local governments are influencing the milieu of people for them to behave healthier, Shannon shows how the fight against obesity starts by defining obesity as something abnormal in respect to a normal healthy way of life.[152] This norm, broadly shared and reiterated with each action that local municipalities take, triggers a governing of the self. Unfortunately, Shannon does not continue on this self-governance but focuses on the knowledge and risk practices of the state/government alone. He highlights how the municipality programmes often approach obesity by dividing their populations in clusters of high/low obesity and then mapping those clusters geographically. In this process, these programmes identify geographic regions at risk, but also, simultaneously, transform particular geographic factors into the core problem, like the number of fast-food restaurants and supermarkets in an area.[153] In so doing, policymakers define obesity as a supply problem and focus on markets and consumers as they try to provide a broader range of healthier foodstuffs for lower prices.[154] Consequently, they disregard the citizen behind the consumer and 'close off a more systemic interrogation of both food production systems and processes of urban economic and racial segregation'.[155] In other words, the wider questions that discuss why the obese live in the poorer downtown regions with lots of fast-food restaurants and the healthy people mainly live in the suburbs with plenty of supermarkets and very little fast-food restaurants.

Shannon's article beautifully shows three important points discussed so far. First, that governing takes place through a physical milieu. The construction of healthier restaurants and shops, the promotion of healthier food, and the organization of healthier and cheaper food for those particular neighbourhoods, indicate that the focus is not on the obese but on their environment, which is reorganized in such a way that their possibilities increase and decrease. Second, Shannon's article shows how the problem definition itself is not neutral. Initially, the problem shifted from the behaviour of the obese to the food itself. Later, food was approached in terms of availability, ease of access, and cost: all related to the organization of supply in concrete buildings (shops, restaurants). At every step, other potential issues are excluded, ranging from a lack of cooking courses to the supermarkets themselves, not as saviours and suppliers of healthy food, but as monopolists within the global food production system pressuring production prices and thereby decreasing actual production. Third, it shows that when things can act human-like then humans can be approached thing-like.[156] Initially, biopolitics implied just that: to study (human) populations with statistics, to define the normal and abnormal and then govern the conduct of conduct of those behaving abnormally. The obese persons in Shannon's article are aggregated as part of the overall city population and within that population are grouped together in degrees of obesity. During this process, 'men … became calculable and measurable and could be conceived of as physical phenomena themselves'.[157] Obese people in this example are transformed into physical thing-like phenomena as they are made visible, problematized, and thereby governable as they are categorized and mapped.

6.4.2 *Materialization through calculation*

The core problem shared by new materialists and those working on security is that it is only possible to govern the things that we know. The power/knowledge nexus is Foucault's way of describing the close linkages between these two. It describes how knowledge and its systematic gathering, categorization and analysis always already contain ways to structure and dominate.[158] As Rouse argues, 'a more extensive and finer-grained knowledge enables a more continuous and pervasive control of what people do, which in turn offers further possibilities for more intrusive inquiry and disclosure'.[159] The power/knowledge nexus describes the practice of governing a group of people (a population) by gaining knowledge over that group and by defining, during the gathering of knowledge, what is normal and abnormal. This subjectification of people, witnessed in the obesity example, is a necessity for people and things 'to have an ontological existence at all' in public life.[160] Nothing material and no person or thing exists in public life that is not somehow structured by knowledge gathering practices. Two observations follow from this argument.

First, while matter and reality are real, the ontology that people use to describe our reality is historically constructed and thus comes in multiple versions (multiplicity) and is open to change.[161] Second, earlier in this chapter power was defined in terms of materialization, as the conflation of discourse and non-discursive practices and matter. This implies that all matter and bodies are imbued with power when they act relationally to other things and bodies. Energy and food in this reading are powerful things that enable us to live a particular lifestyle that would not have been possible without them. Simultaneously, they are part of 'power struggles' as they are part of the milieu through which other humans and things are governed.[162] Power is thus based on knowledge and knowledge is based on power; the two are not identical but relational, yet so intricately related that 'there is no point of dreaming of a time when knowledge will cease to depend on power'.[163]

The power/knowledge nexus already briefly returned in the example from Shannon above. An even better example of how calculative principles help identify and subjectify humans and things – and consequentially make something initially ungovernable and unproblematic into a problem that can be governed – can be found in Amoore's book *The politics of possibility*. Amoore provides an interesting Foucauldian-inspired reflection on the role of accountants and their methods towards food scarcity in Great Britain during World War II.[164] She starts by noting that the British government did not act on its domestic food supplies and commodities pricing during the first 18 months of the war. The reason, according to Amoore, was an 'absence of a defined problem of scarcity'.[165] It was not that the problem of food shortages and price increases were unknown, but that the controls to counter them were unavailable. Hence, the problem was not seen as a governable problem that could be acted on. Amoore then describes how the British Board of Trade subsequently started to identify the problem not in terms of scarcity, but in terms of a lack of statistical knowledge and data about the normal consumption patterns of its population. Without such data, it was deemed impossible to anticipate future consumption, let alone decide upon exceptional measures (like rationing):[166]

> In the absence of accurate census data, the board authorized accountants from the firm Price Waterhouse to devise techniques for accounting for the population and to administer new restrictions on supply: 'The need to control and monitor the workings of an economy at war necessitated the recruitment of accountants as administrators and advisers, many being granted considerable *executive authority*'.[167]

Amoore returns to Foucault to analyse this moment. A moment when accountants helped open up the unknown world of food distribution through their methods of accounting and statistics. The resulting data enabled the government to act upon the food markets by steering the flows of food commodities and their exchange as if they were known in full.[168] In this process, Amoore argues that the accountants gained 'executive authority' as they decided on what trade and consumption practices were allowed, meaning that they had 'the capacity to decide upon the norm'.[169] Amoore concludes that this had two consequences: it helped 'organize' a wartime economy centred on the army, and it reified the techniques and methods used for future government practices. The latter is the main result for Amoore, as 'a changed system of accounting does not simply change the measure but also the world and how we see it, how we apportion it, how we differentiate and divide it'.[170] In other words, it changes our ontology, helps identify new problems (by subjectification) and enables new ways of governing. With knowledge comes the ability to act, thereby making knowledge a goal in itself. To reach this goal, a method is developed (statistical risk calculation), which promises to make the future known. This is such a strong promise, in fact, that the absence of knowledge and the subsequent inability to act can become a risk itself.[171]

These calculative practices develop constantly. Foucault and Amoore highlight the use of statistics, while Shannon discusses geographical and visual mapping (GIS).[172] Elsewhere, Barry discusses the governing of geography and territory through common measurement systems, infrastructure standards and qualification standards (skills).[173] All three of these practices are shared ways of gaining knowledge and not one of them is 'fixed' as they are continuously adjusted and improved. Callon and MacKenzie *et al.* discuss another calculative technique when they independently analyse the performativity of economic formulas.[174] For these authors, economic formulas and models do not describe or represent the economic reality 'out there' but they see these formulas as constituting that reality (in line with Searle's social fact of money).

Someone who pushes the argument that economic calculative practices shape reality even more is Mitchell.[175] More so than Foucault, who sees neo-liberal economics and its calculative practices as separating politics from economics, Mitchell argues that the main function of neo-liberal economics lies in the artificial boundary that it creates to separate the political from the natural. According to Mitchell, in the shift towards governmentality and its focus on political economies, nature became something 'excluded from politics by practices of calculation'.[176] While the sciences define what nature is, economics defines how it is approached in sociopolitical life by creating 'the large no-man's land between the two'.[177] Mitchell refers to the politics surrounding oil and gas reserves, in particular the distinction between above ground politicized relations and the below-ground geological reserves. Mitchell argues that any discussion of oil and gas reserves needs to incorporate the 'space of uncertainty, of economic possibility' that economics (e.g. the oil industry) carves out in calculating the distinction between proven, probable and possible reserves.[178] In short, for Mitchell, 'the appeal to nature shortcuts political debate and contestation'.[179]

6.4.3 Securing circulation

The combination of these three – the power/knowledge nexus, the governing through the milieu, and the desire to organize freedom of circulation for the benefit of the population – results in practices of security to identify and counter undesired futures. Foucault's example of scarce food supplies highlights this combination quite clearly. In the neo-liberal acceptance of the 'reality of grain', Foucault argues, what is accepted is 'the reality of fluctuations between abundance/scarcity, dearness/cheapness'; this is a reality that is governed 'not by trying to prevent it in advance' but by installing 'an apparatus ... which is, I think, precisely an apparatus of security'.[180]

Such a security apparatus, is, like his concepts of discourse or non-discursive, never explicitly defined by Foucault. In one of the few broad descriptions of a security apparatus, Foucault discusses them as consisting of 'discourses, institutions, architectural forms, regulatory decisions, laws, administrative measures, scientific statements, philosophical, moral and philanthropic propositions'.[181] Elsewhere, Foucault summarizes his study of security dispositifs as studying (1) 'spaces of security', (2) 'the treatment of the uncertain' (what Nally describes in terms of 'management of the uncertain or "aleatory"'), (3) 'the form of normalization' and (4) the 'emergence' and 'reality' of the population as 'both the object and subject of these mechanisms of security'.[182] Dillon describes these security dispositifs as a combination of different security technologies that assemble under a singular logic.[183] Schouten takes a similar approach, but combines insights from Foucault with ANT to define a security dispositif or assemblage as 'the totality of relations structured by security apparatus, or the shifting – discursive, material, institutional, practical – "milieu" upon which a security apparatus acts in order to render it secure'.[184] In turn, he defines a security apparatus as 'a set of "socio-technical" arrangements that mediate relations and interactions within a specific sphere of activities, black boxing some concerns and threats while foregrounding others'.[185] Returning to Foucault, perhaps this concept is another one of his that should not be defined but instead just be described by what it does. What a security apparatus does, according to Foucault, is that it indicates the set of relations of a multiplicity of humans and things; it highlights the nature of these relations and its effects; and it highlights the strategic function of such a set of relations.[186] In other words, it is the identification of a specific set of relations based on its shared goal or strategy. It is within these sets that one can analyse the performativity of such a network.[187]

Above this chapter briefly discussed such a strategy by examining the shift from mercantilism to liberalism and the subsequent shift in security apparatus from a direct management of things towards an indirect management via the observation and protection of circulation. However, lastly, circulation is secured from at least five directions.[188] First, the critical security literature takes Foucault primarily as discussing the security of circulation in terms of directly separating good and bad products within the circulatory flow at specific points or gateways where a decision is made on the thing's further mobility, as in the literature on airport security and migration policies (direct governing of circulation). Second, Foucault himself provides the scarcity example and describes how the supply and consumption within the circulation of food should not be governed directly but indirectly through the neo-liberal markets and the milieu (indirect securing of circulation). However, third, this example excludes the protection of the circulation itself and its potential total absence. Within energy security debates, the fear is not whether the oil is good or bad but whether the supplies themselves are secure (the protection of circulation itself against outside influences). Instead, with the example of scarce food, Foucault himself reinforces the neo-liberal separation of politics, economics and nature, while neglecting that scarce food could also have been organized differently, through diversification or other political alternative ways of organizing the circulation of food. While these options most likely cost more and therefore will never result from the markets, they do not fall back into a direct mercantilist governing of supply and demand. This enables a fourth form of protecting circulation, namely that the security of circulation also entails the protection of the idea of free circulation itself against alternative modes of organizing circulation (introduced by movements like La Via Campesina, Occupy Wall Street and communes). Lastly, the security chapter also briefly discussed how security and risk processes themselves are circular, with failure as an incentive to do better and move on.

Securing circulation thus entails more than separating good from bad or leaving the markets to its bidding. Energy security for example highlights how it is not just the product itself that is secured, or the nodes that enable the circulation of these products, but also the idea of free markets, the consequences of the form of circulation, the lifestyles that it enables, and so on. In other words, security needs to be problematized on multiple dimensions. This includes 'refraining from making a priori assumptions about the ontology of (in)security, instead considering it as itself at stake in – and hence the outcome of – security governance efforts'.[189] In other words, like liberalism, security itself changes with security practices. For example, after accepting and observing 'the reality of grain', a set of relations of discursive and non-discursive humans and things was enacted that empowered/materialized a particular form of security, which Foucault identified as biopolitics. Security, like neo-liberalism, is not singular.

6.5 Reflection

This chapter focused on the later work of Foucault in order to combine and deepen many of the insights on security and materiality from the previous chapters to further the study of energy security as a security practice. In particular, this chapter focused on the politics of security, combining the performativity of modern security theories with the performativity of a materialdiscursive world. It tried to answer how we can make sense of the politics and power behind security, narrowly in terms of how it works, and more broadly as part of society?

Section 6.2 drew on Foucault's ontology to introduce the core elements of security. It surmises that governmentality builds on techniques like the *power/knowledge* regimes as well as notions like *biopolitics* and *security apparatuses* to analyse a modern form of (bio)power that is aimed at populations and every-thing that 'makes life live', versus the historic sovereign power 'to kill or let live' or the disciplinary power exercised over individuals to make them behave as part of the norm. Power is key for Foucault in these (and other) political processes and is understood to be intangible, relational and affective, as electri-city instead of the light switch. Once administered through shared strategies, this form of biopower becomes biopolitics. Biopolitics governs life as it regulates the circulations of people and things. It does so by influencing the desires of individuals through the milieu in the interest of the population, which is only possible after knowledge has been gathered over populations. A process that defines it and subjectivizes people to this population. Without knowledge, there is no problematization and hence no ability to act. This turns biopolitics into a security apparatus that organizes and defends freedom. The freedom that allows circulation to take place and which allows life and the relationships that consti-tute life to gather and splinter.

The particular manner or strategies through which biopolitics is applied, through technologies of the self and the market (conduct of conduct), together with the gathering of knowledge about populations, is part of what Foucault describes as governmentality. Section 6.3 hence described the outward politics of security by approaching governmentality as a practice that is constantly balancing governmental (security) practices with society and economy, each with their own biopolitics. The economy, for example, includes its own (neo-)liberal biopolitics based on the freedom of consumers and producers to act within markets. It is in the constant rearticulating of this balance, among others by the liberal argument of the unknowability and hence uncontrollabil-ity of the economy, that economy and security meet. In the search for profit and the need for security, both seek to know the radical uncertain future as best as they can. This turns risk into a core technique to rule the lives of iden-tified populations by distributing 'security' and the accompanying material benefits.[190]

Section 6.4 discussed in more detail how Foucault approaches the material world, by discussing the milieu and circulation, and by continuing the discus-sion on risk. The goal of this chapter was not to differentiate Foucault from new materialist and modern security studies or alternative understandings of perfor-mativity. On the contrary, by reading Foucault through a material lens that focuses on materialization (of power), which looks at the close connection between calculation, politics of ontology, the governing of circulation and security apparatuses, what becomes obvious is how closely related all these different theoretical fields are. It showed how Foucault's idea of productive security is strongly performative of itself and of nature and society. However, above all, his notion of the power/knowledge nexus bring out both the political role of calculations and knowledge gathering practices as simultaneously meas-uring, defining and differentiating, as well as the materialization of these dis-courses through non-discursive acts and their enactment in the milieu of the humans and things that are recognized and subjected to these knowledge practices.

In terms of energy security, this chapter offered an alternative to the way in which energy security is studied in regular policy debates and academia. Simultaneously, it offered the theoretical grounding behind many of the conclusions and insights from the earlier theoretical chapters. Moreover, it added to those theoretical chapters by seeing (energy) security as a security apparatus that: (1) is productive, (2) is based on knowledge gathering practices with their inherent differentiation, (3) is a form of governing and materialization and (4) facilitates in drawing boundaries on a social level between nature, economics, the political and society. With such an understanding, energy security becomes a set of relations between men and things, a set with strategic intent that is constantly performed and disrupted, and part of the circulation of energy. Such a set of relations is enacted by other sets in and through a milieu, while it acts on the milieu of other sets. In short, each call for energy security is a performative act for a particular understanding of energy security and the work of Foucault helps us understand the governance and politics of energy security and how (energy) security acts politically towards other forms of governance.

Notes

1 With some exceptions, as Foucault has been used for energy broadly, with work from Klauser, Paasche and Söderström 2014; Hargreaves, Nye and Burgess 2013; Mitchell 2013; Tyfield 2014; Waitt *et al.* 2016; Gailing 2016.
2 Foucault 2003, 2007, 2008.
3 See, for example, Dillon and Lobo-Guerrero 2008; Dillon 2008.
4 Lemke 2002, 50. However, see Michel Senellart's course context discussion in Foucault 2007, 339, note 126, where Senellart argues that this contraction is a translation error and governmentality instead is the noun of governmental just as musicality derives from musical.
5 Lemke 2002, 50.
6 Ibid.
7 Foucault 1991, 91.
8 Foucault 2007, 193.
9 Dean 2010, 17.
10 Gordon 1991, 3. This thesis follows Dean 2010, 24, who defines rationality as: 'any way of reasoning, or way of thinking about, calculating and responding to a problem, which is more or less systematic, and which might draw upon formal bodies of knowledge or expertise'.
11 Lobo-Guerrero 2012, xvi–xvii.
12 Dean 2010, 19.
13 Gordon 1991, 7.
14 Dillon 2010, 63.
15 Lobo-Guerrero 2007, 330.
16 Foucault 1982.
17 Foucault 2003, 241.
18 Foucault 1991, 90.
19 Foucault 2003, 35.
20 Foucault 1991, 91.
21 Foucault 2007, 12.

22 Ibid., 56.
23 Foucault 2003, 38.
24 Foucault 2007, 57.
25 Foucault 1991, 102.
26 Foucault 2003, 247.
27 Dean 2010, 119.
28 Ibid.; Foucault 2003, 2008.
29 Foucault 2003, 250.
30 Foucault 2007, 19, 44.
31 Ibid., 45.
32 Ibid.
33 Ibid., 8. What Foucault 1991, 102, has called the 'sovereignty-discipline-government' triangle.
34 Collier 2009, 94; Foucault 2007, 11–12; Dillon and Lobo-Guerrero 2008, 266; Watts 2004b. For a problem to be governable, it needs a problem space. Methmann describes how the earth's carbon cycle has become such a problem space based on the technological ability to monitor carbon emissions and their effects. Within this problem space, the population is defined as those people and institutions that are related to the emission of carbon. See Methmann 2013, 78.
35 Lobo-Guerrero 2007, 331.
36 Foucault 2003, 246.
37 Collier 2009, 83; Foucault 2003, 2007; Dillon and Lobo-Guerrero 2008.
38 Campbell 2005, 950.
39 Foucault 1991, 99.
40 Foucault 2007, 77.
41 Gordon 1991, 11.
42 Foucault 2007, 323–326.
43 Ibid., 315.
44 Gordon 1991, 19.
45 Foucault 2003, 253. See also Massumi 2009, 157; Foucault 1991, 92.
46 Foucault 2007.
47 Ibid., 31.
48 Ibid., 33.
49 Foucault 1991, 98.
50 Foucault sees mercantilism as the first serious attempt to gather knowledge/data on an issue to help govern the problem of food shortages and economic growth in general. See Foucault 2007, 102.
51 Ibid., 36.
52 Dean 2010, 137.
53 Foucault 2007, 96.
54 Ibid.
55 Foucault 1991, 95.
56 Foucault 2007, 354.
57 Ibid., 349, 354.
58 Gordon 1991, 14.
59 Ibid., 16.
60 Foucault 2007, 78, 2003, 245.
61 Foucault 2007, 20–21.
62 Compare to the discussion of Bryant in Section 5.4.
63 Dillon and Reid 2001, 47; Campbell 2005, 951.
64 Foucault 2007, 296.
65 Ibid., 20.
66 Dillon and Reid 2001, 48. See also the quote by Mitchell Dean in Watts 2004a, 55.
67 Renzi and Elmer 2013, 48.

68 Dillon 1996, 34.
69 Amoore 2013, 65.
70 Foucault 2007, 108.
71 Foucault 1991, 103; Lemke 2002, 58.
72 Foucault 2007, 109.
73 Dean 2010, 220.
74 Foucault 2007, 173, 184–185.
75 Ibid., 129.
76 Gordon 1991, 12.
77 Dean 2010, 224.
78 Foucault 2007, 348.
79 Ibid., 231, note†.
80 Hayek 1979, 163. As quoted by Dean 2010, 182–183. See also Dillon 1996, 10.
81 And nature; see Mitchell 2013 on the manner in which economics creates nature as something outside of politics.
82 Foucault 2008, 280–282.
83 Ibid., 319. As Best 2007, 90 argues: 'Paradoxically, while the economy is often the exception to politics as usual, it is an exception that simultaneously enables and constrains the possibility of exercising sovereignty itself'.
84 Foucault 2008, 32. Dean 2010, 184, reflects on Hayek and notes that Hayek, contra Foucault's naturalness, translates his non-natural state of freedom to the market, which he sees as neither 'natural' nor as an 'organized system'. Instead, Hayek sees markets as 'spontaneous social order[s]'.
85 Foucault 2008, 286.
86 Ibid., 296.
87 Ibid., 296, 319. Aradau and Van Munster 2008, 34 argue that 'Rather than a formal guideline, law is part of the material reality of society'.
88 Foucault 2008, 301, 302.
89 Ibid., 303.
90 Dean 2010, 21.
91 Ibid., 24.
92 Dillon and Lobo-Guerrero 2008, 271.
93 Ibid.
94 Foucault 2007, 48; Dillon and Lobo-Guerrero 2008, 282.
95 Lundborg and Vaughan-Williams 2011, 374; Foucault 2007, 315; Dillon 2008, 314.
96 Foucault 2007, 5–6.
97 Foucault 2003, 254–255.
98 Ibid., 254, 258.
99 Dean 2010, 164.
100 Ibid., 156.
101 Foucault 1988, 83–84; Selby 2007, 332.
102 Foucault 2007, 201–202.
103 Dean 2010, 182.
104 Lundborg and Vaughan-Williams 2011, 375. Evans and Reid 2013, 84 actually argue that 'the underlying ontology of resilience, therefore, is actually vulnerability. To be able to become resilient, one must first accept that one is fundamentally vulnerable.'
105 Evans and Reid 2013, 87.
106 See also Collier 2009, 100, who argues that the overwhelming focus on the concept of governmentality overshadows any critical readings of (neo-)liberalism.
107 Burchell 1991, 143. See also Best 2007, 91.
108 Lemke 2002, 60.
109 Collier 2009, 100. Collier comments on the limited number of thinkers introduced and analysed by Foucault to make this point, and the lack of attention of current scholars towards the fact that this is actually a process (supported by Foucault).

110 Dean 2010, 132.
111 Foucault 2008, 312; Dean 2010, 63.
112 Best 2007, 92.
113 Lemke 2002, 59.
114 Ibid., 58; Foucault 2008, 112.
115 Foucault 2007, 72–73, 73.
116 Rose 1999, 85–89.
117 Foucault 2008, 65.
118 Ibid.
119 Compare with Figure 3.1.
120 Foucault 2008; Dean 2010, chaps 2 and 8.
121 Dean 2010, 73.
122 Ibid., 259.
123 Nally 2011.
124 Ibid., 49.
125 Ibid.
126 Ibid.
127 Ibid.; Sen 1983.
128 Massumi 2009, 177.
129 Lemke 2002, 56.
130 Lobo-Guerrero 2012, 2, who continuous from Thrift 2005, 1.
131 Renzi and Elmer 2013, 48; Nitzan and Bichler 2009, 280–282, 294; Bichler and Nitzan 2012.
132 Massumi 2009, 176.
133 Lemke 2002, 59.
134 Ibid.
135 Lupton 2006, 14; Amoore and De Goede 2008, 12.
136 Ewald 1993, 222.
137 Aradau and Van Munster 2008, 29.
138 Dillon 2007b, 45.
139 Dillon 2007a, 22. See also Luhmann 1993.
140 Amoore 2013, 5.
141 Foucault also never discussed the connections between humans and non-humans; see Lemke 2015, 5.
142 Foucault 2002, 114, 120–121, 54.
143 Ibid., 77, 179–180.
144 Foucault 1977, 30, 1980, 57–58.
145 Butler 1993, 10–11; Lemke 2015, 13.
146 Hardy and Thomas 2015, 681, 682; Lundborg and Vaughan-Williams 2015, 19.
147 Foucault 2007, 96.
148 Lemke 2015, 9.
149 Foucault 2007, 22.
150 Lemke 2015, 10; Latour 2005; Preda 1999, 358; Bennett 2010.
151 Shannon 2014, 257.
152 Ibid., 255.
153 Ibid., 250.
154 Ibid., 261, 258.
155 Ibid., 250, 259.
156 See also Lemke 2015.
157 Ibid., 10.
158 Foucault 1980.
159 Rouse 2005, 96–97.
160 Hekman 2010, 57.
161 Ibid., 58; Mol 2002.

162 Preda 1999, 358.
163 Foucault 1980, 52.
164 Amoore 2013, 32–39.
165 Ibid., 34.
166 Ibid., 35.
167 Ibid., 36 quotes: Edgar Jones (1995) *True and Fair: A History of Price Waterhouse*, London: Hamish Hamilton, 12 [emphasis added by Amoore].
168 Ibid., 38.
169 Ibid., 47.
170 Ibid., 39.
171 Luhmann 1993.
172 Related, Elden introduces the concept of geometrics and geopower as an alternative to biometrics and biopower, believing that biopower focuses too much on humans and not enough on territory and geography. My reading of Foucault's biopolitics above is more material than Elden's, so I do not follow along in his argument. Elden 2007, 2013; Bridge 2015.
173 Barry 2006.
174 Callon 1998; MacKenzie, Muniesa and Siu 2007; Fine 2005.
175 Mitchell 2013.
176 Ibid., 251.
177 Ibid., 241.
178 Ibid., 247.
179 Ibid., 246.
180 Foucault 2007, 37.
181 Foucault 1980, 194; Aradau and Van Munster 2007, 97.
182 Foucault 2007, 11; Nally 2011, 38.
183 Dillon 2008, 311; Dillon and Lobo-Guerrero 2008, 266.
184 Schouten 2014, 30.
185 Ibid.
186 Foucault 1980.
187 Aradau *et al.* 2015.
188 Kester 2018.
189 Schouten 2014, 24. See also the discussion on observation in Section 5.5.
190 Dillon and Reid 2001; Dillon 2008; Amoore 2013.

Bibliography

Amoore, Louise. 2013. *The politics of possibility: Risk and security beyond probability*. Durham, NC, and London: Duke University Press.

Amoore, Louise, and Marieke de Goede. 2008. Introduction: Governing by risk in the war on terror. In *Risk and the war on terror*, edited by Louise Amoore and Marieke de Goede, 5–20. London and New York: Routledge.

Aradau, Claudia, Martin Coward, Eva Herschinger, Owen D. Thomas and Nadine Voelkner. 2015. Discourse/materiality. In *Critical security methods: New frameworks for analysis*, edited by Claudia Aradau, Jef Huysmans, Andrew Neal and Nadine Voelkner, 57–84. London and New York: Routledge.

Aradau, Claudia, and Rens van Munster. 2007. Governing terrorism through risk: Taking precautions, (un)knowing the future. *European Journal of International Relations* 13 (1): 89–115.

Aradau, Claudia, and Rens van Munster. 2008. Taming the future: The dispositif of risk in the war on terror. In *Risk and the war on terror*, edited by Louise Amoore and Marieke de Goede, 23–40. London and New York: Routledge.

Barry, Andrew. 2006. Technological zones. *European Journal of Social Theory* 9 (2): 239–253.

Bennett, Jane. 2010. Thing-power. In *Political matter: Technoscience, democracy, and public life*, edited by Bruce Braun and Sarah J. Whatmore, 35–62. Minneapolis, MN: University of Minnesota Press.

Best, Jacqueline. 2007. Why the economy is often the exception to politics as usual. *Theory, Culture & Society* 24 (4): 87–109.

Bichler, Shimshon, and Jonathan Nitzan. 2012. The asymptotes of power. *Real-world Economics Review* 60: 18–53.

Bridge, Gavin. 2015. Energy (in)security: World-making in an age of scarcity. *The Geographical Journal* 181 (4): 328–339.

Burchell, Graham. 1991. Peculiar interests: Civil society and governing 'the system of natural liberty'. In *The Foucault effect: Studies in governmentality*, edited by Graham Burchell, Colin Gordon and Peter Miller, 119–150. Chicago, IL: University of Chicago Press.

Butler, Judith. 1993. *Bodies that matter: On the discursive limits of 'sex'*. London and New York: Routledge.

Callon, Michel, ed. 1998. *The laws of the markets*. Sociological review monograph series. Oxford and Malden, MA: Blackwell/Sociological Review.

Campbell, David. 2005. The biopolitics of security: Oil, empire, and the sports utility vehicle. *American Quarterly* 57 (3): 943–972.

Collier, Stephen J. 2009. Topologies of power: Foucault's analysis of political government beyond 'governmentality'. *Theory, Culture & Society* 26 (6): 78–108.

Dean, Mitchell. 2010. *Governmentality: Power and rule in modern society*. 2nd edn. London: SAGE.

Dillon, Michael. 1996. *Politics of security: Towards a political philosophy of continental thought*. London and New York: Routledge.

Dillon, Michael. 2007a. Governing terror: The state of emergency of biopolitical emergence. *International Political Sociology* 1 (1): 7–28.

Dillon, Michael. 2007b. Governing through contingency: The security of biopolitical governance. *Political Geography* 26 (1): 41–47.

Dillon, Michael. 2008. Underwriting security. *Security Dialogue* 39 (2–3): 309–332.

Dillon, Michael. 2010. Biopolitics of security. In *The Routledge handbook of new security studies*, edited by J. Peter Burgess, 61–71. London and New York: Routledge.

Dillon, Michael, and Luis Lobo-Guerrero. 2008. Biopolitics of security in the 21st century: An introduction. *Review of International Studies* 34 (02): 265–292.

Dillon, Michael, and Julian Reid. 2001. Global liberal governance: Biopolitics, security and war. *Millennium – Journal of International Studies* 30 (1): 41–66.

Elden, Stuart. 2007. Governmentality, calculation, territory. *Environment and Planning D: Society and Space* 25 (3): 562–580.

Elden, Stuart. 2013. Secure the volume: Vertical geopolitics and the depth of power. *Political Geography* 34: 35–51.

Evans, Brad, and Julian Reid. 2013. Dangerously exposed: The life and death of the resilient subject. *Resilience* 1 (2): 83–98.

Ewald, François. 1993. Two infinities of risk. In *The politics of everyday fear*, edited by Brian Massumi, 221–228. Minneapolis, MN: University of Minnesota Press.

Fine, Ben. 2005. From actor-network theory to political economy. *Capitalism Nature Socialism* 16 (4): 91–108.

Foucault, Michel. 1977. *Discipline and punish: The birth of the prison*, translated by Alan Sheridan. New York: Vintage.

Foucault, Michel. 1980. *Power/knowledge: Selected interviews and other writings, 1972–1977*, edited by Colin Gordon. New York: Pantheon.

Foucault, Michel. 1982. The subject and power. *Critical Inquiry* 8 (4): 777–795.

Foucault, Michel. 1988. *Politics, philosophy, culture. Interviews and other writings 1977–1984*, edited by Lawrence D. Kritzman, translated by Alan Sheridan. London and New York: Routledge.

Foucault, Michel. 1991. Governmentality. In *The Foucault effect: Studies in governmentality*, edited by Graham Burchell, Colin Gordon and Peter Miller, 87–104. Chicago, IL: University of Chicago Press.

Foucault, Michel. 2002. *The archaeology of knowledge*. London and New York: Routledge.

Foucault, Michel. 2003. *Society must be defended: Lecutures at the Collège de France 1975–76*, edited by Mauro Bertani and Alessandro Fontana, translated by David Macey. New York: Picador.

Foucault, Michel. 2007. *Security, territory, population: Lectures at the Collège de France 1977–1978*, edited by Michel Senellart, translated by Graham Burchell. New York: Palgrave Macmillan.

Foucault, Michel. 2008. *The birth of biopolitics: Lectures at the Collège de France 1978–79*, edited by Michel Senellart, translated by Graham Burchell. New York: Palgrave Macmillan.

Gailing, Ludger. 2016. Transforming energy systems by transforming power relations: Insights from dispositive thinking and governmentality studies. *Innovation: The European Journal of Social Science Research* 29 (3): 243–261.

Gordon, Colin. 1991. Governmental rationality: An introduction. In *The Foucault effect: Studies in governmentality*, edited by Graham Burchell, Colin Gordon and Peter Miller, 1–52. Chicago, IL: University of Chicago Press.

Hardy, Cynthia, and Robyn Thomas. 2015. Discourse in a material world. *Journal of Management Studies* 52 (5): 680–696.

Hargreaves, Tom, Michael Nye, and Jacquelin Burgess. 2013. Keeping energy visible? Exploring how householders interact with feedback from smart energy monitors in the longer term. *Energy Policy* 52: 126–134.

Hayek, Friedrich A. 1979. *Law legislation and liberty. Vol. 3: The political order of a free people*. Chicago, IL: University of Chicago Press.

Hekman, Susan J. 2010. *The material of knowledge feminist disclosures*. Bloomington, IN: Indiana University Press.

Kester, Johannes. 2018. Governing electric vehicles: Mobilizing electricity to secure automobility. *Mobilities* 13 (2): 200–215.

Klauser, Francisco, Till Paasche and Ola Söderström. 2014. Michel Foucault and the smart city: Power dynamics inherent in contemporary governing through code. *Environment and Planning D: Society and Space* 32 (5): 869–885.

Latour, Bruno. 2005. *Reassembling the social: An introduction to actor-network-theory*. Oxford: Oxford University Press.

Lemke, Thomas. 2002. Foucault, governmentality, and critique. *Rethinking Marxism* 14 (3): 49–64.

Lemke, Thomas. 2015. New materialisms: Foucault and the 'government of things'. *Theory, Culture & Society* 32 (4): 3–25.

Lobo-Guerrero, Luis. 2007. Biopolitics of specialized risk: An analysis of kidnap and ransom insurance. *Security Dialogue* 38 (3): 315–334.

Lobo-Guerrero, Luis. 2012. *Insuring war: Sovereignty, security and risk*. London and New York: Routledge.

Luhmann, Niklas. 1993. *Risk: A sociological theory*. Berlin and New York: Walter de Gruyter.

Lundborg, Tom, and Nick Vaughan-Williams. 2011. Resilience, critical infrastructure, and molecular security: The excess of 'life' in biopolitics. *International Political Sociology* 5 (4): 367–383.

Lundborg, Tom, and Nick Vaughan-Williams. 2015. New Materialisms, discourse analysis, and international relations: A radical intertextual approach. *Review of International Studies* 41 (1): 3–25.

Lupton, Deborah. 2006. Sociology and risk. In *Beyond the risk society: Critical reflections on risk and human security*, edited by Gabe Mythen and Sandra Walklate, 11–24. Maidenhead: McGraw-Hill.

MacKenzie, Donald, Fabian Muniesa and Lucia Siu, eds. 2007. *Do economists make markets: On the performativity of economics*. Princeton, NJ, and Oxford: Princeton University Press.

Massumi, Brian. 2009. National enterprise emergency steps toward an ecology of powers. *Theory, Culture & Society* 26 (6): 153–185.

Methmann, Chris. 2013. The sky is the limit: Global warming as global governmentality. *European Journal of International Relations* 19 (1): 69–91.

Mitchell, Timothy. 2013. *Carbon democracy: Political power in the age of oil*. London: Verso.

Mol, Annemarie. 2002. *The body multiple: Ontology in medical practice*. Durham, NC, and London: Duke University Press.

Nally, David. 2011. The biopolitics of food provisioning. *Transactions of the Institute of British Geographers* 36 (1): 37–53.

Nitzan, Jonathan, and Shimshon Bichler. 2009. *Capital as power: A study of order and cre-order*. London and New York: Routledge.

Preda, Alex. 1999. The turn to things: Arguments for a sociological theory of things. *The Sociological Quarterly* 40 (2): 347–366.

Renzi, Alessandra, and Greg Elmer. 2013. The biopolitics of sacrifice: Securing infrastructure at the G20 summit. *Theory, Culture & Society* 30 (5): 45–69.

Rose, Nikolas. 1999. *Powers of freedom: Reframing political thought*. Cambridge: Cambridge University Press.

Rouse, Joseph. 2005. Power/knowledge. In *The Cambridge companion to Foucault*, edited by Gary Gutting, 92–114. Cambridge: Cambridge University Press.

Schouten, Peer. 2014. Security as controversy: Reassembling security at Amsterdam Airport. *Security Dialogue* 45 (1): 23–42.

Selby, Jan. 2007. Engaging Foucault: Discourse, liberal governance and the limits of Foucauldian IR. *International Relations* 21 (3): 324–345.

Sen, Amartya. 1983. *Poverty and famines*. Oxford: Oxford University Press.

Shannon, Jerry. 2014. Food deserts: Governing obesity in the neoliberal city. *Progress in Human Geography* 38 (2): 248–266.

Thrift, Nigel. 2005. *Knowing capitalism*. London: Sage.

Tyfield, David. 2014. Putting the power in 'socio-technical regimes': E-mobility transition in China as political process. *Mobilities* 9 (4): 585–603.

Waitt, Gordon, Kate Roggeveen, Ross Gordon, Katherine Butler and Paul Cooper. 2016. Tyrannies of thrift: Governmentality and older, low-income people's energy efficiency narratives in the Illawarra, Australia. *Energy Policy* 90: 37–45.

Watts, Michael. 2004a. Resource curse? Governmentality, oil and power in the Niger Delta, Nigeria. *Geopolitics* 9 (1): 50–80.

Watts, Michael J. 2004b. Antinomies of community: Some thoughts on geography, resources and empire. *Transactions of the Institute of British Geographers* 29 (2): 195–216.

7 Energy security politics in the Dutch natural gas debate

7.1 Introduction

Where the pervious chapters engaged with three strands of literature to understand the politics of energy security, and before we sum up and reflect in the conclusion, this chapter illustrates how such a performative reading of energy security could look like.[1] As such it draws heavily on the previous chapters to analyse the discussion about the natural gas debate in the Netherlands, a topic heavily debated in the author's region at the time he wrote this book and one that shows strong energy security politics. As discussed in the introduction and hopefully clearer after the theoretical chapters, it is difficult to provide a detailed operationalization of how performativity works as that itself performs one particular reality on top of the fact that each case is highly contextual.[2] This chapter specifically draws on a combination of the security theories and ANT, as this combination helps to highlight the intra-action between events, observation and governmentality in this particular case. Another example, published elsewhere, focuses more on Foucault's *conduct of conduct* to highlight the same intra-action in relation to the governance of consumers through smart grids.[3] However, even though they follow different theories, discuss different aspects of energy (fossil fuel and electricity) and focus on different levels of materialization (the gas infrastructure is established, while the smart grids are under construction), in both cases the eventfulness of matter is problematized, interpreted and defined through a politics of ontology. And, in both cases, the issues are addressed by governing 'men in its relationship with things' through the milieu.[4] In the gas example below, this returns primarily with the lowering of the volume of gas that is extracted but also with the reinforcement of buildings.

Furthermore, in both illustrations energy security returns as a dominant discourse. Yet, it is a reading that builds on a certain level of absence of energy security within these debates. The phenomenon of energy security is so dominant, and yet so openly defined, that it hardly leaves traces and acts as a black box that drives people to act on others in their relationship with things in order to fulfil their desire for energy. Only in the gas example is energy security, in its narrow security of supply definition, mentioned as an argument. It is also here that energy security is reified through its opposition, as the opposition focused on the costs and safety decisions of a secure energy supply and not the supply of energy itself. In contrast, in the smart grid example energy security is hardly ever mentioned but only because it is generally accepted as the core driver behind the development of these technologies and their security apparatus. Moreover, that energy security is relatively absent does not mean that its meaning is static (both cases show how energy security itself changes). All of these reflections are for the conclusion, however, after the actual illustration on the earthquakes and natural gas extraction in the Netherlands.

In short, the Netherlands has been developing natural gas fields since the discovery of a large field in the region of Groningen in the 1950s. By 2015, this had resulted in €275 billion of state revenue as well as an infrastructure that connected almost all Dutch households to these gas fields for heating and cooking purposes. Simultaneously, the Groningen gas field has been drained to roughly one-third of its original low-calorific reserves (680 of its original 2,800 billion m^3). Unfortunately, from the mid-1980s onwards the areas above the fields have experienced light earthquakes, which have been increasing in magnitude and frequency (Figure 7.1, below).[5] For local residents, the everyday experience with and consequences of these earthquakes are conflicting with the long-standing national economic and security of supply concerns of the Dutch government and European energy markets. For a long time, the concerns for earthquakes remained limited to a small number of Groningen inhabitants.[6] This changed with the 2012 Huizinge earthquake, which, as the strongest and most heavily experienced earthquake in the Groningen area to date, led to a large public debate and a string of reports on all aspects of the Dutch natural gas extraction and ultimately to a cap on extraction as of 2014. Consequently, the question is why, after years of neglect, the security concerns of an initially small number of local residents suddenly superseded the energy security concerns of policymakers and energy scholars working on the Dutch gas and energy supplies. In other words, this chapter studies the security politics behind an understanding of energy security.

As mentioned in Chapter 2, the literature has described energy security as a 'slippery', 'fuzzy' and 'multidimensional' concept.[7] Definitions vary widely but simultaneously often share common points of interest building around notions of security of supply, vital systems, environmental and economic energy (in)security concerns.[8] As such, 'the energy security concept nicely weaves together disparate policy issues into one basket'.[9] Consequentially, the discussion on how energy security is used and defined seems ultimately a context-bound one.[10] As Pasqualetti remarks in his reflection on a two-day meeting of 40 energy security experts, 'Any discussion of energy security must recognize that it varies from one place and one culture to another, especially at the household level'.[11] Chapter 3 discussed the multiple ways through which this is resolved. More traditional historical and geopolitical policy analyses draw conclusions from the debates they describe.[12] Another prevalent approach is to map and develop the range of indicators and metrics used to analyse energy security.[13]

In a similar line, Cherp and Jewell, two strong proponents of a contextual approach, confirm the importance of 'social reality in shaping perceptions of truth' and identify a range of storylines about energy security, which they subsequently categorize into a framework that can be used for further analysis.[14]

Elsewhere, however, these same authors argue that 'energy security is an instance of security in general' and thus needs to inquire about the often-taken-for-granted values and assumptions behind energy security.[15] This chapter follows this latter position and argues that energy security, whether defined by scholars or as a shared understanding of participants, is part of a wider political spectrum. However, instead of defining what energy security is, it approaches the context-bound nature of energy security by studying *how* it works. How one of its elements, in this case security of supply, becomes what those involved understand it to be, how it changes over time and how it shapes debates about energy production, transport and consumption. And, while 'the need for empirical investigation into the ramifications of using … energy security [claims], for what purpose and by whom' is not a new question, it remains an imperative one,[16] especially given its small sample size, as the energy security literature mainly studies it from a constructivist perspective on language and discourse[17] or from securitization theory.[18]

The discussion below builds on these studies in two ways. First, the gasquake debate offers an analysis of a central energy security concept, security of supply, in its broader societal context.[19] As such, it does not study competing understandings of energy security[20] or the linguistic construction of a specific energy security understanding.[21] Instead it shows how the Dutch security of supply understanding is influencing the debate and in turn is shaped by the resistance it faces coming from the safety concerns of the local population. The repetitive intra-action between these two security concerns builds on a broader relational understanding that is at the heart of this chapter. It is a relationality that, second, extends the discursive focus above by incorporating ideas of securitization into the flat relationality offered by new materialist studies, in particular actor-network theory.[22] A flat relationality puts the shared understandings of security of supply and safety on an equal footing to the materiality of the earthquakes and the models used by the knowledge institutes. In other words, it reduces the analytical importance of the security claims by forcing the observer to study the security claims as part of their wider constantly changing context.

The analysis itself builds on media coverage, news briefs, (court) statements and a number of reports, among them the 2015 report by the Dutch Safety Board (DSB) on the decision-making process behind the Dutch natural gas extraction from 1959 until 2014.[23] Although the debate is still ongoing (January 2018 saw another earthquake of magnitude 3.4 on the Richter scale and reignited the debates about the speed of the reduction of gas extraction and damage compensation procedures), this chapter focuses specifically on the period following the Huizinge earthquake in 2012 up to the autumn of 2015, as by then most of the major policy changes had taken place, including the decision to cap the extraction volume.[24]

This chapter continues in Section 7.2 with an explication of the theory and subsequent contribution of this chapter. Section 7.3 introduces the Huizinge earthquake and its consequences. Besides a discussion of the gasquake itself, this section touches in particular on a report from the main regulatory body (the State Supervision of Mines (SSM)), which studied the Huizinge earthquake and shows how it is this report that actually shifted the value judgement behind the assessments of the decision makers. Section 7.4 discusses the internationally encapsulated position of the gas-industrial complex, while Section 7.5 looks more closely at the safety and security claims of the locals. Section 7.6 moves on to discuss the knowledge politics behind the earthquakes in order to highlight the struggle over the uncertainty behind the scientific models and how security considerations played a role in this process as well. The reflection brings these lines together.

7.2 Contextualizing security in a flat performative relationality

This chapter offers four main additions to the literature mentioned above. First, it completely conflates the distinction between security and politics. Second, it offers a long-term illustration that enforces a dynamic securitization analysis. Third, by placing security of supply in opposition to safety arguments, this debate not only studies two competing securitization processes but also places the resistance against current energy extraction practices in a Western context (contrary to insights from development studies on mining in Latin America or Africa),[25] with an immediacy and geographical focus that are not always present when energy security is for example studied in relation to climate security. Lastly, the debate studies this immediacy and how it increased over time by analysing the security claims in relation to the actual gasquakes and the scientific knowledge about them. The reinforcing interaction between these elements and the actual material presence of the gasquakes in turn supports the theoretical argument that security should be placed in a flat relationality.[26]

First, the question was raised whether the below offered a discussion of energy security or instead was about energy politics.[27] The relation between security and politics has in fact long been a core issue within critical security studies, and one that is gaining traction once again.[28] It also lies at the heart of securitization theory, discussed in depth in Chapter 4, when it proposes that security is a category separate from regular political and non-political issues.[29] In this theory, security is reserved for those extraordinary issues, like war, where an existential threat is believed to exist and extraordinary action is taken without concern for other social parties (e.g. outside normal political and economic routines).[30] As Chapter 4 concludes, energy security does not often fit that category and if it does it seems to be subject to economic security, climate security or military security.[31] In this sense, a discussion on energy security (contributing to its concepts and theories) as removed from a discussion on energy politics makes little sense as the former is always part of the latter and – as per the question above – the interaction itself deserves closer study.

This is reflected in other security theories, where the distinction is more conflated. For instance, in Foucault's biopolitics[32] or the security practices literature[33] security is not taken as a separate exceptionality but as a thoroughly routinized political process closely linked to knowledge practices (the ways people try to gain knowledge of the world) and the exercise of power. And, while these three theories approach the relation between security and politics differently, all share the view that security acts as a call for urgency based on distinctions between friend and enemy, safe and unsafe, risk and no risk, insecurity and security.[34] They also share an understanding that threat images are performative, first, because the wording of these threats help shape the world we live in by defining an event (and, in doing so, defining not only the event or enemy but also oneself and the (referent) object in need of security), and, second, because people act in the present to prevent these imagined future realities and through these acts materialize an alternative future.[35] On a political level, this implies that policymakers, scholars and other actors are responsible not only for a failure to counter threats but also for the threats that they propose themselves: for the distinctions between friend/enemy, for the choice of what to protect and for the resources drawn from other areas in terms of actual resources and agenda setting.[36]

Second, this chapter moves beyond the static nature of securitization theory with its implicit focus on a security claim made by a speech actor towards a single audience.[37] With its focus on the speech act, that moment when a securitizing actor identifies and presents a future event as a threat and subsequently asks the audience for support to counter it, the theory is predicated on single acts from the perspective of the speech actor. While it would be fairly simple to write the Groningen gasquake debate solely in terms of the local population securitizing their safety concerns, it would offer a description of one actor (a representative of the local population) who calls for the threat (future consequences of more gasquakes) in the hope to convince the respective audience (decision maker). However, the illustration below shows how neither the speech actor nor the audience was a single entity and that they constantly evolved, as the growing audience acceptance of the gasquake threat subsequently meant a growing mass of speech actors, each calling for the gasquake threats in their own way and wording (see Section 7.5).

Third, even though a more dynamic long-term reading of securitization theory would pick up on this, it would still only focus on one event and its accompanying security claim (the threat of future gasquakes). While there is some work done on conflicting energy security claims and interpretations[38] and competing security claims are one of the main reasons for issues to lose their urgency,[39] most of the work done on how energy security relates to other concerns sees energy security as subject to military and economic concerns (above) or as involving negotiations in line with the energy trilemma.[40] In contrast, the gasquake debate offers a case with two active security processes, a case where the securitization of the safety concerns of the local inhabitants interacts with the institutional security of supply concerns that dominate the debate.[41] For, even though security of supply considerations often remained implicit, as the debate primarily focused on safety concerns, compensation and extraction volumes, it was central to it. For the governing bodies and gas industry, security of supply was one of the core reasons to continue with business as usual. And therefore it was also central to the local population as it presented the boundary of what they could achieve. Irrespective of popular calls for a complete halt of extraction, on a political and legal level the argument focused on safe extraction levels and a minimalization of volumes (see Section 7.5). The negotiations and subsequent actions of the actors involved actually reproduced security of supply as a central motif, albeit with a redefined understanding of what it meant. In contrast to an earlier shift in the meaning of security of supply (from its initial unlimited extraction to the strategic 'small gas field policy') that resulted in equal measure from economic and security of supply reasoning (see Section 7.4), this security debate redefined the Dutch security of supply understanding away from economic gains to the minimal extraction necessary for a continuation of energy demand within the existing sociotechnical infrastructure.

Lastly, the debate nuances the discursive nature of security, something that comes across most strongly in the idea in securitization theory that security is 'a self-referential practice' and that threats are always imaginary (as they have not happened yet) and hence have no material standing.[42] As Van Wijk and Fischhendler argue in relation to risk, 'the question of whether risk is genuine or not is irrelevant. What matters instead is the actualisation of risk in policy processes in general.'[43] Yet, even when agreeing that threats are imaginary, the gasquake debate offers two ways in which material elements do play an active role. On the one hand, the support for the safety claims of the local population grew with the tangible experience of ever more and stronger gasquakes. In time it was accepted that (1) the gasquakes threatened local lives and livelihoods (a clear sharable referent object even with people not directly threatened), that (2) a reduction of extraction volumes was an effective (and potentially the only) solution, and, most of all, that (3) the causal relationship between extraction, gasquakes and increasing damage was undisputable.[44] On the other hand, the security of supply understanding has always been closely related to the existing gas infrastructure in the Netherlands. It is the existing infrastructure, including the conversion and extraction capacity and the gas-fired boilers in households (with resulting demand for gas), and the expected rate of change of that infrastructure, which offers the boundaries of minimum extraction capacity and thereby the current boundary of the local safety claim.

In other words, the debate highlights the need for (energy) security scholars to focus on the interaction between threat images, material events and especially the knowledge practices that mediate between these two. Contrary to the facilitating conditions that securitization theory offers, where material elements are subject to security,[45] this chapter places such elements in a flat relational ontology that equalizes them to security images. Such a flat relational ontology is proposed in the field which, by lack of a better term, is called 'new materialism'.[46] Scholars in this broad field have long been uneasy with a sole focus on linguistic explanations in constructivist work, while not wanting to refer back to more traditional realist and objectivist approaches that lose the performative insight that our shared social understandings of the world help shape it. While Chapter 5 concluded with the work of Barad and Foucault, for simplicity's sake this chapter uses the popular relational alternative offered by actor-network theory (ANT).[47] To repeat, this theory depicts the world in terms of networks of nodes, nodes which themselves are networks, and so on. These networks are irreducible and flat, meaning that one should not and cannot prefer one element over another. Whether that element is a social explanation (energy security), something material (a gas well), a law or a newspaper article, all these elements together form our current world. Importantly, as each node exists out of its own networks, theoretically, if any of these nodes is missing, the world is not the same. In other words, security claims and images are only one element out of many and they only have their specific meaning as part of a broader security apparatus.[48] As Latour summarizes the goal of ANT, 'It simply means not to impose a priori some spurious asymmetry among human intentional action and a material world of causal relations'.[49] Instead of assuming who acts (the speech actor) the idea is to actually study who acts by observing the traces that are left when relations change (the damage after a gasquake, a changed interpretation in reports, a new scientific model, etc.). Luckily, the core assumption is that networks are constantly changing and that stability is actually a product of hard work. In this sense, a security argument is the associative work done to create some semblance of stability in an ever-changing environment.

The reading below shows how the local inhabitants, the Grunningers in their dialect, here represented by the *Groninger Bodem Beweging* (GBB, which translates as Groningen Ground Movement), have been increasingly successful in securitizing the gasquakes as a threat to their livelihood. They have managed to put the induced earthquakes on the political agenda with a sense of urgency, while achieving a reduction in gas extraction and an increase in monetary compensation. The lesson however is that they were not believed until the number of measurements increased (which only occurred after repeated security claims), nor granted their urgency until the materiality of the gasquakes became visible through those measurements and material effects. Just calling for the threat of the gasquakes had little effect, as shown by the duration of the debate, but including the scientific uncertainty in those safety arguments ultimately did, especially as the uncertainty led to more seismographs, which led to more measured gasquakes, thereby strengthening the claims of the local population. Simultaneously, one can witness within government and industry a debate geared towards the weighing of the benefits of natural gas extraction and the risk and consequences of these earthquakes. For these institutions, in a typical risk logic, the debate itself rarely changes so much as the numbers and valuation behind it. Consequently, these assessments (weighing security of supply, safety and profit) and the uncertainty behind the scientific knowledge over these tremors lie at the core of the struggle between the local population and the gas-industrial complex (*het Gasgebouw*):[50] the small and closely connected group of companies and institutions in charge of Dutch natural gas extraction.[51]

7.3 The Huizinge earthquake, its interpretation and subsequent reactions

With a magnitude of 3.6 on the Richter scale, the Huizinge earthquake of 16 August 2012 was the strongest ever experienced in the Groningen area.[52] To understand its impact, it is necessary to place it in the ongoing debate on the potential relation between gas extraction and earthquakes. This includes the history that the Grunningers have with an increasing number of such earthquakes, which also have been of steadily higher magnitude (see Figure 7.1), and their struggle for acknowledgement of these quakes. Moreover, it includes the public pressure that resulted a year later from the news that 2013 turned out to be a record year, both in terms of an exceptionally high extraction volume with subsequent revenues[53] and in terms of a record number of 119 tremors, of which about twenty could be felt by inhabitants.[54] Within the debate on the gasquakes in Groningen, the Huizinge earthquake thus acts as a turning point, not only because its magnitude and subsequent public attention made the Grunningers start to protest in earnest (while allowing them a media platform) but also because it turned out to be the event that made officials acknowledge the need for a shift in their values. In this respect, the unsolicited report of the SSM in response to the Huizinge earthquake turned out to be especially important.[55]

As the official supervisory body, the SSM is responsible for ensuring that any mining activities in the Netherlands are in accordance with mining law.[56] Even though the Huizinge earthquake fell below the maximum of 3.9 on the Richter scale that was calculated in earlier risk assessments, the SSM initiated a study in

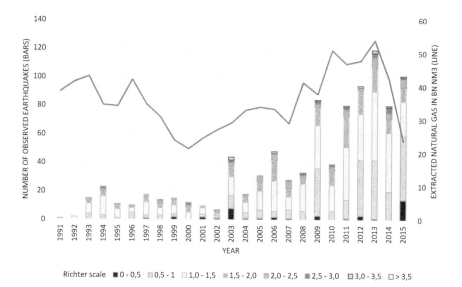

Figure 7.1 Frequency and magnitude of Groningen earthquakes.

Sources: author; adapted from NAM 2015a, with data from KNMI 2015 and NAM 2015a.

response to the growing unrest under the local population.[57] In this unsolicited report, the SSM, until 2015 still part of the Ministry of Economic Affairs (and thus part of the gas-industrial complex), openly and strongly questioned the constant adjustments and increases in the maximum magnitude that risk assessments have put forward since the early 1990s. The SSM combined this with earlier discussions on methodological uncertainties (see Section 7.6), and for the first time put these uncertainties up front. In fact, it concluded that it is impossible to estimate a possible maximum magnitude for the induced earthquakes in Groningen, even going so far as to take a magnitude of 5.0 as a valid possibility. To prevent this, it advised the Minister of Economic Affairs to reduce the output of the Groningen gas field as quickly and drastically as possible.

The SSM's shift came as a surprise to the other parties within the gas-industrial complex and its advice was not immediately accepted by the Ministry of Economic Affairs.[58] Instead the minister called for more research on the relation and effects of the earthquakes and the gas extraction.[59] He did so even though he acknowledged the possibility of higher-magnitude quakes and agreed with the NAM on a sum of €100 million for preventive construction measures.[60] The SSM report meanwhile influenced the regional government, the Province of Groningen, to initiate its own study, which repeated the main conclusions of the SSM and thereby confirmed the local concerns. In turn, the local population used these reports in their protests.[61]

In late 2013 the debate heated up once more following the publication of the range of reports requested by the minister, which confirmed many of the concerns voiced up to that moment, as well as the news that 2013 turned out to be a record year.[62] This time the government heeded the concerns and decided on a range of issues. These included, among others, the organization of an open dialogue among all affected private and public parties.[63] The government also tasked the NAM to conduct a full-scale below-ground survey (which had been missing thus far) and to reduce the extraction in the most effected clusters (while making up for the losses in other clusters). Simultaneously, it increased construction standards and preventive measures, while also improving the administrative procedures behind the compensation claims. And it offered the region an overall package to improve its economic and employment perspectives.[64] These measures were reinforced in the winter of 2014–2015, at which point the Minister of Economic Affairs initiated a first provisional cap on the total gas extraction from the Groningen field, which has since been extended.[65]

7.4 Balancing security of supply, profits and gasquakes

Even though the Ministry of Economic Affairs reduced production at specific clusters and initiated a cap on the total extracted volume, there remains a strong political debate about the installation of permanent extraction quotas. Currently, the safety concerns of the Grunningers are acknowledged. However, the parties responsible for gas extraction are arguing that they are bound to produce whatever is needed in response to contractual and seasonal demand from the Dutch consumers and the European countries that have bought Groningen gas on long-term contracts, and as such cannot limit themselves by installing a definite extraction cap.[66]

For instance, in its 2013 reaction to the reports from the SSM and other institutes on the Huizinge earthquake, the ministry argued that:

> In the near future, the Groningen gas extraction cannot be substituted by gas imports or other measures. A diminished availability of the Groningen natural gas will have serious consequences for the Dutch society and the societies in our surrounding countries.[67]

Likewise in 2015, after the initial decision to cap the volume, the ministry stated that:

> The consequences of long-term gas extraction in Groningen have become increasingly clear in recent years.... Simultaneously, the gas extraction is of essential importance for the energy supply in the Netherlands. Both the mixture of the gas and the fact that the gas from Groningen, due to its size, can be used flexibly, makes that a reduction from the Groningen gas field could lead to problems with the heating of buildings or other usages. In addition, for multiple decades the gas extraction is an important source of income for the Dutch state.[68]

This position has since been confirmed – but simultaneously limited – with a ruling from the highest administrative court in the Netherlands.[69] In its ruling, the court argued that in the assessment of the balance between the safety of the local population and security of supply (which the court defines as the low-calorific natural gas needed to comply with the demand for this type of gas) the minister had not explained why he chose the demand from a harsh winter scenario as the minimal supply benchmark instead of other more averaged demand scenarios.[70] As such, the court considered that the lowest minimal production was not $30\,\text{bn}\,\text{Nm}^3$ as favoured by the Ministry of Economic Affairs but that it should follow a more average scenario of $27\,\text{bn}\,\text{Nm}^3$ (with upward allowances for harsh winters).

This debate should be placed in an energy security context where the role of gas is already shifting for the Netherlands. Before the 1960s, the Dutch did not experience gas insecurity, simply because the level of gas consumption was minimal. Nowadays, the Netherlands is highly gas-dependent but not seen as gas-insecure because most of its gas is extracted domestically. With the draining of the Groningen gas field and other Dutch natural gas reserves this is expected to change. In the near future, the Dutch will be gas-insecure precisely because they have come to rely on it. Similarly, while the Netherlands is one of the least dependent European countries on Russian gas, it does import Russian gas and expects to increase its imports in the future to balance the reduction (and capping) of its emptying domestic fields – negatively influencing its security of supply position. To counter this position in a post-gas era, the Dutch state has launched an ambitious strategy to become the 'gas roundabout' of north-western Europe, combining its central position and the empty gas fields as natural storage facilities.[71] This gas roundabout idea aims to profit from the material (empty gas fields, pipelines and pumping and conversion capacity), legal (national and European long-term contract law and other regulations) and social (knowledgeable and influential gas elites) infrastructure that supports current gas extraction practices.

It is especially the latter social framework and the practices resulting from it that the DSB describes as encumbering the incorporation of the everyday safety of individual citizens in the gas extraction decisions. The board describes the everyday decision-making of these organizations as driven by three main paradigms: (1) maximum profits and winnings, (2) an optimal and strategic use of the natural resources, and (3) a continuity of Dutch gas supplies for both citizens and industry.[72] All three are captured in the 1974 small fields policy that replaced the initial unstructured pumping of gas in the early 1960s with a more strategic and economic long-term vision, based on an optimal development of new small gas fields by giving those fields priority on the Dutch gas market while using the Groningen field more sparingly as a swing field to fulfil the remaining demand.[73] In addition, the board also concluded that 'all efforts within the gas-industrial complex are aimed towards an imperceptible extraction of natural gas'.[74] Together these four maxims for a long time structured the everyday practices within the gas-industrial complex concerning the Groningen natural gas field. Importantly, they excluded the safety and insecurity concerns of the locals, except as a condition to be met for the other goals.[75] This, in turn, preconditioned the initial response from the organizations to claims of insecurity by locals and it explains why these responses, for a long time, have been soothing instead of informative and why they only followed the scientific updates of the magnitude – without repeating the mentioned uncertainties and knowledge gaps.[76]

Up until the debate following the SSM report, the gasquakes were considered an externality of the gas extraction, to be paid off through damage payments. Security of supply arguments simply meant business as usual and an optimal utilization of the Dutch gas fields. With the SSM report and the increasing pressure of the Grunningers, media and other parties (like local governments, safety regions, environmental groupings and so on), the discussion for the gas-industrial complex shifted to more extensive compensatory measures and mitigation practices, while opening up the question of when precisely the Dutch will be gas-secure. Looking back, the gasquake protests and subsequent shift from the SSM and other knowledge institutes forced the government to look closer at its understanding of security of supply. In doing so, it renewed its security of supply considerations that structured the energy debates in the Netherlands, but this time no longer interpreted it in economic or strategic terms but in terms of minimal gas extraction, specifically the minimum extraction that is required to fulfil the expected demand within the current soci-otechnical gas infrastructure, including the technical capacity to fulfil this demand with alternative supplies.

7.5 Calling on safety and scientific uncertainty to securitize the gasquakes

Of course, the local inhabitants above the Groningen gas field do not primarily deal with energy security concerns, contractual obligations and other risk assess-ments. Instead, they deal with a steady increase in frequency and magnitude of induced earthquakes caused by the natural gas extraction, a reluctant acknowledgement of the causality between extraction, quakes and damages, the difficulties in getting their direct and indirect earthquake damages reimbursed, decreasing house prices, a soothing communication by the gas-industrial complex and the perceived unequal distribution of the gas benefits.[77] These grievances and concerns are being voiced through media channels, legal proced-ures and letters of complaint to official institutions both regionally (like the safety region of Groningen and municipalities, which in turn also started to petition) and nationally (the SSM, parliament, the Minister of Economic Affairs and other regulatory and political institutions). In addition, the street protests grew in number and size to gatherings of hundreds of people by late 2014 (a number that is still growing).[78] These protests mainly focused on three claims. First, an overall demand for more attention and acceptance of the urgency of their problems with banners like 'Groningen a ticking time bomb'.[79] Second, especially later in the debate, showcasing their distrust towards the gas-industrial complex and in particular the NAM and the Minister of Economic Affairs with banners like 'Groningen tremors, but The Hague will quiver'.[80] And of course, the need to prevent further gasquakes by calling for a reduction of the natural gas extraction, with banners reading 'Kamp Gas Terug Nu', calling on Kamp, the Minister of Economic Affairs, to take his foot of the gas throttle.[81]

Obviously, some Grunningers have been aware of the gasquakes since the early 1990s and have tried to make themselves heard over time, either as indi-viduals[82] or through well-organized associations like the Groninger Ground Movement[83] or the more activist Shocking Groningen.[84] Looking back into the debate, it is illustrative that it took seven years and a large interdisciplinary study after the first earthquake in 1986 for the government and the NAM to officially acknowledge that the quakes were directly linked to the gas extrac-tion.[85] Until that study in 1993, the NAM ridiculed any claims from individuals and organizations that proposed such a link.[86] Once recognized, it took another twenty years for the official parties to start taking the risks and potential con-sequences of these induced earthquakes seriously enough to adapt their extrac-tion volumes. In those twenty years, every couple of years NAM, government and knowledge institutes have been forced to increase their estimates on the frequency and magnitude of potential quakes.

This eventful material reality and the decades of uncertain knowledge claims that accompany it (only reinforced by the slow response and delaying tactics of the gas-industrial complex since the Huizinge earthquake)[87] have led to feelings of insecurity and distrust.[88] That it took until 2013 for the uncertainty behind the earthquakes to become widespread public knowledge can be explained, so the argument goes, by the idea that the Grunningers were loyal and felt a sense of pride for helping their country to develop as a whole.[89] This slowly changed with the constant adjustment of the risk analyses and maximum magnitude of the earthquakes. In their search for answers, ever more people started to read the actual reports. They called on the uncertainty itself – in depth – in their letters of complaint to official institutions, for example to parliament.[90] The SSM report can be described as a turning point in this respect as well, as it not only informed the gas-industrial complex on the uncertainty in the analyses used so far but also supported and legitimized earlier readings of the Grunningers. As Van der Voort and Vanclay argue, 'the publication of the SSM report was an impact in itself with people becoming more anxious about what will happen to them'.[91] With the report and the media attention following it, a broader group of people learned that there was no certainty in store for them. What is more, the subsequent decision of the Minister of Economic Affairs to not directly follow the advice from the SSM gave the local population further ammunition and a clear focus for their grievances.

One of the largest and most organized interest groups is the GBB, which is actively lobbying, securitizing and litigating against the gas-industrial complex. In terms of security of supply, the GBB has constantly maintained that 'the extraction is reduced or halted until independent research shows at what level extraction can take place safely and securely'.[92] More importantly, 'if "safe extraction" is technical impossible, the GBB demands a total halt to the gas extraction'.[93] The GBB, together with other interested parties, made this tangible in their appeal to the highest administrative court in the Netherlands.[94] Building on their earlier call that the minister was not acting, they argued that legally the Ministry of Economic Affairs had not sufficiently substantiated the decision to cap the gas extraction. The ministry based its decisions on the certainties it had (the budgetary necessity of the gas benefits and security of supply), as opposed to the many uncertainties that accompany the gas extraction.[95] During the hearing, they called for a preferred reduction to 12 bn Nm^3, which the SSM in 2013 argued was a safe extraction level,[96] only accepting 21 bn Nm^3 if practical circumstances (read minimal security of supply and international contractual obligations) dictated otherwise in line with the bottom bandwidth of the GTS report.[97] Although they were unhappy with the legal ruling that confirmed the prevalence of security of supply concerns and set the level at 27 bn Nm^3,[98] this and the second option show that the GBB is forced to accept security of supply as a primary consideration in the debate. In other words, while the local population does not primarily discuss the gasquakes in terms of security of supply, the Dutch security of supply considerations are a constant absent presence in their claims for recognition, safety and a reduction of natural gas extraction.

7.6 The politics behind the gasquake science

Behind the debate on the minimal extraction volume lies the lack of knowledge over the tremors, both in terms of the availability of seismographs to actually monitor them and in terms of the uncertainty of the scientific models that are used to analyse and predict the gasquakes. In this respect, the Groningen gas debate shows (1) that what is not monitored and measured cannot be known, (2) that researchers had little incentives to work on the uncertainties in their models, especially (3) when the institutions using and sponsoring the results are happy with the outcomes. For the argument of this chapter, the debate shows that the decision to monitor is just as political as the decision to cap the extraction, and thus just as much a security decision, in other words that these decisions are heavily influenced by the interests and (energy) security positions of the parties involved, while simultaneously the parties feel justified in their positions by the subsequent outcomes of the studies.

For example, the only reason why the 1986 earthquake near Assen, a town just south of the Province of Groningen, which has its own small gas field, was identified as an earthquake, contrary to other orally reported 'air' tremors,[99] was because it was strong enough to be picked up by the sensors of the Royal Netherlands Meteorological Institution (KNMI) in the middle of the country. One of the main results of the debate that followed was that the Dutch Parliament influenced the Minister of Economic Affairs to order the KNMI – for which the earthquake was unexplainable as it lacked any longitudinal data – to install a number of seismographs around the Assen field in 1989 and around the Groningen field in 1992.[100] Reflectively, this brings up the question whether the start of Figure 7.1 resulted from the first true Groninger gasquake or was actually a result of the capacity to monitor them.

Either way, new waves of attention and research followed, among others in 1993, 1995, 1997, 2000, 2003, 2004, 2006 and 2009, owing to both earthquakes and regulatory changes. Of these, 2004 is of interest on two accounts: first, because the NAM for the first time publicly acknowledged that the maximum magnitude could be corrected if necessary, thereby implying that these cannot be estimated upfront, and, second, because the 2004 KNMI report not only increased the maximum magnitude to 3.9 after an update of its database, but also acknowledged that it was using static models for a situation that was not static (as the earthquakes result from shifting levels of gas extraction). However, it stated that it simply lacked the tools and subsurface information to cope with the fluctuating gas extraction and its relation to the induced earthquakes.[101]

It took until the Huizinge earthquake and the report by the SSM for the number of studies to increase dramatically (as did the number of seismographs). Many of these reports were commissioned as part of the large interdisciplinary study on the gas supply chain by the Ministry of Economic Affairs, which was receiving conflicting advice from the parties involved. Before 2013, the Ministry of Economic Affairs relied on the reports of the KNMI and other knowledge institutes and it expected these reports to be paid for by the NAM after its legal obligation to take the necessary safety precautions. However, as the DSB concludes, the NAM, as the exploiter most knowledgeable of the gas fields, welcomed the results from these reports that the earthquakes would only have a minimum impact and hence saw no cause to order additional studies on the uncertainties mentioned in the reports.[102] To be fair, it also took the semi-independent SSM until 2012 to put forward the uncertainties behind the scientific models and risk assessments.

With the NAM unwilling to study the scientific uncertainties, the ministry passively relying on advice and the SSM (and other expert councils) confirming the official reports, there was little incentive for the KNMI and other geological knowledge institutes to build alternative models. They tried, in part by looking at international research, but then quickly ran in to the unique material qualities of the Groningen gas field.[103] What remained were the static models and their outcomes, which 'focused on the number, the estimated maximum magnitude'.[104] In the end, this focus on the number worked both ways. It simplified matters for the gas-industrial complex as it constantly reinforced their position that the gasquakes did not pose a safety concern but over time also fuelled the distrust and uncertainty of the Grunningers, for whom the message not to worry contrasted with the constant adjustments and their experience with the actual earthquakes. The 2013 SSM report in this sense is interesting as it shows the importance of reflexivity within an energy security and safety debate, in particular the awareness that security of supply still needs a value judgement. Clearly, the Grunningers, with their focus on safety (and their search for answers), judged this threshold differently than the gas-industrial complex which looked at the balance between costs, profits, legal obligations and security of supply.

7.7 Reflection

The Groningen gasquake debate offers an example of a security debate in a developed country that puts security of supply considerations in a broader political context (in this case human security arguments). The analysis built on the interaction between three lines of enquiry. First, it took seriously the material reality of the earthquakes and their impacts, but also the gas field itself and the infrastructure around it, which keeps the debate localized (no earthquakes outside Groningen) and situated in a Northern European market through its pipelines at the same time. Second, it highlighted the politics over these earthquakes in terms of their origin and their potential impact, as well as the knowledge politics related to the scientific uncertainty of the models behind the earthquakes and their future trends. Third, it illustrated the struggle by the Grunningers to attribute a sense of urgency to both the materiality of the earthquakes and their future uncertainty. While successful, the above also shows that the local population could not escape the assessments of the gas-industrial complex.

In fact, in order to break with the conservative force stemming from the unreflective use of security of supply and in order to increase the audience acceptance of their safety claim, the local population needed, first (and painfully), the frequency and magnitude of the earthquakes as well as the visibility of their impact. Second, they helped to speed this up by focusing on the scientific uncertainties in the reports, slowly convincing neighbours and local authorities and then media, semi-regulatory institutions and so on. Third, once the SSM accepted the claim and published the report that legitimized the safety claim, the focus shifted to the decisions of the Minister of Economic Affairs. While this was initially a decision not to act, later the focus shifted to the decision about the level at which the natural gas extraction was capped. That said, while deciding to wait, the minister had already demanded the report from the GTS on the minimum security of supply levels, indicating an early acceptance to review the Dutch security of supply position.

In reflection, this illustration highlights the importance of a contextual and broader political understanding of security of supply. Throughout the debate, the gas-industrial complex slowly increased its willingness to accept and compensate for the consequences of the gas extraction. It was not until it had compromised on almost all aspects of the gas supply chain that it was willing to consider a closer look at the meaning of security of supply and reduce the extracted volume for safety concerns. Similarly, the case showed that, while the Grunningers called for a further reduction, they ultimately took a forced pragmatic legal stance towards a minimum extraction volume based on security of supply considerations. The debate thus centred on the meaning of security of supply as it relates to the low-calorific natural gas of the Groningen gas field, the estimated demand and the available technical capacity to substitute the Groningen gas. From a security perspective, however, the local population through their resistance against the gas extraction practices helped reify the principle of security of supply. Even though their concerns fitted a potential wider understanding of human energy security, they never really successfully questioned the security of supply principles behind the decision-making processes. Consequently, security of supply has been reproduced while it structured the debate by setting the outermost boundaries of acceptable actions and reductions. Still, it has not been reproduced the same: the gasquakes have challenged the Dutch understanding of security of supply, with natural gas no longer seen as a silent and bountiful resource but as a necessity to which the country is addicted.

From this we can draw three lessons. The first is the need to study the use of security and threat images in their wider political context. This should include the sociotechnical energy infrastructure, material causal events, and especially how security practices relate with other knowledge practices that are used to make sense of these events. Second, besides the insight that people who use security language are morally responsible for the distinctions they make, the agenda-setting power they exert and the resources that are drawn from other options, there is the lesson that security is simultaneously about urgency *and* conservation. It is about protecting and conserving a certain situation, except that it always fails as security changes the referent object itself. Protecting the existing gas extraction volumes had clear impacts (the gasquakes), just as arguing for the safety and living standards had an impact on the actual gas extraction (a cap). Security is never static and the search for the definition of what energy security is can therefore only be described as an active political intervention itself. Energy security scholars should be aware of this and not only study 'new' security threats or categorize old ones but explicitly focus on existing energy security practices, their distinctions and the constant renegotiation and hard work that keep them stable.

Notes

1 This chapter is a lightly altered version of an article published in the journal *Energy Research & Social Science* and reproduced under a Creative Commons Attribution 4.0 International License (CC BY); see Kester 2017 (doi:10.1016/j.erss.2016.12.019).
2 Then again, not providing such an operationalization also performs a reality, although it offers one open to free assemblages and association on the side of the reader.
3 For the purpose of this chapter, the choice of debate is thus second to the idea to highlight the performative approach. Another example, with another performative approach can be found in relation to smart grids, see Kester 2016.
4 Foucault 2007, 96.
5 NAM 2015a; KNMI 2015.
6 Van der Voort and Vanclay 2015.
7 Chester 2010; Valentine 2011.
8 Sovacool 2011; Winzer 2012.
9 Fischhendler and Nathan 2014, 152.
10 Cherp and Jewell 2011; Chester 2010.
11 Pasqualetti 2011, 278.
12 Luft and Korin 2009; Yergin 2012.
13 Ang, Choong, and Ng 2015; Kruyt *et al.* 2009; Sovacool 2011.
14 Cherp and Jewell 2011, 334.
15 Cherp and Jewell 2014, 415.
16 Fischhendler and Nathan 2014, 153.
17 Herbstreuth 2014; Littlefield 2013.
18 Buzan, Wæver and de Wilde 1998. Christou and Adamides 2013; Fischhendler, Boymel and Boykoff 2014; Fischhendler and Nathan 2014; Natorski and Herranz Surrallés 2008; Nyman 2014.
19 Christou and Adamides 2013.
20 Fischhendler and Nathan 2014.
21 Herbstreuth 2014; Natorski and Herranz Surrallés 2008.
22 Barad 2007; Bennett 2005; Coole and Frost 2010. On ANT, see Latour 2005; Mol 2002.
23 DSB 2015.
24 Ministerie van Economische Zaken 2015d.
25 Bebbington *et al.* 2008.
26 This comes with a strong moral responsibility for the observer, as it is they who decide what to study as part of this relationality or network: Latour 2002.
27 Many thanks to an anonymous reviewer for bringing this up.
28 Mandelbaum, Kristensen and Athanassiou 2016; Wibben 2016.
29 Buzan, Wæver and de Wilde 1998, 23–24.
30 Ibid., 26.

31 Buzan, Wæver and de Wilde 1998; Christou and Adamides 2013, 509–510; Natorski and Herranz Surrallés 2008, 74.
32 Foucault 2007.
33 Balzacq *et al.* 2010.
34 Booth 2007.
35 These insights are related to a performative reading of energy security; see also Bridge 2015, where actors are seen to be directed in how they approach the world by earlier practices and understandings, and subsequently, when acting (re)produce those or other new social and material practices and effects.
36 Balzacq 2011, xiii.
37 Balzacq 2005; Roe 2008.
38 Fischhendler, Boymel and Boykoff 2014; Fischhendler and Nathan 2014.
39 de Wilde 2008.
40 WEC 2015.
41 This can be read as implying that safety concerns about energy production are not part of energy security itself, which I would argue against in line with the focus on the social/environmental acceptability of vital energy systems. Here, however, I make an analytical distinction to better contrast the positions of the two parties (which together with the choice for specific spokespersons is another analytical choice to simplify the debate).
42 Buzan, Wæver and de Wilde 1998, 24.
43 Van Wijk and Fischhendler 2016, 22 quoting Adam and Van Loon, 2000.
44 Natorski and Herranz Surrallés 2008, 74.
45 Buzan, Wæver and de Wilde 1998, 33.
46 Barad 2007; Bennett 2005; Coole and Frost 2010.
47 Latour 2005; Mol 2002.
48 Foucault 2007; cf. Schouten 2014.
49 Latour 2005, 76.
50 All translations from Dutch are by the author, but I am grateful to the editors and reviewers for offering a better translation of this term.
51 The Netherlands has a framework that distributes the legal ownership, extraction rights and profit sharing between the Dutch state and the companies involved, through a range of legal entities and subsidiaries, which nowadays is bundled under the heading *het Gasgebouw* (see for example Van Gastel, Van Maanen and Kuijken 2014). In this tight network, Shell and ExxonMobil have the licence to operate the Groningen natural gas field through their ownership of the Nederlandse Aardolie Maatschappij (NAM). Both also own shares of GasTerra, the company responsible for the sale of the natural gas. The Dutch state (read the Ministry of Economic Affairs) is directly involved through a legal entity called EBN. The NAM and EBN both cooperate in and own the Maatschap Groningen, which is responsible for the actual exploitation of the natural gas fields. The Dutch state also owns shares of GasTerra both directly (via the Ministry of Finance) and indirectly (through EBN). All in all, the DSB (2015, 8, 75, 88) concludes that, through these constructions and the close personal connections between the boards of GasTerra and the Maatschap Groningen, the decision-making on Dutch natural gas is made in a closed system that is effectively owned by Shell, ExxonMobil and the Dutch state: a system devoid of opposition and ruled by ten persons at most.
52 Although not the strongest ever experienced in the Netherlands (which was a natural earthquake in Roermond, 1992), and not nearly close to the magnitude of some of the recent US shale gas-induced earthquakes. The Richter scale is logarithmic and its magnitude highlights the energy released. Everything below 3 on the Richter scale is hardly perceptible. That said, the actual experienced magnitude depends on multiple factors (energy released, wave speed, ground conditions, force, duration, depth and so on), not all of which relate one-on-one to the

earthquakes in Groningen. In particular, the minimal depth between 1 and 3 km, the ground conditions (clay, high groundwater levels) and the fast speed of the ground waves mean that people experience them earlier than the Richter scale would indicate. Other complicating factors are the uncertainty within the Richter scale itself (±0.1) and the delay of about a year between the gas extraction and the earthquakes.

53 Up to 54 billion Nm^3; see NAM 2015b.
54 Out of 133 total in the Netherlands; see KNMI 2015.
55 SSM 2013.
56 Ministerie van Economische Zaken 2008.
57 SSM 2013; see also DSB 2015, 66; Muntendam-Bos and De Waal 2013.
58 DSB 2015, 77.
59 GTS 2013.
60 Ministerie van Economische Zaken 2013a, 2013b, 2013c; Commissie Meijer 2013.
61 Provincie Groningen 2013; Commissie Meijer 2013.
62 KNMI 2015; NAM 2015a; SSM 2014a, 2014b.
63 Kabinet, Provincie Groningen and NAM 2014.
64 Ministerie van Economische Zaken 2014.
65 Ministerie van Economische Zaken 2015b, 2015a.
66 Ministerie van Economische Zaken 2015d, 2015a.
67 Ministerie van Economische Zaken 2013a, 4.
68 Ministerie van Economische Zaken 2015c, 4.
69 RvS 2015b; RvS 2015a.
70 GTS 2013.
71 Ministerie van Economische Zaken 2006.
72 DSB 2015, 70–71; comparable: SSM 2014a, 4.
73 Steen *et al.* 2013.
74 DSB 2015, 74.
75 Ibid., 71; GBB 2015a.
76 DSB 2015, 81–82, 86.
77 GBB 2013b; Havermans 2015; Van den Berg 2015; Van der Voort and Vanclay 2015, 7–9.
78 FocusGroningen 2014.
79 RTL Nieuws 2014.
80 OOG TV 2015.
81 De Telegraaf 2015.
82 See Van Hamersvelt 2013 on Van der Sluis. Or, more recently, Dwarshuis 2015; Groeneveld 2015.
83 Groninger Bodem Beweging, see GBB 2011, 2013b.
84 Schokkend-Groningen.nl 2013.
85 BOA 1993.
86 Van Hamersvelt 2013.
87 GBB 2014.
88 Van der Voort and Vanclay 2015.
89 Commissie Meijer 2013, 21.
90 See GBB 2013a.
91 Van der Voort and Vanclay 2015, 8.
92 GBB 2015b, 4.
93 GBB 2013b, 1.
94 Plas Bossinade Advocaten Notarissen 2015.
95 GBB 2015a, 7.
96 Muntendam-Bos and De Waal 2013.
97 GTS 2013.
98 GBB 2015c.

99 Van den Berg 2015.
100 Commissie Meijer 2013; Havermans 2015; Meij 1994; Van den Berg 2015.
101 Van Eck *et al*. 2004; see also Dost and Kraaijpoel 2013 for a similar study after the Huizinge earthquake; or the BOA 1993 report for a predecessor.
102 DSB 2015, 65–66.
103 See note 3; Ibid., 64.
104 Ibid., 63.

Bibliography

Ang, B. W., W. L. Choong and T. S. Ng. 2015. Energy security: Definitions, dimensions and indexes. *Renewable and Sustainable Energy Reviews* 42: 1077–1093.

Balzacq, Thierry. 2005. The three faces of securitization: Political agency, audience and context. *European journal of international relations* 11 (2): 171–201.

Balzacq, Thierry. ed. 2011. *Securitization theory: How security problems emerge and dissolve*. PRIO New Security Studies. London and New York: Routledge.

Balzacq, Thierry, Tugba Basaran, Didier Bigo, Emmanuel-Pierre Guittet and Christian Olsson. 2010. Security practices. In *International Studies Encyclopedia Online*, edited by Robert A. Denemark. Oxford: Blackwell. Available from www.blackwellreference.com/public/book.html?id=g9781444336597_9781444336597.

Barad, Karen. 2007. *Meeting the universe halfway: Quantum physics and the entanglement of matter and meaning*. Durham, NC, and London: Duke University Press.

Bebbington, Anthony, Denise Humphreys Bebbington, Jeffrey Bury, Jeannet Lingan, Juan Pablo Muñoz and Martin Scurrah. 2008. Mining and social movements: Struggles over livelihood and rural territorial development in the Andes. *World Development* 36 (12): 2888–2905.

Bennett, Jane. 2005. The agency of assemblages and the North American blackout. *Public Culture* 17 (3): 445–465.

BOA. 1993. *Eindrapport multidisciplinair onderzoek naar de relatie tussen gaswinning en aardbevingen in Noord-Nederland*. Begeleidingscommissie Onderzoek Aardbevingen.

Booth, Ken. 2007. *Theory of world security*. Cambridge and New York: Cambridge University Press.

Bridge, Gavin. 2015. Energy (in)security: World-making in an age of scarcity. *The Geographical Journal* 181 (4): 328–339.

Buzan, Barry, Ole Wæver and Jaap H. de Wilde. 1998. *Security: A new framework for analysis*. Boulder, CO: Lynne Rienner.

Cherp, Aleh, and Jessica Jewell. 2011. Energy Challenges: From local universalism to global contextualism. In *The Routledge handbook of energy security*, edited by Benjamin K. Sovacool, 330–355. London and New York: Routledge.

Cherp, Aleh, and Jessica Jewell. 2014. The concept of energy security: Beyond the four As. *Energy Policy* 75: 415–421.

Chester, Lynne. 2010. Conceptualising energy security and making explicit its polysemic nature. *Energy Policy* 38 (2): 887–895.

Christou, Odysseas, and Constantinos Adamides. 2013. Energy securitization and dese-curitization in the New Middle East. *Security Dialogue* 44 (5–6): 507–522.

Commissie Meijer. 2013. *Vertrouwen in een Duurzame Toekomst: Een Stevig Perspectief voor Noord-Oost Groningen*. Groningen: Commissie Duurzame Toekomst Noord-Oost Groningen.

Coole, Diana, and Samantha Frost, eds. 2010. *New materialisms: Ontology, agency, and politics.* Durham, NC, and London: Duke University Press.

De Telegraaf. 2015. VVD beweegt nog niet in gasdebat. Available from www.telegraaf.nl/binnenland/23676051/__VVD_beweegt_niet_in_gasdebat__.html. Accessed 9 October 2016.

de Wilde, Jaap H. 2008. Environmental security deconstructed. In *Globalization and environmental challenges*, edited by Hans Günter Brauch, Úrsula Oswald Spring, Habil Czeslaw Mesjasz, John Grin, Pál Dunay, Navnita Chadha Behera, Béchir Chourou, Patricia Kameri-Mbote and P. H. Liotta, 595–602. Hexagon series on human and environmental security and peace 3. Berlin Heidelberg: Springer.

Dost, Bernard, and Dirk Kraaijpoel. 2013. *The August 16, 2012 earthquake near Huizinge (Groningen).* De Bilt: Koninklijk Nederlands Meteorologisch Instituut.

DSB. 2015. *Aardbevingsrisico's in Groningen: Onderzoek naar de rol van veiligheid van burgers in de besluitvorming over de gaswinning (1959–2014).* The Hague: Onderzoekraad voor Veiligheid [Dutch Safety Board].

Dwarshuis, Kor. 2015. Gronings gas een ramp in slow motion. Available from www.dwarshuis.com/aardbevingen-groningen/menu/. Accessed 19 May 2016.

Fischhendler, Itay, Dror Boymel and Maxwell T. Boykoff. 2014. How competing securitized discourses over land appropriation are constructed: The promotion of solar energy in the Israeli desert. *Environmental Communication* 10 (2): 147–168.

Fischhendler, Itay, and Daniel Nathan. 2014. In the name of energy security: The struggle over the exportation of Israeli natural gas. *Energy Policy* 70: 152–162.

FocusGroningen. 2014. Groningen massaal in actie tegen gaswinning. Available from www.focusgroningen.nl/groningen-massaal-in-actie-tegen-gaswinning. Accessed 9 October 2016.

Foucault, Michel. 2007. *Security, territory, population: Lectures at the Collège de France 1977–1978*, edited by Michel Senellart, translated by Graham Burchell. New York: Palgrave Macmillan.

GBB. 2011. Ontstaansgeschiedenis Groninger Bodem Beweging. Available from www.groninger-bodem-beweging.nl/index.php/geschiedenis. Accessed 14 April 2015.

GBB. 2013a. Inbreng van de vereniging Groninger bodem beweging t.a.v. commissie onderzoek bodemdaling. Groninger Bodem Beweging.

GBB. 2013b. *Hoofddoelen van de GBB.* Groninger Bodem Beweging.

GBB. 2014. Besluit gaswinning wederom vertraagd. Available from www.groninger-bodem-beweging.nl/55-besluit-gaswinning-wederom-vertraagd. Accessed 18 May 2016.

GBB. 2015a. *Nieuwsbrief nr. 19.* Groninger Bodem Beweging.

GBB. 2015b. *Nieuwsbrief nr. 20.* Groninger Bodem Beweging.

GBB. 2015c. *Nieuwsbrief nr. 30.* Groninger Bodem Beweging.

Groeneveld, Hilda. 2015. Onder Groningen. Available from www.ondergroningen.nl. Accessed 19 May 2016.

GTS. 2013. *Mogelijkheden kwaliteitsconversie en gevolgen voor de leveringszekerheid. Groningengas op de Noordwest-Europese Gasmarkt.* Groningen: Gasunie Transport Services B. V.

Havermans, Onno. 2015. Groningse gasboringen: Ramp in slow motion. *TROUW*, 2015–02–18 edition.

Herbstreuth, Sebastian. 2014. Constructing dependency: The United States and the problem of foreign oil. *Millennium – Journal of International Studies* 43 (1): 24–42.

Kabinet, Provincie Groningen, and NAM. 2014. *Vertrouwen in herstel, herstel van vertrouwen.*

Kester, Johannes. 2016. Conducting a smarter grid: Reflecting on the power and security behind smart grids with Foucault. In *Smart grids from a global perspective*, 197–213. Cham: Springer.

Kester, Johannes. 2017. Energy security and human security in a Dutch gasquake context: A case of localized performative politics. *Energy Research & Social Science* 24 (Supplement C): 12–20.

KNMI. 2015. *Geïnduceerde aardbevingen in Nederland*. De Bilt: Koninklijk Nederlands Meteorologisch Instituut. Available from www.knmi.nl/seismologie/geinduceerde-bevingen-nl.pdf. Accessed 4 November 2015.

Kruyt, B., D. P. Van Vuuren, H. J. M. De Vries and H. Groenenberg. 2009. Indicators for energy security. *Energy Policy* 37 (6): 2166–2181.

Latour, Bruno. 2002. Morality and technology: The end of the means. Translated by C. Venn. *Theory, Culture & Society* 19 (5–6): 247–260.

Latour, Bruno. 2005. *Reassembling the social: An introduction to Actor-Network-Theory*. Oxford: Oxford University Press.

Littlefield, Scott R. 2013. Security, independence, and sustainability: Imprecise language and the manipulation of energy policy in the United States. *Energy Policy* 52: 779–788.

Luft, Gal, and Anne Korin. 2009. *Energy security challenges for the 21st century: A reference handbook*. Santa Barbara, CA: Praeger.

Mandelbaum, Moran, Anna Maria Friis Kristensen and Cerelia Athanassiou. 2016. De/Re-constructing the political: How do critical approaches to 'security' frame our understanding of the political? *Critical Studies on Security* 4 (2): 133–136.

Meij, Wim. 1994. KNMI helpt oliemaatschappijen. *Algemeen Dagblad*, 1994–09–24 edition.

Ministerie van Economische Zaken. 2006. *Visie op de gasmarkt*. ET/EM/ 6009634.

Ministerie van Economische Zaken. 2008. State Supervision of Mines: Organisation. Available from www.sodm.nl/english/organisation. Accessed 19 April 2015.

Ministerie van Economische Zaken. 2013a. *Gaswinning Groningen veld*. DGETM-EM/13010946.

Ministerie van Economische Zaken. 2013b. *Toezending stukken naar aanleiding van gedane toezeggingen in Algemeen Overleg gaswinning Groningen*. DGETM-EM/13021701.

Ministerie van Economische Zaken. 2013c. *Nadere informatie over Groningen gaswinning en aardbevingen*. DGETM-EM/13052090.

Ministerie van Economische Zaken. 2014. *Gaswinning in Groningen*. DGETM/14008697.

Ministerie van Economische Zaken. 2015a. *Instemming gewijzigd winningsplan Groningen-veld*. ETM/EM /13208000.

Ministerie van Economische Zaken. 2015b. *Gaswinning Groningen*. DGETM-EM/ 15015030.

Ministerie van Economische Zaken. 2015c. *Kabinetsreactie op OVV-rapport Aardbevings-risico's in Groningen*. DGETM-EM/15042994.

Ministerie van Economische Zaken. 2015d. *Besluit Gaswinning Groningen in 2015*. DGETM/15086391.

Mol, Annemarie. 2002. *The body multiple: Ontology in medical practice*. Durham, NC, and London: Duke University Press.

Muntendam-Bos, A. G., and J. A. De Waal. 2013. *Reassessment of the probability of higher magnitude earthquakes in the Groningen gas field*. The Hague: State Supervision of Mines.

NAM. 2015a. Aantal aardbevingen in het Groningen-gasveld. Available from http://feitenencijfers.namplatform.nl. Accessed 4 November 2015.

NAM. 2015b. Gaswinning. Available from http://feitenencijfers.namplatform.nl/gaswinning. Accessed 4 November 2015.

Natorski, Michal, and Anna Herranz Surrallés. 2008. Securitizing moves to nowhere? The framing of the European Union's energy policy. *Journal of Contemporary European Research* 4 (2): pp. 70–89.

Nyman, Jonna. 2014. 'Red storm ahead': Securitisation of energy in US–China Relations. *Millennium – Journal of International Studies* 43 (1): 43–65.

OOG TV. 2015. Protest en toezeggingen bij bezoek minister Kamp. Available from www.oogtv.nl/2015/01/protest-en-toezeggingen-bij-bezoek-minister-kamp. Accessed 9 October 2016.

Pasqualetti, Martin J. 2011. The competing dimensions of energy security. In *The Routledge handbook of energy security*, edited by Benjamin K. Sovacool, 275–290. London and New York: Routledge.

Plas Bossinade Advocaten Notarissen. 2015. *Beroep instemmingsbesluit januari 2015. Namens GBB; Milieudefensie; Stichting Natuur en Milieufederatie Groningen; Landelijke Vereniging tot Behoud van de Waddenzee*. Groningen: Plas Bossinade Advocaten N. V.

Provincie Groningen. 2013. *Standpunt inzake aardbevingsgevoeligheid Groningse gasveld*. 2013–05059/5, BJC.

Roe, Paul. 2008. Actor, audience (s) and emergency measures: Securitization and the UK's decision to invade Iraq. *Security Dialogue* 39 (6): 615–635.

RTL Nieuws. 2014. Groningers zetten protest voort in ander dorp. *RTL Nieuws*. Available from www.rtlnieuws.nl/nieuws/binnenland/groningers-zetten-protest-voort-ander-dorp. Accessed 9 October 2016.

RvS. 2015a. *Uitspraak 201501544/4/A4*. ECLI:NL:RVS:2015:1712. The Hague: Raad van State.

RvS. 2015b. *Uitspraak 201501544/4/A4*. ECLI:NL:RVS:2015:3578. The Hague: Raad van State.

Schokkend-Groningen.nl. 2013. Available from http://schokkend-groningen.nl/website/schokkend-groningen-nl. Accessed 19 May 2016.

Schouten, Peer. 2014. Security as controversy: Reassembling security at Amsterdam Airport. *Security Dialogue* 45 (1): 23–42.

Sovacool, Benjamin K. 2011. Introduction: Defining, measuring, and exploring energy security. In *The Routledge handbook of energy security*, edited by Benjamin K. Sovacool, 1–42. London and New York: Routledge.

SSM. 2013. *Aardbevingen in de Provincie Groningen*. 13010015. The Hague: State Supervision of Mines.

SSM. 2014a. *Aanbieding advies 'wijziging winningsplan Groningen 2013' en 'meet- en monitoringsplan'*. 14005929. The Hague: State Supervision of Mines.

SSM. 2014b. *Risico analyse aardgasbevingen Groningen*. The Hague: State Supervision of Mines.

Valentine, Scott Victor. 2011. The fuzzy nature of energy security. In *The Routledge handbook of energy security*, edited by Benjamin K. Sovacool, 56–73. London and New York: Routledge.

Van den Berg, Jurre. 2015. Hoogstens zou het servies een keertje rammelen. *De Volkskrant*, 18 February 2015, sec. Ten Eerste.

Van der Steen, Martijn, Nancy Chin-A-Fat, Jorren Scherpenisse and Mark van Twist. 2013. *Van een zachte landing naar een verlengde vlucht: Een reflectie op het Kleineveldenbeleid*. The Hague: Nederlandse School voor Openbaar Bestuur.

Van der Voort, Nick, and Frank Vanclay. 2015. Social impacts of earthquakes caused by gas extraction in the Province of Groningen, The Netherlands. *Environmental Impact Assessment Review* 50: 1–15.

Van Eck, Torild, Femke Goutbeek, Hein Haak, and Bernard Dost. 2004. *Seismic hazard due to small shallow induced earthquakes*. De Bilt: Koninklijk Nederlands Meteorologisch Instituut.

Van Gastel, Marcel, Geert van Maanen, and Wim Kuijken. 2014. *Onderzoek toekomst governance gasgebouw*. The Hague: ADBTOPConsult.

Van Hamersvelt, Willem. 2013. Van der Sluis had gelijk maar sloeg onzin uit. *Dagblad van het Noorden*, 2013-2-2 edition.

WEC. 2015. *Priority actions on climate change and how to balance the trilemma*. World Energy Trilemma. London: World Energy Council & Oliver Wyman.

Wibben, Annick T. R. 2016. Opening security: Recovering critical scholarship as political. *Critical Studies on Security* 4 (2): 137–153.

Van Wijk, Josef, and Itay Fischhendler. 2016. The construction of urgency discourse around mega-projects: The Israeli case. *Policy Sciences* 50 (3): 469–494.

Winzer, Christian. 2012. Conceptualizing energy security. *Energy Policy* 46: 36–48.

Yergin, Daniel. 2012. *The quest: Energy, security, and the remaking of the modern world*. Updated revised edition. New York, NY: Penguin.

8 Conclusion

Performativity, disclosure and the politics of energy security

8.1 The tightrope walker

The philosopher Achterhuis, in one of his books on scarcity, described the world we live in with the metaphor of a tightrope walker: a world where society acts as an agent who is constantly collecting goods, yet needs to keep moving to stay upright. With each good the agent becomes heavier and more packed, forcing him to speed up to keep his balance and able to move to the next good, always forwards at increasing speeds, never able to look back and reflect on what he carries or leaves in his wake.[1] Achterhuis uses this metaphor to criticize the insatiable desire of relative scarcity that lies behind modern resource use and the consequential imbalance that this creates with local and planetary environmental boundaries. The *desire* for more and the *fear* of falling are also two core elements that shape the politics of energy security. Neither of these has received much attention in the literature on energy security. Perhaps because there is no need, for who does not know what is desired and feared when discussing energy security? Who would object to the shared concern that energy needs to be secured and who does not agree that all humans are entitled to a shared minimum energy consumption? Yet, even the brief personal reflection that opened this book indicates that there is not a single energy security but that what is secured differs across time, space, person and purse.

This view is confirmed in the first two chapters, both dealing with the current energy security literature. Chapter 2 provided a brief historical perspective of the meaning of energy security and its proliferation in terms of referent objects and scale. It found a concept that has evolved and proliferated from an initial understanding in terms of security of supply into a concept that also covers economic, environmental, human rights and systemic aspects in line with the growing importance of energy in society. Chapter 3 subsequently reflected briefly on the different methods and approaches that the energy security literature uses to make sense of its issue area. It discussed the qualitative and quantitative methods used to define energy security, in addition to the theorization of and the search for underlying logics hidden behind energy security. In short, the first chapters argued that the search for a definition of energy security might repeatedly add new variables but does not provide any understanding as to why it constantly proliferates nor what its effects are. Moreover, they reflected that the use of current methods and theories seems to help shape a specific form of energy security (in this particular reading at least). As such the book argues that the search for a central definition or the core logics of energy security provides a form of closure that will always be hiding the virtuality and the differences that result from the actual energy security associations and is therefore inhibitive of a deeper understanding of energy security and its underlying social processes.

To be clear, this is definitely not a call to drop the search for such definitions, to give up scenarios and modelling, or to throw away the study of the theories and logics behind energy security. It is simply an observation that the currently literature on energy security misses a set of questions and literature, which focuses on this proliferation as it analyses the politics of energy security *in use*. What for instance causes the proliferation of energy security definitions? Is it problematic that each author and report upholds their own definition? And how do we study energy security politics, not just energy security? For the latter question in particular, the chapters above move beyond energy to the broad literature on security. In other words, how can the focus be shifted from *energy* security to energy security *as* security in order to ask what security is and how security works (Chapter 4)? And how do the social and linguistic focus of current critical security studies relate to the materiality of the systems behind energy production, transport and consumption (Chapter 5)? Another question to study is how security acts politically in relation to other social processes (Chapter 6). In short, the chapters offered initial answers to these questions by unpacking energy security with critical social theory from the field of critical security studies, new materialism and governmentality studies.

Chapter 4 argued that security is not one thing or one logic but that there are multiple forms of insecurity, different techniques that can be used to identify undesired futures and several security logics that enable a person to act in the present on such futures. Security hence was defined *as the mode through which people identify undesirable futures and act upon them in the present*. The latter half of the chapter discussed security as a performative act. It finds a mode of reasoning that (1) always discriminates, as there are always things and persons excluded from that what is to be secured, which (2) is productive and not just conservative as it helps create the values that it tries to secure, and which (3) is called upon in political arenas to provide a level of urgency to its referent object. And it is a mode of reasoning (4) that through risk assessments and insurance practices to a large extent structures our daily lives. Above all, this chapter sketched an image of security as inherently empty and constantly bound to new referent objects. For the moment that people think themselves secure is also the moment that new insecurities arise: a disturbing conclusion but also a hopeful one, as it means that we can secure increasingly more specific or 'luxurious' aspects of life.

Chapter 5 started from the question how the materiality of the energy systems relates to the social- and linguistic-driven explanations of security. For an answer, this chapter theorized the relationship between knowledge and mate-riality to understand the durability, spatiality and eventfulness that spring from these resources and infrastructure systems. Through multiple theories, ranging from critical IR theories to a number of theories squared under the header of 'new materialism', this chapter makes four points. First, it built on the critical literature and its epistemological argument that all observations are pre-structured by previous knowledge, with the realization that the material/knowledge duality is a post hoc explanation that does not exist in reality but nevertheless is needed academically to understand the world we live in. Second, this chapter, building on the new materialist literature, argued that we should study the political processes through which matter comes to matter, in terms of both knowledge and its effects, and give ample voice to the mediating role of matter in these processes. Third, to study these processes, what needs to be studied are the knowledge practices through which we get to know matter. More specifically, this chapter ended with the idea that observation, by humans, objects or a mix of both, is based on the creation of distinctions between that what is and what is not observed. As in the case of security, such distinctions are ultimately both ethical and material choices, as each observation assembles and folds a set of relations together that make up what we understand as the ontology of an (unknown or uncertain) phenomenon. Together these new materialist theories offer a world of *materialdiscursive* relationships, their becom-ing and breaking apart, a world of artificial distinctions and boundaries custom-ized in social laws but also a world of artefacts and other hard material achievements.

Chapter 6 continued with the closing remarks on the politics of matter in the previous chapter and the insights on risk in the security chapter, which both pointed to the later work of Michel Foucault and one main question: if we see security as a performative practice that shapes a messy materialdiscursive world, then how can we make sense of the politics and power behind it, not just the politics of the application of security but also more broadly the role of security in society? This chapter continued the discussion on the relationship between events, observation and the materialdiscursive world, by turning to Foucault's insights on power/knowledge, biopolitics, conduct of conduct, and governmen-tality. In particular, it paid special attention to the exercise of power that Foucault describes in terms of the indirect governing of processes of circulation (goods, people and so on) by influencing the milieu of these circulations. After this chapter it is possible to read energy security in terms of a political process that (1) is productive, (2) is based on knowledge gathering practices, (3) acts as a form of governance and materialization and (4) not only interprets events but helps draw deeper social and sociotechnical boundaries by differentiating between nature, economics, the political and society.

On their own, each of these chapters further problematized the current understandings of energy security, and each of these chapters offered alternative insights and mechanisms to study energy security differently. At the same time, all of these chapters are connected through several core critical insights. All chapters dealt with being (what is) and becoming (how something is enacted or performed) and highlight a strong ethical dimension of this becoming. They all focused on the creation of boundaries and distinctions but offered different ways of seeing the world and different logics through which to analyse and define issues. They all dealt with the relation between knowledge and the material, and the 'ethico-onto-epistem-ology' sets of relations that make up the durability and vibrancy of life.[2] All chapters deal with the relation between matter, economics, politics and ethics by analysing the broader political economies of (energy) security. After these theoretical chapters, energy security is no longer only something to be achieved but has turned into a governing technique aimed at energy circulations that consist of a set of materialdiscursive relations which are constantly performed and disrupted and which consist of humans, things, knowledge, morality, practices and so on. In this reading, each call for energy security is a performative act that has been produced and is producing a particular understanding of energy security and the materialdiscursive world around it.

This was highlighted in Chapter 7 with an example of a performative reading of energy security of the Dutch natural gas debate, which since the late 1980s has been witness to an increasing number of ever-stronger gasquakes. This chapter offered a security analysis of the accompanying debate on the material consequences and organization of the gas extraction between the threatened local population, the knowledge institutes analysing the gasquakes, and the government and extraction industry. The chapter studied how these parties make sense of the gasquakes through a combination of securitization theory and the flat relationality offered by new materialism, which forces the conflicting securitization claims to be analysed in their local sociotechnical context. The resulting analysis showed how the gas debate is structured by a shared security of supply understanding, but that this understanding has for a long time been questioned by the local population on its safety and cost implications. Still, it took 25 years for these claims to be accepted and the security of supply understanding shifted to a focus on minimum extraction volumes. The analysis showed how this time frame can only be explained through a self-reinforcing combination of security claims, experienced materialdiscursive events, increasing measurements (following security calls), shifting value judgements and increasing audience acceptance (creating additional speech actors).

8.2 Towards a performative reading of energy security

Where the current literature tries to get to the heart of what energy security is, this book thus aimed to disclose the concept of energy security by discussing its performative practices. It approached these practices from multiple angles, disciplines and theories in order to come to an understanding of what energy security does. In other words, to open the intuitive common sense behind energy security to an actual discussion of its underlying sociopolitical processes. In doing so, it does not argue that this approach is better than the current literature and policy work on energy security – it goes against its performative approach to even claim such. Instead, the book offered an additional way of thinking about the phenomenon of energy security. It offered an alternative that moves away from the primary concerns within energy security and its self-reinforcing logics to its use and the practices that shape it. In other words, the value of a performative approach lies in the interruption of many ontological and epistemological a priori assumptions that characterize current studies on energy security, in addition to a reflection on its effects or how it is used instrumentally to govern life. As Der Derian argues:

> A [performative] response is not, then for all its purported relativism, axiomatically apolitical or amoral: It is in fact an attempt to understand – *without* resort to external authorities or transcendental values – why one moral or political system attains a higher status and exercises more influence than another at a particular historical moment.[3]

The chapters above introduced such a performative approach, not by offering *a* theory, method or specific performative reading but via a broad performative mode of reasoning that is open to multiple theories and methods. As an approach, it fits a small (but growing) body of performative work in relation to energy. The work of Bridge on energy security as 'world-making' has been mentioned, but equally interesting albeit slightly beyond energy is the work of Elden and others on *geo*politics and *geo*metrics (a geological play on biopolitics), which points to the ontological politics of observing our natural world.[4] Another alternative, on energy broadly, includes the work on *energo*power from Boyer and colleagues (a play on biopower), who study the 'power over (and through) energy' and concentrate on the interaction between energy utilization and democratization.[5]

Although reluctant to operationalize my own approach beyond the specific theories introduced in this book, my chapters do share a certain performative assemblage of five elements which can be used to describe the epistemology and ontology behind energy security. Such an assemblage starts (1) with a definition of performativity. Performativity, or the practice of how matter comes to matter, was described in Chapter 5 with the help of Butler as 'a reiterative practice by which discourse produces the effects it names ... the boundaries, fixity and surface we call matter'.[6] Her focus is on how discourse affects the non-discursive as it tries to stabilize it through definitions and interventions even though these are inherently incomplete and rife with virtuality. However, based on the rest of the new materialist literature, performativity can be extended to *a reiterative assemblage/folding of sets of materialdiscursive relationships* where 'discourse produces the effects it names' but the non-discursive and already-actualized materialdiscursive relationships simultaneously produce the discourses that it disrupts.

The next step would be (2) to offer a materialdiscursive, flat and relational ontology with multiple sets of relationships that are inherently unstable unless they actively stabilize themselves, and in so doing enable or inhibit each other's circulation in different milieus. Such an ontology (3) is governed through the differences that are created with observation and the further materialization of such differences by the folding/assemblage of new sets of relationships. Observation here is understood as the attribution of meaning through either the identification of undesired futures or the post hoc identification of events, while folding refers to the strategies (intentional or not) that guide materialdiscursive elements to come together, whether through causality, chaos or politics (gathering support for alternative measures). Both observation and folding are part of security politics, although one can also find them in the distinct strategies for properly folded and assembled economic, judicial or cultural/social spheres. Like the differences between these spheres, such strategies are also at work to differentiate energy from non-energy and thus help perform the referent object of energy security. Important here is the observer distinction between the things we observe as facts or objects and the things we see as things and matters of concern. Facts/objects are stabilized and black boxed sets of relationships that are of no political concern, that is until they break down, achieve new connections or wilfully change because then these objects become things and need to be reassembled and interpreted.

With this and the critical security literature in mind, it becomes possible (4) to define energy security as *the mode through which people identify undesirable energy futures and act upon them in the present*. Subsequently, (5) a scholar's focus shifts to these modes or strategies of governmentality, which come to light by studying *events* (surprises or achievements, imagined or post hoc observed), *observations* (practices of knowledge gathering, including security techniques, statistics and so on) and *assemblages* (practices of folding elements in new relationships, including gathering political support, constructing new oil pipelines with reverse flow capacity, demand response algorithms and so on). Of course, the iterative nature of performative processes implies that these three are inseparable except post hoc, as an event can be an observation, an observation an assemblage, and an assemblage an event (see Figure 8.1). Chapter 7 provided an example where the observations of the gasquakes was both an assemblage of elements (seismographs, models, final report etc.) and an event that spurred local response.

Irrespective of how one operationalizes it,[7] a performative reading of energy security has two benefits. First, it allows scholars to escape the real-life energy language of these debates and the urgency that comes with the use of security, by building on its own languages and ontology that places such debates in a wider context. This implies, for example, a move away from the state-centrism often attached to energy security considerations (as opposed to the household-level focus in food security or the individual level in human security or terrorism studies). It also lets one escape the security concerns themselves. In line with earlier remarks that it is not possible to study a system of communication from within that system, someone worried about whether a country is energy-secure cannot properly reflect on what they are doing. In other words, a performative

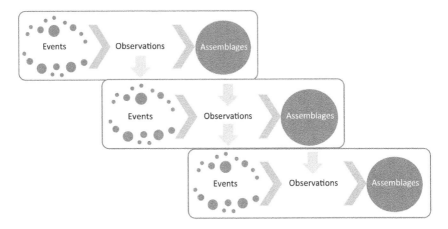

Figure 8.1 The ontology of a performative reading of energy security.
Source: author.

reading of energy security allows one to reflect on how such security concerns evolve and what their impacts are. Following from this, second, a performative approach enables scholars to disclose the inherent assumptions in such a 'system' or materialdiscursive assemblage of relationships. For many, questions like these and the resulting understanding on how humans act socially are enough to justify a critical performative approach (together with any follow-up questions). For others, the lack of modelling and applied theorization means that these understandings might be interesting but less than useful in real life. Clearly, this book argued for the former, if only for the awareness to exclusions that these performative studies offer citizens, consumers, policymakers, economists, scientists and so forth, and thereby highlights the importance of disclosing the self-evident and find other ways to perform our materialdiscursive society.

What results is an understanding of energy security that is both (re)produced and productive. Among others, it is produced by the theories and observations that claim to observe it. It is produced by the ontological politics of security that try to imagine, define and control surprising events and undesired futures. It is produced by individuals who use both descriptive and proscriptive elements in their definitions. It is produced through policies of diversification, contract law or price fluctuations in energy markets. It is produced in the construction of new back-up capacity, the installation of reverse flow techniques and the overhaul of the electricity infrastructure from fossil fuels to renewable sources. In short, energy security is continuously produced and reproduced with each iterative use of the concept, its practices and the energy system itself. These practices are inherently fragile and always open to resistance and change. Energy security proliferates, not because it cannot be defined but because its usage changes constantly. Simultaneously, energy security is productive. It reifies concerns of absolute scarcity and the neorealist geopolitical concerns that come with this. It reifies inherent assumptions on passive consumers that justify a further governing of them.[8] It reproduces a technical and capital-intensive mode of reasoning to solve fundamental social problems. Most importantly, it conserves current ways of life, even if it has to change itself to make that happen.

Counterintuitively, by studying the practices that shape energy security, the search for a fuller understanding of what energy security *does* also results in a new understanding of what energy security *is*. What emerged in this book was a multiplicity of energy security, as energy security is simultaneously energy *insecurity*, a speech act with strong normative consequences, a risk calculation, a teleology (a goal to be reached if one behaves in a particular way), a discourse that structures thought, a localized node of actor-networks within a network of actor-networks, a materialdiscursive phenomenon based on an agential cut, a set of relations with strategic intent, and a way to govern the present by conducting the conduct of people in their relationship with things. It is all of these *in addition* to the more traditional understandings of security of supply and the security of energy systems, resources, services and so on, which together bring energy security into being as a distinct desirable reality. With this in mind, it can be concluded that even though the proliferation of energy security definitions is driven by demands for a more emancipated, complete and truthful definition, the closure offered by such a perfectly emancipated definition of energy security will always remain incomplete as it hides the multiplicity of energy security.

8.3 A brief reflection on a performative reading of energy security

While the previous section specified a bit more how a performative reading of energy security could look like, the metaphor of a tightrope walker in effect captures four additional general insights.

First, the balancing act itself does not just refer to the relation between environmental boundaries and unlimited desires, but also illustrates the constant balancing between (energy) security and (energy) insecurity, between scarcity and abundance, between materiality and language, between construction and deconstruction, between the freedom to choose and the governing of those who choose wrongly. In other words, it refers to politics. And, yes, politics is central to this book, ranging from discussions on the politics of energy security to the distinction between politics of security and insecurity, the shifts in securitization theory (from the non-political via the political to the extraordinary), knowledge politics, ontological politics and biopolitics. All of these touch on different forms of politics. To be clear, politics relates here to the techniques and distinctions that enable or close the *political*: the space of contestation where debate takes place (making things into objects and objects in to things).[9] Choosing one over the other, arguing that security is a subset of biopolitics or that knowledge politics is a prerequisite for ontological politics is an observer distinction and thus a politics on its own.

Second, the relentless forward movement of a tightrope walker not only refers to the unlimited desire for goods but also to the desire for knowledge. Often considered progress, in case of energy systems this desire for knowledge seems limited to a particular mode of thought: a capitalist-driven search for more data and better technology. This is a mode known to be unable to reflect on its own practices, co-opting resistance into its own existing practices instead of engaging it reflexively, and therefore unable to think society differently.[10] In hindsight, it is knowledge, and the politics around it, that is so paradoxical for a critical and performative understanding of energy security. On the one hand, the search for knowledge by the 'traditional' literature is argued to be blind for its own performative effects. Yet, on the other hand, those same knowledge practices are the object of study for performative approaches, meaning that a performative approach cannot do without the more traditional studies on energy security. A performative approach, in a sense, is just as empty as security. It needs positivist knowledge to make its claims. More importantly, it will always find something to criticize in these positivist approaches because it focuses on the exclusionary practices that are inherent to any form of positivist observation.

Third, the agent or tightrope walker is also of interest. For whom or what is the agent balancing on the tightrope? An individual? A group of people? Do we include 'things' or objects as part of these groups? Perhaps society as a whole? Which society? The moment the black box of society is opened, the multitude and constantly shifting sets of relations between humans, animals, technology, economy, nature and so forth come forwards, only to be differentiated by the distinctions of the observer, irrespective whether scholars observe the agent or the agent observes its environment. With these differences should come an awareness of *ethics*, in line with Barad's claim that ethics results from the differences that are part of an assemblage's observation, but which are identified post hoc as separate from the ethico-onto-epistem-ology that is our world.[11] By disclosing this relationship, she and others point to a broader 'us' which includes oneself, the other, the ignored others and the things that mediate these differences. This awareness of visible and invisible others comes with the ethical obligation to care for and give the marginalized a voice or, if we follow Booth, even reorganize subsequent assemblages in favour of those less well off.[12]

A last theme, one not explicitly discussed in the chapters but constantly returning, is *resistance*. A consequence of the boundaries that are drawn in knowledge gathering practices, security decisions, speech acts, the successful association of a set of relations or the materialization of discourse is that something is always excluded. When everything stems from difference, as Bryant argues, this implies that with each performativity comes the option of resistance, whether as failure, achievement or wilful act.[13] In the case of energy security, from a developed country's perspective, the circulation of energy supplies is governed through a political economic assemblage of energy (resources, infrastructure), security (biopolitics, geometrics, security logics) and markets. This assemblage secures, on the one hand, the access to and production of energy (e.g. an energy intensive lifestyle with both its environmental consequences and comfort and health benefits) and, on the other hand, the flow and circulation of energy according to its respective mobile norms.[14] Simultaneously, these forms of governing are constantly resisted, by humans as well as by black boxed uncontrolled causal relationships, something the natural gas illustration showed with the resistance and securitization of the local inhabitants to official sedimented gas extraction practices as well as the gas extraction-induced earthquakes that entered the frame of reference of inhabitants and officials.

8.4 A research agenda and some implications

These reflections lead to five topics that deserve further research and four core implications for energy security scholars and policymakers. The research suggestions include a call to overcome the fear of philosophy and theory, to link the energy *security* literature to the broader work in critical security studies, and to further the performative energy security approach, theoretically and by utilizing its insights to disclose the specific assumptions behind energy security. In turn, the policy implications centre on the additional reflexivity that a performative reading offers.

First, and before anything specific, it should be noted that, while this book has tried to move the energy security debate beyond its realist confirmations and sometimes simple applications of securitization theory to a range of theoretical sources that could be used to understand the processes behind energy security instead of defining them, this theorizing is nowhere near finished. Energy security and theory are not enemies. And in fact, it is easy to foresee a range of PhD projects engaging with the works in this book or the many other philosophical works out there, among which the works of Deleuze and Guattari, Wittgenstein, Habermas, Adorno or an updated reading of Marx. Moreover, such projects would not be complete without looking to geography, feminism and architecture for truly fresh theoretical thinking.

Second, this book's focus on the security aspect of energy security comes with a call to take security more seriously, with its logics, politics and use, to flesh out how energy security differs from the broader security literature by focusing on the 'strategies' behind its ontological politics,[15] because not only could energy security gain from insights from security studies but energy security could contribute to it as well, in line with this book, by comparing the differentiation and assemblage strategies of energy security to those of human security, terrorism studies, economic security or the range of food, water and climate securities. For example, the thesis behind this book compared energy security to food security, which is witness to a similar proliferation of definitions as energy security but simultaneously faces stronger resistance against the traditional solution of more industrial food production and is focused on a different level of analysis (households instead of nations or systems).[16] Another potential avenue is to contrast and compare different forms of energy security, specifically to see how a politics of energy *security* relates to a politics of energy *insecurity*. While the energy security literature clearly differentiates between haves (producers) and have nots (consumers), and the broad security literature looks at how *we* safeguard ourselves from threats, missing seems to be a comparison of the security strategies that are followed by people at different stages of security. In other words, missing is a comparison of how the security strategies of those who are trying to protect current volumes of energy (effectively securing abundance) differ from those who are trying to gain said resources (e.g. securitizing scarcity).

Third, another core aspect that has a lot of potential is the security literature on risk. A further discussion and application of risk, as discussed in Section 4.5, offers a whole new approach to more routine security decision-making and the commodification of those decisions. This literature has the potential to open up the energy security field beyond the use of risk in investment decisions to the security actions that follow insurance and engineering calculations on, for example, the risk decisions behind the level of overcapacity in electricity grids or the amount of back-up generation and spinning reserves or the distance between a major gas pipeline or storage facility and a block of houses,[17] in other words to study the everyday of energy security by following the energy security practices, calculations, scenarios, decisions and debates on a very local level within companies, academia and policymaking, to focus on the desks and processes that lead to declarations and outcomes instead of those declarations and outcomes themselves.

Fourth, a deeper understanding of security, one that discloses the hidden differentiations behind (routine) security practices, calls for more research on the relationship between energy security and ethics. To look for energy security debates and disclose as many of the ethical positions behind them with the help of the literature on energy justice, energy poverty and natural resource distribution. This was part of Chapter 7. For, although it was not put forward (instead highlighting the theoretical and methodological value of the case), it is truly painful that the Dutch gasquake debate is still ongoing in one of the most developed, highly organized and socially oriented countries in the world, especially as it seems to falter on the legal position of who is financially responsible for the compensation and how this should be organized (even if a very legitimate position on its own). This situation is extra peculiar as it is known that the earth will keep settling and thus generating earthquakes for a number of years after the gas extraction stops. Simulteneously, while this is the core concern, a performative focus on the ethics in this debate should look beyond this particular 'agential cut', and for instance notice that the decision to lower extraction volumes also has ethical consequences, as it likely leads to higher heating prices and thus potentially to more people suffering from energy poverty.

Lastly, in addition to a more theoretical reflection, a direct follow-up would be to build on the illustrations, here and elsewhere, and provide for a number of actual case studies that study how energy security is made and how security practices work in energy and how this affects society in doing so. This would enable a deeper understanding of specific performative practices and it would fine-tune the theories from where these performative readings originate; to continue where the illustrations stopped, by analysing the relationality of energy security at the intersection of knowledge practices, security claims and materialization on both local and international levels, for example by studying the performativity of the International Energy Agency as a knowledge broker by tracing the politics behind its statistics and models.

Turning from the research agenda to the implications, there are a couple of implications for traditional energy security scholars and energy policymakers that can be derived from this study. First, this book is not an attempt to convince policymakers that what they do is performative, one the one hand, because the goal of policymaking is to shape the reality of energy and, on the other, because a performative approach does not help them as it does not offer positivist projections or blueprints on how to proceed. Instead it offers a moment to step outside the daily affairs and discourse of energy security and thereby draws attention to the policymaker's position in the overall relationality of energy security. For example, this book starts with a personal reflection precisely to show that this is a work on energy security written by a well-to-do white guy living in the western hemisphere. Most definitely the analysis above would be different if written by somebody else – notwithstanding how fundamental, meticulous and abstract it is. The point being that a performative reading is contextual, reflexive and, in my opinion, additional to existing research directions.

Second, this reflexivity in turn makes it possible to argue for an ethical and normative awareness that extends beyond the self, a particular political economy or a sociotechnical system. On a political level, this implies that policymakers, energy security scholars and other actors are responsible not only for a failure to counter threats but also for the threats that they propose themselves: for the distinctions between friend/enemy, the choice of what to protect, and for the resources drawn from other areas in terms of actual resources and agenda setting.[18] Patterson's argument is worth keeping in mind here: what people really want to secure are not the current production and transmission infrastructures but the services that energy enables them to enjoy.[19] Interestingly, those services are never truly measured. Instead we measure kWh, oil barrels, cubic metres of gas: things that are quantifiable and commodified (a clear case of ontological politics). Likewise, we know that, while the logic of security intrinsically is geared to remove doubts and thus dispels any reflexivity about third party victims (those who become victims in the struggle between you and the threatening other), security threats are not fixed in stone. Hence, energy security measures might become counterproductive. Moreover, the security dilemma implies that more energy security could lead to less security.

Third, researchers have a duty to make sure that the theory they use to analyse a given aspect of energy security is politically valid as well. Realism and liberalism are great theories, but are they so because they explain the world or because the world is performed to behave in that particular way? And would the use of such a theory and its reiterated strengthened principles actually be beneficial to energy security? I for one would minimize my realist analyses with their conflictual geopolitics, not because these theories fail to explain a case or because the energy markets are suddenly full of trust and all happy to trade but because it reiterates certain principles that in certain political contexts need not always be repeated. Basically, this is ANT's main lesson: trace the actual relationships instead of trusting the socio-economic definitions and theoretical explanations. For instance, be aware that scenarios, modelling and algorithms used to test energy security threat levels are constructed on the assumption that we are in danger in the first place; it is not often that one finds a scenario that negates the threat.

That brings us to a last implication. In line with the two remarks above and the reflection that performativity needs positivist scholarship, a certain reflexivity is required of performative scholars as well. Even though the core focus of a performative approach lies in it disclosing the assumptions behind existing practices and existing materialdiscursive assemblages, I share Latour's view that disclosure alone is not enough reason to disclose. We live in a world seemingly characterized by information overload, 'fake news', media highlights and other brief attention spans, and in such a world critical scholars too have a responsibility for what they study and how they report their results, especially as the disclosure of certain scientific facts – how well intended and justified – might not be scientific or political expedient. Climate change is a case in point. Latour in particular reflects on the misinterpretation by positivists (who think the lesson is that everything is language) and conspiracy theorists (who take from it that everything is questionable) of deconstructive theories as only highlighting the uncertainty behind 'matters of fact':

> I myself have spent some time in the past trying to show '*the lack of scientific certainty*' inherent in the construction of facts. I too made it a 'primary issue.' But I did not exactly aim at fooling the public by obscuring the certainty of a closed argument – or did I? After all, I have been accused of just that sin. Still, I'd like to believe that, on the contrary, I intended to *emancipate* the public from prematurely naturalized objectified facts. Was I foolishly mistaken? Have things changed so fast?... While we spent years trying to detect the real prejudices hidden behind the appearance of objective statements, do we now have to reveal the real objective and incontrovertible facts hidden behind the *illusion* of prejudices?[20]

Performative scholars have an obligation to highlight that what an outsider perceives as a move away from facts to the uncertainty behind it is in fact a translation of those 'matters of facts' into 'matters of concern'. Such a translation indeed discloses potential ethical implications, hidden paradoxes, missing relations and voices; however, the goal is not just to deconstruct but also primarily to *reinforce* and *deepen* these facts beyond simplistic 'this is it' claims.

8.5 In closing

In closing, a performative reading of energy security offers an additional way to study energy security as it opens up the political origins and implications of this concept and practice. Above in the conclusion I've argued that this leads to a better understanding of how energy security works, as it highlights the hard work necessary to stabilize our current understanding of energy security in light of materialdiscursive resistance. This understanding is reached by looking at energy security as a security practice in use, for which it shifts the focus to security and introduces the broader security logics and how they relate to the materiality of energy systems and act politically within society.

While it is difficult to formulate a specific performative approach for energy security (owing to its contextualized nature), the brief performative assemblage that was introduced to summarize and connect some of the core elements across the theoretical chapters already offers a range of insights for energy security with its focus on events, observations and assemblages. First, in line with the question that started this book on why the definition of energy security keeps proliferating, it can be concluded that energy security proliferates, not because it cannot be defined but because (1) it is relative, because (2) its usage and context changes constantly and because (3) it is based on empty security logics wherein failure and success always leads to more security. As such, the search for a central definition – while admirable and politically useful (for some) as it makes energy manageable and helps spread awareness of the many facets of energy security – is simultaneously hiding the virtuality and differences of energy security and is thereby inhibitive of a deeper understanding of the phenomena and its underlying social processes. Once defined as *the mode through which people identify undesirable* energy *futures and act upon them in the present*, energy security is no longer solely something to be achieved but emerges as a governance technique aimed at energy circulations that consist of a set of materialdiscursive relations which are constantly performed and disrupted. In this reading, every use of energy security is a performative act that has been produced and is producing a particular understanding of energy security and the materialdiscursive world around it. Subsequently, trying to define energy security/insecurity is not just a discussion about power; it is the exercise of a form of power through meaning attribution and materialization.

All in all, the response of Cherp to Sovacool that a definition of 'energy security takes more than asking around' is interesting in light of the above as this book's performative stance would argue that it is exactly that – a shared relational understanding.[21] At the same time, it argues that energy security entails much more than a shared social understanding, as it includes the work to generate these shared understandings as well as its effects in terms of materialization and forms of governing. Most of all, the above reflects that energy security is forever out of reach of humans, not because it cannot be reached but because, the moment we do, our focus shifts to another element and the process starts again. The proliferation of energy security definitions, the totalizing tendency of security and the constantly growing desire for energy are all indications that the tightrope walker will keep moving forwards. Of course, along the way we might be getting better at managing it, perhaps even for a wider 'us', but unfortunately these management practices remain part of current logics and sociotechnical systems. In contrast, a reflexive performative reading steps outside of them and thereby offers a first step to an actual transformation of our current energy logics and systems.

Notes

1 Achterhuis 1988, 106–107.
2 Barad 2007.
3 Der Derian 2009, 193 (emphasis in original).
4 Bridge 2015; Elden 2007, 2013.
5 Boyer 2011, 5, 2014; Mitchell 2009, 2013.
6 Butler 1993, 2.
7 For an alternative performative, deeply theoretical and practical analysis focused on natural gas security in the UK, see: Forman 2017, 2018.
8 Kester 2016a.
9 Barry 2002, 270–271.
10 See Byrne and Toly 2006.
11 Barad 2007.
12 Bellacasa 2011, 100. Booth 2005.
13 De Goede 2012.
14 Kester 2016a, 2018.
15 Kester 2018.
16 Kester 2016b.
17 Forman 2017, 2018.
18 Balzacq 2011, xiii.
19 Patterson 2008.
20 Latour 2004, 227.
21 Cherp 2012, p. 841; Sovacool 2011. Also Sovacool *et al.* 2012.

Bibliography

Achterhuis, Hans. 1988. *Het Rijk van de Schaarste: van Thomas Hobbes tot Michel Foucault.* Baarn: Ambo.

Balzacq, Thierry, ed. 2011. *Securitization theory: How security problems emerge and dissolve.* PRIO New Security Studies. London and New York: Routledge.

Barad, Karen. 2007. *Meeting the universe halfway: Quantum physics and the entanglement of matter and meaning.* Durham, NC, and London: Duke University Press.

Barry, Andrew. 2002. The anti-political economy. *Economy and Society* 31 (2): 268–284.

Bellacasa, Maria Puig de la. 2011. Matters of care in technoscience: Assembling neglected things. *Social Studies of Science* 41 (1): 85–106.

Booth, Ken. 2005. Security. In *Critical security studies and world politics*, edited by Ken Booth, 21–25. London: Lynne Rienner.

Boyer, Dominic. 2011. Energopolitics and the anthropology of energy. *Anthropology News* 52 (5): 5–7.

Boyer, Dominic. 2014. Energopower: An introduction. *Anthropological Quarterly* 87 (2): 309–333.

Bridge, Gavin. 2015. Energy (in)security: World-making in an age of scarcity. *The Geographical Journal* 181 (4): 328–339.

Butler, Judith. 1993. *Bodies that matter: On the discursive limits of 'sex'*. London and New York: Routledge.

Byrne, John, and Noah Toly. 2006. Energy as a social project: Recovering a discourse. In *Transforming power: Energy, environment and society in conflict*, edited by John Byrne, Noah Toly and Leigh Glover, 1–32. New Brunswick, NJ, and London: Transaction.

Cherp, Aleh. 2012. Defining energy security takes more than asking around. *Energy Policy* 48: 841–842.

De Goede, Marieke. 2012. *Speculative security: The politics of pursuing terrorist monies*. Minneapolis, MN: University of Minnesota Press.

Der Derian, James. 2009. *Critical practices in international theory: Selected essays*. London and New York: Routledge.

Elden, Stuart. 2007. Governmentality, calculation, territory. *Environment and Planning D: Society and Space* 25 (3): 562–580.

Elden, Stuart. 2013. Secure the volume: Vertical geopolitics and the depth of power. *Political Geography* 34: 35–51.

Forman, Peter J. 2017. *Securing natural gas: Entity-attentive security research*. PhD thesis, Durham University.

Forman, Peter J. 2018. Circulations beyond nodes: (In)securities along the pipeline. *Mobilities* 13 (2): 231–245.

Kester, Johannes. 2016a. Conducting a smarter grid: Reflecting on the power and security behind smart grids with Foucault. In *Smart grids from a global perspective*, 197–213. Cham: Springer.

Kester, Johannes. 2016b. *Securing abundance: The politics of energy security*. PhD hesis, Groningen: University of Groningen.

Kester, Johannes. 2018. Governing electric vehicles: Mobilizing electricity to secure automobility. *Mobilities* 13 (2): 200–215.

Latour, Bruno. 2004. Why has critique run out of steam? From matters of fact to matters of concern. *Critical inquiry* 30 (2): 225–248.

Mitchell, Timothy. 2009. Carbon democracy. *Economy and Society* 38 (3): 399–432.

Mitchell, Timothy. 2013. *Carbon democracy: Political power in the age of oil*. London: Verso.

Patterson, W. 2008. *Managing energy wrong*. Energy, Environment and Resource Governance Working Paper. Managing Energy: for Climate and Security. London: Chatham House.

Sovacool, Benjamin K. 2011. Evaluating energy security in the Asia Pacific: Towards a more comprehensive approach. *Energy Policy* 39 (11): 7472–7479.

Sovacool, Benjamin K., S. V. Valentine, M. Jain Bambawale, M. A. Brown, T. de Fátima Cardoso, S. Nurbek, G. Suleimenova, J. Li, Y. Xu and A. Jain. 2012. Exploring propositions about perceptions of energy security: An international survey. *Environmental Science & Policy* 16: 44–64.

Index

Printed and bound by CPI Group (UK) Ltd, Croydon, CR0 4YY
01/05/2025
01858426-0007